THE PRAISES OF ISRAEL

PSALMS 1–72

THE PRAISES OF ISRAEL

Volume One

Psalms 1-72

Dudley Fifield

First Published 2008

ISBN 978-0-85189-177-4

© 2008 The Christadelphian Magazine and Publishing Association Limited

Printed and bound in England by:

THE CROMWELL PRESS
TROWBRIDGE
WILTSHIRE BA14 0XB

CONTENTS

Two further volumes are in preparation:
VOLUME 2 – BOOKS III, IV– PSALMS 73–106;
VOLUME 3 – BOOK V – PSALMS 107–150

v

PREFACE

THIS work on the Book of Psalms was written over a period of some twenty-five years; Psalms 107 – 150 (see Volume 3) being the product of recent study. Consequently it is possible that readers will detect a development in style between earlier and later studies. The writer is, after all, twenty-five years older!

Originally they appeared in the pages of *The Bible Student* and we are grateful to the Editors of that magazine for agreeing so readily to their reproduction.

Inevitably, given the period of time involved, our thinking on some of the Psalms has changed. It would, however, have been a monumental task to have made substantial changes in those that were written in earlier years. We have therefore, apart from some minor editing, left them in their original form.

Because they were written in this way there is also some repetition of thought and ideas. However, as readers are most likely to read the Psalms on an individual basis, 'dipping in' as it were, this might prove to be more of a benefit than a disadvantage.

When this venture began it was not anticipated that the study of all 150 psalms would be completed, or that they would be published in book form. I am grateful to the Christadelphian Magazine and Publishing Association, the Editor and his staff for making this possible.

This is the first volume of a proposed three-volume work. This volume contains Psalms 1–72.

INTRODUCTION
THE FIVE BOOKS OF THE PSALMS

MOST readers will be aware that the Psalms are divided into five books. The Revised Version correctly indicates the divisions at the appropriate places. The books are as follows:

> Book 1 – Psalms 1–41
> Book 2 – Psalms 42–72
> Book 3 – Psalms 73–89
> Book 4 – Psalms 90–106
> Book 5 – Psalms 107–150

Instinctively one is drawn to make a comparison with the Pentateuch, the five books of Moses. Any attempt, however, to relate the substance of the book of the Psalms to the corresponding books of Moses is fraught with difficulty. We have a recollection of Brother L. G. Sargent once expressing a sense of bewilderment at attempts to accomplish this aim and we share his feelings at what we have come to consider a pointless exercise. There is, however, a suggestion of a possible solution that has nothing to do with the substance of the Psalms or the books of Moses.

In his book *Hymns of The Temple* (pages 18,19), Dr. Norman Snaith suggests that there is evidence that in Palestine it was customary to read a portion of the law, a psalm, and a closing reading from the prophets each sabbath day. Over a three year cycle, all of the books of Moses and of the Psalms would be read. Based on the lunar year, this meant that there would be 146 sabbaths in the period. If we accept that every third year an intercalary month was introduced into the calendar to harmonize the lunar and solar years, then the additional four sabbaths correspond to the last four psalms, making the total 150.

The writer developing his argument says; "Working on this basis, we find the curious state of affairs that Exodus was begun on the 42nd sabbath, Leviticus on the 73rd, Numbers on the 90th, and Deuteronomy on the 117th. But 1, 42, 73, 90, 107 are the first psalms in the five books of the Psalms. This can scarcely be a coincidence. Four of the numbers coincide".

Snaith conjectures over the difference between 107 and 117 and we lack the background knowledge to comment with any confidence on his conclusions. However, we find his suggestion compelling as in a sense the division of the Psalms would correspond to our own Bible Reading Companion.

It must be said that there are several aspects of the argument outlined above that might be open to question, but overall it has an appeal and, we feel, a sense of rightness that makes it worthy of readers' consideration.

PSALM 1

IT would seem to be completely inappropriate for the opening psalm, which can in a sense be regarded as a preface to the entire book of Psalms, to be anything other than Messianic in its content. It is a strange thing but a perusal of about half-a-dozen works on the Psalms did not produce a single reference to the Lord Jesus Christ. Yet he who is the substance of so many prophetic utterances in the Psalms, whose heart and mind is revealed in so many of the crises of his life through "his spirit" in the writers, must surely be *the man* of whom the psalm speaks.

Of course, in general terms it can be said to contrast the righteous with the ungodly; but it is worthy of note that in verses 1 to 3, where the unrighteous are described in the plural, the contrast is with a single individual – "the man", "his delight", "he meditated", "he shall be like a tree" etc., and it is only the Lord Jesus who has fully realised the language of the psalm, for he is pre-eminently "the righteous one", "the ideal man". Of course, the psalm's words have meaning for all God's servants, but only inasmuch as they reflect the example of the perfect man, in that measure in which they have followed the footsteps of their Lord.

It is interesting that the psalm in its description of the righteous one should allude in a most obvious way to earlier scripture. Where the language here is a positive assertion of the attributes of the godly, the words echo God's exhortation to Joshua: "... that thou mayest prosper whithersoever thou goest ... thou shalt meditate therein day and night ... then thou shalt make thy way prosperous" (1:7,8). Joshua, in leading the people to their promised rest, was a wonderful type of the Lord Jesus Christ and bore the same name; and emphasised the fact

3

(following the death of Moses) that "what the law could not do" would be accomplished by God sending His Son in the likeness of sinful flesh. That the Lord delighted in God's law as no other, is evident from the Gospel records. His temptation particularly illustrates the benefits of his constant meditation upon the word of God, as oft times he resorted to some solitary place to continue in prayer and meditation throughout the long hours of the night. Thus he could rebut the suggestions of the temptation with his firm assertion, "It is written"; and it is particularly significant that his three quotations are drawn from within the space of three chapters in Deuteronomy (two from chapter 6 and one from chapter 8), in the context of which it was recorded:

"And these words, which I command thee this day, shall be in thine heart: and thou shalt teach them diligently unto thy children, and shalt talk of them when thou sittest in thine house, and when thou walkest by the way, and when thou liest down, and when thou risest up. And thou shalt bind them for a sign upon thine hand, and they shall be as frontlets between thine eyes." (Deuteronomy 6:6-8)

True Happiness

"Blessed is the man that walketh not in the counsel of the ungodly, nor standeth in the way of sinners, nor sitteth in the seat of the scornful. But his delight is in the law of the LORD; and in his law doth he meditate day and night. And he shall be like a tree planted by the rivers of water, that bringeth forth his fruit in his season; his leaf also shall not wither; and whatsoever he doeth shall prosper." (Psalm 1:1-3)

"Happy is the man" (verse 1, RV margin) cries the Psalmist, who disassociates himself from every evil work and from all ungodly men. It is a truth that the world fails completely to comprehend. Sometimes even those who seek to serve God do not appreciate fully the divine desire that men should be happy. Too often religion is presented as a doleful way of life that requires men to deny themselves those things that make for happiness. In fact, the reverse is true, for real and lasting happiness is not found in material things or in the ways of man's own

4

devising, but is achieved through an understanding and practical application of the revealed will of God. In other words, God's laws are not given as "burdens grievous to be borne", but rather are designed to make men happy by regulating their lives and guiding them into spiritually healthful habits that will result in peace of mind and a complete absence of the unrest and disquiet that are characteristics of the fleshly mind. So Moses could write:

"Happy art thou, O Israel: who is like unto thee, O people saved by the LORD?"　　(Deuteronomy 33:29)

Similarly the Psalms declare:

"Happy is that people, that is in such a case: yea, happy is that people, whose God is the LORD."

(Psalm 144:15)

"Happy is he that hath the God of Jacob for his help, whose hope is in the LORD his God."　　(Psalm 146:5)

Thus that righteous man who is constantly sustained by drawing on the word of God in which he delights, is likened to a tree which is nourished by a constant supply of water, without which, under the burning eastern sun, it would wither and die. The tree, of course, is frequently used as a figure of the righteous:

"I am like a green olive tree in the house of God."

(Psalm 52:8)

"The righteous shall flourish like the palm tree: he shall grow like a cedar in Lebanon. Those that be planted in the house of the LORD shall flourish in the courts of our God. They shall still bring forth fruit in old age."　　(Psalm 92:12-14)

"... that they might be called trees of righteousness, the planting of the LORD, that he might be glorified."

(Isaiah 61:3)

The Ungodly are not so

"The ungodly are not so: but are like the chaff which the wind driveth away. Therefore the ungodly shall not stand in the judgment, nor sinners in the congregation of the righteous."　　(Psalm 1:4,5)

In describing negatively those works and men which the righteous eschew, the psalm covers every aspect of human activity: walking, standing, sitting, and points the way to the road to ruin.

The parallelism is striking:

walketh	counsel	ungodly
standeth	the way	sinners
sitteth	the seat	scornful

The word translated "ungodly" is a general word for human sin, often rendered "wicked". Particularly relevant, however, is the root from which it is derived, which emphasises the difference between the happiness and peace of heart of the righteous and the lack of fulfilment and satisfaction that must ever be the lot of the wicked. It means 'to disturb, to vex', hence 'unrest, disharmony', and is wonderfully descriptive of the disquiet that sin brings into the heart which is lacking in self-control. Isaiah says:

"The wicked are like the troubled sea, when it cannot rest, whose waters cast up mire and dirt. There is no peace, saith my God, to the wicked." (57:20,21)

In this "way of the ungodly" the righteous will not walk. He refuses to be influenced by their "counsel". He will not adopt the principles that govern the lives of the wicked. As the Proverb says, "My son, if sinners entice thee, consent thou not" (1:10); and again, "My son, walk not thou in the way with them; refrain thy foot from their path" (1:15).

Similarly, the word rendered "sinner" is commonly used throughout the Old Testament. It has often been pointed out that its basic meaning is 'to miss the mark', and this is powerfully illustrated by Paul's words, "for all have sinned, and come short of the glory of God" (Romans 3:23). Particularly relevant, however, is the fact pointed out by several writers that the intensive form of the word in this instance is indicative of habitual offenders. So also the word rendered 'stand' means literally 'to stand still', hence 'to stay', 'to abide' or 'to continue'. Thus to "stand in the way of sinners" is to persist in the ways and practices of habitual sinners.

The "scornful" are a class of people who are described predominantly in the book of Proverbs, where they stand in contrast to the wise. Apart from two or three isolated

6

instances, all occurrences of the word are to be found in this book. A selection of references might help us to get a better insight into the stubborn and rebellious heart of the scorner:

"Reprove not a scorner, lest he hate thee." (9:8)
"A scorner heareth not rebuke." (13:1)
"Proud and haughty scorner is his name, who dealeth in proud wrath." (21:24)

The scornful, then, are proud and self-sufficient, arrogant men who contemptuously disregard both God and man when rebuked for their foolishness. Of such are the scoffers who ask, "Where is the promise of his coming?", for these in their scorn will not shrink from openly mocking and defying the things that belong to God's Truth. With such the righteous will keep no company. Never will he sit in their seat (i.e. their assembly), deliberately associating himself with these cynical and hard-hearted sinners.

The true meaning and full power of the words of Psalm 1 is perhaps emphasised by comparison with other scripture. Thus Psalm 15, in answer to the question, "LORD, who shall abide in thy tabernacle? who shall dwell in thy holy hill?" states:

"He that *walketh uprightly*, and *worketh righteousness*, and *speaketh the truth* in his heart."
(verses 1,2)

Jeremiah 17 is particularly helpful, for as Psalm 1 quotes Joshua 1, so Jeremiah in turn alludes unmistakeably to the psalm:

"Thus saith the LORD; Cursed be the man that trusteth in man ['the counsel of the ungodly'] and maketh flesh his arm ['stands in the way of sinners'] and whose heart departeth from the LORD ['sitteth in the seat of the scornful']. For he shall be like the heath in the desert, and shall not see when good cometh; but shall inhabit the parched places in the wilderness, in a salt land and not inhabited. Blessed is the man that trusteth in the LORD, and whose hope the LORD is. For he shall be as a tree planted by the waters, and that spreadeth out her roots by the river, and shall not see when heat cometh, but her leaf shall be green; and shall not be careful in the year of drought, neither shall cease from yielding fruit." (verses 5-8)

The Destruction of the Wicked

Unlike the enduring spiritual prosperity of those who love Jerusalem and feed continually upon God's word, the ungodly are likened to the chaff which, when the wheat is winnowed, is blown away by the wind. They would not stand in the judgement. They would not be vindicated before God in a time of reckoning, and no place would be found for them in the congregation of the righteous. For their way was but vanity and vexation of spirit, an aimless and purposeless life with no ultimate goal; for them, the nothingness of the sinners' doom – only the coldness and stillness of the tomb, for they will perish in their way.

The Providential Hand of God

Not so the righteous, however, for their way is known to God, not only in God's awareness of their way, but in His active participation:

"For the LORD *knoweth* the way of the righteous: but the way of the ungodly shall perish." (Psalm 1:6)

The word "knoweth" carries this connotation: its significance has been variously rendered 'keeps his eye upon', 'takes note of', 'cares for', 'has a loving regard towards'. It is illustrated by the events of the Exodus: "And God looked upon the children of Israel, and God had respect unto them" (AV margin, "knew them") (Exodus 2:25).

In practical terms, it means that there is not a step that the righteous takes, but God is there watching, protecting, guiding. If the psalm is in a measure built around Joshua, his example is the perfect illustration. God promised him that although the unbelieving generation would perish in the wilderness, nothing would prevent him from entering the land. Thus through the privations and hardships of the wilderness, he had no need to fear, for his way was known to God. He had given His angels charge concerning him.

In similar fashion, God is with us, and the happiness of the man of God is seen grounded in the two foundation principles that govern God's work in the lives of His servants: firstly, the power and influence of His word, and secondly, His providential care. Perhaps the message of the psalm generally can be summed up in Paul's words to Timothy:

"The Lord knoweth them that are his. And, Let every one that nameth the name of Christ depart from iniquity." (2 Timothy 2:19)

PSALM 2

IT is a sad commentary upon human nature, that so many should find it necessary to conjecture as to who the author of Psalm 2 might be, and what historical circumstances caused it to be written. There is, of course, no room for dissension in this matter as far as the authorship is concerned, for we have the authority of scripture (Acts 4:25) for our assurance that the words were first uttered by David himself. Clearly the theme of the psalm is based upon the covenant that God made with David when He promised the everlasting stability of his throne and kingdom through the one God would raise up, to whom He would be a Father and who would be His Son (1 Chronicles 17:11-14).

If the psalm has a historical setting, there would appear to be only one period in David's life to which it could refer, and that is the period at the very end of his days when Solomon was anointed king, and various factions sought to take advantage of the occasion to promote their own ambitions. David himself was under no illusions as to the divine choice:

"And of all my sons, (for the LORD hath given me many sons,) he hath chosen Solomon my son to sit upon the thone of the kingdom of the LORD over Israel. And he said unto me, Solomon thy son, he shall build my house and my courts: for I have chosen him to be my son, and I will be his father."   (1 Chronicles 28:5,6)

The king himself speaks in verses 7 and 8, and it might be that originally the substance of the psalm was the basis of a conversation between David and his son. It is interesting that it is said in Acts 4, "... who by *the mouth* of thy servant David hath said ..." (verse 25), i.e. the words were not written, but spoken. In any event, the grand theme of the psalm far transcends any incipient

10

fulfilment that it might have had in the experiences of Solomon, for it declares for all succeeding generations the immutability of God's purpose, and the utter futility of all human endeavours to frustrate His pleasure. Here is the true significance, the real message of the psalm; and it gives us a wonderful insight into the character of Bible prophecy. It is sometimes said that prophecies have a dual or secondary meaning. It is, perhaps, more correct to say that certain prophecies have recurring fulfilments. That is, because God never changes, He always reacts to certain situations which have a common factor, in the same way. Thus, whenever men are confederate together to rebel and to exalt themselves "against the LORD and against his anointed", their efforts are doomed to failure, for "He that sitteth in the heavens shall laugh: the LORD shall have them in derision ... Yet have I set my king upon my holy hill of Zion" (Psalm 2:2-6).

Thus the psalm could have an incipient fulfilment in the life of Solomon when all the evil counsels of his enemies were brought to nothing. Similarly, it was particularly relevant to the experiences of Hezekiah when Jerusalem was besieged by the Assyrian host. Hezekiah seems to have appreciated its significance, for his prayer and God's response to it recorded in Isaiah 37 contains obvious echoes of Psalm 2:

"Thou art the God, even thou alone, of all the kingdoms of the earth: thou hast made heaven and earth." (verse 16)

"Hear all the words of Sennacherib, which hath sent to reproach the living God." (verse 17)

"Now therefore, O LORD our God, save us from his hand, that all the kingdoms of the earth may know that thou art the LORD, even thou only." (verse 20)

"This is the word which the LORD hath spoken concerning him (Sennacherib); The virgin, the daughter of Zion, hath despised thee, and laughed thee to scorn." (verse 22)

"I know ... thy rage against me. Because thy rage against me, and thy tumult, is come up into mine ears ..." (verses 28,29)

(See also Psalm 46 in this connection, which is associated with the same event – N.B. verse 6.)

Perhaps the most remarkable application of the psalm is that made by the apostles in Acts 4:23-30. It is doubtful if we, without the guidance of the Spirit, would ever have applied it in this way. What is significant about the apostles' prayer is the way in which they not only quote Psalm 2, but also pick up the reference from Isaiah 37 produced above: "Lord, thou art God, which hast made heaven, and earth" (verse 24, cp. Isaiah 37:16). The apostles then proceed to apply the words of David to the manner in which, acting from their own particular point of view, men had been confederate together to crucify the Lord Jesus. Herod, Pilate, the Gentiles and the people of Israel were joined together to perform, unwittingly, what God's hand and counsel had determined before to be done. And when Jesus died, that, they thought, was the end of him. The embarrassment he caused them, the threat to their way of life, the challenge of his sinless life – all gone, disposed of, leaving them free to pursue their own ways. But He that sitteth in the heavens laughed. The Lord had them in derision, for on the third day He raised His Son from the grave, and thereby gave assurance to them that "He hath appointed a day, in the which he will judge the world in righteousness by that man whom he hath ordained" (Acts 17:31). A day will come when God will say, in the face of all man's efforts to frustrate His purpose, "Yet have I set my king upon my holy hill of Zion" (verse 6).

Further fulfilments of the psalm remain, the first being when the Lord will come again and sit on the throne of his glory, when all nations will be subdued before him. Revelation 19 refers to this time (verses 11-21) and the words of the psalm are quoted in verse 15:

"And out of his mouth goeth a sharp sword, that with it he should smite the nations: and *he shall rule them with a rod of iron*: and he treadeth the winepress of the fierceness and wrath of Almighty God."

Secondly, we can look to the end of the Millennium, when the Psalm has its final fulfilment in the last great surge of human rebellion (Revelation 20:7-9).

The declaration by the king of the divine decree which recognised him as God's Son and promised him universal dominion is not without difficulty. The passage already quoted from 1 Chronicles 28 is a clear indication that Solomon, when anointed king and elevated to the throne of the Lord over Israel, became the adopted son of God. "I will be to him a father, and he shall be to me a son." This has its origins in the relationship between God and His people Israel:

"And thou shalt say unto Pharaoh, Thus saith the LORD, Israel is my son, even my firstborn."

(Exodus 4:22)

"Do ye thus requite the LORD, O foolish people and unwise? is not he thy father that hath bought thee?"

(Deuteronomy 32:6)

Nationally, Israel were God's son, His firstborn. The king who sat on Zion's throne did not reign in his own right. It was the throne of the Lord and he was therefore God's representative upon that throne. Similarly, the national heritage of Israel – all that they stood for before God – was summed up in the office of this one man, so that there was a sense in which it could be said of every man who sat as rightful heir on David's throne, that when he was anointed king the decree was proclaimed, "Thou art my son, this day have I begotten thee". He became the adopted son of God and in this sense there was a perpetual fulfilment of the psalm's words throughout the first kingdom whenever a son of David was anointed king in his royal line. Of course, herein is the solution to the problem created by the words, "If he commit iniquity, etc."; and a study of Psalm 89 throws further light on this aspect of David's royal line.

This might appear to cause difficulty when we consider the case of the Lord Jesus, for in him the words of the psalm find their deepest and truest expression. Each king before him had in a measure pointed forwards to the ultimate fulfilment when the words would have a literal meaning never before known in the experience of men. For at his birth he was Son of God through the power of the Holy Spirit, and Son of David through the lineage of Mary his mother. In retrospect, he could declare the divine decree made at that time, for being born the heir of all things, he was the only begotten Son of God.

Dare we suggest, however, that notwithstanding the fact that Jesus was literally the Son of God, the words of the psalm have their fullest significance in the resurrection of the Lord, when, having overcome the power of sin and broken the bonds of death, he was begotten again, this time from the darkness of the tomb to become "the firstborn from the dead"? It is worth contemplating that the greatness of God's Son is not seen simply in the fact of his miraculous birth. Throughout his life he proved himself worthy of the "name" he inherited by birth. He gave that name practical expression in the life he lived and in the victory he achieved. Herein is to be found his true greatness and it was sealed with the divine authority by his resurrection from the dead, when with a more profound significance than ever before God could say, "Thou art my Son, this day have I begotten thee". As Paul writes:

"Concerning his (God's) Son Jesus Christ our Lord, which was made of the seed of David according to the flesh; and declared to be the Son of God with power, according to the spirit of holiness, by the resurrection from the dead."   (Romans 1:3,4)

Paul's address at Antioch (Acts 13) also seems to support this view:

"God hath fulfilled the same unto us their children, in that he hath raised up Jesus again; as it is also written in the second psalm, Thou art my Son, this day have I begotten thee."   (verse 33)

We are aware in this instance that a case can be made through the RV for applying the words to the birth of the Lord, but we suggest that the theme of the psalm (developed in this study) lends itself to the time of the Lord's resurrection, when, having proved himself in every sense to be the Son of God, the way was prepared for God to say of him as of all David's line, "Yet have I set my king upon my holy hill of Zion"; and in the further development of His purpose, "Ask of me, and I shall give thee the heathen for thine inheritance, and the uttermost parts of the earth for thy possession". Is there here an echo of the covenant with Abraham? The words "inheritance" and "possession" are characteristic of the promise of the land (Genesis 17:8; Acts 7:5; Hebrews 11:8). The Abrahamic covenant with its promise of the land for an everlasting possession is seen to be inextricably bound up with the Davidic covenant, as now the emphasis on a throne, a kingdom and a house is enlarged to encompass the whole earth when all nations will be blessed in Abraham's seed.

With the futility of human rebellion so clearly emphasised, it is fitting that the psalm should conclude with an appeal to the nations to be wise and to listen to instruction. Nothing could frustrate God's purpose: therefore to serve Him with fear, to rejoice with trembling, to manifest obedience by submitting to the Son and giving one's allegiance to him, was the only viable course of action. This homage was represented by the act of kissing the Son (Psalm 2:12). Thus men acknowledge him as the Lord's anointed – God's King – His representative on David's throne. How telling, then, is the condemnation of Judas Iscariot, who, filled with bitterness and disillusion, chose to betray the Son of Man with a kiss – the token of recognition and submission to the Lord's anointed!

How powerfully this psalm dominated the thinking of faithful men and women is demonstrated by scripture; for the allusions to it, in the recognition that Jesus was both Lord and Christ, Son and King, abound – of which the following are a few notable examples:

"And Simon Peter answered and said, Thou art the Christ, the Son of the living God." (Matthew 16:16)

"Nathanael answered and saith unto him, Rabbi, thou art the Son of God; thou art the King of Israel." (John 1:49)

"She (Martha) saith unto him, Yea, Lord: I believe that thou art the Christ, the Son of God, which should come into the world." (11:27)

"But these are written, that ye might believe that Jesus is the Christ, the Son of God; and that believing ye might have life through his name." (20:31)

Truly, we can say with the Psalmist, "Blessed are all they that put their trust in him" (Psalm 2:12).

PSALMS 3 & 4

THE word 'Selah' occurs five times in Psalms 3 and 4. Most are agreed that its basic meaning is 'to lift up', 'to elevate', and again there seems to be a consensus of opinion that it is a musical instruction. Some say that it is a direction to lift up the voice in relation to that which follows (J. W. Thirtle, *The Titles of the Psalms*); others, that it refers to the playing of unaccompanied music creating a break in the flow of thought and offering opportunity to meditate, i.e. to lift up the heart in contemplation of the words that have gone immediately before (Wm. Kay, *The Psalms with Notes*). In any event, it indicates a break between that which has gone before and that which follows. As the word occurs at the conclusion of Psalm 3, there would seem to be a clear indication that Psalms 3 and 4 are closely connected and were either sung together, or intended to be read together. There are other verbal links between the psalms which confirm the connection:

Psalm 3	Psalm 4
"LORD, how are they increased that trouble [lit. 'distress'] me!" (verse 1).	"Thou hast enlarged me when I was in distress" (verse 1).
"Many there be which say ..." (verse 2).	"There be many that say ..." (verse 6)

The two psalms lend themselves to the description of a morning song (3:5) and an evening hymn (4:4-8). And perhaps in this context we might refer them to a day in the life of David – not any day, but a particular day, a day of trouble and of great anxiety, for, as the historical information at the head of Psalm 3 tells us, it is "A Psalm of David, when he fled from Absalom his son". The historical background, then, is to be found in 2 Samuel 15

16

and 16, and the main events described in these chapters may be summarised as follows:

1. Absalom by devious means captures the hearts of the people of Israel (15:1-12).
2. David and his servants flee from Jerusalem (15:13-23), but David is encouraged by the loyalty and devotion of men like Ittai the Gittite (verse 21).
3. David sends the ark of God back to Jerusalem in the keeping of Zadok and Abiathar the priests (15:24-29).
4. David and those with him leave the city precincts by the way of the ascent of Mt. Olivet, and as he journeys, he is told of the treachery of his former friend Ahithophel.
5. At Bahurim he is met by Shimei, who curses him; but he refuses to allow Abishai to take vengeance, deferring rather to the will of God (16:5-13).
6. The section ends with: "And the king, and all the people who were with him, arrived weary at the Jordan; and there he refreshed himself" (16:14, RSV).

It is at this particular juncture that the psalms are seen to be relevant to this sequence of events in the life of David. There can be no more trying experience for a godly man who has been a true shepherd of God's flock, than to hear those for whom he has cared speak evil of him and prove themselves in difficult and changing circumstances to be his adversaries. "LORD", cries David, "how are mine adversaries increased! Many are they that rise up against me" (Psalm 3:1, RV). Many there were who said, "There is no help for him in God" (verse 2). How truly these words reflect the situation in which David found himself is expressed in the historical record: "The conspiracy was strong; for the people *increased* continually with Absalom" (2 Samuel 15:12); and after the crisis was over and the danger averted, Cushi comes with the news, "The LORD hath avenged thee this day of all them that *rose up* against thee" (2 Samuel 18:31). Compare also the cursing of Shimei (2 Samuel 16:7,8), where he accuses David of being a man of Belial who has been deserted by God.

David's response to this situation, however, reveals the man: "But thou, O LORD, art a shield for me; my glory, and

17

the lifter up of mine head" (Psalm 3:3). David was accompanied by his mighty men. No doubt he carried his personal weapons, including his shield. Humanly speaking, he had taken all possible precautions; but nevertheless his trust was in God, for all those things that were so necessary for his safety during his eventful life, his shield and buckler, the cliffs and rocks in which he took refuge from his enemies, were to him but symbols of the care and protection afforded him by God, and without which he could never have been delivered out of the hands of his enemies (see Psalm 18:2). How vital a lesson for us! We must play our part; we must do what we can, but in and through the events of life, however ordinary they may be, we must have the faith and the perception to see the hand of God and appreciate in the expression of His loving care that we are indeed workers together with Him.

David could find consolation in the knowledge that he was the Lord's anointed. God was his glory, and the lifter up of his head. Men sought now to turn this glory which God had given him into shame, to deprive him of his throne and kingdom by espousing false hopes and lying words ("leasing", lying – Psalm 4:2). But David knew that He was faithful who had promised. God had chosen and anointed him; He had promised him the everlasting stability of his throne and kingdom. As background to these phrases consider Psalm 21:1-6, which celebrates his coronation, and Psalm 89:20-29.

At this juncture it is perhaps appropriate to emphasise the fact that David was the Lord's anointed. Consequently, he who rebelled against him defied also the Lord who had appointed him. His enemies were God's enemies, and the psalm reflects this truth. This is a matter we shall need to return to as we continue our meditations in the Psalms; but for the moment it should help us to appreciate that there was nothing personal or vindictive in David's response to his enemies. Indeed, we are conscious of the Messianic element within the psalms, the very spirit which is reflected in Jesus' parable: "Those mine enemies, which would not that I should reign over them, bring hither, and slay them before me" (Luke 19:27).

David cried unto the Lord (Psalm 3:4). The verb expresses continuity and emphasises the urgency and the persistency with which David presented his pleas before God. The Lord heard him out of His holy hill, and here in these words we have, perhaps, a tacit reference to the carrying back of the ark. It was the symbol of God's presence in the midst of His people, but it should never have been regarded as some kind of talisman which afforded protection to those who carried it forth with them. God could not be confined in such a way, and David recognised that his prayers were heard in God's dwelling place and His presence continued with him to bless, for the Most High was not constrained in any way by the location of the ark.

So in these thoughts David was refreshed, and in the midst of all his troubles could lay down in sleep, clear in his conscience and firm in his faith, for the Lord sustained him, and he knew he had no cause to fear his enemies, however numerous they might be (verse 6; see also Psalm 27:3).

When the ark of the covenant was carried forth Moses spoke these words:

"Rise up, LORD, and let thine enemies be scattered."
(Numbers 10:35; Psalm 68:1)

With these thoughts of God's guidance and protection foremost in his mind, David recalled the language of Moses: "Arise, O LORD; save me, O my God: for thou hast smitten all mine enemies upon the cheek bone; thou hast broken the teeth of the ungodly" (Psalm 3:7). Like angry, ferocious beasts they had sought to tear and rend; but God had smitten and subdued them, that the victory and the dominion should be His. So, through the spirit, David could affirm that "Salvation belongeth unto the LORD: thy blessing is upon thy people" (verse 8). God was the sole possessor and dispenser of salvation; through it His blessing is upon His people. The word "blessing'" should always be noted carefully. In many instances, as the context here appears to demand, it is an overt reference to the blessing of Abraham which has particular reference, of course, to the forgiveness of sins (see Psalm 32:1,2; Acts 3:25,26; Romans 4:1-8), a thought which leads smoothly on to the opening words of Psalm 4: "Hear me when I call, O God of my righteousness."

He could not stand in his own strength. He was what he was by the grace of God, from whom his righteousness came. Like Abraham, he "believed God, and it was counted to him for righteousness"; and as in earlier days he had reflected upon the qualities necessary for a man to approach God in His holy hill, he was still conscious that only by hungering and thirsting after righteousness would he ultimately "receive the blessing from the LORD, and righteousness from the God of his salvation" (Psalm 24:3-5).

In his distress (literally in the *straitness* of his circumstances), when persecuted and hemmed in by his enemies, when the pressures of life had weighed heavily upon him, God had given him enlargement, deliverance and relief from those restrictions that hindered and impeded the path he trod. He had brought him, as it were, from the straitness of some narrow mountain path to the freedom of a large and open space. It was in the confidence born of such experiences that David could beseech God to continue to show His graciousness (AV margin) unto him (Psalm 4:1).

Evidently the words and deeds of those who led the rebellion against him were known to David. It is these whom he addresses (verse 2) as "men of high degree" (AV, "sons of men", Psalm 62:9) – that group, confederate with Absalom, who had organised and led the rebellion. They had spoken defamatory words against David, slandering and maligning him in an endeavour to undermine his authority and royal dignity. In behaving thus they had forgotten he was the Lord's anointed. In their pursuit of personal ambition they had espoused a false hope and given themselves to a vain and empty pursuit of their own aggrandisement (N.B. they "love vanity", they "seek after leasing").

In contrast (verse 3), David calls upon them to recognise the stamp of divine approval manifest in his experiences as chosen and anointed of God, one with whom the Lord had made an everlasting covenant. The word "godly", sometimes rendered "saint" (Hebrew, *chasid*), seems to be

20

descriptive not only of the quality of life such men live, but also of the covenant relationship they have established with God (see Psalm 50:5 for a definition of the word). How foolish, then, were their aspirations to worldly greatness and honour! They represent the typical rebel both in the world, and (sadly) sometimes in the ecclesia too, who in pursuit of personal ambition says in his heart, "I will not have this man to reign over me".

When assailed by hard, rebellious thoughts, when resentment burns because of self-will and self-indulgence, when one would prefer not to honour the Lord's anointed, then remember the greatness of God and consider your own finiteness. Think of the arrogance that leads to such feelings – "Stand in awe (of God), and sin not: commune with your own heart upon your bed, and be still" (verse 4). Let not such evil thinking find a place in one's heart, but even as you lie upon your bed let your meditations in the 'night watches' cause you to reflect upon your folly, that wiser, calmer thoughts may prevail; that, resting in God, your troubled heart may be still, finding peace once more by submitting to the divine will before the eyes are closed in sleep.

The words are quoted by Paul in Ephesians 4:26 with significant differences: "Be ye angry, and sin not: let not the sun go down upon your wrath." There is no need to question the verbal difference or to ponder whether Paul is quoting the Septuagint. The Spirit is its own interpreter, and through Paul the essential meaning of the words of the psalm is applied to the particular circumstances of the Ephesians. They too felt resentment one against another; but anger was not allowed to fester within the breast. Human weakness may on occasions give rise to such emotions, but they must never be allowed to take root; they must be resolved before the end of the day, and never carried forward to the dawn of another day, for "let not the sun go down upon your wrath", but "be still and know that I am God".

It is then, prepared in heart and mind (perhaps having agreed with your adversary quickly in the way – Matthew 5:21-25), that the sacrifices of righteousness can be offered

– that is, presented before the Lord in a right spirit (Psalm 4:5).

There were many in Israel who grumbled and murmured. "There be many that say, Who will shew us any good?" (verse 6). Their discontent was as a fruitful field for those who sowed the seed of rebellion. Perhaps even amongst those who were with David there were some who were filled with dismay and fear because of the apparent uncertainties and dangers that lay before them. In seeking the remedy for such faint-heartedness, David reveals himself as a true shepherd of God's flock, numbering himself with the malcontents and, indeed, all God's people, by referring to the beautiful words of the priestly benediction (Numbers 6:24-26): "LORD, lift thou up the light of thy countenance upon *us*." The blessing was pronounced by the priest when he emerged from the tabernacle where God dwelt.

Absalom and his associates were in Jerusalem; there the ark was, but David was confident that his prayer would be heard. The location of the ark placed no constraint on Israel's God; indeed, the use of this blessing might reflect David's assurance that God would bless the people out of Zion, that the hearts of the people might be knit together once more, the present folly abandoned and he himself restored to his throne. His confidence that God would sustain and deliver him finds expression in the words of verse 7: "Thou hast put more joy in my heart than they have when their grain and wine abound" (RSV). David had a deeper joy, a greater peace, that did not depend upon material blessings to sustain it. It was in God, in the fellowship he enjoyed, in the spiritual blessings that God bestowed upon him.

The words allude to Deuteronomy 33:28,29, where the thoughts of Psalm 4 in particular seem to have a foundation. As if in contrast to the more material blessings that gladdened men's hearts, David looks beyond to the deeper spiritual things in which he himself delighted. They related to eternal things that could not be affected by external circumstances and events. They gave therefore an abiding joy, a continuing peace with God that nothing but sin could destroy. It is a testimony to the character of this man after God's own heart that he could write in spite of the troubles on every hand, "I will both lay me down in peace, and sleep: for thou, LORD, only makest me dwell in *safety*" (see Deuteronomy 33:28,29 again).

PSALM 5

THERE are some psalms to which it is difficult to give a precise historical setting. Perhaps Psalm 5 falls into this category, for its message is not affected unduly by the absence of the particular circumstances against which the Spirit moved David to write it. On the other hand, bearing in mind its association in the order of psalms with two songs (3 and 4) that have an undoubted reference to the time of Absalom's rebellion, it does not seem unreasonable to presume that Psalm 5 was also connected with this period of David's life. In fact, when all three psalms are read together, there does seem to be a continuity of thought and a similarity of language that brings a conviction that this is indeed the case.

Once again we appear to be confronted with a morning hymn:

"My voice shalt thou hear in the morning, O LORD; in the morning will I direct my prayer unto thee, and will look up." (verse 3)

One wonders, however, if in fact this is precisely the case; for if Psalms 3 and 4 had reflected the experiences of David at one of the darkest hours of his life, then he would have looked in faith beyond the blackness of that night of trouble and adversity to the morning of deliverance that would eventually dawn. This, of course, is not a thought uncommon in the Psalms:

"Weeping may endure for a night, but joy cometh in the morning." (Psalm 30:5)

"I wait for the LORD, my soul doth wait, and in his word do I hope. My soul waiteth for the LORD more than they that watch for the morning: I say, more than they that watch for the morning." (Psalm 130:5,6)

David's plea is wrought in sorrow: "Give ear to my words, O LORD, consider my meditation. Hearken unto the

24

voice of my cry, my King, and my God: for unto thee will I pray" (Psalm 5:1,2).

The Hebrew word rendered "meditation" is instructive. It has been variously interpreted as "silent musing" and as "a low murmuring", connected particularly with grief and mourning. The idea of "silent musing", of carrying on a conversation with oneself within, is beautifully expressed by the words of Psalm 4: "Commune with your own heart upon your bed, and be still" (verse 4). And the connection with mourning and sorrow is illustrated in the life of Isaac, for when Abraham's servant brought Rebekah to be his wife, the record tells us that "Isaac went out to meditate in the field at the eventide" (Genesis 24:63), and the chapter concludes with the statement that after their union, Isaac "was comforted after his mother's death" (verse 67 – see also Isaiah 38:14).

We would not wish to give the impression that meditation springs only out of sorrow and adversity; but it is nevertheless true that when we are in trouble, when faced by the harsh realities of life, sobered perhaps by grief, it is then that we find it easier to reflect in silent contemplation upon the relevance of God's word and the reality of His presence about us. It is in this context that it is sometimes difficult to make a distinction between meditation and prayer, for the one passes so easily and naturally into the other. Our inmost thoughts and desires are recognised and acknowledged by God, though having no audible expression. Oftentimes, though, meditation will lead to the pouring out of our hearts before God, as David made his cry unto his King and God. The associations of the word "cry", when traced with a concordance, show that it has an intensity associated with it that springs from adversity and leads the godly man to implore God to hearken to his voice (see Psalm 22:24; 28:2 etc.). The spirit of David, "the LORD's anointed" who sat on the throne of the Lord over Israel, is surely seen in all its loveliness as, with his own position threatened as wicked men sought to depose him from his throne, he could recognise the sovereignty of his God who was truly his King and on whose behalf he reigned. It was God's Kingdom, and he but His earthly representative.

The RV has some interesting variations with regard to David's reference to the morning (verse 3): "In the morning will I order my prayer unto thee, and will keep watch." The word rendered "order" has an instructive background, for it is associated with the setting in order of the wood for the burnt offerings (Genesis 22:9, Leviticus 1:7) and also with the arranging of the parts of the sacrifice upon the altar (Leviticus 1:8). Like the morning sacrifice, David's prayer would ascend, knowing as he did that what the Lord valued above all else was a broken and a contrite spirit, which would never be despised. A similar thought is expressed in Psalm 141:2: "Let my prayer be set forth before thee as incense; and the lifting up of my hands as the evening sacrifice." So David would keep watch like the watchmen upon the tower (see Habakkuk 2:l; Micah 7:7), looking expectantly for God's deliverance, waiting for an answer of peace.

That God would hearken to his cries and deliver him, David was confident, for he knew the character of the One who had exalted him to be His anointed. He has no pleasure in the wickedness of men, and consequently David's enemies, those who sought to do him harm, could never prevail:

"For thou art not a God who delights in wickedness; evil may not sojourn with thee. The boastful may not stand before thy eyes; thou hatest all evildoers. Thou destroyest those who speak lies; the LORD abhors bloodthirsty and deceitful men."   (Psalm 5:4-6, RSV)

Note particularly here that the "foolish" of the AV are described as "boastful" (verse 5). Literally, the word means "shiners", and it is an apt and telling description of those whose main preoccupation was the display of self. As the Lord Jesus warned, 'Do not your works to be seen of men', for "many will say to me in that day, Lord, Lord, have we not prophesied in thy name? and in thy name have cast out devils? and in thy name done many wonderful works? And then will I profess unto them, I never knew you: depart from me, ye that work iniquity" (Matthew 7:22,23). Again the phrase "workers of iniquity" in the psalm (verse 5) describes a class of people who habitually practise iniquity; it is characteristic of their whole outlook on life.

They pursue iniquity "as if it were a trade or profession" (Wm. Kay, *The Psalms with Notes*). Such phrases might help us to appreciate more readily the type of men that David had to contend with and the grief it caused him that they should prosper in Israel. Yet his confidence in God brought with it the assurance that ultimately these men would not prevail, for all such were hated and abhorred by God and would not be tolerated indefinitely. This should be a source of comfort and consolation to us also, for the world remains full of evil men who pursue iniquity as if it were a trade or profession. Yet if we love righteousness and hate iniquity, we can be confident that the day is near when the sinners shall be consumed out of the earth and when the wicked shall be no more (Psalm 104:35). Some might shrink away from such sentiments; but the more we assimilate God's word, the more readily we shall see things as He sees them, and appreciate also the great responsibility we have and the urgency of our task to preach the word and to turn everyone of them from his iniquity.

In contrast, David looks forward to the day when, because of God's faithfulness, he would come again into His house and worship towards His holy temple (Psalm 5:7). The references to God's house and holy temple have led some to conjecture that the psalm must have been written after the construction of the temple and consequently could not have been written by David. Such presumptions are unnecessary and unfounded. The simple use of a concordance will establish that the phrase "house of the LORD" was applied both to the tabernacle built by Moses (Exodus 23:19; 34:26; Deuteronomy 23:18 etc.) and also to the word "temple" (1 Samuel 1:9; 3:3). Psalm 27 actually brings all three together and uses them in close conjunction:

"One thing have I desired of the LORD, that will I seek after; that I may dwell in the house of the LORD all the days of my life, to behold the beauty of the LORD, and to inquire in his temple. For in the time of trouble he shall hide me in his pavilion: in the secret of his tabernacle shall he hide me." (verse 4,5)

In any event, it is possible that David was in fact thinking of the temple in heaven of which God's house on earth was but the symbol, for this is not an uncommon thought in the Psalms (see Psalm 11:4; 18:6; 29:9).

As he contemplates his plight, the apparent power of his enemies and his own weakness, David reflects that humble spirit of dependence upon God in which He delights:

"Lead me, O LORD, in thy righteousness because of mine enemies; make thy way straight before my face."

(Psalm 5:8)

It is the spirit of the prayer Jesus taught his disciples to pray: "Lead us not into temptation, but deliver us from evil." We can have no confidence in our own ability, but we rest in the boundless love and providential care of God. The word rendered "straight" opens a wonderful vista for us. Literally, it means "plain or smooth", and it is the word used in Isaiah 40 concerning the work of John the Baptist:

"The voice of him that crieth in the wilderness, Prepare ye the way of the LORD, make straight (i.e., plain or smooth) in the desert a highway for our God."

(verse 3)

The figure behind these words has often been remarked upon. It describes how one would go before some dignitary, a prince or a king, to remove all the obstacles that might hinder or cause to stumble and fall, thus making the way straight or plain before him. Thus God is pleased to deal with us as kings. He has gone before – He leads and removes from our path all things that might cause us to stumble. It is important, however, to appreciate the fullness of the lesson. It does not mean that there will be no difficulties for us in life, no trials of faith to face and overcome. It does mean, however, that because God has gone before and prepared the way, there are no circumstances of life, no problems or tests of character, that are too great for us to overcome triumphantly by His grace. If we fail, we cannot blame God, for He has made straight the way before us; but it is entirely due to our own inadequacies – our own lack of faith in the Lord who leads us in faithfulness and righteousness.

PSALM 5

In David's case, he was particularly conscious of this
need for God's guidance, for he could have no confidence in
the smooth, flattering words of his adversaries. They were
unscrupulous and hypocritical enemies who, though they
flattered with their tongues, sought only his destruction.
So their throats were like an open sepulchre, like a
yawning grave to swallow up and devour the unwary
(Psalm 5:9).

In contemplation of their malice, David can restrain
himself no longer, but calls upon God to pass judgement on
these rebellious men (verses 10-12). It is not personal
vindictiveness that moves him, but the understanding
that those who lift their hands against the Lord's anointed
commit a treasonable act against God whom he
represents. "Destroy them" (RV, "hold them guilty"); may
their own counsels, the evil machinations of their hearts,
be turned against them, that they may be instrumental in
bringing about their own downfall. "Cast them out", or,
alternatively, "thrust them down" from the elevated
position they have sought for themselves – "for they have
rebelled against thee" (verse 10). There is the heart of the
matter. In their downfall the righteous rejoice because
thereby God has vindicated both them and His name.
They love God's name whereby His character and
attributes are revealed and His purpose made known.
How great, then, is their joy when He proves Himself true
to all He has promised! (verse 11).

"For thou, LORD, wilt bless the righteous; with favour
wilt thou compass him as with a shield."   (verse 12)

29

PSALM 6

PSALM 6 is the first of what are regarded as the seven penitential psalms (6,32,38,51,102,130,143). Nevertheless, the Messianic character of the song is beyond dispute. It was quoted by the Lord Jesus when he referred to the manner in which many human assessments of their own worth would be reversed at the final judgement:

"Not every one that saith unto me, Lord, Lord, shall enter into the kingdom of heaven; but he that doeth the will of my Father which is in heaven. Many will say to me in that day, Lord, Lord, have we not prophesied in thy name? and in thy name have cast out devils? and in thy name done many wonderful works? And then will I profess unto them, I never knew you: depart from me, ye that work iniquity."

(Matthew 7:21-23; last phrase taken from Psalm 6:8)

The quotation, however, poses an interesting question, for it is prefaced and followed by words that express the writer's deep conviction about his enemies:

"Mine eye is consumed because of grief; it waxeth old because of all mine enemies. Depart from me, all ye workers of iniquity; for the LORD hath heard the voice of my weeping. The LORD hath heard my supplication; the LORD will receive my prayer. Let all mine enemies be ashamed and sore vexed: let them return and be ashamed suddenly." (Psalm 6:7-10)

The conclusion is inescapable. These enemies were not openly antagonistic. They were not seeking his hurt or discomfort in any obvious manner; but as the words of Matthew indicate, they considered themselves to be disciples with an association with him and his work. Yet it was all a sham, no more than a vain show, for their hearts were far from him. Far from counting them his friends, he dissociates himself from them completely – "I never knew you … ye that work iniquity" – and such was the depth of his feeling because of their double standards, their hypocritical approach to him, that he counted them as enemies whose conduct was to him the source of profound sorrow and anguish. There is surely no deeper grief than the knowledge that apparent friends and fellow-workers are in fact treacherous and unreliable, motivated by selfishness and personal ambition rather than love and affection. The matter here, though, is coloured by a deeper perspective, for they were "workers of iniquity"; and the Lord Jesus (for it is surely established that it is an insight into his thoughts and feelings that the Psalm reflects) is shown to have an uncompromising attitude towards them that is completely inconsistent with personal animosity.

Another psalm provides the key:

"Surely thou wilt slay the wicked, O God: depart from me therefore, ye bloody men. For they speak against thee wickedly, and thine enemies take thy name in vain. Do not I hate them, O LORD, that hate thee? … I hate them with perfect hatred: I count them mine enemies."
(Psalm 139:19-22)

The sorrow that the godly man feels because of human wickedness (and this, of course, is particularly true of the experiences of the Lord Jesus) is clearly expressed in the 119th Psalm:

"Horror hath taken hold upon me because of the wicked that forsake thy law." (verse 53)

"Rivers of waters run down mine eyes, because they keep not thy law." (verse 136)

"I beheld the transgressors, and was grieved; because they kept not thy word." (verse 158)

Here then, in part at least, is the cause of the groaning, the tears and the grief (Psalm 6:6,7), and surely now we can begin to build up a picture of the true significance of the psalm. It is, remember, the first of the penitential psalms and it has, therefore, to do with sin and man's reaction to it. It takes us, however, into the mind of a sinless man, and it is only in the fullness of our understanding of the atonement, in the enlightenment

31

that the Truth brings, realising that "he also himself likewise took part of the same (flesh and blood); that through death he might destroy him that had the power of death" (Hebrews 2:14), that we can appreciate the manner in which he could associate himself with all those with whom, through Adam, he shared a common experience, a heritage of weakness, temptations and death, except that he alone never succumbed to the power of sin.

Thus it is from the vantage of the judgement that came by one (Adam) upon all men to condemnation (Romans 5:16,18) that the sinless one could cry that his might not be the common lot of all men: "O LORD, rebuke me not in thine anger, neither chasten *me* in thy hot displeasure" (Psalm 6:1). As with all humankind, the nature he bore was prone to corruption; therefore "have mercy upon me, O LORD; for I am weak" (lit. withered away like the sapless tree or the faded flower, for "all flesh is grass, and all the goodliness thereof is as the flower of the field" – Isaiah 40:6). He, too, needed deliverance from the dreadful effects of Adam's transgression that had been imposed upon him as upon all men – "O LORD, heal me; for my bones are vexed" (Psalm 6:2). Just as he felt bodily weakness, so also there was an anguish of spirit: "My soul is also sore vexed" (verse 3); but he did not doubt or question the wisdom of God, for his only reaction to this human situation was, "Return, O LORD, deliver (lit. 'snatch out') my soul; oh save me for thy mercies' sake" (verse 4). Why? "For in death there is no remembrance of thee: in the grave who shall give thee thanks?" (verse 5). As with all of Adam's posterity, there was no escape from the hand of death. He could not evade it, but he could be saved out of it ("snatch out my soul"). There in the coldness and blackness of the tomb all man's opportunity is lost, all communion and fellowship with God broken. Only through his victory and God's deliverance out of death could there be hope for any man. This burden the Lord carried, for without his will to overcome, all men would have perished. The travail of his soul is seen in the expressions of his inner conflict and torment: "I am weary with my groaning; all the night make I my bed to swim; I water my couch with my tears" (verse 6).

How grievous his sorrow, how deep his anger, for those who spurned the opportunity so hardly won, so wonderfully provided by God's grace! Truly, in neglecting so great a salvation, they proved themselves to be the enemies of God; and in rejecting the one who had suffered so willingly for them, they demonstrated also that they had nothing in common with the righteous one. So it was inevitable that they must "depart from me, all ye workers of iniquity", for God had heard his supplication and hearkened to the voice of his prayer (verse 9). He had emerged from the grave victorious. For them there was but shame, trouble and great vexation (verse 10).

The psalm appears to form a background to at least two New Testament scriptures – John 12 and Hebrews 5. Perhaps the links are best seen in both instances by setting the respective records in parallel columns:

Psalm 6	John 12	Hebrews 5
"My soul is also sore vexed (troubled, RSV): but thou, O LORD, how long? Return, O Lord, deliver (lit. *'snatch out'*) my soul: oh *save me* for thy mercies' sake." (verses 3,4)	*"Now is my soul troubled*; and what shall I say? Father, save me from this hour: but for this cause came I unto this hour." (verse 27)	"Who in the days of his flesh, when he had offered up *prayers* and *supplications*
"I am weary with my *groaning*; all the night make I my bed to swim; I water my couch with my *tears*." (verse 6)		with *strong crying and tears* unto him that was able to *save him from death* (lit. *out of death*), and was heard in
"For the LORD *hath heard* the voice of my weeping. The LORD hath heard my *supplication*; the LORD will receive *my prayer*." (verses 8,9)		that he feared; though he were a Son, yet learned he obedience by the things which he suffered." (verses 7,8).

John 12

The Lord's reference to the words of Psalm 6, and his interpretation of those words in terms of his own

33

experiences, help us to appreciate more fully the anguish of his soul. He was troubled; "O LORD, how long?" asked the psalm, "What shall I say? Father, save me from this hour", describes the Lord's anguish as recorded by John. But the spirit of the psalm prevails ("how long?") – "But for this cause came I unto this hour. Father, glorify thy name" (John 12:27,28). We know that the Lord Jesus experienced great physical pain and distress in his death by crucifixion, and not for one moment would we wish to minimise this. The words of John and the theme of the psalm, however, help us to see another perspective. This concerned his desire to be snatched out of death, for in death there was no remembrance of God; in the grave, none could give Him thanks. The Lord Jesus had experienced an unbroken fellowship with God. But now in that "horror of great darkness" in the coldness and stillness of the tomb, where he would lie as still and unknowing as any man, his relationship was to be broken. It could only be restored if God in His faithfulness would save him, not from death, but "out of death", for this was the means, not just of his own deliverance, but of all those who by faith will ultimately share his victory. How deep the grief he felt, the earnestness and fervour of his prayers, the psalm reveals, indicating by his weariness and the effect upon his eye (verse 7) the very real physical suffering produced as a result of his mental agony. The latter verses of the psalm (verses 8-10) assure us of the faithfulness of God who heard his prayer, hearkened to his supplication, and delivered him.

Hebrews 5

The words in italics indicate the striking similarity in the language of these two portions of scripture. Clearly Hebrews is expanding the psalm, and we need say little more in the light of what we have already written to clarify this point. Perhaps to emphasise "in the days of his flesh" lends weight to the development of the theme of the sinless one as a man among men. Particularly interesting, though, are the words which tell us "though he were a Son, yet learned he obedience by the things which he suffered". How did he learn obedience by these things, for he never disobeyed, and sin was never part of his experience?

34

Surely in our reflections on Psalm 6 we have, if but dimly, an insight into the answer. The burden he carried with his awareness of the sinfulness of his fellow men was to him a continual source of grief (Psalm 119, etc.). He knew that there was no hope for any man if he failed to overcome. Thus there was strong crying and tears as he sought the strength he needed and as he contemplated the awful consequences of failure, not just for himself, but for all of Adam's race without exception. It was the realisation of this awesome responsibility, which he reflected upon in grief and tears and vexation of soul, that taught him obedience, that sustained the conviction that there must for him be no disobedience, for the consequences were too dreadful to contemplate.

Truly, the gospels tell us of the events that occurred in the life of our Lord Jesus; but it is in the psalms that we so often get that fuller insight into what his sacrifice cost him, as they take us into the innermost recesses of his heart and mind and reveal just what he felt and thought. Such a song is Psalm 6.

PSALM 7

THERE can be little doubt as to the historical background to Psalm 7. It is clearly associated with that period of David's life when he was driven from the royal court by the hatred of Saul and hunted by the king as though he were some kind of wild animal. To fully appreciate the appropriateness of the psalm to this time in David's life, it would be helpful to read chapters 21–26 of 1 Samuel; for not only do these chapters give us historical detail, but also, in the words spoken by David and Saul, insight into the minds of both these men.

It is interesting to reflect upon the theme of the psalm, for while expressing his confidence in God and pleading for His deliverance from those who would rend and tear him like wild beasts (verses 1,2), David's principal concern is to protest his innocence in the face of those who falsely accused him (verses 6-10), confident in the knowledge of God's perpetual anger against the wicked and the certainty of His ultimate judgement upon them (verses 14-16). In this respect, it can truly be described as a song for the righteous, beginning in the experiences of David, but so aptly reflecting the feelings of God's servants in all ages when faced by the slander and lies of evil men, and, perhaps, finding its fullest and deepest expression in the life of the Lord Jesus Christ, of whom another psalm testifies: "Let not them that are mine enemies wrongfully rejoice over me: neither let them wink with the eye that hate me without a cause" (Psalm 35:19, cited of Jesus in John 15:25). For "when he was reviled, (he) reviled not again; when he suffered, he threatened not; but committed himself to him that judgeth righteously" (1 Peter 2:23). We often speak of 'Messianic' psalms; but considerations such as these lead us to wonder whether all the psalms can be regarded as reflecting the mind, the life and the experiences of the Lord Jesus Christ in some way or another. Perhaps as we progress through the psalms, this fact might become more evident and bring us to a greater appreciation and a deeper realisation that the writers of these songs, by the Holy Spirit, do indeed testify in a most wondrous manner to the sufferings of Christ and the glory that should follow (1 Peter 1:11).

The heading to the psalm says, "Shiggaion of David, which he sang unto the LORD, concerning the words of Cush the Benjamite". The word "Shiggaion" is said to mean 'something erratic' in the sense of 'to wander', and hence conveys the idea of excitement or indicates that the words which follow are the product of intense emotional experience resulting in expressions of passionate feeling. In the event, the tone of the psalm does not convey the idea of a deep cry of anguish in adversity and tribulation, but rather a sense of indignation – righteous anger at the slanderous allegations of his enemies and a yearning and longing for God to vindicate him and judge the wicked, that the righteous might at last be established in the earth. The identity of Cush the Benjamite has caused much speculation. The close association in word and thought with the historical record of 1 Samuel already referred to, and in particular the words of verse 4 ("yea, I have delivered him that without cause is mine enemy"), have led some to suppose that it is Saul himself who is referred to under the pseudonym "Cush", so named because of his 'dark, black hatred of David', or again to one of his retinue 'who was as Ethiopian in heart as his master'.

Whether or not it was Saul himself or one of his associates, possibly of Ethiopic origin, it is evident that men were fostering Saul's hatred of David by bringing him false and slanderous reports that David was plotting to take his life, perhaps thus hoping to gain favour with the king, but in reality only further disturbing his already unbalanced mind. The words of 1 Samuel reveal his mental derangement:

"All of you (Benjamites) have conspired against me." (22:8)

"Why have ye conspired against me (the priests of Nob), thou and the son of Jesse?" (22:13)

"And David said to Saul, Wherefore hearest thou men's words, saying, Behold, David seeketh thy hurt?"
(24:9)

Then Saul's anger was kindled against Jonathan, and he said unto him ... do not I know that thou hast chosen the son of Jesse to thine own confusion ... For as long as the son of Jesse liveth upon the ground, thou shalt not be established, nor thy kingdom. Wherefore now send and fetch him unto me, for he shall surely die."
(20:30,31)

Saul knew that David had been anointed by Samuel. His own stubbornness and rebellion had caused the Lord to leave him. It was a situation that he could not bring himself to accept. It produced within him a conflict, and tensions that he could not cope with; and it was these that revealed the man and contributed to his own destruction. The words of Psalm 7 illustrate this warped and twisted characteristic of human nature. It is seen, as it were, written large in the life of Saul; but this insidious, cankerous growth of jealousy and hatred is characteristic of all sinful men who are unable to find that peace which belongs to them that love God's law.

"He hath also prepared for him the instruments of death; he ordaineth his arrows against the persecutors. Behold, he travaileth with iniquity, and hath conceived mischief, and brought forth falsehood. He made a pit, and digged it, and is fallen into the ditch which he made. His mischief shall return upon his own head, and his violent dealing shall come down upon his own pate."
(Psalm 7:13-16)

The mind of David is also revealed in contrast to that of Saul, and we set out in tabulated form the words of the psalm for easy comparison (see overleaf).

David's integrity, his understanding of the situation in which he stood, is clearly seen. He would not take matters into his own hands to promote his own personal interests; he would not sin by lifting up his hand against the Lord's anointed. Patiently he rested in the Lord to whom he had committed his cause, trusting in His righteous judgement.

So the psalm reflects the spirit of all true servants of God. They do not seek their 'rights' as men would interpret them; they do not seek recompense from those who show themselves to be their enemies, but, like the Lord Jesus, they commit their cause to Him that judgeth righteously, knowing that He has said, "Vengeance is mine; I will repay, saith the Lord" (Romans 12:19).

They long for the day when God will finally judge and destroy the wicked that the earth might be glorified by His salvation. Theirs is the spirit of those slain for the word of God and the testimony that they held, under the fifth seal: "How long, O Lord, holy and true, dost thou not judge and avenge our blood on them that dwell on the earth?" (Revelation 6:10).

It is a perspective that perhaps many of us would shrink from, but nevertheless it remains the theme of Psalm 7, one of the songs that God has given to sustain us in the long night of Gentile power (see Psalm 42:8).

PSALM 7	1 SAMUEL
"O Lord my God, in thee do I put my trust: save me from all them that persecute me, and deliver me." (verse 1)	"And David fled from Naioth in Ramah, and came and said before Jonathan, What have I done? what is mine iniquity? and what is my sin before thy father, that he seeketh my life?" (20:1)
	"And David arose, and fled that day for fear of Saul, and went to Achish the king of Gath." (21:10)
	"As thy life was much set by this day in mine eyes, so let my life be much set by in the eyes of the Lord, and let him deliver me out of all tribulation." (26:24)
	(See also 23:7-12; 19-24)

PSALM 7

1 SAMUEL

"O LORD my God, if I have done this; if there be iniquity in my hands; if I have rewarded evil unto him that was at peace with me ... Let the enemy persecute my soul, and take it; yea, let him tread down my life upon the earth, and lay mine honour in the dust."
(verses 3-5)

"And David said to Saul, Wherefore hearest thou men's words, saying, Behold, David seeketh thy hurt? Behold, this day thine eyes have seen how that the LORD had delivered thee to day into mine hand in the cave: and some bade me kill thee: but mine eye spared thee; and I said, I will not put forth mine hand against my lord, for he is the LORD's anointed ... know thou and see that there is neither evil nor transgression in mine hand, and I have not sinned against thee; yet thou huntest my soul to take it." (24:9-11)
(See also 26:8,9; 17-20)

"Arise, O LORD, in thine anger, lift up thyself because of the rage of mine enemies: and awake for me to the judgment that thou hast commanded." (verse 6)

"The LORD judge between me and thee, and the LORD avenge me of thee: but mine hand shall not be upon thee." (24:12)
"David said furthermore, As the LORD liveth, the LORD shall smite him; or his day shall come to die; or he shall descend into battle, and perish. The LORD forbid that I should stretch forth mine hand against the LORD's anointed." (26:10,11)

"The LORD shall judge the people: judge me, O LORD, according to my righteousness, and according to mine integrity that is in me. Oh let the wickedness of the wicked come to an end; but establish the just: for the righteous God trieth the hearts and reins." (verses 8,9)

"The LORD render to every man his righteousness and his faithfulness: for the LORD delivered thee into my hand today, but I would not stretch forth mine hand against the LORD's anointed." (26:23)
"As saith the proverb of the ancients, Wickedness proceedeth from the wicked: but mine hand shall not be upon thee." (24:13)
"The LORD therefore be judge, and judge between me and thee, and see, and plead my cause, and deliver me out of thine hand." (24:15)

PSALM 8

MANY readers will be aware of the suggestion developed by J. W. Thirtle in his book *The Titles of the Psalms*, that the words "for the Chief Musician" (AV, "to the chief Musician") which prefix fifty-five psalms, together with the accompanying words, such as "Gittith", "Shoshannim", "Alamoth" etc., through error in compilation, have been placed at the head of the psalm following, whereas in fact they refer to the preceding psalm. In developing this idea Thirtle argues that the literary information, i.e., the author, the description of the writing (whether song or michtam etc.), its historical circumstance or the object for which it was written (e.g., "to bring to remembrance", Psalm 38), are always placed at the head of the psalm; whereas the musical information (i.e. information as to when they were to be sung etc.) always came at the conclusion of the psalm.

Thus the words, "For the Chief Musician; set to the Gittith" (RV) which appear at the head of Psalm 8 actually refer to Psalm 7. It is said that the word "Gittith" has to do with the winepress, and hence by association with the Feast of Tabernacles. The winepress in scripture is indicative of judgement, and we have already pursued this theme in our study of the previous psalm (in this connection note particularly Psalm 7:5).

Similarly, the musical information at the head of Psalm 9 is not relevant to that song, but to the preceding psalm, which is the subject of our present study. It bears the inscription, "For the Chief Musician; set to Muthlabben" (RV). The Jewish paraphrase known as the Targum renders the phrase "Muth-labben" as "concerning the death of the champion", or again, "regarding the death of the man who went out between the camps". The reference to Goliath of Gath is unmistakeable. In fact he is twice

41

referred to as "a champion" in the text of 1 Samuel 17 (verses 4,23).

A champion, or one who stood between two camps, was one who presented himself for single combat, with the final outcome of the conflict between the rival armies being dependent on the victory of the champion. By his victory the battle could be decided and the warfare terminated. Thus Goliath hurled his taunts, his scorn and his ridicule upon Israel and their God. The historical setting for Psalm 8 then, indicated through the musical directions at its subscription, is the defeat and death of Goliath of Gath. There is, perhaps, no more striking example of the value of Thirtle's work than that on Psalm 8, seen as written by David to celebrate his victory over the Philistine. At first consideration, we might feel that there is no clear reference to that event, but a comparison of the psalm with the record in 1 Samuel 17 produces some remarkable verbal allusions.

PSALM 8	1 SAMUEL 17
"O LORD our Lord, how excellent is thy name in all the earth!" (verse 1)	"That all the earth may know that there is a God in Israel." (verse 46)
"Out of the mouth of babes and sucklings hast thou ordained strength because of thine enemies." (verse 2)	"Thou art but a youth." (verse 33) "And when the Philistine looked about, and saw David, he disdained him: for he was but a youth." (verse 42)
"Thou madest him to have dominion over the works of thy hands; thou hast put all things under his feet." (verse 6)	"So David prevailed over the Philistine ... Therefore David ran, and stood upon the Philistine." (verses 50,51)
"All sheep and oxen, yea, and the beasts of the field; the fowl of the air, and the fish of the sea ..." (verses 7,8)	"And the Philistine said to David ... I will give thy flesh unto the fowls of the air, and to the beasts of the field. Then said David ... I will give the carcases of the host of the Philistines this day unto the fowls of the air, and to the wild beasts of the earth." (verses 44-46)

These verbal links establish beyond all reasonable doubt that David was inspired to write this psalm to celebrate his victory over Goliath.

The psalm has a particular spiritual emphasis. Clearly the challenge of Goliath and his subsequent defeat by the representative of the God of Israel has a typical and symbolic meaning in relation to the purpose of God that stands for all ages. Goliath, on the one hand, represents all the glory of flesh, proud and arrogant in his abuse and defiance of the armies of Israel and of the God whose purpose in the earth was to be carried forward through them. David, in contrast to this human colossus, was but a youth without military experience, going forth without the military accoutrements that flesh would have regarded as essential for such a conflict, yet confident in his trust that God who had helped him slay the lion and the bear would also deliver this Philistine, so beastlike in his outlook and approach, into his hand. The victory was the Lord's, and it stands as a token of the ultimate conquest of sin in all its manifestations. The divine behest that man should "have dominion over the works of his hands" was shown to be certain of realisation, for it was the upright that should "have dominion over them in the morning"; and David's own understanding is perhaps indicated by the fact that after his victory, he took the head of Goliath to Jerusalem and buried it there. The suggestion that this became Golgotha, the place of the skull, where the Lord Jesus was crucified, is particularly appealing when considered against the background of the psalm.

The historical background is seen, then, to throw enlightenment on the grand theme that is developed in the psalm. It is interesting to note that the Lord Jesus alluded to the words of this psalm, linking them with another scripture (Isaiah 14) which tells of the downfall of Babylon, yet another symbol of human pride and arrogance – the very epitome of human rebellion, representing in its worship and culture everything that the God of heaven hates. Truly a colossus amongst the nations!

THE PRAISES OF ISRAEL (PSALMS 1–72)

The background is the sending forth of the seventy (Luke 10) and the words of condemnation spoken by the Lord Jesus concerning those principal cities in which they should preach. Once again we set out the scriptures in tabulated form for easy reference:

LUKE 10	ISAIAH 14	PSALM 8
"And thou, Capernaum, which art exalted to heaven, shalt be thrust down to hell." (verse 15)	"I will ascend into heaven, I will exalt my throne above the stars of God." (verses 13,14)	"Who hast set thy glory above the heavens." (verse 1)
"And he saith unto them, I beheld Satan as lightning fall from heaven." (verse 18)	"Hell from beneath is moved for thee to meet thee at thy coming." (verse 9) "Thy pomp is brought down to the grave." (verse 11) "Yet thou shalt be brought down to hell." (verse 15) "How art thou fallen from heaven, O Lucifer, son of the morning!" (verse 12)	
"Behold, I give unto you power to tread on serpents and scorpions, and over all the power of the enemy." (verse 19)	"For out of the serpent's root shall come forth a cockatrice, and his fruit shall be a fiery flying serpent." (verse 29)	"Thou hast put all things under his feet: all sheep and oxen, yea, and the beasts of the field." (verses 6,7) "That thou mightest still the enemy and the avenger." (verse 2)

"In that hour Jesus rejoiced in spirit, and said, I thank thee, O Father, Lord of heaven and earth, that thou hast hid these things from the wise and prudent, and hast revealed them unto babes." (verse 21)

"Out of the mouths of babes and sucklings hast thou ordained strength." (verse 2)

"All things are delivered unto me of my Father." (verse 22)

"Thou hast put all things under his feet." (verse 6)

In the success of his disciples' work Jesus saw the earnest of the final victory over all the power of sin, of the fall of Babylon, and the assurance that God would indeed subdue all things under his feet.

In this context of God's purpose to give man dominion over the works of His hands, it is perhaps appropriate to draw attention to the manner in which the language of Genesis 1, which of course the psalm quotes, is applied to the dominion of Nebuchadnezzar; for in him is seen exemplified the rebellious spirit of man that would seek to frustrate the purpose of God and usurp the dominion and sovereignty that belongs to God alone and those who represent Him:

"The leaves thereof (of the tree) were fair, and the fruit thereof much, and in it was meat for all: the beasts of the field had shadow under it, and the fowls of the heaven dwelt in the boughs thereof, and all flesh was fed of it." (Daniel 4:12)

Nebuchadnezzar sought for dominion, but he could not achieve it; instead, he himself became like a beast (verses 16,17). This is why human empires are likened unto beasts which tear and rend one another in their desire for dominion over the earth (Daniel 7). When men forget God, they themselves become like the beasts of the field.

"I have made the earth, the man and the beast that are upon the ground, by my great power and by my outstretched arm, and have given it unto whom it seemed meet unto me. And now have I given all these lands into the hand of Nebuchadnezzar the king of Babylon, my servant; and the beasts of the field have I given him also to serve him" (Jeremiah 27:5,6 – see also 28:14).

The scriptures, then, establish spiritual truths made plain by the historical background to Psalm 8. With these considerations before us, we shall turn our attention now to the manner in which the psalm provides us with a divinely inspired commentary on the words of Genesis 1.

In the first part of our study we established the historical background to the psalm, finding in David's triumph over Goliath the token of God's ultimate victory over all the arrogance and pride of flesh. We saw how this typical significance was echoed in other scripture, notably by the Lord Jesus as he beheld the success of his disciples in their preaching mission and saw therein the fall of Babylon the Great, linking together in his language Psalm 8 and Isaiah 14 (Luke 10).

The manner, however, in which against this background the psalm describes the ultimate fulfilment of the purpose of God in man is a profound expression of the divine intent in creation. It is at once a divinely inspired commentary on Genesis and a prophecy of the ultimate fulfilment of those words in the Lord Jesus Christ:

"And God said, Let us make man in our image, after our likeness: and let them have dominion over the fish of the sea, and over the fowl of the air, and over the cattle, and over all the earth, and over every creeping thing that creepeth upon the earth. So God created man in his own image, in the image of God created he him; male and female created he them. And God blessed them, and God said unto them, Be fruitful, and multiply, and replenish the earth, and subdue it: and have dominion over the fish of the sea, and over the fowl of the air, and over every living thing that moveth upon the earth" (Genesis 1:26-28).

The use of the word "dominion" is illuminating, for, of course, it is associated with the idea of sovereignty. It conjures up the picture of a kingdom. Thus we might say

46

that in these words we have the first reference to the kingdom of God in scripture. It is linked with the fact that God made man in His image and likeness. The implication seems obvious: made in the image of God, man was intended to represent the Almighty. He was to be Lord of Creation, not in his own right, but as regent on God's behalf, representing Him in the midst of all that His hand had made. This is surely the message of the psalm.

It is sometimes assumed that the manner in which David expresses his wonder at the majesty of the heavens (Psalm 8:3) and then poses the question, "What is man, that thou art mindful of him? and the son of man, that thou visitest him?" (verse 4) is drawing attention to the apparent insignificance of man. But upon reflection this is seen to be only partly true. Man is an insignificant, transient creature of the dust when considered apart from the purpose of God. The psalmist, however, in contemplating the splendour of the heavens, is filled with awe and amazement not by the boundless realms of space, but by the fact that for all the wonder of God's handiwork, it is not through this medium that God's glory will be seen to its greatest effect, but through man, who, in the orbit of God's purpose, has been chosen to represent God and to glorify Him in that most magnificent of commissions given at creation, "to have dominion over the works of thy (God's) hands". It is through man, weak and frail though he may be, that God intends to carry His purpose to its ultimate fulfilment.

Of course, man created in God's image failed to rise to the greatness of that calling. He came under subjection to sin and death (see Psalm 19:13; 119:133; Romans 5:7,21; 6:14). But the purpose of God was not frustrated by this failure of man, and the psalm is an eloquent testimony to the fact that ultimately God will fulfil this purpose in one designated "son of man".

It should be noted that the psalm opens and closes with the words, "O LORD our Lord, how excellent is thy name in all the earth". We know from our own experiences and observations that this is not a description of the earth at present. Far from the excellence of God's name being acknowledged, it is blasphemed and dishonoured by evil men. So our minds are directed to the fact that the psalm is really a prophecy, an affirmation of God's ultimate intention to be glorified in man when He will give him the dominion promised. This dominion, however, is to be achieved through the one styled "son of man" – one who should be the embodiment of everything that God intended man to be. In the words, "Thou hast put all things under his feet" we have the assurance of how this representative man would triumph over the serpent-power of sin, for it embraces the promise of Genesis 3:15 – "It shall bruise thy head, and thou shalt bruise his heel".

The title "Son of man" is perhaps the most common title used of the Lord Jesus in the Gospel records. It should be noted that it is never used of him by others, but it is always he who uses it of himself. Clearly it is a Messianic title, and it is not intended to indicate only that he was of Adamic stock (true though that is). Some New Testament passages point unmistakably to Daniel's prophecies of the Son of man (e.g., Daniel 7:9-14 – see for instance Matthew 24:30; 26:64; John 5:27). Daniel's theme, however, is but an extension and elaboration of the divine theme of "dominion" arising from Genesis 1 and expounded in Psalm 8.

The title "Son of man" is therefore a declaration by the Lord Jesus Christ that he is representative of the human race – the perfection of manhood in whom is embodied everything that God intended man to be when He created him. And in breaking the power of sin within himself, thus showing that he was capable of ruling all the latent tendencies to sin that he shared with other men, he indicated also that he alone was fit to exercise the dominion promised and to rule the world as God's future King.

It is, of course, the epistle to the Hebrews that brings Genesis 1 and Psalm 8 into focus in the person of the Lord Jesus Christ. Notice the reference in chapter 1 (which deals with the Lord's superiority over the angels) to the fact that he has obtained "a more excellent name" – an obvious allusion to the opening and closing words of Psalm 8. Chapter 2, however, directly relates the words of the psalm to the redemptive work of the Lord Jesus. "For unto the angels hath he not put in subjection the world to come, whereof we speak" (verse 5). The dominion is not theirs, but his; and not his alone – for through him comes dominion over sin and death (verses 6-9).

"It became him, for whom are all things, and by whom are *all things*, in bringing many sons unto glory, to make the captain of their salvation perfect through sufferings." (verse 10)

The emphasis upon "all things" is obvious. Two simple words – yet whenever we encounter them in scripture we do well to examine the context and consider whether in fact they are being quoted from Psalm 8 with all its associations (see Romans 8:32; 1 Corinthians 15:27,28; Philippians 3:21; Ephesians 1:10 etc.).

PSALMS 9 & 10

IT is not intended, even if space allowed, to give a verse-by-verse exposition of every psalm. Our hope is that we might stimulate further study by indicating the general theme of the psalms, and on occasions deal more fully with particular examples that assume a more obvious importance because of their use in the New Testament.

We have already drawn attention to the fact that certain psalms are linked, by the order in which they are presented, with that which follows (e.g., Psalms 1 and 2; 3 and 4); and a consideration of the substance of Psalms 9 and 10 leads to a similar conclusion in this instance.

The association between the psalms is based initially on three facts:

1. There is no note of authorship to Psalm 10. It is usually assumed in such instances that this is an indication that it is from the pen of the author of the previous psalm. In fact, in the Septuagint, the two psalms are regarded as one.

2. Psalm 9 is the first of the 'alphabetic psalms' – that is, psalms that appear to be structured on the alphabet. For instance, each stanza of the psalm commences with the successive letters of the Hebrew alphabet through to the eleventh. The first verse of Psalm 10 begins with the twelfth; but at this point the sequence is broken, only to be reintroduced at verse 12, when the sequence continues through the last four letters of the alphabet. It is suggested that the use of the alphabet was an aid to memory. This may be true, but it does not account for the irregular use we encounter here, or, indeed, for the most prominent and wonderful example in Psalm 119, where every verse refers in some way to the word of God.

The letters of the Hebrew alphabet are the foundation of the language through which God was pleased to reveal Himself to men. They form the framework with which God has constructed the manifestation of His purpose. It is therefore significant that verses 2 to 11 of Psalm 10, which turn away from the alphabetic structure, should be describing men who have no place for God in their lives, and who consider themselves to be secure from all judgement and retribution because God, if He exists at all, is not interested in them or their works. Could it not be an indication that for all such, because of their separation from the word of God that liveth and abideth for ever, there is no part or place in the purpose of God revealed in that word? They are outside the orbit of His grace.

3. Finally, there are the linguistic links between the psalms. These are best appreciated by setting them out below in parallel columns:

PSALM 9

PSALM 10

"in times of trouble" (verse 9)   "in times of trouble" (verse 1)

(this particular phrase does not reoccur in any other part of the Old Testament record)

"oppressed" (verse 9)   "oppressed" (verse 18)

(literally 'downtrodden'; the Hebrew word only occurs once more outside the context of these two psalms)

"that the nations may know themselves to be but men" (verse 20)

"man who is of the earth" (verse 18, RSV)

"He forgetteth not the cry of the humble" (verse 12)

"forget not the humble" (verse12)

"for ever and ever" (verse 5)   "for ever and ever" (verse 16)

"Arise, O LORD" (verse 19)   "Arise, O LORD" (verse 12)

"all the nations that forget God" (verse 17)

"All his thoughts are, There is no God" (verse 4, AV margin)

It is difficult in these particular psalms to ascribe them to any particular historic events in the life of David, although the internal evidence of the songs would suggest a time in the later years of David's reign, certainly after the bringing up of the Ark from the house of Obed-edom, for God is spoken of as "the LORD, which dwelleth in Zion" (Psalm 9:11). Also, there is reference to the "daughter of Zion" (verse 14). The use of this phrase, which personifies the inhabitants of Zion as her daughter and thus stands also for the city itself (see Isaiah 22:4; 52:2; Jeremiah 4:31 etc.), surely demands the consolidation of the place of Zion in the purpose of God that has its foundations in the covenant that God made with David. Again, the description of the wicked (Psalm 10:2-13) points not to the heathen, but rather to those who existed in the midst of Israel itself like a canker, corrupting the very body of the nation. This also would seem to be more appropriately ascribed to the plotting and scheming associated with David's latter years, after his sin in the matter of Bathsheba and Uriah the Hittite, when David appears to have been less decisive in the exercise of his authority and many factions flourished, both in the court of the king and in the nation abroad, spreading discontent.

There is on this count a sharp contrast between the two psalms. The predominant theme through both seems to be an emphasis upon the sovereignty of God (see Psalm 9:3,4,7,8,11,16,19; 10:12,14-18). Psalm 9, however, is concerned with the manner in which God has judged, and will again judge the heathen (nations) (see verses 15,16,17,20, and in particular verse 5: "Thou hast rebuked the heathen, thou hast destroyed the wicked, thou hast put out their name for ever and ever").

Whatever incipient fulfilment the words of verse 5 might have had, they are clearly prophetic of God's ultimate triumph over all human pride and arrogance. There is a clear allusion to Amalek, that great type of all the nations that oppose themselves to God and His people: "Thou shalt blot out the remembrance of Amalek from under heaven" (Deuteronomy 25:19).

The words of verse 6 have been rendered, "As for the enemy, they are extinct" (Kay – *The Psalms with Notes*). In contrast to the eternal desolation that will overtake the wicked, Yahweh endures for ever, and He has prepared

His throne for judgement (verse 7). Consequently, He will
judge the world in righteousness (verse 8). This is just one
of a number of similar references (see also Psalm 96:10,13)
which seem to be the basis of the apostle's words to the
Athenians:

> "He (God) hath appointed a day, in the which he will
> judge the world in righteousness by that man whom he
> hath ordained; whereof he hath given assurance unto
> all men, in that he hath raised him from the dead."
> (Acts 17:31)

Even the thought of the resurrection of the Lord Jesus
seems to find expression in the psalm: "When he maketh
inquisition for blood, he remembereth them" (verse 12). It
points back to the divine principle declared to Noah
(Genesis 9:5,6) but portends also the words of those who
called upon themselves the blood of the Lord Jesus: "His
blood be on us, and on our children" (Matthew 27:25). But
he who suffered of them that hated him could rejoice
because God had lifted him up from the gates of death
(Psalm 9:13) that he might yet show forth all His praise in
the gates of Zion, and rejoice in His salvation (verse 14).

It is because of these things which are "faithful and
true" that the psalmist can even now rejoice in the fact
that "the LORD also will be a refuge for the oppressed, a
refuge in times of trouble. And they that know thy name
will put their trust in thee: for thou, LORD, hast not (lit.
'never') forsaken them that seek thee" (verses 9,10). To
know His name encompasses an understanding of the
whole will and purpose of God, and in the particular
context of the psalm recalls the manner in which God has
revealed Himself in history for the salvation of His people;
and herein is the assurance that He will fulfil all that He
has promised.

Perhaps the words of verse 17 regarding "all the nations
that forget God" serve as a useful bridge between the two
psalms. Literally, the word "forget" is 'are forgetful', the
tense of the verb implying a habit or rule of life. It
suggests a wilful neglect of God, a deliberate act of will to
shut Him out of one's life and experience.

The words of Psalm 9, however, which speak of the
heathen are reflected in Psalm 10, when the psalmist

turns to consider not the nations whom God has judged, but those in Israel who have adopted the "Babylonish" way of life. They, too, as a deliberate choice, have disregarded God and, like the heathen around them, have elected to live as though God did not exist:

"The wicked, through the pride of his countenance, will not seek after God: all his thoughts are, There is no God." (verse 4, see AV margin)

"He hath said in his heart, I shall not be moved." (verse 6)

"He hath said in his heart, God hath forgotten: he hideth his face; he will never see it." (verse 11)

"Wherefore doth the wicked contemn God? he hath said in his heart, Thou wilt not require it." (verse 13)

The wicked in these passages is not the atheist, the man who thinks that he can prove by intellectual reason that God does not exist. These are men who publicly acknowledge Him, but in their heart as they pursue their wickedness, they speak to themselves by way of assurance the words of self-delusion: "There is no God", "God hath forgotten", "He will not require it". They assure themselves that, if there is a God, then He is not really interested in them; and consequently they are free to cast off all moral restraint and do that which is right in their own eyes, for they say, "There is no day of judgement, no hour of reckoning, no time of retribution". Faced by such wickedness in the midst of God's people by those who, unlike the heathen, had a knowledge of the revealed will of God, the psalmist is moved to cry, "Why standest thou afar off, O LORD? why hidest thou thyself in times of trouble?" (Psalm 10:1). It is a perplexing experience that is part of the spiritual training of all God's children, that sometimes He seems to have left them. They feel bereft of His help; they are conscious of a desolating sense of separation from Him. But it is in the midst of such experiences that God looks for that resolute and steadfast spirit that will not let go those eternal things which He has committed to our trust. It is part of the chastening of the Lord, one of the means by which He tries and proves us to see if we will keep His word, that He might know all that is in our hearts (see Deuteronomy 8:2; 2 Chronicles 32:31).

For all the cunning, deceit and oppression of the poor (Psalm 10:3-10), however, David is not deceived. He knows that God has seen it: "For thou beholdest mischief and spite, to requite it with thy hand" (verse 14) . His prayer is that God will break the power of the wicked, seeking him out until none of his evil works remain (verse 15).

So he declares that the Lord is King for ever and ever; the heathen are perished out of His land (verse 16). Is it a reference back to the theme of Psalm 9, or is David recognising that the wicked in Israel were no better than the heathen? They were Israelites by birth, but Canaanites at heart, who, when God answers the cries of the poor and humble, will perish out of His land as finally and thoroughly as God will blot out the name of Amalek, in that day when the man who is of the earth will no more have the dominion and oppress the poor and humble (verses 17,18).

55

PSALM 11

WHEN David came to the court of King Saul he soon grew in stature and was recognised and held in favour and esteem by the people (1 Samuel 18:13,16). Saul with that twisted thinking that became a characteristic of his bitterness and hatred towards David, had in his madness twice tried to kill him (verse 11). Filled with fear and foreboding, he appointed David as captain over a thousand, with the evident intention of removing him from the immediate sphere of influence in the court itself, and increasing the possibility that as an active soldier he would sooner or later fall in battle, or act imprudently and so lose influence and esteem (verse 13). David, however, continued to prosper and grow in favour with the people. He clearly took his responsibilities seriously and regarded himself increasingly, with his widening authority, as a shepherd in Israel, for he "went out and came in before the people" (verses 13,16).

A time came when Saul openly expressed his desire to have David killed (1 Samuel 19:1). At this juncture, as the record reveals, it became necessary for David to take measures to protect himself and eventually to flee for his life and become a fugitive. In the time preceding his flight, his life in the royal court must have been full of uncertainty. There were probably few like Jonathan, whom he could trust implicitly, and there must have been many false friends who, while actually loyal to Saul and seeking to destroy or discredit him, suggested how he should behave to ensure his safety. It is against this background that Psalm 11 appears to have been written.

The counsel of false friends was 'get away while you can', 'take refuge in the caves and rocks of the mountains which offer you safety'. David, however, conscious of the fact that he was the Lord's anointed and that it was necessary to behave in a manner fitting this status, while remaining loyal to Saul, showed concern for "the flock of God" and conducted himself with dignity, recognising the responsibility laid on him. To take flight before it was necessary would have been an act of cowardice; a shirking of responsibility that was an indication of a lack of real faith in the God whom he had made his refuge in those troubled times. David's response was typical of the man:

"In the LORD put I my trust: how say ye to my soul, Flee as a bird to your mountain? For, lo, the wicked bend their bow, they make ready their arrow upon the string, that they may privily shoot at the upright in heart. If the foundations be destroyed, what can the righteous do?" (verses 1-3)

The advice to flee is based upon the fact that the wicked were dominant in the kingdom. They were prepared to destroy David, either literally or by character assassination, for the figure of the bow is used to describe slanderous accusations in other scriptures (see Psalm 64:3-6). This they did privily ("in darkness", RV) for fear of the people, with whom David enjoyed great popularity. Likening the kingdom to a building, they asserted that the very foundations of righteousness, truth and justice on which it was built had been eroded away, and in such circumstances they argued, "What can the righteous do?" – a rhetorical question demanding the answer, 'Nothing!'

The obvious similarity between the experience of David and the circumstances of the Lord Jesus Christ is an indication of how all the psalms in their various ways reveal the mind and spirit of Messiah. It also emphasises the exhortation to us to take "the shield of faith, wherewith ye shall be able to quench all the fiery darts of the wicked" (Ephesians 6:16).

The advice to flee to the mountain is particularly telling. It recalls the urgent words of the angel to Lot (Genesis 19:17). Lot, however, would not go to the mountains, out of fear for his safety, and sought refuge instead in the little city of Zoar. Was it not, then, a subtle suggestion to tempt David to think that, as with Lot, it was God's will for him to seek refuge in the mountains rather than remain in the city? That the thought is

57

implicit in the false counsel seems evident from David's description of the judgement of the wicked in terms of the destruction of Sodom and Gomorrah: "Upon the wicked he shall rain snares, fire and brimstone, and an horrible tempest" (verse 6).

In response to the pressure of worldly advice that would have destroyed his faith, David refers them to the true grounds of his confidence – facts which, if the righteous remained true to their God, would leave them in an unassailable position, for:

"The LORD is in his holy temple, the LORD's throne is in heaven: his eyes behold, his eyelids try, the children of men. The LORD trieth the righteous: but the wicked and him that loveth violence his soul hateth."

(verses 4,5)

To men, the unrighteous might appear to prevail. Truth and justice might seem to have perished out of the earth. Men who are not 'God-conscious' might, as a consequence, looking at the events of the moment, imagine indeed that the foundations have been destroyed. The eye of faith, however, sees beyond the outward appearance to the reality of God's throne in heaven, from whence He exercises His sovereignty over all the affairs of men. Here is one who judges righteously and is unaffected by all the prejudices and evil passions that influence men in their assessment of their fellows. If men have been faithful to God, then however painful the experience might be for the moment, it doesn't really matter what others might think or what opinions they might hold concerning them; for "the foundation of God standeth sure, having this seal, The Lord knoweth them that are his" (2 Timothy 2:19). Thus the Lord "beholds" from heaven; the word suggests "a discerning, penetrating gaze" (*Cambridge Bible*). The idea of the eyelids trying the children of men is an extension of this definition. The contraction of the eyelids conveys the sense of close scrutiny and examination. Men are tried like metals are refined in the furnace, that the fine gold and dross might be separated from each other. Thus the trying of the righteous is a means of proving them, that they might come forth as purged gold; whereas the wicked are shown to be as the dross, and the Lord as a result of His scrutiny knows them that are His. The wicked and those that love violence are rejected for, because of their works, He hates them.

God's judgements described in verse 6 recall (as previously indicated) the destruction of Sodom. Note, however, that the fire and brimstone are preceded by the rain of snares from heaven. Literally, the idea presented is of the wicked caught in the snare so that there is no escape from their punishment. The thought is of the unexpectedness by which they are overtaken. The Lord said of his coming that "as a snare shall it come on all them that dwell on the face of the whole earth" (Luke 21:35).

The snare, however, is basically of their own making, for, forgetting God, they allow themselves to be "overcharged with surfeiting and drunkenness, and the cares of this life" (verse 34). Enmeshed by these things, they are trapped, and there is no escape when God's judgements are finally poured out. It is a solemn warning for us, as for all men, for we, too, can forget the reality of God in an obsession with everyday cares and anxieties. Because the judgement is God's and not man's, we can be sure that it is just and measured, the due reward for all the sins of the wicked, for "this shall be the portion of their cup".

The confidence of the righteous lies, then, in the knowledge that in the midst of all men's plotting and scheming, "the righteous LORD loveth righteousness" (Psalm 11:7). He is unchanging. True to His own nature, He abideth faithful and constant, and because of this, "the upright shall behold his face" (verse 7, RSV).

This is a concept which is common to Old and New Testament alike, expressed in the following passages:

"Blessed are the pure in heart: for they shall see God." (Matthew 5:8)

"It doth not yet appear what we shall be: but we know that, when he shall appear, we shall be like him; for we shall see him as he is." (1 John 3:2)

To behold His face is the inestimable blessing of those whom God will vindicate in the sight of men. It means that they will be like Him, for the righteous Lord, seeing the characteristics of His own holiness in His children, loves righteousness. And when finally He manifests Himself in the earth, those who have put their trust in Him and maintained their faith will be elevated to the divine nature, that with their spiritual perception perfected, they may in glorious spirit nature "see him as he is".

Psalm 11 is a song that we might so easily neglect because of its apparent insignificance, but it has an abiding message that has particular relevance for us today.

Our community too could experience a time of trouble, when the pessimistic might say that the very pillars of the Truth, the foundations, are destroyed. Such an atmosphere can so easily breed mistrust, with slanderous allegations being made about brethren and sisters. Some might say that there is no remedy but to flee to our mountain, to get away from it all; but, like David, we have a responsibility to shoulder. In a sense we are all shepherds with a duty towards the flock. If we remain true to God, holding fast the sound words of the Gospel, then though some might criticise and make slanderous accusations that (like the arrows of the wicked) can wound, causing hurt and sorrow, we know that God is in His Holy Temple. He tries the hearts of all men, and whatever human assessment might be made, the Lord God is faithful to Himself. "The righteous LORD loveth righteousness." He knows who are His, and as He causes His countenance to shine upon them, so they also shall see His face.

PSALM 12

THE series of psalms we are considering (Psalms 10-13) all have reference to the same period in the life of David, and consequently are similar in tone and emphasis, though each with its own characteristic message. The historical background, as already emphasised in Psalms 10 and 11, has to do with the days when David was the target of Saul's hatred and was finally compelled to flee from his presence to live the life of an exile and outlaw.

In each of these psalms the emphasis is upon the unscrupulous nature of David's enemies who, while not always seeking to harm him physically, carried on a scurrilous campaign against him with their tongues, often while feigning friendship. Again, there were always those who, if the opportunity arose, were prepared to betray him to Saul. We have examples of the kind of treachery which confronted David in the attitudes of the men of Keilah (1 Samuel 23:11) and the Ziphites (verse 19).

It is difficult to imagine the debilitating effect that the hypocrisy and untrustworthiness of men can have upon the human spirit, unless one has experienced it personally. It is sometimes hard to credit the duplicity of men – the way in which they will twist and distort one's words, break their own promises and generally behave in such a way as to leave the man who seeks to live uprightly completely disillusioned and, as far as the human perspective is concerned, with a feeling of helplessness and despair.

So David spoke of the evil men of his generation: "They speak vanity every one with his neighbour: with flattering lips and with a double heart do they speak" (Psalm 12:2).

Man's words are vanity, empty and without substance, spoken to deceive or distort for personal advantage and

61

favour. He has a "double heart", literally 'a heart and a heart'. In other words, he is thoroughly unreliable, for he thinks one thing and says another, and there is no constancy or consistency about his behaviour.

It was in these circumstances, feeling that he was friendless and alone, that David cried unto his God, "Help, LORD; for there is no longer any that is godly; for the faithful have vanished from among the sons of men" (verse 1, RSV).

This must have been how Noah felt in his generation, for with the passage of the years he had witnessed the line of Cain, the seed of the serpent, becoming dominant in the earth. In the development of the two lines, it is interesting to reflect on the emphasis in Genesis 5 upon the godly line. After the particulars of the lives of each of the early patriarchs, it is recorded with marked emphasis "and he died" (see verses 5,8,11,14,17, etc.). While indicating the dire consequences of Adam's sin upon all those who were born in his likeness and image, there is also an air of finality about each pronouncement. It was as if with the death of those patriarchs, one of the faithful vanished from the earth, and a light went out in the darkness of the world that perished in the flood, until at last God saw that the wickedness of men was very great, and only "Noah found grace in the eyes of the LORD" (Genesis 6:8; see also 7:1).

Such experiences, as the day of the Lord draws nearer, must inevitably become more and more a part of the pressure of living the Truth in this wicked and adulterous generation, as the 'faithful few' seek to maintain constancy in their service to the Lord.

As it was for David, and surely for Noah also, we too must become increasingly aware of the brazen self-assertive arrogance of the words of men's lips. Such utterances (to use the words of the psalm) as "With our tongue will we prevail; our lips are our own: who is lord over us?" (verse 4).

In the life of David, the words probably describe those in the court of King Saul who unscrupulously sought to achieve their ends by slander, flattery and disregard for the truth – men who in their arrogance thought they were in control of the situation and had no need to fear retribution. They were inebriated by their own assessment of their ability to prevail over men like David, because of their facility for working mischief and delighting in it. The world is full of men like that. God forbid that there should be any with such characteristics in the household of faith; but it is a daunting thought that there were such in the first century ecclesias (read, for instance, 2 Peter 2:1-3,10-14,18,19). Can we be confident that our community is free from such perversions? For one of the characteristics of such individuals, as Peter's words imply, is that they are not easily identified and recognised.

All such, however, in whatever generation they live, are hated by God (Psalm 12:3). And when His children sigh because of such oppression by men of flattering lips and proud tongues, God gives His assurance that He will arise and set the poor and needy "in safety from him that puffeth at him" (verse 5). There seems to be some obscurity about the Hebrew text with regard to the words rendered "puffeth at him". The Cambridge Bible presents alternative understandings of the words:

1. "I will set him in the safety he panteth for" (RV margin) – "for which he longs" (RSV).
2. "I will set him in safety when they pant for him", i.e. like wild beasts, hunting down their prey; ravening wolves that would swallow up the righteous.

In any event, the assurance remains that God will act on behalf of His children. In this generation His providential hand will keep them, and ultimately He will save them when His judgements are in the earth and His purpose brought to fruition, for "Thou shalt keep them, O LORD, thou shalt preserve them from this generation for ever" (verse 7).

In the face of the hypocrisy, flattery and lying lips of men, however, the righteous have that on which to lean and to call to their aid, which is completely dependable. It will never fail, for "The words of the LORD are pure words: as silver tried in a furnace of earth, purified seven times" (verse 6). God's word has been given to strengthen and comfort, to give light to our path and to provide us with the means of overcoming all the power of the enemy.

With such a living power in our lives, and with the providential hand of God at work co-operating, as it were, with His word, what more do we need in our pilgrimage to provide for that safety from evil that God has promised, and to bring us ultimately to our haven of rest?

In conclusion, we might note the word "godly" used in verse 1, for it describes the very antithesis of all the evil speaking, treachery and double-mindedness of sinful men. It is from the same root as the Hebrew *chesed*, variously rendered "mercy", "lovingkindness", "goodness", and expressing, when used of God, the constancy of His love in the bonds of the covenant. But when it is used of men who have been "taught of God to love one another", it reflects their constancy and love of truth and judgement – not only Godwards, but also in their dealings with their fellow men (see Hosea 4:1,2; 12:6 for instance, where the word is rendered "mercy").

In the midst of all the duplicity and untrustworthiness that is so characteristic of worldly-minded men, the godly, in contrast, must maintain their integrity and remain a model of truth and constancy in their dealings with all men, for thus they show forth the same steadfast and unchanging qualities that are characteristic of the God they serve.

PSALM 13

IN many ways the psalms are like mirrors. They record the experiences of godly men of old, covering the whole spectrum of human emotions. And though we are separated from these men by time, and though our social background may be completely different, we share the same human nature and the same spiritual aspirations. Consequently, we share a common pilgrimage, and we have the same problems and the same sources of comfort and strength that were available to them. When we read the psalms, therefore, we can see reflected our own experiences, both in joy and sorrow, both in temptation and in victory over sin and the world.

Some might find difficulty in the words of the first two verses of our psalm:

"How long wilt thou forget me, O LORD? for ever? how long wilt thou hide thy face from me? how long shall I take counsel in my soul, having sorrow in my heart daily? how long shall mine enemy be exalted over me?"

Clearly God cannot forget in the ordinary sense of the word. The idea is rather of disregarding – and we know that God does not regard the wicked. As another psalm says, "If I regard iniquity in my heart, the Lord will not hear me" (66:18). However, although God hides His face from the wicked, He never forgets or disregards the needs of His children. He does, nevertheless, on occasions, allow circumstances to arise in which it might appear to men that He has forsaken His servants, that through these experiences He might prove them and know all that is in their hearts (Deuteronomy 8:2; 2 Chronicles 32:31).

In this situation, the man of God might plunge into the very depths of despair, but we must not make the mistake of equating such a reaction with sin. It is not sin to feel despair and despondency. It is not sin to feel afraid and to be troubled in soul. It is how we react when we experience these human emotions that is important, for it is then that we show the true quality of our faith. Although it might appear that God has forgotten us, if we cling tenaciously to the conviction that He will never forsake us, we show that we have not forgotten God, and we come through the trial with a proved faith and a character that has been fashioned a little more into the image of what God desires us to be.

Thus the writer of Psalm 13, almost certainly David during the time of his exile and persecution at the hands of Saul, takes us through the range of human emotions and illustrates in these first two verses that he has not forgotten God, although God might appear to have forgotten him. Indeed, he is confident that God will eventually act on his behalf, for the burden of his cry is, "How long?" – a plea which he repeats four times. Some suggest that the phrase "How long shall I take counsel in my soul?" should have the words 'by night' added to balance the next line, "having sorrow in my heart daily". The idea would then be of the plans and schemes to produce an alleviation of suffering, conceived in the night watches, dashed and frustrated in the cold light of day; and instead of relief, sorrow fills his heart. It is, perhaps, appropriate to remind ourselves that in all our plans and counsels, God remains sovereign, and whatever we might determine to do, we must remember that it is subject to the will of God.

As the psalm progresses, so David rises above the despondency produced by his troubles:

"Consider and hear me, O LORD my God: lighten mine eyes, lest I sleep the sleep of death; lest mine enemy say, I have prevailed against him; and those that trouble me rejoice when I am moved."   (verses 3,4)

The words express a calmer spirit, and reflect a greater sense of confidence. He has grappled with the feelings of despair that had seemed to overwhelm him, and now his faith is shown in a more reasoned and balanced way. It would appear from the phrase "lighten mine eyes, lest I sleep the sleep of death", that David had experienced a serious illness which had contributed to his despondency.

The eyes are regarded as an indication of health and vitality. Thus another psalm states:

"For my loins are filled with a loathsome disease: and there is no soundness in my flesh ... my heart panteth, my strength faileth me: as for the light of mine eyes, it also is gone from me."   (38:7,10)

Thus David prays that God will revive him, that the 'dimness' of his vision that reflected the darkness of his situation might be enlightened by God's blessing. Thus his enemies will not be able to rejoice over him. It is worth remembering that, if indeed David is the writer, then he was the Lord's anointed, and if the adversaries prevailed over him, they would frustrate the purpose of God and God's honour also would be in jeopardy.

It was because he knew that God is faithful and His word steadfast that David, rising completely above the circumstances that had enveloped him, is able to cry:

"But I have trusted in thy mercy; my heart shall rejoice in thy salvation. I will sing unto the LORD, because he hath dealt bountifully with me."
(Psalm 13:5,6)

He had trusted in God's mercy. Once again it is the word *chesed*, which describes God's faithfulness and constancy to those with whom He has made a covenant (see previous chapter on Psalm 12). It must be the inevitable experience of those who have such a faith that, though the vicissitudes of life might on occasions cause despondency and anxiety, the joy of God's salvation will always triumph. The comfort of the Truth will always restore that joy in the Lord that no earthly disaster can ever destroy, or totally take away from us.

It is a measure of David's confidence that he can now recognise God's hand in all the circumstances of his life. He acknowledges that even his tribulation and adversity have been controlled by God for his good, however bleak the situation might have appeared at the time; therefore he will "sing unto the LORD, because he hath dealt bountifully with me" (verse 6).

By His Spirit God has caused these things to be written, that we might learn from the experiences of our brethren of old, that we might find comfort and consolation in the knowledge that they were of "like passions", and that they have trodden the road before us, that we in our day might follow in their footsteps.

PSALMS 14 & 53

I T is appropriate that we consider these two psalms together, for with certain variations, the text of Psalm 14 is reproduced in Psalm 53.

There are two main differences between the psalms. First of all, where the covenant name Yahweh occurs in Psalm 14 (verses 2,4,6,7) the word 'Elohim' is substituted in Psalm 53. Secondly, verses 5 and 6 in Psalm 53 differ substantially from verses 5 and 6 in Psalm 14. These are best compared by setting them out in parallel columns:

PSALM 14:5,6

"There were they in great fear: for God is in the generation of the righteous. Ye have shamed the counsel of the poor, because the LORD is his refuge."

PSALM 53:5,6

"There were they in great fear, where no fear was: for God hath scattered the bones of him that encampeth against thee: thou hast put them to shame, because God hath despised them."

There seems little doubt that Psalm 14 precedes Psalm 53 in time, and that it was written by David. It seems reasonable to assume, therefore, that under the guidance of the Spirit of God, Psalm 14 was reproduced in its amended form (53) to meet a situation for which it was particularly relevant, and that the changes were made to take account of the different historical circumstances that form the background of the later psalm. In this event, if we can identify the appropriate history that called forth its repetition, then verses 5 and 6 should be seen as an inspired exposition of Psalm 14:5,6, in relation to the different circumstances.

It is sufficient at this point to say that, outside the critical schools of thought, Psalm 53 is almost universally acknowledged as belonging to the time and possibly the pen of King Hezekiah.

Psalm 14

The mention of Zion in verse 7 places the psalm in the latter part of David's life. The reference to "the captivity of his people" need not be a cause of difficulty, for scriptural usage indicates that the word "captivity" does not always apply in the strictly literal sense in which we might understand it, as for instance of the exile in Babylon. It sometimes has to do with the period of trouble which precedes the restoration of blessing, as, for example, when "the LORD turned the captivity of Job" (Job 42:10; see also in this connection Hosea 6:11 and Zephaniah 2:7).

In the light of these reflections, we might appropriately link the writing of the psalm with the troublous times of Absalom's rebellion and the subsequent years, which were certainly amongst the most difficult of David's life. We have previously remarked in connection with Psalm 10:4,6,11,13, that David was confronted by men in Israel who, while openly acknowledging Yahweh, in their hearts practised self-delusion. They were whispering, as it were, in their own ear that there was no God of whom they must take account in their lives, and consequently they were free to pursue their own ambitions without fear of judgement. Such men were fools (Psalm 14:1). The word "fool" does not imply ignorance or weakness of intellect, but rather describes moral perversity; and the psalm highlights a great truth, for whenever men disregard God in their hearts in this way, the consequence is always the moral degeneracy and corruption described in verses 1 to 3. Folly is, in effect, practical disbelief in God.

Against the background of Absalom's rebellion, we can appreciate how he and those who supported him were seeking to frustrate the declared purpose of God contained in the promises covenanted to David. Following his death, we still find dissension: there were those who followed Sheba the son of Bichri, a Benjamite. His words in rallying his supporters were, "We have no part in David, neither have we inheritance in the son of Jesse" (2 Samuel 20:1). The words are surely echoed in the Lord's parable: "We will not have this man to reign over us" (Luke 19:14).

In the ruthless pursuit of their personal ambitions, such men as Absalom and Sheba were seeking to frustrate the purpose of God. They caused chaos and anarchy in Israel. In the words of the psalm, they "eat up my people as they eat bread, and call not upon the LORD" (Psalm 14:4). But God, in frustrating their aims and bringing home to them the futility of their rage against His anointed, made them realise their folly and the impending doom they had brought upon themselves by their actions. "There were they in great fear", knowing as their purposes failed that God's presence dwelt in the midst of His people; and though they had sought to "put [them] to shame" (RV), mocking and deriding them because their counsel was to seek refuge in the Lord, the faith of the poor had been vindicated and Yahweh had triumphed over the enemies of His people (verses 5,6).

It was in these troublous times that David longed for the restoration of blessing, that God would turn again their captivity, that Jacob might rejoice and Israel be glad (verse 7). If, however, we are right in our suggestion that the precise historical background to the psalm was the days of Absalom's rebellion, there are nonetheless allusions in the language that carry us back in history to the early chapters of Genesis and also to earlier events in the life of David when his life had been threatened by wicked men.

Genesis
The idea of a fool who said in his heart "There is no God" is certainly appropriate to the days of Noah. He lived in a society that was completely blind to the reality of God because of people's obsession with material things, "eating and drinking, marrying and giving in marriage ... and knew not until the flood came, and took them all away" (Matthew 24:38,39). The language also has certain similarities with Genesis 6 (see comparison overleaf).

Also there are, perhaps, echoes of the thought of God looking down and perceiving the wickedness of man in Genesis 11:5 and 18:21.

71

GENESIS 6	**PSALM 14**
"And GOD saw that the wickedness of man was great … and that every imagination of the thoughts of his heart was only evil continually." (verse 5)	"They are corrupt, they have done abominable works, there is none that doeth good." (verse 1)
"The earth also was corrupt before God, and the earth was filled with violence. And God looked upon the earth, and, behold, it was corrupt." (verses 11,12)	"The LORD looked down from heaven upon the children of men, to see if there were any that did understand, and seek God. They are all gone aside, they are all together become filthy: there is none that doeth good, no, not one." (verses 2,3)

David's Early Life

One interesting suggestion, originating, we believe, with Brother Harry Whittaker, is that it was the events connected with Doeg the Edomite that form a background to the psalm. The reference to those who "eat up my people as they eat bread" would then have direct reference to the slaying of all the priests at the command of Saul.

Again, the Hebrew word rendered "fool" is linked directly with that churlish man, Nabal. Truly it was written of him, "For as his name is, so is he; Nabal is his name, and folly is with him" (1 Samuel 25:25). There are, of course, clear similarities in the attitude of Nabal and the spirit of the age before the flood; this becomes particularly evident when we realise that this man is the prototype of the foolish rich man in the Lord's parable (Luke 12:19-21).

Psalm 53

If the use of the covenant name Yahweh is an indication that Psalm 14 is directed primarily toward those within Israel who demonstrated practical disbelief by their attitude towards God and towards David His anointed, then the change to 'Elohim' is an indication that the "fool" who disregards God is now to be found amongst the Gentiles.

The association with Hezekiah seems conclusive when we reflect how appropriate the words of the psalm, as amended, are to the host of Sennacherib smitten by the angel of God as they encamped against His city (see Psalm 53:5,6 with Isaiah 37:10-13,16-20,35-38). Psalm 53 is therefore directed against Gentile pomp and arrogance, whereas Psalm 14 speaks of those in Israel itself who behaved themselves foolishly.

How, then, do we understand the differences between the words of verses 5 and 6 of the two psalms? Surely the words of Psalm 53 are an application of the thoughts of Psalm 14 to the destruction of Sennacherib's host. The point can be illustrated by bringing the words of the two psalms together in the following paraphrase:

'Proud and arrogant in their approach, with no fear in their hearts, they were reduced to great fear, for God was in the generation of the righteous; and consequently He scattered the bones of those who encamped against them, though they sought to put the poor to shame by deriding them for putting their trust in the LORD their refuge. It was in fact God who put the oppressor to shame, since they were despised in His eyes because of their wickedness.'

Conclusion

In the light of these things, could it not be that the psalms also reflect the spirit of Christ shown on two different occasions? Psalm 14 could refer to his perception of the people of Israel who showed themselves 'fools' at his first coming, and Psalm 53 to his reaction to Gentile arrogance at his second coming. That Jew and Gentile are in focus in these psalms is, perhaps, emphasised by the Apostle Paul when he quotes the words of the psalms in relation to human wickedness in his epistle to the Romans:

"... we have before proved both Jews and Gentiles, that they are all under sin; as it is written, There is none righteous, no, not one: there is none that understandeth, there is none that seeketh after God."

(Romans 3:9-11)

PSALM 15

THERE are seven psalms traditionally associated with David bringing up the ark to Zion, and of these Psalm 15 is the first. (See also Psalms 24, 68, 87, 96, 105 and 132.) It bears a striking similarity to the second section of Psalm 24 (verses 3-5), particularly in the question posed in the opening words, "LORD, who shall abide in thy tabernacle? who shall dwell in thy holy hill?" (Psalm 15:1) compared with "Who shall ascend into the hill of the LORD? or who shall stand in his holy place?" (Psalm 24:3).

Detailed consideration of the historical background is dealt with under Psalm 24. Suffice it to say that the great lesson David learned at this time was that God must be sought "after the due order" (1 Chronicles 15:13) and that it was necessary for those who would come into His presence to sanctify themselves first (verse 12). It was because of the failure to recognise this principle and to do "as Moses commanded according to the word of the LORD" (verse 15) that Uzzah perished and David was filled with fear and apprehension (1 Chronicles 13:11,12).

The physical requirements that needed to be met to bring up the ark to Zion, and to dwell with God whose presence was manifest from between the cherubim, served only to emphasise that God would be sanctified in all them that came nigh Him (Leviticus 10:3). David clearly had the spiritual perception to appreciate that this sanctification extended beyond the physical and ceremonial emphasis, to encompass the personal holiness of heart and mind of the man who would seek to dwell with God by ascending into His holy hill. It would appear that Psalm 24 is the more imminent of the two psalms, in the sense that it was probably written in close proximity to the event, and captures all the urgency of the occasion;

whereas Psalm 15 contemplates the qualities of a true citizen of Zion in a more measured fashion, as it was written, we believe, some time later after the ark had been established for a little while in its new resting place, the tabernacle of David.

There is an interesting distinction in the words of verse 1. The word rendered "abide" means literally 'to sojourn'. Its associations have to do with temporary habitation, and the abiding, significantly, is in God's tabernacle. Appropriately, the sojourning is in the tabernacle or tent, for this too speaks of a temporary habitation. The word rendered "dwell", however, speaks of a settled and permanent abiding (see Psalm 37:29), and the thought of the psalm seems to encompass the days of David with the tabernacle in their midst and extend to the establishment of God's kingdom when He would dwell in Zion for ever, a fact of which the tabernacle of David was but a shadow and a type.

The description of the righteousness of those who belong to Zion, which is the substance of the remainder of the psalm, is one that should search the hearts of all seekers of truth who read its words.

To dwell with God one must hunger and thirst after righteousness; and the measure of a man's desire to attain that blessedness is shown by his growth in the qualities that constitute it.

Walking uprightly

"He that walketh uprightly" is the beginning of the description that identifies a true "son of Zion". 'Walking' is a wonderful way to convey the tenor and direction of a man's life. When we walk, every member of the body plays its part, and the word itself implies that there is a goal to be achieved, a destination to be reached. Of the word rendered "uprightly", Gesenius (Hebrew–Chaldee Lexicon) indicates that it had various shades of meaning which are all related to the idea of perfect, entire or complete. It describes a man of integrity – not a double-minded man, a hypocrite, but a whole man, who with singleness of heart and purpose pursues his devotion to God and maintains his sincerity before men. The Greek word used in the LXX to represent the Hebrew adds to our understanding of its significance, for it is translated "without blame" (Ephesians 1:4) and "unblameable" (Colossians 1:22).

Working Righteousness

The word "worketh" implies labour, and as such serves to emphasise the effort that God looks for in His servants as an indication of their earnest desire to attain unto righteousness. Of course, we can never save ourselves. Even one sin would separate us from God and bring with it the condemnation that is its inevitable consequence. The multiplicity of our sins reminds us of our inherent weakness and waywardness. We can only be saved by the grace of God manifest in His forgiveness of our sins. We might feel that it would be so much easier if, as Pentecostals believe, God did it all for us by the direct operation of His Spirit independently of His word. To hold such a view is, however, a serious misunderstanding of scripture which negates the significance of such words as "worketh righteousness" with which the scriptures abound. It is our labour in working righteousness which is the testimony before God and man that, truly, we long to possess righteousness. Any teaching which could have the effect of weakening our resolve and undermining our efforts must therefore be regarded as dangerous and mischievous.

Speaking the Truth in the Heart

Each phrase in verse 2 is an extension of the thought which precedes it. Thus a man's integrity and wholeheartedness is demonstrated by his labour in the performance of good works, and what he appears outwardly is confirmed by the essential quality of the man within, for he speaks the truth in his heart. There is no place for the sham and the counterfeit. It is probably true that there is nothing at which human nature is more adept than putting on an act, usually to impress others or to gain some kind of personal advantage. But we can never be two people, one inside and the other outside. Everything should be done wholeheartedly, with nothing hidden in the dark corners and shadowy recesses of our being which is incompatible with our public profession of faith.

Isaiah 33 has the same message:

"The sinners in Zion are afraid; fearfulness hath surprised the hypocrites. Who among us shall dwell with the devouring fire? who among us shall dwell with everlasting burnings?"   (verse 14)

Backbiting and Reproach

Verses 3 to 5 of Psalm 15 describe in more precise detail how the man of integrity who labours in good works because he treasures the Truth in his heart, behaves himself in his daily life. Strong's Concordance states that the Hebrew word rendered "backbiteth" is from a root meaning 'to walk along', and one translation has the very graphic rendering of the first phrase of verse 3, "he that footeth it not with his tongue". It is the classic picture of the gossip who carries titillating information from place to place and who does not hesitate to slander his brother or sister.

Leviticus 19 conveys the idea perfectly: "Thou shalt not go up and down as a talebearer among thy people" (verse 16). Similarly, in the New Testament Paul expresses the same idea in 1 Timothy 5:13: "... wandering about from house to house; and not only idle, but tattlers also and busybodies, speaking things which they ought not."

The spirit of the slanderer is reflected in another graphic and expressive figure that lies behind the words "nor taketh up a reproach against his neighbour". The word rendered "reproach" is derived from a root which describes the stripping of trees of their autumn fruit (Gesenius). Hence to slander is to strip honour and reputation from those we reproach.

It is an awesome responsibility that we take upon ourselves when we speak evil of our friends (Psalm 15:3, RV). When we judge our brethren and sisters so that by our words we strip them of all honour and reputation, we are in effect pronouncing them to be unworthy of the kingdom of God. Jesus said that the man who calls his brother a fool (and the word carries the idea of moral

77

obliquity, for it is the fool of the Psalms and the Proverbs) is putting himself in danger of the judgement of Gehenna.

We must witness to the Truth in word and deed. Our testimony may reflect upon the teaching and conduct of others, but it is not our place to condemn in the sense of seeking to define their standing before God, for it is to Him that they will stand or fall.

The Company we keep

That some discrimination between persons is necessary is evident from verse 4: "In whose eyes a reprobate is despised" (RV). The righteous man's integrity is manifested by his estimate of men, for whereas he despises (that is, regards with little esteem) those who are void of spiritual judgement (i.e., reprobate) and avoids them, both to maintain his own integrity and to witness against them for their good, he nevertheless honours those who fear Yahweh. As another psalm says, "When thou sawest a thief, then thou consentedst with him" (50:18); and we cannot escape the responsibility we bear for the company we keep. To keep company with, or to show favour to, the wicked is to consent to their deeds and share their condemnation.

The question that must be asked is, 'Do we believe the same things?', or 'Have we the same aims in life?' If there is no common bond of worship and if we are not heirs together of the promises of life, then we can have no real association. The spirit of the man of integrity is reflected in Psalm 119: "I am a companion ... of them that keep thy precepts" (verse 63).

A Man of his Word

The most obvious example of one of whom it might be said, "He that sweareth to his own hurt, and changeth not", is Jephthah who, however we interpret his subsequent actions, certainly regretted his rash words – but showed himself to be a man of honour by his determination to fulfil his promise.

The Lord said, "Let your communication be, Yea, yea; Nay, nay: for whatsoever is more than these cometh of evil" (Matthew 5:37). In the most unequivocal terms Jesus is telling us that we must be true to our word.

78

Commitments, however trivial, should not be cancelled because we subsequently find them inconvenient, or because something more appealing has presented itself. In this connection the use of the words "God willing" might be thought of a little more deeply than is, perhaps, our wont. We need, of course, to recognise in this way that our lives are subject to God's providential hand but, at the same time, what we are affirming is that nothing will prevent us doing this or that, unless it be the will of God. To say, "I will be there, God willing" does not mean we can change our mind if it is "to our hurt" or if we have a subsequent alternative that is more to our liking.

Care for the Poor

"He that putteth not out his money to usury, nor taketh reward against the innocent" (Psalm 15:5). To charge interest on a loan was forbidden by the Law of Moses. It was regarded as an unbrotherly act (see Leviticus 25:35-37; Exodus 22:25-27).

The man of integrity must never take advantage of the predicament of those who are worse off than himself. Whether in time or money, we must be prepared to give. The principle which should motivate our action in these circumstances is emphasised in the Proverbs: "He that hath pity upon the poor lendeth unto the LORD" (19:17). God will repay, not necessarily in material things, but certainly in the abundance of spiritual blessings that will accrue.

The man who does these things shows himself fit, by God's grace, to abide in His tabernacle and to dwell in His holy hill. Even more, "He that doeth these things shall never be moved" (Psalm 15:5). His place in God's purpose is assured. Nothing can threaten his eternal security, for it is the Father's good pleasure to give him the kingdom.

PSALM 16

PSALM 16 bears a title: it is a "Michtam of David". This form of words appears at the head of six psalms (16 and 56-60 inclusive) and there is little unanimity among so-called 'authorities' as to its meaning. Suggestions vary from an obscure musical instruction to "a golden Psalm" (AV margin), with supposed reference to the preciousness of its contents. The possibility of it being a musical term cannot be dismissed completely, but it seems unlikely to this writer; whereas most of the other explanations, like that of the "golden Psalms" have an inherent weakness, in that what is suggested is true of every psalm because of their divine authorship. On balance, the view put forward by Thirtle (*The Titles of the Psalms*) appears to have much to be said for it.

It is pointed out that one of the psalms (60) gives an indication of its purpose, for it says "Michtam to teach". Further, it is emphasised that all the psalms involved could be described as personal prayers or meditations. Thus it is suggested that, while being of a distinctive personal nature in their origin (with perhaps another proposed meaning of 'an inscription' being relevant, for the themes were so dear and close to the heart of David that they could be described as being written or inscribed on his heart), they had been adopted for public worship for one specified purpose, 'to teach'.

Background

The opening words of the psalm (verse 1), "Preserve me, O God: for in thee do I put my trust", are an indication that the circumstances in which the song was written were such that David was placed in great danger.

Again, the references to such words as "portion", "inheritance", "lot", "heritage" (verses 5,6) – used not of the land and not referring to the literal portion of his

80

inheritance that had been divided to his family by lot (Joshua 14–17) but of God Himself, whom he acknowledges as his portion and his heritage – is an indication that David was in exile. He was cut off from his natural inheritance and found solace in the fact that he had an association with God that more than compensated him for that which he had lost, albeit temporarily.

This view is reinforced by the words of verse 4 (RV): "Their sorrows shall be multiplied that exchange the LORD for another god: their drink offerings of blood will I not offer, nor take their names upon my lips." We can compare David's words here with the words of his enemies, to which he refers when he flees from Saul to the wilderness of Ziph, and thus associate that particular time with the writing of this psalm:

> "For they have driven me out this day from abiding in the inheritance of the LORD, saying, Go, serve other gods." (1 Samuel 26:19)

David, however, was not influenced by such pressures. He was not deluded into thinking that Yahweh's sovereignty only extended to the borders of Israel and that other gods exercised authority over the territory of surrounding nations. There would be no offerings to Baal (Lord) or Molech (king), and he could not even bring himself to utter their names, lest by so doing he be thought to recognise the supposed power and dignity that was implicit in them.

It is interesting to notice that those who indulge in idolatry will have "their sorrows ... multiplied", which is a reference to the sentence on Eve, "I will greatly multiply thy sorrow and thy conception" (Genesis 3:16), and the verb rendered "hasten" in the AV is associated elsewhere with the giving of a dowry for a wife (Exodus 22:16). Possibly the common scriptural practice of likening apostasy to an adulterous liaison is implicit in the words.

David's Outlook on Life

> "I have said unto the LORD, Thou art my Lord: I have no good beyond thee. As for the saints that are in the earth, they are the excellent in whom is all my delight." (Psalm 16:2,3, RV)

81

Here is the true spirit of the godly man. Apart from God and those things that belong to His purpose, there is nothing that can bring abiding happiness. There is no real fulfilment or satisfaction in life apart from that which is found in Him. Once it is realised that His fulness is sufficient for all our needs, then we have a perspective on life that is able to sustain us in all its vicissitudes and adversities. The corollary to this is that we find no pleasure in the company and activities of those who do not share our faith. Our desire will be to seek continually the fellowship of those whom God recognises as His saints. It is not the company of the rich and influential that we should cultivate, but that of the holy (saints) – the truly noble (AV, "the excellent") in the earth in whose fellowship alone we can find real delight, for we share a common heritage.

David develops this thought of God as his supreme good in verses 5 and 6:

"The LORD is the portion of mine inheritance and of my cup: thou maintainest my lot. The lines are fallen unto me in pleasant places; yea, I have a goodly heritage."

The language is figurative, for David is emphasising that God was more to him than that portion of land that was allotted to him, and yet implicit in that fact was the recognition that because God was his chief joy, all he hoped and longed for, then all that God had promised was sure and every circumstance was directed by Him. David was secure from all the evil plans of men, and whatever befell him he accepted cheerfully, knowing that it was of the Lord. It was He who gave him his cup to drink and maintained or controlled his lot.

The experience of the abiding presence of God in life is not a mystical indwelling in the heart, but is a practical outworking of the hand of God in our lives. He fills the cup we drink. He maintains our lot. He is not in us, but He is with us, and knowing that all things work together for good, we can say with David, "The lines are fallen unto me in pleasant places; yea, I have a goodly heritage".

The thought of God as our heritage is drawn from the promise made to the Levites:

"Thou shalt have no inheritance in their land, neither shalt thou have any part among them: I am thy part and thine inheritance among the children of Israel."

(Numbers 18:20)

The Levites, however, were representative of the nation as a whole who were "a kingdom of priests" (Exodus 19:6), and thus not only was God the portion of the individual believer, as in Psalm 16 (see also Psalm 73:26; Lamentations 3:22-24), but also He is described as the "portion of Jacob" (Jeremiah 10:16). In this latter passage Jeremiah introduces another emphasis, for he describes Israel as "the rod of his (God's) inheritance", and this introduces us to another fruitful source of scriptural allusion, for:

"The LORD hath taken you ... to be unto him a people of inheritance, as ye are this day." (Deuteronomy 4:20)

"Yet they are thy people and thine inheritance ..."
(9:29)

"For the LORD's portion is his people; Jacob is the lot of his inheritance." (32:9)

Both strands of thought – the Lord our portion, and we His inheritance – seem to meet in the Epistle to the Ephesians, where a certain ambiguity in the text appears to bring both ideas together (1:11):

AV – "In whom also we have obtained an inheritance;"

RV – "In whom also we were made a heritage."

For these blessings David could give God thanks, for the counsel received from His word which had taught of them and, cognisant of the outworking of God's hand in his life, it was also the subject of his meditations in the quiet of the night (Psalm 16:7).

The Ground of Confidence

Because he sought no good beyond his God, David lived in the abiding consciousness of His presence: "I have set the LORD always before me: because he is at my right hand, I shall not be moved" (verse 8). The result was that there permeated his being a joy and confidence that transcended all earthly sources of happiness. "Therefore my heart is glad, and my glory rejoiceth: my flesh also shall rest in hope" (verse 9). It is worth emphasising that flesh does not rest (lit. 'dwell confidently') in the grave. It is part of the living organism that with the soul and the heart make up the whole man. Note that the Apostle Paul refers in a similar context to "spirit and soul and body" (1 Thessalonians 5:23). "Spirit" here stands for the heart, and provides an important expositional point in the understanding of one of the uses of the word 'spirit' in the New Testament. David experienced a pervading joy and confidence, not just because of the care of God in this life, but because his portion and inheritance in the Lord was also an assurance to him of life beyond the grave through the resurrection from the dead. "For thou wilt not leave my soul in hell; neither wilt thou suffer thine Holy One to see corruption" (Psalm 16:10). Life from the dead and the joy of unbroken and unending fellowship with God were his dominant desires, for God had revealed to him the life that was life indeed, in which alone true happiness and fulfilment is to be found:

"Thou wilt shew me the path of life: in thy presence is fulness of joy; at thy right hand there are pleasures for evermore."
(verse 11)

Although we have laboured to show the relevance of the psalm to the life of David in which it had an initial application, there can be no doubt that the words find their fullest expression in the Lord Jesus Christ. That which David experienced in his longing for God and his delight in those things that are eternal, were but imperfect reflections of the longing and desires of the Holy One of God, whose perfection stands as an example to men of all ages.

There can be no cavil about the Messianic nature of the psalm, for it is twice quoted by the apostles (Acts 2:25-31; 13:34-37) in their preaching, with particular reference to the fact that, although the words might express his hope in the resurrection, there was no sense in which it could be said that David did not see corruption. These words were realised only in the Lord Jesus Christ who was raised up the third day.

The fulness of the spirit of Christ in the psalm is seen, however, not just in this particular phrase, but in the whole context in which it appears. This becomes evident by a comparison between the words of the psalm and the language of Hebrews 12. We set the passages in parallel columns for comparison:

PSALM 16	HEBREWS 12
"I have set the LORD always before me." (verse 8)	"Looking unto Jesus the author and finisher of our faith." (verse 2)
"In thy presence is fulness of joy." (verse 11)	"Who for the joy that was set before him endured the cross." (verse 2)
"At thy right hand there are pleasures for evermore." (verse 11)	"… is set down at the right hand of the throne of God." (verse 2)
"I shall not be moved." (verse 8)	"Consider him that endured such contradiction of sinners against himself, lest ye be wearied and faint in your minds." (verse 3)

The use of the psalm in Hebrews is illuminating, not just for the way in which it shows the spirit of Christ revealed there, but also for the manner in which the language is adapted to our own circumstances, that we might learn from him.

Jesus set the Lord always before him. It was that fulness of joy that was to be experienced in his Father's presence (the joy set before him) that enabled him to endure the cross, together with the help given him by God, for because he was at His right hand, he was not moved (weary and faint in his mind).

So we, too, must have a like experience, looking unto Jesus, the captain (AV, "author") who has gone before us to show us "the path of life" and who stands, as it were, at the end of the way, the finisher of our faith, for he is our portion and our heritage. The prize we seek is to be like him, transformed into his image, that through him we, too, might know that fulness of joy associated with the presence of God. Now, in this life, we have an earnest of it, that our hearts might rejoice and our tongues be glad, until the Lord come and, with mortality swallowed up of life, we know that pleasure for evermore in his presence.

PSALM 17

AN examination of the text of Psalm 17 reveals several verbal links with Psalm 16, and these are sufficient in themselves to link the two psalms together:

PSALM 17	**PSALM 16**
"Thou hast visited me in the night." (verse 3)	"My reins also instruct me in the night seasons." (verse 7)
"... that my footsteps slip not." (Hebrew, 'be not moved') (verse 5)	"I shall not be moved." (verse 8)
"... in thy paths." (verse 5)	"... the path of life." (verse 11)
"O thou that savest by thy right hand." (verse 7)	"... because he is at my right hand." (verse 8)
"... which have their portion in this life." (verse 14)	"The LORD is the portion of mine inheritance." (verse 5)
"I shall be satisfied, when I awake, with thy likeness." (verse 15)	"I have set the LORD always before me." (verse 8); "In thy presence is fulness of joy." (verse 11)

We can therefore assume that Psalm 17 refers historically to the same period of David's life as does Psalm 16, and also that its Messianic significance is an extension of the thoughts and theme of that psalm.

A careful reading of both psalms tends to leave the impression that, whereas there is a sense of calmness and serenity about the tone of Psalm 16, there is a note of urgency running through the language of Psalm 17, because the danger that was anticipated in Psalm 16 is now imminent. In a sentence, the faith of calmer days is now being put to the proof.

86

For convenience we divide the psalm into three parts:

1. An appeal to God's justice, based on the writer's integrity (verses 1-5)
2. An appeal for God's protection from the hatred of his enemies (verses 6-12)
3. A further plea to God, based on the worldly man's satisfaction with earthly things contrasted with David's desire for a closer and abiding relationship with God (verses 13-15).

God's Justice and the Integrity of the Righteous

One of David's greatest trials, as we have seen in earlier psalms, was the manner in which wicked men who hated him sought to vilify and slander him by making all manner of false accusations and spreading malicious rumours in an attempt to discredit him before the people.

It was, of course, equally true in the experience of the Lord Jesus Christ, and it is one of the most difficult and grievous of all burdens that the righteous man must bear – the reviling, the taunts, the misrepresentations and the accusations of unscrupulous men, particularly when they do these things under a cloak of righteousness. So David's appeal, as he found himself in this situation, was for God to vindicate him in the sight of his enemies, and its basis was the integrity of his heart, the single-minded way in which he had sought to tread the path of righteousness.

"Hear the right (AV margin, 'justice'), O LORD, attend unto my cry, give ear unto my prayer, that goeth not out of feigned (no falsehood or hypocrisy) lips" (Psalm 17:1). There is in this psalm, as in Psalm 16, an emphasis upon David's awareness of the presence and omniscience of God, for as his prayer does not arise out of "lips of deceit" (AV margin), he beseeches God to pass "sentence" or give judgement, that his cause may be seen to be just, for he knows that God's eyes "behold with equity" (RV margin). His judgement is complete and impartial (see also Psalm 11:4). Such a plea before God can spring only from the boldness of a good conscience that knows that God has tried and proved the heart and that, like gold refined in the furnace, there was no dross – for "thou findest no evil

87

purpose in me; my mouth shall not transgress" (verse 3, RV margin).

Once again there is reference to this process taking place "in the night" (verse 3 – see Psalm 16:7). It is, of course, true of human experience that it is in the night season, when we are able to relax and cast aside the burdens and cares of the day, with perhaps all its show of respectability and endeavour to maintain appearances, that the real man emerges. When unrestrained, the things that really matter pass through the mind.

The godly man who, like David and Paul, can say, "I have lived in all good conscience before God" (Acts 23:1), will of course not be the subject of such double-mindedness, for he will "commune with (his) own heart upon (his) bed, and be still" (Psalm 4:4). As the Psalmist says, "My mouth shall praise thee with joyful lips: when I remember thee upon my bed, and meditate on thee in the night watches, because thou hast been my help" (Psalm 63:5-7).

The wicked, however, will devise mischief upon his bed (Psalm 36:4) like Ahab (1 Kings 21:4). Micah's testimony is particularly powerful:

"Woe to them that devise iniquity, and work evil upon their beds! when the morning is light, they practise it, because it is in the power of their hand. And they covet fields, and take them by violence; and houses, and take them away: so they oppress a man and his house, even a man and his heritage." (Micah 2:1,2)

So, conscious of the two ways before him, David could say:

"As for the works of men, by the word of thy lips I have kept me from the ways of the violent. My steps have held fast to thy paths, my feet have not slipped." (Psalm 17:4,5, RV)

How these words received a practical expression in the life of David can be seen by his reaction to the occasion when God delivered Saul into his hand (1 Samuel 24:10) and also when he was restrained from taking revenge on Nabal by the intervention of Abigail (1 Samuel 25:32).

This section of the psalm, which emphasises the integrity of the righteous before God and man, presents a yardstick for all who seek to follow the Lord Jesus Christ and to measure themselves against him. The singleness of purpose, the good conscience which we should have, is an indication of our motives. Everything should be done with the intention of doing what is right in the sight of God. It doesn't mean that we shall never make mistakes. Because of our human fallibility we might be guilty of a serious lack of judgement as to the proper thing to do. Nevertheless, nothing will be done out of envy and jealousy; there will be no vindictiveness or malicious feeling towards others. Foolish we might be, but we shall not blatantly and defiantly show a preference for this world rather than for the kingdom of God. If, when we judge ourselves by these standards, we can say that we have acted in all good conscience before God, then whatever the taunts and accusations of men, we can still say with David, "Let my sentence come forth from thy presence" (Psalm 17:2).

Appeal for God's Protection

In pleading for God to vindicate him, David undoubtedly looked forward ultimately to the kingdom of God and the eternal inheritance that he should enjoy then (verse 15 is surely an indication of this fact!). At the same time, however, surrounded by enemies who sought to do him mischief, he was conscious also of how great a need he had of the divine protection, which itself, by the continued deliverance out of all his troubles, was a token of God's favour and vindication.

Observe first the way in which David describes the determination and ferocity of his enemies that rose up against him (verse 7):

"They have shut up their heart (RV, margin): with their mouth they speak proudly. They have now compassed us in their steps: they set their eyes to cast us down to the earth. He is like a lion that is greedy of his prey, and as it were a young lion lurking in secret places." (verses 10-12, RV)

89

They are depicted as men with closed hearts and minds, contemptuous of all appeals to show judgement and mercy. They have set their eyes upon him, an indication of their malicious spirit that could only be satisfied by his death: they compassed him about (see 1 Samuel 23:26) and they pursued him relentlessly, besetting his every step. As David said to Saul, "Thou huntest my soul to take it" (1 Samuel 24:11). Saul was, in fact, like a ravening lion waiting to pounce on his prey (see also Psalm 10:8,9).

Thus David looked to God, beseeching Him to show His "marvellous lovingkindness" (Psalm 17:7). The Hebrew rendered "marvellous" has the root meaning 'to distinguish', 'to set apart, separate', and would seem to indicate the distinctiveness of God's "lovingkindness", for whatever the odds against David in human terms, the power of God was unique and exercised in loving-kindness (Hebrew, *chesed*, with its associations with 'faithfulness'). He would manifest Himself to save those who put their trust in Him from those who in arrogance disregarded God and the power of His right hand.

David's plea to God is drawn from the language of Deuteronomy (32:10,11). "Keep me as the apple of the eye, hide me under the shadow of thy wings" (Psalm 17:8). Strong's Concordance says that the literal meaning of the word rendered "apple" is 'the little man, hence the pupil', and the idea is of that which was dearest and tenderest, that because of its preciousness was guarded and preserved. Linked with this figure is the idea of sheltering under the shadow of God's wings, a figure expanded in Deuteronomy:

"He kept him as the apple of his eye. As an eagle stirreth up her nest, fluttereth over her young, spreadeth abroad her wings, taketh them, beareth them on her wings: so the LORD alone did lead him."   (32:10-12)

The care of the mother eagle for her young, which so beautifully illustrates the love of God for His children, is reflected in other psalms besides 17 (see 36:7, 63:7, 91:4). It is perhaps interesting also to note as we come to the last section of Psalm 17 and remember our study in Psalm 16 concerning the words "lot", "portion", "inheritance", that in that same context of Deuteronomy it is written: "For the

90

LORD's portion is his people; Jacob is the lot of his inheritance" (32:9).

The Portions of the Wicked and the Righteous

The final prayer is introduced in language that is associated with the going forth of the ark of the covenant:

"Arise, O LORD, confront him, cast him down: deliver my soul from the wicked by thy sword; from men, by thy hand, O LORD." (Psalm 13,14, RV)

In this connection the words of Moses are particularly relevant:

"And it came to pass, when the ark set forward, that Moses said, Rise up, LORD, and let thine enemies be scattered; and let them that hate thee flee before thee." (Numbers 10:35; see also Psalm 68:1; 2 Chronicles 6:41; Psalm 3:7; 7:6; 9:19; 10:12; 12:5 etc.)

It was a plea for the Lord of all the earth (Joshua 3:11) to rise up in judgement upon His enemies, for inasmuch as they sought to lift up their hand against the Lord's anointed, they revealed their antagonism not only against David, but also against the God who had chosen him.

The psalm concludes with a most telling contrast between the desires of the man of the world and the man who looks for his satisfaction in God:

"Deliver my soul … from men of the world, whose portion is in this life, and whose belly thou fillest with thy treasure: they are satisfied with children, and leave the rest of their substance to their babes. As for me, I shall behold thy face in righteousness: I shall be satisfied, when I awake, with thy likeness." (Psalm 17:13-15, RV)

That "the fashion of this world passeth away" (1 Corinthians 7:31) is one of the most difficult lessons for men to learn. Because they appeal to men's baser appetites and appear to offer instant pleasure and satisfaction, it is the transient and fleeting things that capture men's hearts. They are deluded into thinking that these are lasting and abiding, and sin's greatest delusion is in convincing men that somehow they will live for ever. Of course, they know that they will die; but they still live as though it will never happen to them, and all that they desire or hope for is to be found within the confines of this mortal life. These, in scriptural terms, are "the children of this world" (Luke 16:8) who "mind earthly things" (Philippians 3:19). Their portion is in this life; they are satisfied with the material things that God gives from His treasures when He causes His sun to rise on the just and the unjust. They find fulfilment in their children. Psalm 49 takes us right into the heart of such men and emphasises their ultimate end:

"Their inward thought is, that their houses shall continue for ever, and their dwelling places to all generations; they call their lands after their own names. Nevertheless man being in honour abideth not: he is like the beasts that perish." (verses 11,12)

Of such was Cain, who called the name of the city he built after the name of his son Enoch (Genesis 4:17), and Absalom who, because he had no son, reared up a pillar in the king's dale and called it by his own name, that he might be kept in remembrance after his death (2 Samuel 18:18). The reality of the situation is that those who have their portion in this life want to see themselves reflected in their sons; but those who hunger and thirst after righteousness, who want God to be their portion (Psalm 16:5), want God to be reflected in them.

David, in contrast to the man of the world, expressed this truth beautifully as he thought of the consummation of all God's work in his life when he would be raised from the dead and receive God's gift of eternal life. So many scriptures express the same truth as that expressed in Psalm 17:15 (e.g., Philippians 3:21; Revelation 22:4). But perhaps a comparison with the words of the Apostle John would be most appropriate:

PSALM 17:15	1 JOHN 3:1,2
"I will behold thy face in righteousness: I shall be satisfied, when I awake, with thy likeness."	"The world knoweth us not, because it knew him not. Beloved, now are we the sons of God, and it doth not yet appear what we shall be: but we know that, when he shall appear, we shall be like him; for we shall see him as he is."

The satisfaction and fulfilment that the godly man longs for will finally be consummated when he is changed into His image; and this transformation, when mortality is swallowed up of life, will bring that enlarged vision and perfection of understanding for which he now longs, for he shall see him as he is.

John's exhortation for us is most apposite: "Every man that hath this hope in him purifieth himself, even as he is pure" (1 John 3:3).

PSALM 18

THE information at the head of Psalm 18 tells us that it is "a Psalm of David, the servant of the LORD, who spake unto the LORD the words of this song in the day that the LORD delivered him from the hand of all his enemies, and from the hand of Saul". It is therefore a psalm of deliverance, a song of victory, and it is particularly remarkable on two counts. First of all, throughout its fifty verses, it sustains a continuing emphasis upon the fact that all that had been accomplished is attributable not to David's prowess in war (although undoubtedly in human terms he was a mighty warrior), but to the work of God, without whom he could have done nothing. It is amongst the most powerful testimonies to the ways of providence in scripture; and the spirit of the writer overflows in praise and confidence as he contemplates the manner in which God has worked through all the troubles and vicissitudes of his life. Secondly, it is manifestly the song of a righteous man. There is no suggestion of sin, and, in fact, the basis of God's deliverance is declared to be the psalmist's righteousness before Him (verses 19-24). However, there is no hint of vainglory in the words. It is not that the psalmist is boasting of his own merit before God; rather, it is an expression of his integrity and his understanding that God is faithful and rewards the steadfastness of His servants accordingly:

"With the merciful thou wilt shew thyself merciful; with an upright man thou wilt shew thyself upright; with the pure thou wilt shew thyself pure; and with the froward thou wilt shew thyself froward." (verses 25,26)

Nevertheless, notwithstanding the application of the psalm to David, the absence of any reference to personal sin and the joy of the victory won through the power of

God is a clear indication that, in Messianic terms, the psalm is a prophecy of the ultimate triumph of the Lord Jesus Christ and the saints. This is an aspect of the psalm that we shall return to later.

The psalm is one of those portions of scripture that is recorded twice. It appears again, with certain variations, in 2 Samuel 22. We know that no word of scripture is wasted. It does not seem therefore to be an adequate explanation of its repetition to say that it is included in the Psalter because it was sung in the temple services, or that the variations between Psalm 18 and 2 Samuel 22 were amendments made to enable the psalm to be more easily used for this purpose. If we might reverse the question – most of the psalms, if not all, were intended to be sung: why then is Psalm 18 repeated in 2 Samuel? A detailed study of the variations would not be appropriate in our consideration of this psalm; but we know that a twofold cord is not easily broken. So important, then, are the lessons of this psalm that God tells us not once, but twice, of the way in which He will work in the lives of faithful men to give them the ultimate victory over sin and death.

The Ways of Providence
The psalmist opens with a declaration of fervent love for the Lord his strength. The particular form of the word for "love" occurs nowhere else in scripture, and indicates the closeness and tenderness of the relationship. David declares in words that recall his days of exile when he fled from the wrath of Saul:

> "The LORD is my rock, and my fortress, and my deliverer; my God, my strength, in whom I will trust; my buckler, and the horn of my salvation, and my high tower." (Psalm 18:2)

The thoughts expressed give us a wonderful insight into the mind of David. In those days when he was hunted as though he had been an animal, it was the rocks of the wilderness which had given him shelter from the heat of the sun and the rage of the storm. It was the cliffs and the high places which had been to him as a fortress against his enemies, and when they had come upon him, his shield and his buckler had been his defence. To the human eye, David had used all these natural surroundings to his best advantage and with his weapons of war had proved more than a match for his adversaries. But David saw them in a different light. To him they were but the tokens of the love and care of God whose hand was manifest in every circumstance to deliver him out of the hand of the enemy.

David knew that God was faithful who had promised. He had been anointed by Samuel to be king over Israel and no human agency could frustrate that purpose if he remained faithful also. Thus in everything he saw and recognised the hand of God and acknowledged that although he had played his part, he could never have succeeded if God had not enveloped him in His love and sustained him by His power. The victory was not his, but God's, and without Him he could never have triumphed over all his enemies:

"It is God that girdeth me with strength, and maketh my way perfect. He maketh my feet like hinds' feet, and setteth me upon my high places. He teacheth my hands to war, so that a bow of steel is broken by mine arms. Thou hast also given me the shield of thy salvation: and thy right hand hath holden me up, and thy gentleness hath made me great." (verses 32-35)

We note that here are the origins of the armour of righteousness developed in Isaiah's prophecy (59:16,17) and expounded finally by the Apostle Paul (Ephesians 6:13-17). Interestingly, we see in Paul the same spiritual perceptions that we observed in David. The Roman soldier who guarded him was the trigger to call to mind all the wonderful imagery and figures of the Old Testament scriptures whereby he, too, was reminded of the work of God for salvation in the lives of faithful men.

The reference to hinds' feet is an indication of sure-footedness in slippery places, and whilst it must have a literal significance for David in his experiences, it clearly means much more. "But as for me, my feet were almost gone; my steps had well nigh slipped" (Psalm 73:2).

In the conflict with sin, God's providential hand is constantly at work to deliver us, for He "is able to keep (us) from falling, and to present (us) faultless before the presence of his glory" (Jude, verse 24).

The words about God's gentleness which had made him great present us with a thought that is truly amazing. The word rendered "gentleness" means literally 'meekness or lowliness'; and it staggers the imagination to find words adequate to describe the condescension of God in humbling Himself to lift up the lowly from their human degradation and to exalt them to a position of greatness in His sight (see Psalm 113:4-6; Isaiah 57:15). This is not greatness as the world understands it, with pomp and arrogance and strutting dignity, but it is found in the place that God had given David in His purpose, in the covenant that He had made with him and with his seed for ever.

This was true greatness, for, like John the Baptist, he was great in the sight of the Lord (Luke 1:15), and humility and contriteness of spirit is one of the chief characteristics of the man for whom God humbles Himself, that he might be exalted before Him. It is the very antithesis of everything that the thinking of the flesh associates with greatness.

Perhaps one verse in particular takes us into the mind of David as it recalls two of the most spectacular victories in his military career:

"For by thee I have run through a troop; and by my God I have leaped over a wall." (verse 29)

The first part of this sentence recalls David's pursuit of the Amalekites who had attacked and sacked Ziklag (1 Samuel 30). The same word rendered "troop" is used to describe the Amalekites in that passage. The second part recalls the capture of Zion (2 Samuel 5:6-8) which was effected in such a spectacular manner, and with apparent ease. Despite its reputation of impregnability, David could be said to have jumped over the wall.

God's Manifestation of Power

Of the days of his calamity David cries, "The sorrows of death compassed me, and the floods of ungodly men made me afraid" (Psalm 18:4). The word rendered "sorrows" means literally 'cords', and the idea seems to be that so close was David to death at the hands of his enemies as

97

they harassed him and encompassed him that, like a flood, they would have swept him away. It was as if he were already bound with the cords of death and the grave.

Thinking of the Lord Jesus, however, we may perhaps be able to extend the thought a little further. Psalm 118 says, "Bind the sacrifice with cords, even unto the horns of the altar" (verse 27). So the man of sorrows was taken by wicked hands, the cords of death compassed him as, in the language of the law, he was bound to the altar, that for the sins of men he might die in accordance with the will of God.

For David, deliverance was from the death his enemies sought to impose upon him. For the Lord Jesus Christ it was from the very real death, even the death of the cross, to which he became obedient. Both could cry, "In my distress I called upon the LORD, and cried unto my God: he heard my voice out of his temple, and my cry came before him, even into his ears" (Psalm 18:6).

The divine response was a dreadful manifestation of power – earthquake, fire, storm, hail, thunderings and lightning (verses 7-19). In the scriptural records there is no event in the life of David which corresponds to the phenomena described. The secret, however, lies in the type of language used. It is reminiscent of the Exodus, when God came down to deliver His people from the bondage of Egypt (see Exodus 15, Habakkuk 3 etc.). So in the life of David (and Jesus) the Lord had won a great victory. He had redeemed him from the power of his enemies and the language is especially appropriate to describe the manner in which God will deliver all His saints from the bondage of sin. The apocalyptic character of the words is emphasised by one phrase, "He rode upon a cherub, and did fly" (verse 10). It was a redemptive work, for the words recall the cherubim who kept the way to the tree of life. The figures that overshadowed the mercy seat in the most holy place where God's glory dwelt in the midst of His people, and which were also wrought into the veil with cunning workmanship, were to remind Israel of the principles by which they could approach their God. All spoke of God's redemptive work, and David had experienced the hand of God throughout his life, active to deliver him from his enemies and to exalt him to the position he now occupied.

Dependence upon the Word of God

Though it may perhaps not be immediately apparent, a careful consideration of Psalm 18 reveals that it is built upon earlier scriptures. This gives us further insight into the faith of David. His confidence in God, his understanding of the work of the Lord in his life, was founded upon his knowledge of the word of God.

In particular, we might compare two earlier passages of God's word, one drawn from the other – Deuteronomy 32 and 1 Samuel 2. Deuteronomy 32 contains the Song of Moses. It concludes with the declaration of God's judgement upon the wicked and the vindication of the righteous (verses 39-43). 1 Samuel 2:1-10 contains the song of Hannah. The language she uses is drawn from Deuteronomy 32, and both scriptures are referred to by David in Psalm 18, showing the extent to which they figured in his meditations upon the work of God in his life. Particularly interesting is the fact that Hannah's song seems to have been already committed to writing at the time of David's song. The following table illustrates this:

DEUTERONOMY 32	1 SAMUEL 2	PSALM 18
"He is the Rock." (verses 4,15,18,30,31)	"neither is there any rock like our God." (verse 2)	"The LORD is my rock." (verses 2,31,46)
"His work is perfect." (verse 4)		"As for God, his way is perfect." (verse 30)
"A perverse and *crooked* generation." (verse 5)		"With the froward (same word) thou wilt show thyself froward." (verse 26)
"For a fire is kindled in mine anger (lit. nostrils)." (verse 22)		"There went up a smoke out of his nostrils." (verse 8)
"To me belongeth vengeance ... their foot shall slide in due time." (verse 35)	"He will keep the feet of his saints." (verse 9)	"He maketh my feet like hinds' feet ... my feet did not slip." (verse 33,36)

99

"I kill, and I make alive." (verse 39)	"The LORD killeth, and maketh alive." (verse 6)	
	"The bows of the mighty men are broken, and they that stumble are girded with strength." (verse 4)	"A bow of steel is broken by mine arms ... for thou hast girded me with strength." (verses 34,39)
	"My horn is exalted in the LORD." (verse 1). "He raiseth up the poor ... and lifteth up the beggar ... to set them among princes, and to make them inherit the throne of glory." (verse 8)	"Thy gentleness hath made me great." (verse 35)

The Messianic Application

Some references have already been made to the psalm's application to the Lord Jesus Christ. The relevance of the song's general theme to Jesus and the saints is obvious. Nevertheless, any doubts are completely dispelled by the use of the psalm in the New Testament. It is quoted twice. In Hebrews (2:13) the words of verse 2 are quoted as the words of the Lord Jesus, "I will put my trust in him", as an indication that "he that sanctifieth and they who are sanctified are all of one: for which cause he is not ashamed to call them brethren".

The context shows that he who is the Captain of salvation (verse 10) , who shared our nature (verse 14), depended on God in the hour of his need, as we and all faithful men (including David) must do if we are to know His salvation. Hence the appropriateness of the psalm to Christ and the saints is established.

The second quotation is taken from the end of the psalm (verse 49) and occurs in Romans 15 in connection with the call of the Gentiles: "As it is written, For this cause I will confess to thee among the Gentiles, and sing unto thy name" (verse 9). It is significant that the passage from the psalm is linked with other quotations, amongst them the words of Deuteronomy 32:43 to which we have already referred.

Thus the psalm is encompassed by these two quotations which establish the application in its entirety to the Lord Jesus Christ – yet not to him only, but also to his faithful brethren. And the closing verses of the psalm link together the covenant with David and the blessing for all nations as it looks forward to the day of the Lord's ultimate triumph:

"Therefore will I give thanks unto thee, O LORD, among the heathen, and sing praises unto thy name. Great deliverance giveth he to his king; and sheweth mercy to his anointed, to David, and to his seed for evermore." (Psalm 18:49,50)

PSALM 19

IT is amazing how many writers assume that because of the apparent difference in style and subject matter that occurs at verse 7, this psalm is the work of two different authors. Perhaps even more surprising is the number of writers who, having made the assertion, then proceed to declare what a happy fusion of ideas it was, and emphasise the spiritual perception of whomsoever it was that made the compilation.

One would have thought that, even without inspiration, if a man could see the appropriateness of the two writings, he would realise that both sections could have been the product of a single mind motivated by the same kind of spiritual genius.

We need, however, concern ourselves no longer with the surmisings of men, for, appreciating the power of inspiration, we know that David, who was almost certainly the author, has expressed thoughts concerning the work of God in creation and the power of His word in men's lives that are completely compatible with, and complementary to, each other.

The Structure

The psalm falls very simply into three sections, the last being an extension of the thoughts of the second:

(1) The glory of God revealed in the heavens which speak unceasingly of His power and might (verses 1-6).

(2) The glory of God revealed in His word, which is powerful to effect transformation in the lives of men (verses 7-11).

(3) The longings and prayers of the psalmist for God to keep him from the effects of sin and wickedness (verses 12-14).

The unity of the psalm is appreciated when once we allow our minds to be directed by the clear teaching of other passages of scripture.

Psalm 33 is particularly appropriate, for it demonstrates the connection between the works of God and the word of God – a connection so close that in reality the two cannot be separated:

"For the word of the LORD is right; and all his works are done in truth." (verse 4)

"By the word of the LORD were the heavens made; and all the host of them by the breath of his mouth." (verse 6)

"For he spake, and it was done; he commanded, and it stood fast." (verse 9)

"The counsel of the LORD standeth for ever; the thoughts of his heart to all generations." (verse 11)

First, the psalm declares that God speaks, and works of physical creation are "done" and stand fast as a consequence; then it moves easily and logically to the moral sphere, where the counsel of God's heart is revealed by the same word, and equally stands fast to all generations.

Thus in the beginning, when the earth was without form and void, God said, "Let there be light: and there was light" (Genesis 1:3), and order was created out of the chaos of that primeval world. Similarly, God who commanded light to shine out of darkness has illuminated our hearts to bring order and harmony out of the chaos of sin, by causing the light of the knowledge of His glory to be revealed in the face of Jesus Christ (2 Corinthians 4:6).

Peter in his second epistle exhorts, "that ye may be mindful of the words which were spoken before by the holy prophets" (3:2); and telling of the scoffers who were to come, he continues:

"For this they willingly are ignorant of, that by the word of God the heavens were of old, and the earth standing out of the water and in the water: whereby the world that then was, being overflowed with water, perished: but the heavens and the earth, which are now, by the same word are kept in store, reserved unto fire

103

against the day of judgment and perdition of ungodly men." (verses 5-7)

It is the same word, revealed through the prophets, by which the heavens were created in the beginning, whereby the world of Noah perished and the present constitution of things stands condemned, and will be judged by fire.

The relationship between the two apparently differing sections of the psalm is now clear. They are both manifestations of the mind of God created by the breath of His mouth. Of the physical creation, Psalm 33 said, "All the host of them by the breath of his mouth". Of the scriptures, the written word of God, Paul writes, "All scripture is given by inspiration of God" (lit. 'the breath of God') (2 Timothy 3:16).

Thus the order and beauty of the natural is a mirror-image of the perfection of the spiritual. In fact, the physical is the product of the word of God, and it is not inappropriate to notice that the words of 2 Timothy 3:16, "God-breathed", form an allusion to the creation of man – "God breathed into his nostrils the breath of life" (Genesis 2:7). Thus God in the beginning gave to man that life-giving energy; so by a similar process, through the transforming power of His word, a new creation is effected in men.

It is such insights which help us to appreciate that it is not just the natural physical heavens that the Spirit refers to in Psalm 19; but that these are an allegory for the new heavens of the Messianic age, which similarly will be founded through the word of God. They represent the redeemed who will shine as the stars for ever and ever with the sun, predominant in its illumination, representing the "Sun of righteousness (who shall) arise with healing in his wings" (Malachi 4:2). The link is therefore between the heavens of the age to come which will reflect the glory of God in its fulness and the transforming power of God's word which is responsible for the establishment of that divine order.

We can now appreciate that the apostle's use of this psalm in his epistle to the Romans (10:18) is more than just the apt use of an appropriate illustration, but is drawn from a psalm which is primarily concerned with the word of God and the surpassing glory of God's coming kingdom (see below). We can now look at the sections in more detail in their original context.

The Heavens declare the Glory of God

The idea in verses 1 and 2 is simple to comprehend. The heavens tell forth God's glory, and the silent witness of the constancy of their light is passed on from each successive day and night to that which follows in a perpetual declaration of the wonder of God's handiwork. "There is no speech nor language, their voice cannot be heard"; yet "their line is gone out through all the earth and their words to the end of the world" (verses 3,4, RV). The reference to "line" is probably to the measuring line by which the very ends of the earth, to which the continuing message is extended, have been compassed.

Paul's word in Romans, however, rendered "sound", means literally an utterance, usually musical, either vocal or instrumental (Strong's), and it is not sufficient to say that Paul is quoting the Septuagint, for the Spirit is its own interpreter. Another look at the Hebrew word "line" reveals that, whereas normally the word is used for a measuring line, it can also carry the idea of the string of a harp (see Gesenius' *Hebrew-Chaldee Lexicon*) and it appears to be this idea that is reflected in Romans, as though the harmony of creation, like the beauty of a symphony in all its complexity, extended throughout the earth to wherever men had senses to perceive.

Note that this is the point of the quotation in Romans 10. The glory of the heavens is seen over all the earth. The future glory of the new heavens will encompass the whole earth. The Gospel therefore was not for Jews only, but for all men without distinction; and the quotation is made particularly with reference to the call of the Gentiles. The fact that God's coming kingdom was to be worldwide was reason enough for the Gospel to be preached in all the earth.

Supreme in the heavens is the sun with its all-pervading energy, and the reference to its influence, to its emergence to pursue its course like "a bridegroom coming out of his chamber" is resonant with scriptural allusion to

105

the work and office of the Messiah. The reference to a strong man running a race, recalling the words of Judges, is also not to be missed: "But let them that love him be as the sun when he goeth forth in his might" (Judges 5:31).

The Word of God

The handicap of being unable to read the word in the original Hebrew is manifest at this point. We are told, but cannot verify it, that in the original text there is a perfect symmetry, for each phrase used to describe the word of God and its effect has exactly the same number of syllables.

There is advantage in setting out this section of the psalm in tabular form:

DESCRIPTION	ITS QUALITIES	ITS EFFECT
The law of the LORD	is perfect	converting the soul
The testimony of the LORD	is sure	making wise the simple
The statutes of the LORD	are right	rejoicing the heart
The commandment of the LORD	is pure	enlightening the eyes
The fear of the LORD	is clean	enduring for ever
The judgments of the LORD	are true	(making) righteous altogether

The transforming quality of the word is perhaps emphasised here more powerfully than in any other part of scripture. The language bears a striking resemblance to the words of Psalm 119; but the concise, concentrated form of the description which is contained in just two verses brings home the absolute importance of the word of God in effecting man's salvation. It was God who, in the beginning, created man, who has also provided His word; and the two are complementary to each other. God knows man's needs; He made him in His image, and consequently He has so structured His word that it is perfectly suited to the requirements of men. God's word and His providential care are sufficient for man's salvation. In the things revealed, in the guidance provided, there is all that is necessary. The passage is a complete answer to those who look for the indwelling of the Holy Spirit to give enlightenment and guidance and to bring about moral change in a man's life.

This is not to say, however, that we must forget the hand of God working in our lives; the last few verses emphasise how David felt the need for such guidance to work in conjunction with the word.

Prayer for God's Guidance

David acknowledges that the weakness lies not with the word of God, but with the infirmity of his own nature:

"Who can understand his (i.e., his own) errors? cleanse thou me from secret faults." (verse 12)

Even with the word to instruct, there was still need to recognise the danger of sins committed inadvertently, through ignorance, of which a man could remain blissfully unaware. For these, when discovered, the law provided an atonement (see Leviticus 4:2; Numbers 15:22); but David, recognising how blind a man could sometimes be, beseeches God for His forgiveness when he lapsed into such sins of inadvertence and ignorance.

Equally, David realised the danger in which he stood from the example and influence of evil men. The word rendered "presumptuous" (verse 13) is elsewhere always referred to proud and evil men. So here David, aware of the railing and mockery of such men who despised righteousness, beseeches God to keep him from their oppression, that they might not have dominion over him. The influence of the world we live in is such that we, too, without God's guidance and care, must surely perish. How much it becomes us, therefore, to separate ourselves from its company, to keep as far away as possible from the temptations to which it would expose us. We stand in enough danger without putting ourselves, of our own choice, in positions where presumptuous, proud and arrogant men can influence us with their godless words and thoughts. Our spirit must be, "I am a companion of all them that fear thee" (Psalm 119:63).

107

If we do these things, we shall be innocent of "great transgression" (AV margin, "much"). We shall be kept from rebellion against God and will show ourselves to be upright – perfect in the sense of wholeness or oneness, men and women of integrity who wholeheartedly serve God.

These things to which God has called us far outweigh in their value anything that the world can offer. The problem is that material things sometimes appear to offer more advantage, and we can be blinded to the reality of the things that are eternal. If, however, we truly love God's word and delight in it, then day by day we shall come to appreciate more and more that everything that men of this world value fades into complete and utter insignificance compared with it:

"More to be desired are they than gold, yea, than much fine gold; sweeter also than honey and the honeycomb. Moreover by them is thy servant warned: and in keeping of them there is great reward."

(Psalm 19:10,11)

If such thoughts dominate our hearts, if day by day we are being changed by the sweet influences of God's words, then with David we, too, can say:

"Let the words of my mouth, and the meditation of my heart, be acceptable in thy sight, O LORD, my strength, and my redeemer." (verse 14)

PSALM 20

THE psalm falls into three sections: first, a prayer on behalf of the king, the Lord's anointed, by his people (verses 1-5); second, the response of the king when the prayer has been answered (verse 6); and third, the rejoicing of the people in the salvation of God wrought through him (verses 7-9).

Apart from the actual substance of the sections, the division of the psalm as outlined above can be readily appreciated by the use of the pronouns "we" and "thee" in sections one and three, and the first person singular, "I", in section two.

There has been speculation as to the historical background of the psalm (see 2 Samuel 8:3); but there is no firm evidence on which to reach a conclusion. This, however, does not detract from the meaning of the psalm or diminish in any way the principles that underlie it, and some suggestions will be seen to emerge from our study.

Prayer on behalf of the King

The people, or the priests who pray on their behalf, clearly recognise that the king is both their representative before God and also God's representative in their midst. Their salvation is bound up with his victory. It is in his success that they also will be exalted. Thus their plea before God is that the king's prayers and sacrifices will be accepted and that in God's response, his enemies might be abased:

"The LORD hear (RV, 'answer') thee in the day of trouble; the name of the God of Jacob defend thee; send thee help from the sanctuary, and strengthen thee out of Zion." (verses 1,2)

The word rendered "trouble" is cognate with that sometimes rendered "adversaries". Consequently, we appreciate that the trouble confronting the king does not

109

arise principally from loss of health or bereavement, or deprivation of goods and possessions. Rather, it is the confrontation with men who are his enemies and, it must be assumed, who seek to destroy him.

The reference to "the God of Jacob" in this context becomes particularly meaningful. Jacob in all his trouble had shown a steadfast faith in God, and God on His part had shown Himself to be faithful in delivering Jacob out of all his afflictions and giving to him comfort and consolation in the midst of his tribulations. In scripture, "the God of Jacob" invariably has reference to the faithfulness of the God who comforts us in all our troubles and delivers us by His providential care. For the basis of this fact, see the following references in the life of Jacob: Genesis 28:10-22; 31:11-13; 32:1,2; 35:1-15; 48:15,16.

We shall take Genesis 28 to illustrate the point in more detail. Jacob was fleeing from the wrath of his brother Esau, his adversary, who sought his life. At Bethel he had this remarkable vision of the angels of God ascending and descending on the ladder that reached up to heaven. The fact that they were going up and coming down is significant. The message to Jacob was that God's angels had already been active in his life, ascending now with that part of their work which had brought him to this place complete. Yahweh Himself stood at the side of the ladder (see RV) and announced, "I am the LORD God of Abraham thy father, and the God of Isaac: the land whereon thou liest, to thee will I give it, and to thy seed" (verse 13). In the reiteration of the promise to Abraham, God declared Himself to be also the God of Jacob, and gave him the wonderful assurance:

"And, behold, I am with thee, and will keep thee in all places whither thou goest, and will bring thee again into this land; for I will not leave thee, until I have done that which I have spoken to thee of."   (verse 15)

This is a promise that, in its scope, gave Jacob a hope of life beyond the grave in fulfilment of the things of which God had spoken. It could only be fulfilled in its entirety by a resurrection from the dead. This, of course, is a fact enlarged on by the Lord Jesus when he silenced the foolishness of the Sadducees. Had they not read that at

110

the bush God had said, "I am the God of Abraham, and the God of Isaac, and the God of Jacob? God is not the God of the dead, but of the living" (Matthew 22:32). Though dead, the fathers 'lived' unto God; and all faithful men who sleep in the dust of the earth have died in faith, knowing that not even death can separate them from the love of God, for He will not leave them until He has done that of which He has spoken to them.

So the call that "the name of the God of Jacob" might defend the king is a plea for that angelic guidance that characterised the life of Jacob to be extended now to His anointed, that by His providential care he might be delivered from his adversaries. It is in the name of Jacob's God that these things will be accomplished – that name of purpose in which is enshrined the whole plan of salvation and which, as we have shown, extends its influence beyond the grave to the resurrection day. It is a fact of some significance when we contemplate the Messianic meaning of the psalm.

The references to the sanctuary and to Zion make it evident that historically the psalm can be placed in two periods. The sanctuary could refer to the tabernacle of David that he provided to house the ark of God in Zion; the anointed for whom the people pray would therefore in the first instance be David. On the other hand, the reference could be to the temple which Solomon built and the words would then be as true of him as of David.

It appears that the Hebrew word for "sanctuary" is used of both tabernacle and temple, so no distinction can be made on that account. However, the response of the anointed in verse 6 is interesting, for in acknowledging that God has heard their prayers, he refers not to the earthly sanctuary, but to the temple of God in heaven: "He will hear him from his holy heaven". It is, of course, a feature of the great prayer of Solomon at the dedication of the temple, that he recognised that no earthly building could confine or contain God and that His response is from heaven, His dwelling place. The refrain that runs through the prayer is, "When they pray towards this place ... then hear thou in heaven thy dwelling place".

It must be acknowledged that David had a similar perspective; but having regard to the emphasis upon the name of God in that prayer, and the fact that it is mentioned three times in this short psalm, together with all the sacrifices offered at the dedication of the temple, and the words of the psalm regarding sacrifice that we now come to consider, we suggest (led more, perhaps, by intuition than by firm evidence) that the psalm was written to express the feelings of the people and the response of Solomon shortly after the glory of God had filled the house that he had built. "Remember all thy offerings, and accept thy burnt sacrifice" (Psalm 20:3).

The word rendered "offering" has specific reference to the meal offering which was offered in association with the burnt offering (Exodus 29:35-42). The plea to "remember" is appropriate, for that part of the meal offering that was burned by the priest was consumed in the flames as a memorial before God (see Leviticus 2:2,9,16). It was intended to bring the worshippers, on whose behalf it was offered, into remembrance before God.

The AV marginal reference for "accept the burnt sacrifice" says, "turn to ashes". The burnt offering was to be completely consumed on the altar. The ashes remaining were the token that God had accepted the sacrifice. The burnt offering represented the total dedication of a man's life to God. The meal offering (and the wine offering), being the fruit of man's labours, represented the dedication of the works of his hands. It is these works, the outward token of an inward dedication of heart, that rise as a sweet-smelling savour and bring men into remembrance before God. There has, it need hardly be said, been only one perfect burnt offering, the Lord Jesus Christ; and the Messianic nature of the psalm is emphasised once more.

The prayer continues by beseeching God to grant him his heart's desire and to fulfil all his counsels. Of course, in the context of the psalm, the desires and counsels that fill the heart of the Lord's anointed are of the highest spiritual calibre. They belong to those things of the kingdom for which we, too, can pray, in the complete assurance that if we ask in faith, God will grant our requests, for they are expressions of our desire, in the knowledge of His counsel, to be incorporated into His eternal purpose. Because God will do these things the faithful can say, "We will rejoice in thy salvation, and in the name of our God we will set up our banners" (verse 5).

Strong's Concordance suggests that the idea behind the banners is that of raising a flag. The word is used in the Song of Solomon: "terrible as an army with banners" (6:4,10). In other words, the flags are raised in triumph as a declaration of allegiance to the king. In the colloquialism of our day we "fly the flag" when we declare our allegiance, when in the face of stern opposition we show ourselves ready to defend the things we stand for. It is in the understanding of the name of our God and the confidence wrought from this appreciation of His faithfulness, that we shall be always ready to give an answer.

The King's Response

With the sacrifice offered and accepted, the Lord's anointed can rejoice in the ultimate victory:

> "Now know I that the LORD saveth his anointed; he will hear him from his holy heaven with the saving strength of his right hand."   (verse 6)

This foundation truth was emphasised in Psalm 2. Though the heathen might rage and the kings of the earth in their anger set themselves against the Lord and against His anointed, it was all to no avail. He that sat in the heavens laughed; the Lord had them in derision, for all their fury would be frustrated, and He would set His King upon His holy hill of Zion (verses 1-6).

The Rejoicing of the People

The conclusions drawn from the prayers expressed, and the victory of the king, lead to a joyous expression of faith on the part of the people:

> "Some trust in chariots, and some in horses: but we will remember the name of the LORD our God. They are brought down and fallen: but we are risen, and stand upright."   (verses 7,8)

Chariots and horses were the symbol of military might in ancient times. A nation's power and standing was

113

measured by the number they possessed. Yet Israel were commanded not to multiply horses, for they were not to rely upon the arm of flesh, but in the strength and power of their God.

Both Elijah and Elisha were the instruments through whom God wielded this power in their day. The distinctive expression used of them both, when their work came to an end, takes us to the very heart of this truth: "My father, my father, the chariot of Israel, and the horsemen thereof" (2 Kings 2:12; 13:14). There was a recognition that the power of God manifest through them was more to Israel than all the chariots and horses of the nations. Thus we have the contrast of Psalm 20: "... but we will make mention of the name of the LORD our God" (RV). It is the hallmark of true servants of God, that it is always their delight to talk together of the things that they hold most dear, to rejoice in the things of the name by which they have been redeemed, by which ultimately the wicked will be abased and they will be exalted.

So the concluding prayer of the people is, "Give victory to the king, O LORD; answer us when we call" (verse 9 RSV).

PSALM 21

WE have discussed previously, when dealing with Psalm 8, the suggestion of Thirtle (*The Titles of the Psalms*) that the superscriptions at the head of many of the psalms refer in fact to the psalm preceding. In this particular instance, the words "Aijeleth Shahar" at the head of Psalm 22 would refer to Psalm 21. The margin of the AV and the rendering of the RSV point to the meaning of the words, "The hind of the morning" and "Hind of the Dawn" respectively.

It is not easy to determine the precise significance of the hind in scripture. We know that it is a gentle creature particularly associated with the hunt. It is associated also with sure-footedness in slippery places, the physical attribute being a token of a spiritual quality. Hence, "He maketh my feet like hinds' feet, and setteth me upon my high places" (Psalm 18:33).

In this context it would speak of David's days of exile, hunted by Saul, and of the joy of deliverance at the breaking of the dawn of the new day – for the psalm has been described as David's "Coronation Anthem". And, of course, it would speak typically of the morning without clouds when the Lord Jesus Christ will enter into his kingdom, when "the Sun of righteousness (will) arise with healing in his wings" (Malachi 4:2).

Structure

The psalm can be divided into two main sections, the first in which Yahweh (verse 1) is praised for the blessings bestowed upon His king (verses 2-7), and the second in which the king himself is addressed and extolled because of his triumphs over his enemies (verses 8-12). Finally, the last verse (13) is a prayer expressing the thanksgiving and praise of the people for what Yahweh has done for His anointed.

115

We might note at this juncture the emphasis in the two main sections. In the first, we are told what God has done for His king:

"Thou hast given him his heart's desire."   (verse 2)

"Thou dost meet him with goodly blessings."
(verse 3, RSV)

"Thou settest a crown of pure gold on his head."
(verse 3)

"He asked life ... and thou gavest it him."   (verse 4)

"Thou hast made him most blessed for ever." (verse 6)

"Thou hast made him exceeding glad with thy countenance."   (verse 6)

In the second, we see what the king is able to accomplish because of the work of God in his life:

"Thine hand shall find out all thine enemies."
(verse 8)

"Thou shalt make them as a fiery oven in the time of thine anger."   (verse 9)

"Their fruit shalt thou destroy from the earth."
(verse 10)

"Therefore shalt thou make them turn their back."
(verse 12)

Application to the life of David

It is the psalms that, time and again, emphasise the humility and faith of the man David. It is hard to appreciate how truly remarkable a man he was, not trusting in the arm of flesh, but always, in every circumstance, every crisis and emergency, recognising how completely he depended upon God who was his strength and his helper. It was in this that David knew a perpetual joy as he gloried in the God of Israel who had upheld him through all adversity (verse 1).

The blessing given in response to his prayer (verse 2) is described in the following verses (3-6) and although they can only be fully appreciated in terms of the experience of the Lord Jesus Christ, they also have a fulfilment, albeit incipient in certain respects, in the life of David.

We do not know precisely when the psalm was written. It does not seem unreasonable to suppose, however, that it was written in the fullness of David's glory, when he was established in Zion, and before his sin in the matter of Bathsheba and Uriah. Indeed, it may be that it was synonymous with the time of the giving of the Covenant, when the desires of David's heart were made plain, and in the words of the Covenant which promised David an eternal inheritance, the words of the psalm would take on a more literal and precise meaning:

"For thou dost meet him with goodly blessings; thou dost set a crown of fine gold upon his head. He asked life of thee; thou gavest it to him, length of days for ever and ever. His glory is great through thy help; splendour and majesty thou dost bestow upon him. Yea, thou dost make him most blessed for ever; thou dost make him glad with the joy of thy presence."   (verses 3-6, RSV)

If we follow this interpretation, then the latter section of the psalm would be fulfilled in the conquests of David described between chapters 7 and 10 of 2 Samuel, and the song describes how utterly God would frustrate all the wicked imaginations of his enemies.

The Lord Jesus Christ

We look in more detail at the words in their application to the Lord Jesus; and as he is the substance in which scripture finds its fulfilment, we shall see also how David's experiences are in measure a reflection, as in a mirror, of the Lord's own deepest longing and desires.

Of the desires of his heart and the words of his lips, the Lord said, "I knew that thou hearest me always" (John 11:42); and in nothing did he pray more earnestly than for deliverance out of death, that he might know the fullness of the joy to be experienced in the presence of his Father (Psalm 16:9-11; Hebrews 12:2). In the days of his flesh, he offered up prayers and supplications to God who was able to save him out of death. Crying and tears characterised the earnestness of his pleas, and because of his godly fear he was heard (Hebrews 5:7,8). God gave him life for evermore, and crowned him with glory and honour (cp. Psalm 21:5 with Hebrews 2:7). Glory and honour are divine attributes and the king, in reflecting them, fulfils the purpose of God in creation when He commissioned

117

man to have dominion over the works of His hands (cp. Genesis 1 with Psalm 8:1,5,6).

One of the things about scripture to which we must always be alert is the way in which key words are intended to remind us of particular aspects of the work of God. Such words are "blessed" and "blessing". Almost invariably they turn the mind back to God's covenant with Abraham. Thus Psalm 21 tells us of the king that "thou hast made him most blessed for ever" (verse 6). Literally the sense is "thou makest him a blessing". Kay (*Psalms with Notes*) writes, "For thou makest him (a source of) everlasting blessing". The king is both the recipient and the mediator of blessing. God told Abraham, "I will bless you, and make your name great, so that you will be a blessing" (Genesis 12:2, RSV). In him and his seed all families of the earth would be blessed (Genesis 22:18). The blessing of Abraham was the forgiveness of sins. Through his seed, men are blessed in being turned every one from his iniquities (Acts 3:25,26).

All this is involved in the sovereignty of the Lord Jesus Christ, and all has been achieved because of his trust in Yahweh through the loving-kindness of the Most High (Hebrew *chesed*, AV "mercy"; expresses 'covenant love', i.e., faithfulness). Because of his trust and God's faithfulness, none will be able to stand before him or escape his anger in the day of his wrath. For the day is coming that shall burn as an oven, when all who do wickedly shall be as stubble (Malachi 4:1; see also Isaiah 2).

The reference to the "time of thine anger" (verse 9) is interesting. The word rendered "anger" is that which is also translated "face", "countenance" and "presence" (Hebrew, *panis*) on other occasions. God lifts up His countenance in mercy, but His face is also turned against those that do wickedly, while to dwell in His presence is the desire of all faithful disciples. The revelation of His presence in the person of the King will bring about also the destruction of those who obey not the Gospel, "who shall be punished with everlasting destruction from the presence of the Lord, and from the glory of his power" (2 Thessalonians 1:9).

The wicked and all their seed are to be destroyed out of the earth, for "they intended evil against thee: they imagined a mischievous device, which they are not able to perform" (verse 11), but God frustrates their endeavours. The language reminds us of man's attempt to thwart the purpose of God in Babel, when God sent confusion of tongues to confound their intentions (Genesis 11). Of the manner in which Herod, Pontius Pilate, the people of Israel and the Gentiles were gathered together to crucify the Lord Jesus Christ, we read in Acts 4:27 that they were unwittingly doing what God's counsel determined before to be done. When God raised His Son from the dead and exalted him to His own right hand, He frustrated their purpose and gave assurance unto all men that, in the appointed day, He would rule the world by him. Psalm 2 remains to be fulfilled in the last days when "the heathen rage, and the people imagine a vain thing", but God who sits in the heavens shall laugh, He will have them in derision. He will establish His King upon His "holy hill of Zion".

It is in this confidence that all who long for that day will pray, "Be thou exalted, LORD, in thine own strength: so will we sing and praise thy power" (Psalm 21:13).

PSALM 22

IT is difficult to imagine that this psalm, with its direct and unmistakable reference to the sufferings of the Lord Jesus Christ, could have a precise historical background that occasioned its writing. One can sympathise with the view that says that the things recorded transcend the limits of an ordinary individual's experience, and that consequently it is in its entirety wholly predictive.

It is the writer's conviction that it is indeed wholly predictive, and that every single word has reference to the sufferings of the Lord Jesus Christ and to the glory that should follow. At the same time, however, this does not necessarily rule out the possibility that it was events in the life of the author that prompted the expression of these thoughts, under the guidance and influence of the Holy Spirit.

Any suggestion as to what the background might be may appear, in the circumstances, to be somewhat tenuous. It is therefore with an element of caution that we propose that the psalm was written by David some time after his sin in the matter of Bathsheba and Uriah the Hittite. There is, of course, no hint of sin, shame or guilt, in the words of the psalm, and bearing in mind its primary significance, this is appropriate. Nevertheless, the expressions of suffering and affliction, the feeling of desolation, of separation from God, are particularly appropriate to describe the effects of David's sin upon him.

It seems certain also that David suffered serious ill health after his sin, possibly a form of leprosy (see Psalms 32, 38, 41 and 51) and this could be reflected in Psalm 22 (verses 14,15). The references to the contempt of his enemies, their cruel delight in his sufferings, would also be true of the latter part of David's reign when, although

120

forgiven his sin, he suffered the consequences of it in trouble and afflictions.

If we consider the sufferings of the Lord Jesus Christ and all his experiences against this background, a certain aptness may be seen. Jesus died for David's sin; indeed, the Lord laid upon him the iniquity of us all. Jesus, of course, died for humankind, for all born in Adam's line, but in the last analysis, it is only those whom he is not ashamed to call brethren who, by their response to his sacrifice, enjoy its benefits. It is difficult for us to appreciate the feelings and emotions of the Lord Jesus, both in his life and on the cross; for, unlike us, he never sinned and consequently knew no personal shame or guilt. Yet by sharing our nature he was daily associating with sinners. It was with strong crying and tears that he cried to be delivered out of death, for he shared that common heritage with us. And when he who knew no sin became sin for us, he willingly recognised our sins and acknowledged them and owned them, on our behalf, as though they were his own. In terms of his experience, it would not be wise to speculate too far as to what all this really meant to him, but perhaps this is as much as we can say. In some sense he shared the sinner's feelings of desolation because of his separation from God. He knew, with all humankind, the feelings of doubt and fear that are not in themselves sin, but only become so when they are nurtured and allowed to dominate thought and action.

Certainly God stood aside from that dreadful scene depicted in the crucifixion, for He could not be associated or identified with sin, and this fact was, we believe, indicated by the withdrawal of the Holy Spirit. As Brother John Thomas expressed it in his usual robust style, "Before he had uttered this exclamation (Psalm 22:1), the Holy Spirit ... had been withdrawn. The Father-Spirit had evacuated the son of David's daughter" (*Eureka Vol. I* pages 13,14).

All these thoughts form a background to our understanding of the opening words of the psalm, which were quoted by the Lord Jesus on the cross: "My God, my God, why hast thou forsaken me?" (Matthew 27:46; Mark 15:34).

121

The psalm falls into two parts:

verses 1-21 – The sufferings of Christ;

verses 21-31 – The glory that should follow.

The Sufferings

That this psalm was the subject of the Lord's meditations on the cross is beyond doubt, having regard to the number of times that it is quoted in connection with that event. To understand the feelings and sentiments expressed in the first twenty-one verses is to share with him his deepest longings and yearnings in those last few hours of his life. Yet it is not confined in its significance to those dying hours, as will be demonstrated.

We have already considered in part the opening words quoted by the Lord Jesus; but in associating them with his offering for sin, we should not overlook the fact that they reflect a common human experience for all who seek to find their fulfilment in God. It is not to be understood as a demand for an explanation of the situation in which he found himself, but rather it is an expression of both the faith and the perplexity that he felt at that moment. His assurance that God was indeed his God is seen in the words, "My God, my God". The wrestling within that all men experience when they are tried is seen in the question, "Why hast thou forsaken me?" He was tempted in all points "like unto his brethren". Sin lies not in the wrestling, but in being overcome by the evil, and the Lord in his victory triumphed gloriously over all doubt and uncertainty.

That the thoughts of the psalm are not confined to the cross is seen by the latter part of verse 1 taken with verse 2:

"Why art thou so far from helping me, and from the words of my roaring (Strong's – 'moaning'; Kay – 'groaning')? O my God, I cry in the daytime, but thou answerest not (RV); and in the night season, but find no rest" (RV margin).

We have in an earlier chapter demonstrated the links between Psalm 6 and Hebrews 5. It might be appropriate to compare verse 6 of that psalm with verse 7 of the chapter from the epistle:

PSALM 6

"I am weary with my groaning; all the night make I my bed to swim; I water my couch with my tears." (verse 6)

HEBREWS 5

"Who in the days of his flesh, when he had offered up prayers and supplications with strong crying and tears unto him that was able to save him from death ..." (verse 7)

Such words may cause some perplexity at what might appear to be lack of trust in God; but note that the text says not "thou hearest not" (AV), but "thou answerest not" (RV), and this is a most important distinction. No man of God could doubt that God hears his prayer. But all must recognise that sometimes God remains silent and does not give an answer immediately (Psalm 10:1; 13:1,2), the purpose being to test the faith of the individual so that God might know all that is in his heart (see 2 Chronicles 32:31). To be tempted in all points like unto his brethren, it was necessary that the Lord Jesus should share this experience with us, and the fact that he did so in no way contradicts scriptural teaching concerning his perfect life and absolute righteousness. Indeed, the next verses (3-5) of the psalm indicate his understanding of the nature and character of God and of the way in which He had manifested His faithfulness to the fathers in times past:

"But thou art holy, O thou that art enthroned upon the praises of Israel (RV margin). Our fathers trusted in thee: they trusted, and thou didst deliver them. They cried unto thee, and were delivered: they trusted in thee, and were not ashamed" (RV).

Of the word translated "inhabitest" (AV), Strong's Concordance indicates that it is from a root meaning 'to sit' – hence the rendering of the RV margin. Both renderings, however, call to mind the Lord "who (dwelt) between the cherubims" (2 Samuel 6:2; 2 Kings 19:15). It was there in the tabernacle and afterwards in the temple that Yahweh was enthroned in the midst of His people. And in a dramatic figure, the praises of Israel (see Psalm 9:11; 65:1) are depicted as being like a cloud of incense ascending through the veil and filling the most holy place – the habitation of Him who never ceases to be worthy of the praise of His people (Exodus 15:11; Isaiah 63:7).

The trust of the fathers had not been misplaced. They had not been confounded, they were not brought to shame as a result of their faith. With the example of God's mercy in their lives before him, the psalmist, and through him the "spirit of Christ" in the psalm, returns to the distress in which he found himself at that time:

"But I am a worm, and no man; a reproach of men, and despised of the people. All they that see me laugh me to scorn: they shoot out the lip, they shake the head, saying, He trusted on the LORD that he would deliver him: let him deliver him, seeing he delighted in him."

(Psalm 22:6-8)

Note first of all the connections with the suffering servant of Isaiah:

"But I am a worm" – Isaiah 41:14

"a reproach" – Isaiah 52:14; 53:2,3

"despised" –   Isaiah 49:7; 53:3

He saw himself as a worm, trampled underfoot, despised and defenceless. The delight of his enemies and their cruel mockings of his sufferings are terrible indictments of the depths of depravity to which men can sink. The enormity of their crime seems even more frightening when we remember that all their gestures of contempt, their use of the very words of this psalm (verse 8) to deride him, were directed at the Son of God.

If we take Matthew's Gospel record (27:39-43) to illustrate the psalm, it tells us that "they that passed by reviled him, wagging their heads". The psalm says, "They open the lip (AV margin), they shake the head" – in shameful mockery of his gaping mouth and rolling head. They made his agony a figure of fun as they wagged their heads in time with his, laughing scornfully at his terrible plight and actually throwing in his face the words of the psalm. "If he delighted in him" is taken up in the words, "If thou be the Son of God, come down from the cross ... He saved others; himself he cannot save. If he be the King of Israel, let him now come down from the cross, and we will believe him. He trusted in God; let him deliver him now, if he will have him: for he said, I am the Son of God" (verses 40-43).

124

The Hebrew says, "He rolled himself on the LORD" (AV margin). Psalm 37:5 and Proverbs 16:3 (marginal renderings) might be noted for use of the same expression. The original figure is of rolling stones or burdens laid upon one. Both in Proverbs and Psalm 37 the words carry the idea of "roll back" (Gesenius, Lexicon), implying that it is God who imposes burdens and trials, and we in faith must roll them back onto Him in order to be able to bear them. Thus they said, 'He claims that God is his Father; let us see if his words are true. Here is the opportunity to test them; let him roll his way upon the Lord and let Him deliver him, if He really delights in him'.

One trembles at the effrontery of such scoffers as they taunted in this way "the only begotten Son of God". Yet the mocking words were true, for (picking up the phrases which they in derision had used against him) the psalmist had said, "Yea, thou art he (lit. translation) that took me out of the womb: thou keepest me in safety (AV margin) when I was upon my mother's breasts. I was cast upon thee from the womb: thou art my God from my mother's belly" (Psalm 22:9,10). In such words we learn much about the sinlessness of the Son of God. Infancy and childhood are periods of the life of Jesus that we find difficult to contemplate; but they are not for useless imagination and speculation. It is enough for us to know that God was in control and kept him even from his mother's womb (see also Isaiah 49:1,2).

Therefore he cried, turning the very words of verse 1 into a prayer, "Be not far from me; for trouble is near; for there is none to help" (verse 11). His enemies, like bulls of Bashan, had encircled him. Like lions with open mouths they were waiting to pounce and devour him (verse 13). Perhaps the words "as a ravening and a roaring lion" are what Peter referred to when he spoke of "your adversary the devil, as a roaring lion, walketh about, seeking whom he may devour" (1 Peter 5:8). It indicates that the devil is not some supernatural tempter, but rather the equivalent, in the experience of the brethren to whom Peter wrote, of those who conspired together to crucify the Lord Jesus Christ.

125

There could be no more graphic picture of a man in the throes of death than that contained in verses 14 to 17: "I am poured out like water" is representative of human weakness, of all strength and energy having ebbed away. A good illustration of the figure is to be found in 2 Samuel 14:14: "For we must needs die, and are as water spilt on the ground, which cannot be gathered up again". "All my bones are out of joint" – not literally, but his whole frame was racked with pain as if in fact every joint had been dislocated. "My heart has become like wax, molten in the midst of my bowels" (Kay – *The Psalms with Notes*) – burning, searing pain was experienced, the vital saps and juices of the body were dried up. "My strength is dried up like a potsherd; and my tongue cleaveth to my jaws". It is worth comparing these words with the description of David's agony of spirit after his sin as described in Psalm 32: "When I kept silence, my bones waxed old through my roaring all the day long. For day and night thy hand was heavy upon me: my moisture is turned into the drought of summer" (verses 3,4).

It seems, as we have already considered, that in some ways the experiences of the Lord Jesus when God made him an offering for sin were similar to the distress of the sinner when the true nature of his actions were brought home to him. Yet all these things had been brought upon Jesus by the hand of God, for it "pleased the LORD to bruise him". It was "by the determinate counsel and foreknowledge of God" that he was taken (Acts 2:23), for "thou hast brought me into the dust of death" (Psalm 22:15).

Dogs had compassed him about; the assembly of the wicked enclosed him. So he says, "They pierced my hands and my feet". It is interesting to notice how the enemies of the Lord are likened to beasts – bulls, lions, dogs – for that is what men become when they forget that they are created in the image of God and give themselves over to all manner of degradation and wickedness. The latter part of verse 16 is, perhaps, the clearest reference to crucifixion in the Old Testament. It is referred to at least four times in later books of scripture, twice in the Gospel records (Matthew 27:35; John 19:23), where it is stated that "they crucified him" and immediately the words are linked with verse 18 of the psalm, which tells how they parted his garments among them and cast lots on his vesture. But it is also referred to in Zechariah 12:10 and Revelation 1:7 as we shall see.

So the picture was complete. As they looked and stared upon him, he could count all his bones, having been reduced to a living skeleton (verse 17). So he cried, "But be thou not far off, O LORD; O thou my succour, haste thee to help me" (verse 19, RV), and "Deliver my soul from the sword; my darling from the power of the dog. Save me from the lion's mouth" (verses 20,21). The use of the word "sword" implies a violent death, perhaps judicially imposed. The word rendered "darling" (RV margin, "my only one") is the feminine form of the word used to describe Isaac, "thine only son", in Genesis 22. Literally it means 'only daughter'. It is a bold figure to describe the preciousness of life which, when lost, can humanly speaking never be regained.

Once again his enemies are likened to dogs – not the domesticated pets that we are used to, but the half wild, dirty, unkempt, hungry and savage creatures that inhabit eastern villages and cities. It was a fitting description for those who, whatever their social standing, were really no better than a common rabble, as with malicious delight they gazed upon the sufferings of the one whom God in His love had given for the sins of the world.

It is in the middle of verse 21 that the tone of the psalm suddenly changes: "From the horns of the wild-oxen thou hast answered me" (RV). It is at this point that the second part of our study, concerning the glory to follow, begins.

Any doubts that readers of the psalm might have about the true significance of verses 1 and 2 are dispelled, as in the joy of deliverance the Spirit of Christ in the psalm cries, "from the horns of the wild-oxen thou hast answered me" (verse 21, RV); and again, "For he hath not despised nor abhorred the affliction of the afflicted; neither hath he hid his face from him; but when he cried unto him, he heard" (verse 24).

In the midst of mortal weakness when God, on occasions, appears to have hidden His face that He might

127

know what is in our hearts, perplexity and adversity become part of the "many wrestlings for the prize" that we must all endure. There may be no evidence that God has heard our prayers, for there is no answer from Him. It is at this point that faith must lay hold on the eternal verities, cling to them and never let go; for in the great day, when we shall stand in the congregation of the redeemed, we shall be able to look back and acknowledge that God heard our prayers and that, whatever outward appearances might have suggested, in faithfulness He afflicted us (Psalm 119:75).

Declaring the Name

The fathers trusted in God and were delivered. Their faith had not been confounded. And now, reflecting on how God had wrought a similar deliverance for him, the Lord was to declare His name – everything that He had proved himself to be – to his brethren (verse 22). But, of course, in the case of the Lord Jesus, this declaration of the name went much further than his own experience of the mercy, grace and faithfulness of God, for he himself was the revelation of that name. In him God was manifest for the salvation of men. The purpose of God enshrined in the Name was worked out in the life and experience of the Lord Jesus, so that he himself is the bearer of the name in the very fullest sense.

Thus Peter could declare:

"Be it known unto you all, and to all the people of Israel, that by the name of Jesus Christ of Nazareth, whom ye crucified, whom God raised from the dead, even by him doth this man stand here before you whole. This is the stone which was set at nought of you builders, which is become the head of the corner. Neither is there salvation in any other: for there is none other name under heaven given among men, whereby we must be saved." (Acts 4:10-12)

Similarly, Paul could write:

"Wherefore also God highly exalted him, and gave unto him the name which is above every name; that in the name of Jesus every knee should bow ... and that every tongue should confess that Jesus Christ is Lord, to the glory of God the Father."

(Philippians 2:9-11, RV)

Jesus himself said, "I have manifested thy name unto the men which thou gavest me out of the world" (John 17:6), and it is these whom he acknowledges as brethren. The manner in which verse 22 is quoted in the Epistle to the Hebrews (2:12) as evidence that he is not ashamed to call us brethren – for he is the first-begotten from the dead of the many sons whom God is bringing unto glory – helps to establish also that the congregation is in fact the ecclesia.

The word "brethren" is most interesting, for it appears to be the origin of a number of single-word quotations in the New Testament:

"Go tell my brethren ..." (Matthew 28:10)

"Go to my brethren ..." (John 20:17)

"The firstborn among many brethren."

(Romans 8:29)

"In all things it behoved him to be made like unto his brethren." (Hebrews 2:17)

The reference from Hebrews 2 is, of course, a development of the argument arising from the quotation from the psalm already referred to, and it establishes the link – the bond that exists between Jesus and his brethren, not just because they are related to him through the work of salvation, but also because they shared a common heritage in Adam. Jesus also partook of our nature, had like experiences and endured temptation, that he might be able to succour us in our times of testing.

The Universal Consequence

The remainder of the psalm describes the effects of his victory and of God's deliverance. Because he declares the name and sings God's praise, there is a response from his brethren, who recognise that he died for them as one of them. His public proclamation leads progressively to all the ends of the world remembering and turning to the Lord (verse 22-27). His victory, won in his lonely conflict, faced by the taunts and jibes of his enemies and the dreadful mocking to which they subjected him, finally results in "all the kindreds of the nations" worshipping

129

God, since all that he has accomplished was to the end that his Father might be glorified: "For the kingdom is the LORD's: and he is the governor among the nations" (verse 28).

The word rendered "kindred" in verse 27 means literally 'families' (Strong's). It is the word used in connection with the covenant made with Abraham (see Genesis 12:3; 22:18; 28:14), and it is a reminder to us that the covenants of promise are the foundation of God's purpose; the references to them run through the pages of scripture like golden threads. To neglect them, or to imagine that somehow we can preach Christ without them, is to reveal a spiritual immaturity that is nothing less than shameful in those who profess to know the name.

The Meek shall Eat and be Satisfied

The reference to the "great congregation" (verse 25) is surely an allusion to the saints of all ages, the Ecclesia of God in the very fullest sense of the term when they are gathered unto the Lord. It began with the declaration to his brethren immediately after his resurrection. It extends to every generation of believers in the days of their pilgrimage; it culminates when all those called out, both Jews and Gentiles (verse 23), join with immortal voices to praise God in His kingdom, when the meek shall inherit the earth, and they "shall eat and be satisfied" (verse 26). The words concerning the meek appear to be an allusion to the book of Deuteronomy (14:29; 26:12). The passages refer to the manner in which the Levite (who had no inheritance), the stranger, the fatherless and the widow were to be provided for in the harvest. So gathered up in the words of the psalm and in the blessing from the mount is the thought that all those who have been pilgrims and strangers in the earth and who have eschewed earthly inheritance that they might look for that city that hath foundations, will have all their hopes and desires fulfilled – for they "shall eat and be satisfied".

The idea of eating and being satisfied is linked with the words, "your heart shall live for ever". The disposition of the meek is to have that humble and contrite spirit that trembles at God's word. It is, above all things, to be receptive to divine teaching. It is the "hearts" of such that will lead to them inhabiting the earth for ever. Another echo of the words of the psalm should not be overlooked. Jesus said, "I am the living bread which came down from heaven: if any man eat of this bread, he shall live for ever" (John 6:51).

It is a mistake to seek to limit these words and similar expressions in the chapter to that which we do weekly in remembrance of him. To eat the living bread is to comprehend all that he is and all that he did. It is to imbibe his words concerning himself and the purpose of God so that they are digested and become part of one's being. The result is that because his word is in us, we think like him and act like him and, by his grace, we shall live for ever, because we have been counted amongst the meek of the earth.

All Kindreds of the Earth wail

The psalm presents us with an insight into the hierarchy of the kingdom, for whereas verses 23 to 26 refer to the saints, the immortal rulers, verses 27 and 29 refer to the mortal nations over whom, with the Lord Jesus, the saints exercise sovereignty.

Reference has already been made to verse 27, and perhaps it would be sufficient to give the sense if we were to quote verse 29 from the RSV: "Yea, to him shall all the proud of the earth bow down; before him shall bow all that go down to the dust, and he who cannot keep himself alive."

Earlier in our study we deferred consideration of verse 16 ("they pierced my hands and my feet") in so far as the words are referred to in Zechariah (12:10) and Revelation (1:7), and it is appropriate to deal with this matter now.

It is clear that Zechariah's prophecy is referring to the words of the psalm when it speaks of a contrite house of David mourning when they look upon him whom they pierced. Now it is sometimes assumed that the words of Revelation 1 are a quotation from Zechariah 12; but this is only partly true. The passage says:

"Behold, he cometh with clouds; and every eye shall see him, and they also which pierced him: and all kindreds of the earth shall wail because of him."

The latter part of this verse is a clear reference to verse 27 of the psalm. Thus the mourning of Zechariah's prophecy, confined to those who pierced him, is extended now to include all families of the earth. It is not a mourning because of the consequences of his coming to them, but a recognition that all humankind were by the manner in which they have neglected and rejected him, caught up in the events of the crucifixion. All humanity was represented there, and all the kindreds of the earth shall wail because of him when it is appreciated what he has suffered on their behalf – and at that time it was as nothing to them.

A Seed shall serve Him

The word 'seed' is one of the most significant words in scripture. It first appears, in the sense of progeny, in the conflict between the seed of the woman and the seed of the serpent (Genesis 3:15). It is prominent in the covenants of promise, for in Abraham's seed all the families of the earth will be blessed, and David's seed is to sit on his throne for ever. All these scriptures have their primary significance in the Lord Jesus Christ; but we know also that "if (we) be Christ's, then are (we) Abraham's seed, and heirs according to the promise" (Galatians 3:29). Our relationship as brethren of the Lord Jesus, emphasised in the psalm and quoted in Hebrews, is linked there with the fact that in sharing our nature, the Lord took upon him the seed of Abraham. Clearly the thought patterns of the psalm are prominent in this part of the epistle.

"A seed shall serve him; it shall be counted unto the Lord for his generation" (Psalm 22:30, RV margin) – a seed, a never failing posterity that is God's generation, a righteous seed. For, having described the qualities of the man who shall ascend into Zion's hill, who shall receive the blessing of righteousness from the God of his salvation, David says, "This is the generation of them that seek him (thee), that seek thy face, O God of Jacob" (Psalm 24:6, with AV margin). They are born out of the travail of soul described in the first part of the psalm.

When the Ethiopian eunuch read from the book of the prophet Isaiah (Acts 8), the chapter he read asked, "Who shall declare his generation? for he was cut off out of the land of the living" (Isaiah 53:8). The implication was that he had no natural progeny. The bewilderment of the eunuch can be appreciated, when two verses later he read:

"When thou shalt make his soul an offering for sin, he shall see his seed, he shall prolong his days, and the pleasure of the LORD shall prosper in his hand."

(verse 10)

Philip "preached unto him Jesus" and, as a result, he was brought to an understanding of the "generation" who would "seek the face of the God of Jacob", the spiritual seed who would in every generation ensure the perpetuity of the "godly seed", for they would declare His righteousness unto a people that would be born (verse 31). It was not a natural birth, of course, but the new birth in Christ by which they themselves would be incorporated into "his generation" – a chain of Truth and Light extending through history until the dawn of the perfect day.

In declaring His righteousness, they would affirm "that he hath done this". It is all of God, who through Christ has done everything that is necessary for our salvation. We wait the consummation of the purpose of God in the glorious manifestation of the sons of God; but effectively, God's purpose with man was assured in the moment of the Lord's victory on the cross. With the psalm still in his thoughts, it was the closing words of the song that he used to affirm this truth that God had done all that was necessary: "It is finished" (John 19:30).

Another psalm combines both the opening and closing thoughts of Psalm 22:

"Commit thy way unto the LORD; trust also in him; and he shall bring it to pass."   (Psalm 37:5)

PSALM 23

IT seems probable that this, undoubtedly the best-known of all psalms, was written by David at the time of Absalom's rebellion. No doubt the language used by the Spirit reflects also the experiences of David in his earlier life when he had cared for the sheep. The way in which God cared for him found a logical expression in those words and figures that were so real to David because of his own care and protection for the sheep placed in his charge.

Historical Background

The evidence that the psalm was written at the time of David's flight from Absalom is based on the historical record in 2 Samuel (chapters 15 to 19) and on comparisons with the language of other psalms of the same period. We notice, for instance, that the words of verse 5, "Thou preparest a table before me in the presence of mine enemies", find a precise counterpart in the kindness of Barzillai, who had provided the king with sustenance when he came to Mahanaim and rested (2 Samuel 17:27-29).

Again, the reference to "the valley of the shadow of death" seems most appropriate to describe the manner in which, when David had gone the way of the wilderness, he had descended into the valley of the Kidron and crossed the brook (2 Samuel 15:23). The name 'Kidron' means 'dusky or shadowy'. It comes from a root which means 'blackness, darkness, mourning' – a most appropriate description for the circumstances in which David found himself as he traversed the valley. Furthermore, the language of verse 2, "He maketh me to lie down in green pastures: he leadeth me beside the still waters", reflects accurately the language of both Psalms 3 and 4, which we have previously shown to be connected with this same period in David's life:

"I laid me down and slept; I awaked, for the LORD sustained me."   (Psalm 3:5)

"I will both lay me down in peace, and sleep: for thou, LORD, only makest me dwell in safety."   (Psalm 4:8)

David, pursued by his enemies, thought not of the dangers they presented but rather of the consolation he found in the knowledge that "goodness and mercy shall follow (lit. pursue) me all the days of my life" (Psalm 23:6).

The closing words of the psalm, "I will dwell in the house of the LORD for ever" (verse 6), should more accurately be rendered, "I will return and dwell in the house of the LORD". These words had an imminent fulfilment for David, for he did return to Jerusalem, and spent the rest of his days close to God's sanctuary and preparing for the "exceeding magnifical" temple that Solomon was to build. Such a fulfilment, however, was but a dim shadow of the future glory, when he will worship God in a temple "not made with hands", a spiritual house built upon the foundation of the apostles and prophets, Jesus Christ himself being the chief cornerstone.

The Lord Jesus Christ

The historical background serves to emphasise that Psalm 23 is pre-eminently the Lord's own, for David's experiences were typical of those of the Lord Jesus when he, too, crossed the brook Kidron and went the way of the wilderness (John 18). The Lamb who now leads us to living fountains of waters was also led of his Father, for he could say, "I am not alone, because the Father is with me" (John 16:32); and on another occasion, "I ... know my sheep, and am known of mine. As the Father knoweth me, even so know I the Father" (John 10:14,15). In effect, he said, 'As I am your shepherd and lead you, so my Father is my Shepherd and leads me. As you know me, so I know the Father'. It is, then, the Lord's psalm. His experiences, through which he revealed his calm serenity and his steadfast trust, are described in the song – and they are, of course, our experiences also in the measure in which we enter into his life and conduct.

135

The Structure

It has been suggested that, although the theme of the shepherd dominates the psalm, it actually falls into three or possibly two sections. Verses 5 and 6 undoubtedly use the figure of a host providing sustenance for an honoured guest. The first four verses can be understood completely in terms of the shepherd's care; but some see verses 3 and 4 as being more descriptive of a guide. Perhaps it would be right, while maintaining the allegory of the shepherd, to regard those verses as describing that aspect of his work which has particularly to do with guiding the flock.

God's Care

God as the Shepherd of His people is one of the most frequent and beautiful descriptions of God's care. The Psalms of Asaph (74–83) are particularly characterised by the use of the figure (see 74:1; 77:20; 78:52; 80:1). What is worthy of note in this context is that it was from these psalms that the Lord Jesus quoted to silence his critics when he had spoken of himself as the "good shepherd" (John 10). "Is it not written in your law, I said, Ye are gods?" (verse 34, quoting Psalm 82:6).

"The good shepherd giveth his life for the sheep" (John 10:11), and the sacrifice of the Lord Jesus is a manifestation of the love of God. It is because of this that we can truly say, "I shall not want", for everything that is necessary for our salvation has been done. There is nothing lacking, for "He that spared not his own Son, but delivered him up for us all, how shall he not with him also freely give us all things?" (Romans 8:32). This supreme sacrifice had been foreshadowed in Abraham's willingness to offer up his only son; but, although Isaac had been spared, there was no such remission for God and the Lord Jesus Christ. Truly Abraham named that place "Yahweh Yireh" in the confidence that God would provide (Genesis 22:8,14), and the shepherding of God embraces our whole life in Christ, which is providentially controlled by Him. The words of Jacob stand as an example:

"God, before whom my fathers Abraham and Isaac did walk, the God which fed me (lit. shepherded me) all

136

my life long unto this day, the Angel which redeemed me from all evil, bless the lads." (Genesis 48:15,16)

The words of the psalm reflect also God's dealings with His people Israel and in this connection Deuteronomy 2:7 and 8:9 should be noted.

Primarily, we "shall not want" because "he maketh (us) to lie down in pastures of tender grass" (AV margin), and "he leadeth (us) beside the waters of quietness" (AV margin). In that hot and arid climate, the sheep need to be properly fed and watered. In the wilderness of the world, God's sheep are also in need of constant spiritual refreshment. Our spirit, like that of the bride in the Song of Solomon, should be, "Tell me, O thou whom my soul loveth, where thou feedest, where thou makest thy flock to rest at noon" (1:7). This feeding and watering comes from the word of God, but the focus for the receiving of this word should be our ecclesial life. The ecclesias are the watering places, the places of refreshment that God has provided for our sustenance in the world. If we neglect the fellowship they offer, if we minimise the quiet comfort and assurance they can give in the midst of the world's mad, hectic rush to attain what is empty and vain, then in reality we have failed to appreciate what our life in Christ is all about.

Equally, if we who must be shepherds of God's flock fail to feed them by providing a proper diet and by creating the right spiritual atmosphere, then it might be that instead of providing a place of quietness and rest amidst the world's incessant roar, we become, in part, responsible for causing some of the sheep to stray (1 Peter 5:1-4).

God's Guidance

God renews and sustains, for "he restoreth my soul". Again the agent is the word of God. The Hebrew word translated "restoreth" occurs again in Psalm 19: "The law of the LORD is perfect, converting ('restoring', RV) the soul" (verse 7). Note the interesting use of the same word, translated "relieve" in Lamentations 1:11,16,19. The word has a wide variety of shades of meaning, and does in certain contexts have the meaning of 'turn again' or 'bring back'. While in no sense could the Lord Jesus be said to

137

need turning or bringing back, we are reminded of how prone we are to stray. Sheep are well described as "silly animals" and it is a characteristic of them that there will always be those who stray from the main flock and choose to graze in dangerous and perilous places. It is a warning to us all and a comfort to know that the Shepherd will not forsake us, but will always seek us out and restore us. It is to this phrase in the psalm that the Apostle Peter refers in what appears to be the only direct quotation from the psalm in the New Testament: "For ye were as sheep going astray; but are now returned unto the Shepherd and Bishop of your souls" (1 Peter 2:25).

The shepherd as a guide is now brought to our attention. "He guideth me (RV) in the paths of righteousness." This He does "for his name's sake". The name declared was "The LORD, The LORD God, merciful and gracious, longsuffering, and abundant in goodness and truth, keeping mercy for thousands, forgiving iniquity and transgression and sin" (Exodus 34:6,7). Such as He has revealed Himself to be, He now seeks to prove Himself to be by His actions, by leading His sheep into paths of righteousness. Such paths will sometimes lead into "the valley of the shadow"; but, in the knowledge that "all things work together for good", His sheep will still follow in trust wherever He leads, for He never leaves them alone – "for thou art with me; thy rod and thy staff they comfort me".

God's continuing presence with His people is their abiding strength and comfort. To Jacob God said, "I am with thee, and will keep thee in all places whither thou goest ... I will not leave thee, until I have done that which I have spoken to thee of" (Genesis 28:15). These words were re-iterated to Joshua: "As I was with Moses, so will I be with thee: I will not fail thee, nor forsake thee" (Joshua 1:5).

These assurances are all the more comforting to us when we appreciate that the word "path" conveys the idea of 'well-trodden', 'marked out'; for others have gone before us: we tread in their footsteps, and their examples are a constant source of encouragement to us as we follow in their paths of righteousness.

We are comforted by His "rod and staff". These are not separate implements, but two descriptions of one. The rod describes the shepherd's crook, and the staff his means of support and defence by which he seeks to defend the sheep from the wild animals that would prey upon the flock.

God as the Host

We have already seen how the words "Thou preparest a table before me in the presence of mine enemies" has a most precise and literal fulfilment in the life of David, when Barzillai heaped his hospitality upon him. It must have been a most bitter experience for David's enemies to see him refreshed and encouraged in this way. It was not something unique to him, for all God's servants in time of hardship and distress will find that God provides a means of sustenance that will revive the flagging spirit and uphold them when, perhaps, all seems lost. Faith recognises that God will provide a table; unbelief questions and doubts and like Israel says, "Can God furnish a table in the wilderness?" (Psalm 78:19).

There is, of course, a permanent table provided to which we come week by week to remind ourselves of God's provision. His goodness is seen in the oil poured out in blessing; His mercy in the overflowing cup that speaks of His forgiveness. Here is a banquet indeed,where we can be refreshed in the memory of the things that pertain to God's salvation. This goodness and mercy will follow us (lit. 'pursue us') all the days of our life. In other words, God will never let us go. Though we wander through foolishness or wilfulness, His love will pursue us relentlessly and the Lord our Shepherd will seek us out. It is such an awareness of the all-embracing nature of the care of the Shepherd that should dispel all fear and anxiety, that should give us confidence and assurance – for because of these things, because no man can pluck us from His hand, we know that nothing (apart from our own perverseness) can prevent us from dwelling in the house of the Lord for ever.

PSALM 24

IN our study of Psalm 15 we drew attention to the seven psalms that are associated with David bringing the ark of God to Zion, and observed particularly the similarities between that psalm and the song at present under consideration. On that occasion we deferred our contemplation of the historical background until this study.

It should be noted first of all that Psalm 24 falls into two well-defined sections: (a) verses 1 to 6; (b) verses 7 to 10. The historical circumstances are of relevance to the structure of the psalm, which is a reflection of David's experience at that time.

Historical Background

It will be recalled that after the Philistines returned the ark, it rested in the house of Abinadab at Kirjath-jearim for twenty years. Long before he became King, David had longed to bring the ark of God to Zion (Psalm 132:2-8), and so, shortly after the capture of the city, he initiated arrangements for it to be brought to the tabernacle that he had prepared for it. The subsequent attempt, however, ended in tragedy. Uzzah and Ahio, the sons of Abinadab, accompanied the ark, and when the oxen stumbled, Uzzah put forth his hand to steady the ark and, as he touched it, God smote him and he died (2 Samuel 6).

It has often been asked why Uzzah should have died in this way. The answer is because of his presumption, not just for a thoughtless moment, but for the manner in which the whole house of Abinadab had conducted themselves throughout the matter. Apart from the irregular manner in which the ark was transported, they had usurped to themselves the duties and privileges that belonged to the Levites (see 1 Samuel 7:2). As a further reflection, it is worth noting that Obed-edom, into whose house the ark was then carried, was a Levite and played a part in bringing up the ark to Zion on the second, successful, occasion (see 1 Chronicles 15:28).

As a result of what happened to Uzzah, David was afraid, and his fear was reflected in the question that he asked at that time, "How shall I bring the ark of God home to me?" (1 Chronicles 13:12). The evidence of scripture is that David meditated upon this problem and his thoughts led him to Exodus 19.

Observe first how the death of Uzzah is described in 1 Chronicles 13: "He put his hand to the ark" (verse 10) and "the LORD made a breach upon Uzza" (verse 11). Hence that place was called Perez-uzza. The Hebrew says literally, 'God broke forth upon Uzzah', and this forges the link with Exodus 19, which describes how God at Sinai descended upon the mount and taught the people the never-to-be-forgotten lesson, "I will be sanctified in them that come nigh me", for God must be approached "after the due order" (1 Chronicles 15:13).

Notice the words of Exodus, and compare them with those from 1 Chronicles quoted above: "Whosoever toucheth the mount shall be surely put to death" (Exodus 19:12); "There shall not an hand touch it" (verse 13). If any did, man or beast, he should be stoned or shot through, i.e., with a dart or spear (verse 13). God said, "Charge the people, lest they break through unto the LORD to gaze, and many of them perish" (verse 21); and again, "... but let not the priests and the people break through to come up unto the LORD, lest he break forth upon them" (lit. "make a breach upon them, Hebrew *Perez*) (verse 24).

So Uzzah touched the ark, and God broke forth upon him. It is interesting to observe that the place where it happened is given two names, "Nachon' s threshingfloor" (2 Samuel 6:6) and "the threshingfloor of Chidon" (1 Chronicles 13:9). "Chidon" means 'to thrust through', i.e., 'as with a dart' (see Hebrews 12:20). It seems likely that the name of the threshing-floor was changed to "Chidon" to commemorate that which happened there.

The ark was the symbol of God's sovereignty – in effect, His throne. It was called "the ark of the covenant of the Lord of all the earth" (Joshua 3:11). This thought is reflected in Exodus 19:5: "for all the earth is mine", and forms also the opening words of David's meditation upon these scriptures in Psalm 24:

"The earth is the LORD's, and the fulness thereof; the world, and they that dwell therein." (verse 1)

We consider now the relevance of the two sections of the psalm. The first (verses 1-6) reflects the lessons learned about man's approach to God – "How shall I bring the ark of God home to me?" (1 Chronicles 13:12) – "Who shall ascend into the hill of the LORD? or who shall stand in his holy place?" (Psalm 24:3). In other words, it arises out of the first, unsuccessful, venture to bring the ark of God to Zion. The next section deals with the second, successful, ascent to Zion, when the ark finally came to its resting place.

Section (a) (verses 1-6)

In addition to the earlier scriptural background to verse 1 which we have just noted, it is interesting to consider the use of the verse by the Apostle Paul in his First Epistle to the Corinthians (chapter 10). The verse is quoted twice (verses 26 and 28) and two different conclusions drawn. It is in the context of meats offered to idols. The first conclusion is that because the earth is the Lord's, and all that it contains belongs to God, then the meats can be received with thanks, for the idols were but vanity; they were no gods. However, there was also the conscience of others to be considered and if in their hearts some considered eating that which had been offered to idols as dishonouring to God, it should be remembered that all must be done to the glory of God (verse 31) who will be sanctified in those that come nigh Him. Nothing is ours in our own right; it all belongs to God and must only be used in ways that are compatible with His character and purpose, "for the earth is the Lord's, and the fulness thereof" (verse 28). This fact is rooted in the foundation truth that God is the Creator, "for he hath founded it upon the seas, and established it upon the floods" (Psalm 24:2; see Genesis 1:2,9,10).

It is in this appreciation of the greatness of God and of His universal sovereignty that David also reveals his understanding of the purpose of God, for the Lord had chosen Zion to be His special dwelling place from where He would exercise His power over all the earth.

Who then "shall ascend into the hill of the LORD? or who shall stand in his holy place?" (verse 3) – stand in the sense of not being found wanting, of one's cause being vindicated before His judgement seat (see Psalm 1:5 and Malachi 3:2). The answer given is in similar terms to the answer in Psalm 15: "He that hath clean hands, and a pure heart; who hath not lifted up his soul unto vanity, nor sworn deceitfully" (Psalm 24:4).

"Clean hands, and a pure heart" speak of an outward innocence and an inward purity of heart and mind, a righteousness that encompasses the whole personality. There is no hypocrisy, but outward deeds reflect inward thoughts. To lift up the soul is 'to direct the mind towards', as in Psalm 25:1, or, again, 'to set the heart upon', as in Deuteronomy 24:15 and Hosea 4:8. "Vanity" is that which is empty and transitory. On occasions it is used to describe false gods, but, of course, it is descriptive also of human life in all its aspects when it is lived without God.

With regard to swearing deceitfully, we have already commented adequately on this in our study of Psalm 15. A further thought regarding the background, however, might be appropriate. The capture of Jerusalem is followed immediately in the records of both Samuel and Chronicles by the arrangements for bringing up the ark. Joab was prominent in the capture of the city, and as a result (because David had sworn that whoever climbed the gutter to enter the fortress should be chief) became captain of the host (1 Chronicles 11:6).

It has often been regarded as something of a mystery that David should have allowed this man the prominence he enjoyed. Perhaps, initially, he never intended that he should be captain, but he had given his word, and Joab fulfilled the conditions. So he wrote in his song at this period, "He that sweareth to his own hurt, and changeth not" (Psalm 15:4), "He shall receive the blessing from the LORD, and righteousness from the God of his salvation" (Psalm 24:5).

We are confronted here with an amazing paradox. "Who shall ascend into the hill of the LORD?" was the question asked. If we were to paraphrase verse 4, we might say that the answer was 'he who practises righteousness'; and it is this man who will receive the blessing, even righteousness from the God of his salvation. Thus righteousness is not just the means of obtaining salvation, but is also the end to be achieved. It is that we should be like Him. This is the "blessing of the LORD", and whenever we read the word 'blessing' it should make us think of God's covenant with Abraham, for the blessing of Abraham is indeed righteousness, or the forgiveness of sins. Abraham believed God, and it was counted to him for righteousness; and it is the imputation of righteousness by God that takes us to the very heart of God's work of salvation.

We are, of course, utterly dependent on God for our salvation; but works are essential, for they are the token of our faith, the evidence that we "hunger and thirst" after the righteousness that, in the last analysis, God alone can give (see Genesis 15:6; Psalm 32:1,2; Acts 3:25,26; Romans 4:3-9,22-25; Galatians 3:6-9 etc.). This, says the psalm, is the generation of them that seek Him, "that seek thy face, O God of Jacob" (Psalm 24:6, RV). In the original text there are two different words which are translated "seek". Nevertheless, both emphasise the diligence and urgency to be shown.

Behind these words is Jacob's experience at Peniel (Genesis 32:24-32). It was here that Jacob wrestled with the angel. He would not let him go unless he blessed him, showing all the tenacity required in that generation that seek the righteousness of God. Because of his endurance, Jacob received God's blessing and, thus blessed, he saw God "face to face" (verse 30).

So these "righteous ones" who seek the face of the God of Jacob constitute that seed who are counted to the Lord for a generation (Psalm 22:30; see also Isaiah 53:8,10).

Section (b) (verses 7-10)

As the first section of the psalm reflects the meditations of David after the abortive attempt to bring up the ark, so the second section speaks of the triumphal procession

144

when the ark was eventually brought to Zion. We observe that David appointed gatekeepers for the ark (see 1 Chronicles 15:23,24, RSV), also singers and musicians (verses 19-22). The journey was about seven miles, and as they progressed they must have sung the psalms of David, particularly those associated with the bringing up of the ark.

We can perhaps speculate that the words of these would have been sung by the choirs:

"Arise, O LORD, into thy rest; thou, and the ark of thy strength." (Psalm 132:8)

"Let God arise, let his enemies be scattered." (Psalm 68:1)

"Glorious things are spoken of thee, O city of God." (Psalm 87:3)

As they reached the gates of the city, David himself, or perhaps the lead singer cried:

"Lift up your heads, O ye gates; and be ye lift up, ye everlasting doors; and the King of glory shall come in." (Psalm 24:7)

The gatekeepers responded:

"Who is this King of glory?" (verse 8)

The answer from the head of the procession:

"The LORD strong and mighty, the LORD mighty in battle. Lift up your heads, O ye gates; even lift them up, ye everlasting doors; and the King of glory shall come in." (verses 8,9)

The gatekeepers again:

"Who is this King of glory?" (verse 10)

The final answer:

"The LORD of hosts, he is the King of glory." (verse 10)

So the ark of God came to its rest in the tabernacle that David had prepared for it.

We look forward to the day when the anti-typical Ark of the Covenant – the glorified Christ – will come to the gates of Zion. May we be with him in that day.

PSALM 25

W E have already considered two examples of psalms structured upon the basis of the Hebrew alphabet, and commented appropriately (Psalms 9 and 10). Our present psalm is the first of seven that are completely, or almost completely, alphabetic in form.

We say 'almost' in this case because there are two instances where the alphabetic form (in which every stage begins with the letters of the Hebrew alphabet, in order) is not adhered to strictly. *Vau* and *Qoph* are omitted, and two verses (18,19) begin with *Resh*. After the completion of the alphabet, a final verse commencing with *Pe* is added.

As we have said previously, we do not think that the use of the alphabet as an aid to memory is an adequate explanation for its use in the psalms. And endeavours by some to amend the text to produce uniformity, looking to errors in transcription as the reason for the omissions referred to above, are completely lacking in supportive evidence. Indeed, the internal evidence of scripture points conclusively to the genuineness of the text, for the next of the alphabetic psalms (34) has precisely the same omissions and additions as Psalm 25. This cannot be coincidence, and must be recognised as design, even if we cannot discern the meaning behind it. We return to this question, when dealing with Psalm 34, but the fact of this precise similarity in structure binds the two psalms together and gives us grounds for establishing a historical background for Psalm 25 which otherwise we might have failed to discern. The historical information at the head of Psalm 34 tells us that it was written when David "changed his behaviour before Abimelech (Achish, margin); who drove him away, and he departed".

This is the occasion when David came to the priests at Nob and was fed with the shewbread and given the sword of Goliath. He was forced to flee to the Philistines because of the treacherous behaviour of Doeg the Edomite who was there at the time and, reporting the matter to Saul, was instrumental in bringing about the resultant slaughter of the priests. We believe these circumstances illuminate the language of the psalm and show the faith and the earnest desire of David's heart in sharper detail.

Structure of the Psalm

The alphabetic nature of the psalm aside, it seems to fall into three clearly defined sections. Verses 1 to 11 constitute a prayer for God's protection, guidance and forgiveness to be extended to him. Verses 12 and 13 speak of one who "feareth the LORD" and whose "seed shall inherit the earth" – a clear allusion, we believe, to the Lord Jesus Christ. Finally, verses 14 to 22, as a result of the things revealed concerning the man spoken of in verses 12 and 13, describe how the prayers and longings of the first section will find fulfilment.

Verses 1-11

The opening words of the psalm give us an insight into the calibre of the man David, and stand as a powerful exhortation to all who seek to follow in his steps and be counted as men "after God's own heart".

Psalm 24 describes the man who ascended into the hill of the Lord as one "who hath not lifted up his soul unto vanity" (verse 4). Kay (*The Psalms with Notes*) renders the words, "who has not let his soul yearn towards falsehood". David lifts his soul unto the Lord. He is filled with an earnest longing for God. The same phrase is rendered 'to set the heart upon' (Deuteronomy 24:15; Hosea 4:8). David's greatest joy was found in his God, and his yearning for spiritual things dominated all other influences and strengthened him in the midst of all life's adversities.

Confronted by the hatred of Doeg, the jealousy of Saul and the suspicion of the Philistines, David could say with all his heart, "Let not mine enemies triumph over me. Yea, let none that wait on thee be ashamed: let them be ashamed which transgress ('deal treacherously', RV) without cause" (verses 2,3).

147

The Hebrew word rendered "wait" means 'to bind together', hence 'to expect' in the sense of 'waiting upon'. David had, as it were, made his will subject to God's will. They were bound together inasmuch as David had developed the mind of God through his meditation upon the word of God. Because of this, he lived in the expectancy of the fulfilment of his deepest longings and spiritual aspirations, and in this sense he waited upon God to answer his prayers. His request was that he should not be *ashamed*. Literally the word means, 'to be disappointed because of misplaced trust; hence, to suffer shame and approbation because of one's foolishness'. None that trusted in God would know such shame; but the Doegs and the Sauls of this world who acted treacherously, and without cause hated and persecuted David, would see all their ambition end in frustrating disappointment.

David must have experienced great perplexity at this time with, it must have seemed, all men's hands against him. His prayer therefore is for God to help him to understand the outworking of His purpose in his life – the methods by which His providence operated: "Shew me thy ways, O LORD; teach me thy paths. Lead ('guide', RV) me in thy truth, and teach me" (verses 4,5).

The plea to be guided in God's truth is not a prayer for fuller knowledge of God's word, but for a deeper appreciation of God's faithfulness. This could only be gained through the experiences of life. The prayer for God to teach him, in this context, is a reminder to us that the circumstances of life together with the word of God, are the twin forces that God uses to mould and fashion our characters.

David's words recall the similar request made by Moses: "Shew me now thy way, that I may know thee, that I may find grace in thy sight" (Exodus 33:13). That David's words are a conscious allusion to the words of Moses is confirmed by the verses that follow. In Exodus the prayer of Moses was answered when God manifested His glory and declared His name:

"The LORD, the LORD God, merciful and gracious, longsuffering, and abundant in goodness and truth,

148

keeping mercy for thousands, forgiving iniquity and transgression and sin." (Exodus 34:6,7)

In Psalm 25 the words of Exodus are reproduced as David seeks for solace in a meditation upon the name of God:

"Remember not the *sins of my youth*, nor my *transgressions*: according to thy *mercy* remember thou me for thy *goodness'* sake, O LORD. Good and upright is the LORD: therefore will he teach sinners in the way. The meek will he guide in judgment: and the meek will he teach his way. All the paths of the LORD are *mercy* and *truth* unto such as keep his covenant and his testimonies. For thy name's sake, O LORD, pardon mine *iniquity*; for it is great." (verses 7-11)

The words indicated show the links in thought. Implicit in the call for God to remember is the desire for God to act, for the second is the necessary outcome of the first. See Exodus 2:24,25: "God heard ... God remembered ... God looked upon (them) ... God had respect unto them."

God had been faithful in the days of old (Psalm 25:6); therefore David longed for Him to manifest the qualities of His name in his life, recognising that it was the meek, those who were of a quiet and humble disposition, who would learn God's ways – for above all else, the meek are teachable. It was this quality that Jesus looked for in his disciples – the ability to receive with trembling heart the sweet influence of his words.

David repeats the same words as Exodus 34 – "sin", "transgression" and "iniquity" – as he pleads for God's forgiveness; and it is on this note, conscious of his human frailty, that the first section of the psalm ends and the second section, consisting of only two verses, begins. The two verses are like a pivot on which the first and third sections balance.

Verses 12,13

"What man is he that feareth the LORD? him shall he teach in the way that he shall choose. His soul shall dwell at ease; and his seed shall inherit the earth."

Kay renders this verse, "Who is the man that fears the LORD?", and the words, we suggest, must be understood in

149

a similar sense to the question of the gatekeeper in Psalm 24, "Who is this King of glory?" (verse 8). There the answer is more specific, in that it refers to a precise historical event; but the principle behind the words of Psalm 25 remains the same. David in the midst of his perplexity, and conscious of his sins, turns his attention to the promised deliverer who would save him out of all his human distress and provide a covering for his sins, in reconciling him to God. Although this is the first of David's psalms where we find an emphasis upon his consciousness of sin, it must not be assumed (as some have) that this places the psalm late in the life of David.

The references are general rather than specific, and the intensity of feeling associated with the penitential psalms written after the sin in the matter of Bathsheba and Uriah is missing. Like all godly men, David must always have been conscious of his human weakness and of the sin "that doth so easily beset us" all. The words of verses 12 and 13 are therefore a prophecy of the promised deliverer. They speak to us of the Lord Jesus Christ.

"Him [the man that fears the LORD] shall he teach in the way that he shall choose." There is an ambiguity about the exact meaning. Is it the way that God shall choose for him, or is it the way that he shall choose to tread himself? It appears sometimes that there is a deliberate ambiguity in the text, and this is one of those occasions, for it will be observed at once that in the case of the Lord Jesus, the way that God chose for him, the way of the cross, was also the way that he consciously and willingly chose to tread himself; for he was obedient even unto death on the cross. In that way he is taught of God, and we remember that it is written of the Lord Jesus that "though he were a Son, yet learned he obedience by the things which he suffered" (Hebrews 5:8) (we have commented more fully on this passage in our consideration of Psalm 6). His soul shall, as a consequence, dwell at ease and his seed shall inherit the earth. Clearly his seed are the meek of whom the psalm has spoken in the first section, for "the meek shall inherit the earth" (Psalm 37:11; see Matthew 5:5).

Although there is no precise verbal link with the Hebrew rendered "dwell at ease", the thoughts of verse 13 are beautifully expressed in the words of Isaiah 53:

"When thou shalt make his soul an offering for sin, he shall see his seed, he shall prolong his days, and the pleasure of the LORD shall prosper in his hand. He shall see of the travail of his soul, and shall be satisfied."

(verses 10,11)

It would be inappropriate if we concluded this section without pointing out that verse 13, with its emphasis upon the seed and the inheritance, is clearly based upon the promises to Abraham, which even before the covenant that God made with him, were held dear by David and were among the foundation truths that formed the basis of his faith.

Verses 14-22

When Moses saw the glory of God on Sinai, he was told, "There is a place by me ... and it shall come to pass, while my glory passeth by, that I will ... cover thee with my hand while I pass by" (Exodus 33:21,22). It is to this occasion that another psalm refers: "He that dwelleth in the secret place of the most High shall abide under the shadow of the Almighty" (Psalm 91:1). The words carry the idea not only of that which is hidden, but also of counsel and friendship. In a literal sense we might say that it speaks of that relationship between friends who take each other into their confidence and who, in the closeness of their fellowship, enjoy a relationship that others cannot enter into and consequently cannot understand.

"There is a place by me", and in that secret place Moses heard the name of God declared. So "The secret of the LORD is with them that fear him; and he will shew them his covenant" (Psalm 25:14). The deep things of God, the wonders of His Truth, the joy of fellowship, are hid from those who are dominated by the thinking of the flesh. They are revealed only to those who continue in the doctrine and, abounding in the life of Christ, enter more fully into fellowship with God and the understanding of His counsels. For "Eye hath not seen, nor ear heard, neither have entered into the heart of man, the things

151

which God hath prepared for them that love him. But God hath revealed them unto us ..." (1 Corinthians 2:9,10; see also in this connection Matthew 6:4,6,18).

Because of this intimacy of relationship David can say, "Mine eyes are ever toward the LORD" (Psalm 25:15) to whom he had lifted up his soul (verse 1).

The spirit of Christ in Psalm 16 takes us into the Lord's own experience: "I have set the LORD always before me: because he is at my right hand, I shall not be moved" (verse 8). So in Psalm 25 David could rejoice in the knowledge that because his eyes were ever towards the Lord in this aspect of expectant prayer, he could have confidence that God would "pluck (his) feet out of the net". He would deliver him from all the perplexities and entanglements that he now found himself to be in because of the actions of treacherous men. As his eyes were ever towards the Lord, his plea was that God would turn unto him and have mercy on him (verse 16). It is the opposite of "hiding the face". If God turned His face unto him then, as if eye met eye, there would be that closeness of fellowship and understanding already referred to.

"The troubles of my heart", or, more literally, "the straitness of my heart" (verse 17) implies the pressures brought upon him through all his distress. It was his desire that these pressures should be relieved or 'enlarged', thus removing the causes of the adversity he experienced, easing the strictures that life laid upon him. But deliverance from trouble was not in itself enough to bring the peace of heart he desired, for sin also must be forgiven if this was to be achieved (verse 18). So the psalm concludes with a reiteration of the thoughts of the opening words of the first section:

"Consider mine enemies [Doeg, Saul, the Philistines, to name but a few]; for they are many; and they hate me with cruel hatred. O keep my soul, and deliver me: let me not be ashamed; for I put my trust in thee. Let integrity and uprightness preserve me; for I wait on thee." (verse 19-21)

It has been supposed that the last verse of the psalm is a later addition, possibly by Hezekiah, to make the words more appropriate to the circumstances of his own day.

Such a conjecture seems unnecessary, for if our identification of the historical background is correct, then the words can be understood very easily against the background of those times:

"Redeem Israel, O God, out of all his troubles."

(verse 22)

To illustrate – it was not loyalty to Saul that moved Doeg the Edomite to betray David, but hatred of Israel. He recognised the potential of this man, the Lord's anointed, and sought to destroy him. His lack of success was compensated for, to some extent, by the slaughter of the priests. Israel, then, with a weak and mentally unbalanced king, had become a victim for predators of all kinds. As God had delivered Jacob from Esau so many centuries before, now David's prayer was that God would redeem Israel from the evil machinations of Doeg the Edomite – a descendant of Esau – and from those who foolishly allowed themselves to be influenced for evil by this godless man.

153

PSALM 26

AS we seek to serve God we are constantly aware of our own inadequacy. If we are not, then there is something lacking in our perception of spiritual realities. Human weakness and our own shortcomings serve to remind us of the need for humility and contrition before God.

These things acknowledged, however, there is also a need to balance our inadequacy with the steadfastness of purpose that should characterise our lives. It is not so much what we might seem to be in the eyes of men, but what with all our heart we long to be and seek to be. As the proverb says, "As he thinketh in his heart, so is he: Eat and drink, saith he to thee; but his heart is not with thee" (Proverbs 23:7).

While recognising the danger of self-deception, the man of God must nevertheless have a confidence and assurance of his own integrity, of the singleness of his purpose and the sincerity of his heart. So sure must he be that he is at one with himself, that there is no schism or division within, he must be prepared to submit himself to the divine scrutiny that he might be vindicated. This is the spirit that pervades Psalm 26. It is an expression of David's confidence, and at a higher level of the Lord Jesus Christ's assurance, that God who knows the hearts of all men would recognise and acknowledge his fidelity.

Walking in Integrity

The opening verses of the psalm reflect the thoughts expressed above:

"Judge (RSV, vindicate) me, O LORD; for I have walked in mine integrity (lit. completeness): I have trusted in the LORD; therefore I shall not slide. Examine me, O LORD, and prove me; try my reins and my heart.

154

For thy lovingkindness is before mine eyes: and I have walked in thy truth." (verses 1-3)

"I have walked in mine integrity ... I have walked in thy truth." This was David's habitual way of life. Note that integrity of itself is not sufficient. Like the word 'sincere', 'integrity' can be a much abused word. It may well be that a man of integrity, a sincere man, will at least be true to his own standards, whereas an unscrupulous man of no principle can never be trusted. Nevertheless, integrity and singleness of purpose is only of real value when it is linked with the Truth of God. It was in faithfulness to this Truth that David walked with consistency throughout his life.

David's singleness of heart in seeking to serve his God was something from which nothing could deflect him. The word "therefore" in the last phrase of verse 1 is not in the original text, and its use is misleading. The words do not describe the consequence of his trust, but rather they are an assertion of his determination to keep it. The RV renders it: "I have trusted in the LORD without wavering"; and Kay (*Psalms with Notes*), "I will not falter".

The Psalmist's conscience in respect of the general tenor of his life was clear. Yet if there remained any taint of evil, any impurity of motive, his desire was that God would purge it away: "Examine ... prove ... try." These are the words that emphasise his willingness for his life to come under the illumination of divine scrutiny. The words rendered "examine" and "try" have to do with the testing and refining of metals. In effect, it is a prayer that through the circumstances of life God would purge away any dross that remained. It is the real test of a man's desire for righteousness that he can actually pray for "the chastening of the LORD". "Try my reins and my heart" was his plea, and the words encompass the whole of the inner man. The word "reins" means literally 'kidneys', and was regarded figuratively as the seat of the emotions and affection. The heart was considered to be the seat of thought and was associated with the human will (see Strong's Concordance and Gesenius' Lexicon). David's confidence was grounded in his knowledge of God: "Thy lovingkindness is before mine eyes"; and there is surely an allusion here to the precept recorded in Deuteronomy (6:8) that God's words should be "as frontlets between thine eyes". It was his resolve never to forget God's word or the constancy of His love towards him.

No Association with Wicked Men

A mark of David's walk in integrity and truth was the manner in which he refused to keep company with wicked men: "I have not sat with vain persons, neither will I go in with dissemblers. I have hated (RV, I hate) the congregation of evil doers; and will not sit with the wicked" (verses 4,5). The words are reminiscent of Psalm 1 (verses 1,2) and they teach the vital lesson of separation from the world which must be acknowledged and practised by everyone who aspires to be a servant of God.

The word 'sat' implies a continued and prolonged association. It is unavoidable that the saint must be in the world, but he can never share its tastes and interests. Whether social, political or religious, these are all vanity, empty and worthless as, in the last analysis, are those who espouse the world's causes and thereby turn their back on the word of God and the purpose it reveals.

A dissembler is the opposite of a man of integrity. Literally the word "dissembler" means 'hypocrite'. It comes from a root meaning 'to veil from sight, to conceal'; in other words, it means to hide the real self and act out a part. The world is full of such men and the danger is that for personal gain, for the fulfilment of ambition or just for ordinary enjoyment, men who profess to serve God can form an association of heart and mind with them.

"The congregation of evil doers" stands in direct contrast to "the congregation" of verse 12. The latter is clearly a reference to a divinely convened assembly, the ecclesia of God. The former would seem to imply therefore the organised assemblies convened by the world – its social, political, charitable bodies etc., which for all their apparent fine intentions, remain the assemblies of evil-doers. The word translated "evil doer" is from a root 'to break in pieces'. In the actual context of the psalm it no doubt had reference in a very literal way to men of violence; but perhaps we can draw the lesson that for the children of God such associations can end only in disaster, in the destruction of faith and the disintegration of the integrity of their life before God.

His Love for God's House

Because of the way in which he kept himself from the company of wicked men, David was able to declare his ability to "wash (his) hands in innocency", and as a consequence to "compass thine altar, O LORD", which in turn made it possible for him to "make the voice of thanksgiving to be heard" (RV) and to "tell of all (God's) wondrous works" (verses 6,7).

Before the priests approached the altar to minister, they were commanded to wash both their hands and their feet (Exodus 30:17-21). This symbolic ritual lies behind the words of verse 6. It was a spiritual reality for David, for to approach the altar he had as it were, not simply to wash his hands, but to do it in innocency, with a clear conscience, the integrity of his life bearing witness to that represented in the rite of washing. The priestly background, however, does pose a problem, for the expression "compass thine altar" seems to imply a priestly function rather than that of a worshipper approaching God through the priest.

This difficulty applies only in relation to David. When the words are projected to the Lord Jesus Christ, they find perfect fulfilment in him who is priest, altar and sacrifice. We do know that David on at least one other occasion seems to have taken upon himself the role of king-priest (2 Samuel 6:12-19) to enact typically the everlasting priesthood of Melchizedek which was central to his faith (Psalm 110:4). He was the Lord's anointed, and as such he was both God's representative on the "throne of the LORD" over Israel and also that of the people of Israel. How far David, acting in faith, was permitted on occasions to act in apparent contradiction of the letter of the law (1 Samuel 21:1-6) is open to debate; but there do seem grounds for recognising that this man "after God's own heart", with his spiritual insight, was allowed in spirit to contravene the letter of the law in deference to a higher order.

Remember that when David brought the ark to Zion, it was to the tabernacle that he had prepared for it, styled "the tabernacle of David" (Amos 9:11), and that consequently there were two tabernacles in existence, "for the tabernacle of the LORD, which Moses made in the wilderness, and the altar of the burnt offering, were at that season in the high place at Gibeon" (1 Chronicles 21:29). The reference to the altar of burnt offering in this context raises the interesting question as to which altar David was referring in Psalm 26.

Undoubtedly, here was a man who in the very best sense of the word was preoccupied with the house of the Lord: "I love the habitation of thy house. and the place where thy glory dwelleth" (verse 8, RV). To "dwell in the house of the LORD for ever" (Psalm 23:6) was the dominant desire of his heart; and after he had brought the ark to Zion, and God had made the covenant with him, it is recorded. "Then went king David in, and sat before the LORD ..." (2 Samuel 7:18). This was the pattern of his life, and in this he emulated another man of God, Joshua, of whom it is written that he "departed not out of the tabernacle" (Exodus 33:11).

It should be noted that the word "dwelleth" in Psalm 26 (verse 8) is literally the word 'tabernacle' (Hebrew, *mishkan*), emphasising all the scriptural associations concerned with God's sanctuary (Exodus 25:8,9).

Conclusion

In the light of his confidence in standing before God in his integrity, his refusal to be associated with wicked men and his overwhelming love for God's dwelling place, David's final plea to God is that he might not share in the fate of the sinner. To understand the end of the wicked, to be conscious of your own weakness and yet to know also that you have walked in integrity before God, must make such a prayer the cry of all that are godly – for thus they will be vindicated:

"Gather not my soul with sinners, nor my life with bloody men: in whose hands is mischief, and their right hand is full of bribes. But as for me, I will walk in mine integrity: redeem me, and be merciful unto me."

(verses 9-11)

Although confident of his steadfastness, David acknowledged that this would be of no avail apart from the mercy of God. It is God who redeems, and our resolve is but the response that God seeks to His work of salvation. But even as he prays thus for God to extend His loving-kindness, faith asserts itself and he recognises that by God's grace he stands in "an even place", a place of security where there is no danger of falling, and because of this he will continue, not in the company of sinners, but in the congregations, the meetings of the saints where he will bless the Lord. Such gatherings together of God's Ecclesia in this present dispensation are but dim reflections of the great assembly of the saints of all ages in God's kingdom, when all those who have walked in integrity and truth will finally be vindicated and will bless the Lord and tell of all His wondrous works (verses 7,12).

PSALM 27

WE have not so far made any reference to the compilation of The Book of Psalms. Clearly, written as they were over a considerable period of time and by a number of authors, they must have been brought together in the form and order which we now have them no later than the days of Ezra and Nehemiah. The evidence suggests that the work of arrangement was progressive, beginning, we believe, under the hand of David himself, and being continued perhaps by Solomon and certainly by Hezekiah, who not only composed, or was the subject of, psalms, but is also credited by many with being the man who, under God's hand, was primarily responsible for the final compilation of the book. There are, nevertheless, a few psalms that would appear to have been written after Hezekiah's days.

We deal with this particular subject and related topics such as the structure of the Psalter in later chapters. However, it seems appropriate to refer to the matter at this juncture because, although they might not all have the same historical background, it does appear that Psalms 24 to 31 are bound together by a common thread. Psalm 24, as we have shown, was connected with David bringing the ark to Zion, to the tabernacle he had prepared. We have already observed in Psalms 25 and 26 David's love for the dwelling place of God and his overwhelming desire to be received into the presence of God; and we shall see in Psalm 27 and the following four psalms expressions of the same earnest longing. It seems that the psalms are arranged in this way because they all reflect in some measure this quality in the man David that marked him out from all his contemporaries as a man after God's own heart.

160

Background and Structure of the Psalm

Psalm 27 appears to fall into three sections. These may be described briefly as follows:

(a) verses 1-6   The declaration of a triumphant and victorious faith.

(b) verses 7-12   The outworking of that faith in a time of trouble and distress.

(c) verses 13,14   Concluding exhortation to confidence in God arising out of His response to David's faith.

As far as the historical background is concerned, there is little to be said of any real substance. The Septuagint adds to the title "A Psalm of David before he was anointed", but with what authority is not evident. Certainly the context of the psalm would be appropriate to the time of David's life when he was hunted by Saul or, indeed, the later time of Absalom's rebellion. If there is a hint in the psalm itself, perhaps it is in the absence of any reference to Zion. For instance, Psalm 3 which refers to Absalom's rebellion says, "I cried unto the LORD with my voice, and he heard me out of his holy hill" (verse 4). In expressing his longing for God's tabernacle, the fact that he did not mention Zion, where he made a home for the ark of God, is possibly a clear indication that the psalm was written in the days before he became king.

Verses 1-6

This particular section of the psalm presents us with a triumphant faith and a glorious hope. It is difficult for men to appreciate that in their natural state they have no "inner light", no instinctive understanding of right and wrong and that, apart from divine revelation and the salvation it brings, they would walk perpetually "having the understanding darkened, being alienated from the life of God through the ignorance that is in them, because of the blindness of their heart" (Ephesians 4:18). It is only when the light of Truth has been perceived that one can really appreciate the hopelessness of the human predicament and, understanding the privilege of God's favour, the confidence that it brings.

161

"The LORD is my light and my salvation; whom shall I fear? the LORD is the strength (lit. stronghold) of my life; of whom shall I be afraid?" (verse 1)

A stronghold is a place of defence, a place of safety. While we remain within the orbit of God's grace we have no cause for fear. Perhaps we have a problem with such expressions of confidence. We know, most of us, from sad experience that life in the Truth is not a kind of insurance policy against the tribulations and adversities of life. Sickness and death will encompass all of us, if the Lord remain away. The Lord himself could not evade the cross with all its shame and ignominy if he was to remain faithful to his Father's will. What we must appreciate is that David had been anointed to be king over Israel. Nothing could frustrate the word of God if he remained faithful to his calling. Thus, although his enemies sought to devour him like wild beasts, they would but stumble and fall (verse 2).

Though hosts gathered against him, though men waged war with him, they could never succeed, for God had promised, and in the light of God's word and the knowledge that God would deliver him out of all these troubles and set him on the throne of Israel, David could say, "In this will I be confident" (verse 3).

For the Lord Jesus and, indeed, for us, the circumstances are different but the principle remains the same. For Jesus it was the cross before the crown and for him God's word is as faithful as it was for David. To us the Lord has said, "I will never leave thee, nor forsake thee. So that we may boldly say, The Lord is my helper, and I will not fear what man shall do unto me" (Hebrews 13:5,6).

His never-failing grace will ensure that we are protected from all spiritual calamity and His faithfulness extends beyond the grave; He will fulfil His word to us. It is this that gives us a different perspective on life – to know that the Lord is our light and our salvation and that "in this will (we) be confident".

We have already written, in dealing with Psalms 23 to 26, of that which was dominant in David's heart. The same thoughts are expressed again in Psalm 27 verses 4 and 6:

162

"One thing have I asked of the LORD, that I will seek after; that I may dwell in the house of the LORD all the days of my life, to behold the beauty of the LORD, and to inquire in his temple."   (verse 4, RV)

It is not necessary to repeat what we have said already about David's longings for God's house; but some additional points emerge. Note that the RV changes "one thing" from a desire to a petition – "one thing have I asked". It teaches us a great lesson about human endeavour and gives us a true insight into the nature of prayer. Except for rare occasions when there is absolutely nothing that we can do except wait upon Him, God expects us to do what we can. It is the token of our faithfulness, of the sincerity of our desire – "one thing have I asked ... that will I seek after". If we want to be righteous, then we must hunger and thirst after it. We must seek to be righteous, and God in His mercy, despite all our inadequacy, will see that we are filled.

The word rendered "behold" implies a sense of wonder and awe – a steadfast gaze to behold the beauty or, more literally, the pleasantness of the Lord. This, of course, encompasses all the wonder of God's character, and we have already commented on the similar thoughts in Psalms 25 and 26. The RV margin, however, suggests for "inquire in his temple" the rendering "consider His temple". In other words, it implies all that God intended the faithful worshipper to learn from surveying the literal tabernacle and perceiving the spiritual realities that lay behind its construction and ordinances. These, of course, were important principles relevant for daily life, but is it not also a scriptural endorsement to study the types and shadows it contained?

"For in the day of trouble he shall keep me secretly in his pavilion: in the covert of his tabernacle shall he hide me; he shall lift me up upon a rock" (verse 5, RV). The word "pavilion" means literally 'a hut, as of entwined boughs' (Strong and Gesenius). It is the masculine form of the word used to describe the booths associated with the feast of tabernacles (see Leviticus 23:42), and also the word 'tabernacles' itself (e.g., Deuteronomy 16:13,16; Isaiah 4:6).

163

Very similar words to verse 5 recur in Psalm 31 (verse 20). In dealing with Psalm 25 we have already drawn attention to the words of Moses and his experience when he saw the glory of God (Exodus 33:21,22). We have therefore at least three allusions to this passage in this group of psalms and, clearly, it was a scripture that was dear to the heart of David. He may in fact have been alluding to the Psalm of Moses (91) which would have been known to him, and which also gives us a divine comment on this event in Moses' life. "He that dwelleth in the secret place of the most High shall abide under the shadow of the Almighty" (verse 1). At any event, it confirms the importance of the written word for the man of God in whatever age or period of human history he lives.

It was because of all these things that David knew God would exalt him above his enemies, and thus he offered to God in His tabernacle the sacrifice of joy and praise (verse 6).

Verses 7-12

If the first section speaks of his confidence – 'tranquil', 'undaunted', 'full of calm faith' (Kay, *Psalms with Notes*), this second section introduces a note of anxiety, a hint of storm after calm, as if the faith declared in time of peace and security is now tested by a sudden change of circumstance – as if David says to God, 'Show now that I have not trusted thee in vain'.

"Hear, O LORD, when I cry with my voice: have mercy also upon me, and answer me. When thou saidst, Seek ye my face; my heart said unto thee, Thy face, LORD, will I seek. Hide not thy face far from me; put not thy servant away in anger: thou hast been my help; leave me not, neither forsake me, O God of my salvation. When my father and my mother forsake me, then the LORD will take me up. Teach me thy way, O LORD, and lead me in a plain path, because of mine enemies. Deliver me not over unto the will of mine enemies: for false witnesses are risen up against me, and such as breathe out cruelty."   (verses 7-12)

164

The obvious tension present in these verses is not to be understood as a weakness in faith; rather, it is faith proved and tested by adversity. Again there is an important lesson to learn. Opportunities must be taken. If we are to stand in the face of tribulation or indeed persecution, then we can only do so if we have prepared ourselves in the day of peace and tranquility. We must use such periods that God gives us to imbibe His word, to grow in our understanding of it, to learn from it the principles by which God works in the lives of faithful men. Without such inner spiritual resources we shall be found in the day of trouble in the same plight as the foolish virgins, albeit, if it is not the day of the Lord's coming, with opportunity still to learn from our mistakes.

When did God say, "Seek ye my face" (verse 8)? Could it be a reference to a particular passage of scripture (e.g., Deuteronomy 4:29), or is it the invitation contained in the totality of God's revelation? To seek God's face is to desire to be in His presence, for the Hebrew word rendered "face" and "presence" is the same in both instances. We might say that understanding the divine call to seek His face, "the answer of a good conscience before God" is able to respond, "Thy face, LORD, will I seek".

It is interesting to refer back at this juncture to the words of Psalm 24; "This is the generation of them that seek thy face, even Jacob" (verse 6, RV margin). We did not refer to this translation in our study of the psalm, but it is, nevertheless, worthy of consideration as an alternative to the AV margin. "The generation who seek even Jacob" is, if this translation be followed, the Israel of God – the ideal people who epitomise the spirit of Jacob. David's words in this context could be catching the very spirit of both God's words to Jacob and His subsequent dealings with him.

Notice the words in italics; "*leave* me not, neither *forsake* me, O God of my salvation" (Psalm 27:9), and compare God's words to Jacob at Bethel: "I am with thee, and will keep thee in all places whither thou goest ... for I will not leave thee, until I have done that which I have spoken to thee of" (Genesis 28:15). Of course, when Jacob wrestled with the angel, he called the place Peniel, for he said, "I have seen God face to face" (Genesis 32:30).

The lives of Moses and Jacob were close to the heart of David, and he longed to know in his life the same privileges and blessings that they had experienced. God's word speaks to our hearts through all the wonderful examples of our brethren and sisters in the pages of scripture. We walk the same path and look for the same spiritual rewards. We want to be there with them in the kingdom of God.

David said, "When my father and my mother forsake me, then the LORD will take me up" (Psalm 27:10). This is said to be a proverbial expression to describe one who is left friendless and alone. However, might it not still be a reference to the life of Jacob when he fled from the wrath of his brother Esau? Isaac and Rebekah were powerless to deliver him. Yet friendless and alone, the Lord found him and took him up at Bethel (Genesis 28).

These words, "the LORD will take me up" are possibly alluded to in the New Testament. When Aquila and Priscilla found Apollos at Ephesus, "they took him unto them" (Acts 18:26). The Greek here is almost exactly that used in the Septuagint to render the words of Psalm 27, and once again it gives a valuable insight into the way in which God works in the life of the believer. Often it is through the kindness and ministrations of those of like faith that God provides comfort and security for those who are lonely and friendless.

As always, David recognised his own inadequacy. If he was to succeed in living the life of God, then he must be taught by God; and with this teaching there must also be the providential guidance that would lead him in a plain (lit. 'even') path where there were no obstructions or stumbling blocks that might cause him to fall (verse 11). Thus he beseeches God to deliver him out of the hand of all his enemies who so actively sought to do him harm (verse 12).

Verses 13 and 14

David concluded his song with a most powerful exhortation growing out of his own experience:

"If I had not trusted to see the goodness of the Lord in the land of the living! ... Oh! wait thou for the Lord; be strong and let thy heart be firm; yea! wait thou for the Lord." (verses 13,14, Kay – *Psalms with Notes*)

The translation above accurately reflects the Hebrew text for verse 13 which contains a broken sentence, an unfinished thought. It can be described as a dramatic device of great power and emphasis, as if the consequences of not trusting were so awful to contemplate that they could not be uttered. Truly, without such faith we are left desolate. We perish in our afflictions. It is a lesson, then, a spiritual verity that we each need to perceive and embrace. In this confidence there is only one proper attitude, that of patience and endurance, waiting upon the Lord. The Hebrew word rendered "wait" means 'to gather together by twisting, to expect' (Strong's). Hence it conveys the idea of two bound together in a common purpose and aim, and, because it is God and His word that we cleave to, we can wait or confidently expect Him to manifest Himself on our behalf. Therefore:

"Be strong, and let thine heart take courage; yea, wait thou on the Lord." (verse 14, RV)

PSALM 28

IT is generally agreed that this short psalm was written against the background of Absalom's rebellion. Certainly the reference to "the workers of iniquity, which speak peace to their neighbours, but mischief is in their hearts" (verse 3) reflects the attitude of those who plotted against David at that time and is consistent with the language of other psalms of this period. There does, however, appear to be an objection to this hypothesis. If we examine the psalms of David's earlier life when, for example, he was hunted by Saul, they are characterised by references to natural and material things which, in human terms, contributed to David's deliverance, but which he recognised and acknowledged as being the symbols of God's protection and providential hand in his life. Obvious examples are "my rock", "my shield", "my stronghold", "my refuge" etc.

The fact is that each of the examples mentioned above occurs in Psalm 28 – "My rock" (verse 1), "my shield" (verse 7), "stronghold" (verse 8, RV) – suggesting that the psalm could belong to an earlier period of David's life. The question to which we address ourselves is, Can the two strands of thought be reconciled? We believe they can, and in bringing them together there is much exhortation for those who faithfully seek to serve God as David did.

Let us accept the view that the psalm speaks of the hypocrites who presented themselves as friends by speaking peace, but secretly plotted mischief. Such double-minded men surrounded David in the days leading up to Absalom's attempt to seize the throne. David, of course, was aware of their duplicity and of the possible consequences of their treachery. As circumstances proved, he was compelled to flee for his life and to go once more "the way of the wilderness" (2 Samuel 15). What therefore was more natural than for David to recall the events of his early life when, as now, he had been a fugitive, and to strengthen and encourage himself by remembering the work of God in his life at that time, whereby he had been delivered, in the same figures and symbols that had been so appropriate then? In effect, David was drawing on his past experience to consolidate his faith at this trying time. In this he stands as an example to us all. If we cannot recognise the goodness of God in our lives, if we have not a fund of personal experience to draw from to encourage us to face the trials and adversities that confront us, then surely we have failed in some respect to appreciate the providential hand of God which works in the lives of all His servants.

These things David recalled and reiterated in the context of the tribulations of his later life. But there is a different emphasis also from the psalms of David's earlier life. These abound with expressions of his confidence in God, characterised in the main by a joyous certainty that God would hear him and deliver. However, after his sin in the matter of Bathsheba, there is a more sombre tone, as if David, though conscious that God had forgiven him, could in a sense not forgive himself. He had to live with that knowledge of his sin, and it brought to him a greater realisation that he had no right to expect God either to hear him or deliver him, though his faith that God in His goodness would do both remained unabated. Thus his cry is:

"To Thee will I cry, O LORD, my Rock; turn not from me as one who hears not; lest, if Thou turn in silence from me, I become like them that go down to the pit."

(verse 1, Kay, *Psalms with Notes*)

David recognises God's goodness in the past, as he acknowledges Him as His Rock – but shows also how he appreciates his absolute dependence on God's continuing mercy, unworthy of it though he might feel himself to be. If God turns His ear away from us, if He hears not when we cry unto Him, then we are without hope. We become as those who are laid in the grave like sheep (Psalm 49:14).

169

David's Prayer

The actual words of the prayer are contained in verses 3 to 5. They are prefaced by a further cry to God to hear him, "Hear the voice of my supplications, when I cry unto thee, when I lift up my hands toward thy holy oracle" (verse 2), and conclude with an acknowledgement that God has indeed responded to his prayer: "Blessed be the LORD, because he hath heard the voice of my supplications" (verse 6).

There are two points we can develop here. The first concerns the "lifting up of the hands", which is the typical attitude of prayer in scripture. What does it signify? First, it shows that one's thoughts and words are directed heavenwards towards God's holy temple; secondly, although different words are used, one thinks of the heave offerings under the law, when, with hands full, the offerer lifted up the sacrifice towards heaven in token that it was presented to God. In similar fashion, the hands lifted up were a token of that spiritual sacrifice, that total dedication of heart and mind of which the prayer was but an expression.

Some interesting New Testament connections might be considered. Take, for instance, the Lord's words to Peter in John 21:18. When Peter was young, he had girded himself and, as it were, gone his own way. In old age, in his spiritual maturity, he would stretch forth his hands in the attitude of prayer, and another (God) would gird him and carry him whither he would not. It is a declaration of how Peter would come to recognise and acknowledge the will of God in his life, and in particular in his death (verse 19).

Another connection is the writer's exhortation to the Hebrews (12:12) to "lift up the hands which hang down". The answer to all human adversity is not to fall into limp submission, a state of despair and despondency, but to "pray always" – that is, "to lift up the hands".

The second point we can consider is the word "oracle". It is the Hebrew word *debir*, a derivation of the word *dabar*, normally translated "word", and it is the precise equivalent of the Greek word *logos*. It is used in this psalm, and in 1 Kings (6:5,16,19,20,23 etc.) and 2 Chronicles (4:20; 5:7,9) to describe the Most Holy Place where God dwelt between the Cherubim, from whence, it might be said, the word of God proceeded in the midst of His people. It gives added meaning and deeper insight to the words of John's Gospel: "And the Word was made flesh, and dwelt (lit. tabernacled) among us, (and we beheld his glory, the glory as of the only begotten of the Father,) full of grace and truth" (1:14). He was "the oracle", the antitype of the Most Holy Place where God spoke with authority in the midst of His people and where His glory resided.

Here, of course, is also the reference in this psalm to the dwelling place of God that binds together Psalms 24 and 31, to which reference was made when considering Psalm 27.

The actual substance of the prayer is directed against false-hearted men who paraded themselves as friends of David, but were in fact workers of mischief (Psalm 28:3). It is worthy of note that though the activity of these men was directed against their neighbours, it is not for that reason that they are primarily indicted. Note the parallel between verses 4 and 5:

"Give them according *to their deeds*, and according to the wickedness of their endeavours: give them after the *work of their hands*; render to them their desert."

(verse 4)

"Because they regard not the *works of the LORD*, nor the *operation of his hands*, he shall destroy them, and not build them up." (verse 5)

The work of their hands which springs out of that which was right in their eyes, from a leaning unto their own understanding, is contrasted with the work of God's hands which they refused to recognise. It was for this cause that David prays for God to give them in justice that which they deserved.

In all periods of human history God's servants have been afflicted and their faith put in peril by such men as these. They were especially active in the days of the Lord Jesus, and the first century ecclesias were warned of such, termed "false brethren" (Acts 20:29,30; 2 Corinthians 11:13; Galatians 2:4; 2 Peter 2:1 etc.).

171

We may not be able to identify them, and it is not our prerogative to judge them in the absolute sense, for the sin is primarily against God. But, sadly, we have to recognise that our age is no different from the time of David or the first century. We too have false brethren, double-minded men whose activities do not promote, but rather destroy, the work of God. We shall not seek to develop this theme, but it serves to remind us of the importance of judging every issue by the word of God and accepting its authority as absolute at all times.

Conclusion

As God had delivered Israel of old and they and Moses had sung a song unto the Lord (Exodus 15:1), so David in thought is carried back to that time, and his exclamation of joyous faith in verse 7 is reminiscent of the words of Moses: "The LORD is my strength and my shield; my heart trusted in him, and I am helped: therefore my heart greatly rejoiceth; and with my song will I praise him" (cp. Exodus 15:2). What is particularly interesting is that the words of Moses contain the phrase, "I will prepare him an habitation". Is this why David's thoughts went to this passage? Is there here yet another indication of the theme that binds this group of psalms together – David's preoccupation with the House of his God?

Verse 8 presents a difficulty, for David exclaims, "The LORD is their strength, and he is the saving strength of his anointed". The pronoun 'their' has no antecedent in the text (the marginal rendering 'his' seems to be without foundation). It obviously refers to the people of Israel or a multitude of some kind. Could the answer be that David understood that ultimately God's habitation would comprise a multitude of humble and contrite spirit, of whom truly it could be said that the Lord was their stronghold and the salvation of their king His anointed?

So the final supplication is on behalf of the people: "Save thy people, and bless thine inheritance". Israel were described as God's inheritance (Deuteronomy 4:20; 32:9). The thought is carried over into the New Testament, for the saints also are spoken of as God's inheritance (Ephesians 1:11, RV; 1:18). There is a remarkable interplay on this idea of a heritage in scripture, for not only are God's people His heritage, but "The LORD is the portion of (our) inheritance" (Psalm16:5,6; see also Lamentations 3:22-24; Psalm73:26). Jeremiah brings the two ideas together:

"The portion of Jacob is not like them ... Israel is the rod of his inheritance." (Jeremiah 10:16)

The idea of God our portion and we His heritage is a means of describing the eternal relationship that will finally obtain between God and His people. It is in fact akin to the idea of God's habitation to which we have already referred (see 1 John 4:13,16). The passages in John have a present application, but nevertheless they illustrate the principle, for the present experience is but a reflection of the perfect fellowship that will be known in the future.

This surpassing love of God for His people is crowned by the final thought of Psalm 28 (verse 9): "Feed them also, and lift them up for ever". The NKJV renders the words, "shepherd them also and bear them up forever". God will provide for their spiritual sustenance and like the shepherd He will bear His sheep, gathering them in His arm and carrying them in His bosom (Isaiah 40:11). Such is the care of God for those who are His. It is unceasing in its operation, and it is intended primarily to bring us at last to His kingdom and glory. David will be there. Our reflections on the words of David should so move and encourage us that we can be assured that we also will be there with him in that day.

PSALM 29

THE substance of this psalm appears to be concerned with the description of a tremendous and, in its fury, almost unprecedented tempestuous thunderstorm. It breaks in the north of the land over Lebanon and Hermon (Sirion, see Deuteronomy 3:9) (Psalm 29:5) and sweeps southward to the wilderness of Kadesh (verse 8). In might and majesty (verse 4), with thunderclap and lightning flash, the very mountains seem to skip like calves, like a young ox (verse 6, RV). Before the hurricane-like wind, the trees are stripped of their bark and with the forks of fire from heaven, the cedars are split asunder.

Such is the fear engendered by the path of the storm that (figuratively) the wilderness trembles and the timid hinds are induced into premature birth-pangs (verses 8,9). Our description remains totally inadequate, and no words of purely human origin could match the grandeur and sheer power expressed by the language of the psalm itself.

Structure
The manner in which one is swept along by the fury of the tempest, by these manifestations of God's power in natural phenomena such as thunder and lightning should not, however, blind us to the structure of the psalm. In the very nature of things storms are chaotic and violent. They give the impression of causing arbitrary damage by blind uncontrollable fury. It is therefore of no little significance that in the original Hebrew text the storm is described with precise symmetry (verses 3-9). This is matched by the perfection of poetic form of the prelude (verses 1,2) and the conclusion (verses 10,11).

We have abstracted this information regarding the Hebrew text from *The Psalms* Volume 1 (J. J. Perowne), based apparently on the original analysis of Ewald. The conclusions drawn, however, are our own, based we trust on the enlightenment that understanding of the Truth brings.

It is stated that the psalm is divided into five parts: the prelude, a central section consisting of three strophes, followed by the conclusion or epilogue. Both the prelude and the conclusion are constructed in similar fashion, comprising two verses, each containing two members. In the central section the three strophes are constructed in such a way as to describe the beginnings of the storm (verses 3,4), the storm at its height (verses 5-7), and finally its last burst of fury before dying away over Kadesh (verses 8,9). Furthermore, each of the three strophes is constructed with the same characteristic double line, i.e., "The voice of the LORD is upon the waters ... The LORD is upon many waters" (verse 3).

We do not elaborate further, because the majority of readers, like the writer, being unable to read the original Hebrew text, would not be able to appreciate fully the force of the structure at first hand. Given, however, that this symmetry exists in describing what man regards as capricious and disorderly, what a powerful message is being conveyed to reinforce the words of the psalm itself!

"The LORD sat as king at the Flood; yea, the LORD sitteth as king for ever."   (verse 10, RV)

God is in complete control. The raging of the elements, the tumult of the storm are subject to His counsel and wisdom, and in its every aspect He speaks and it is done; He commands and it stands fast (Psalm 33:9). In it all there is purpose and design: "For the word of the LORD is right; and all his works are done in truth" (Psalm 33:4).

Seven times in this central section the voice of God speaks to emphasise His absolute authority:

"The voice of the LORD is upon the waters." (verse 3)

"The voice of the LORD is powerful."   (verse 4)

"The voice of the LORD is full of majesty."   (verse 4)

"The voice of the LORD breaketh the cedars."

(verse 5)

"The voice of the LORD divideth the flames of fire."

(verse 7)

175

"The voice of the LORD shaketh the wilderness."

(verse 8)

"The voice of the LORD maketh the hinds to calve."

(verse 9)

Reference to a concordance will indicate that the Hebrew word *kohl*, rendered "voice" here, and on numerous other occasions, is also rendered "thunder" in various contexts, and clearly in Psalm 29 the thunder and the voice of God are both implicit in the use of the word. There seems to be an obvious reference to the seven thunders of Revelation 10, and we make further reference to this connection in the conclusion.

From an exhortational point of view, we can take comfort in the psalm on at least two levels. First, in all the storms of life, however chaotic events may seem, however keen the adversity and the tribulation, what occurs is all part of the work of God in our lives. He is in control. Similarly with the raging of the nations and the fury of the storm of world events – wars, famine, civil unrest, natural catastrophes are all subject to the voice of God. He rules in the kingdom of men; His purpose cannot be frustrated, and the God who rides the storm speaks peace to those who put their trust in Him: "The LORD will give strength unto his people; the LORD will bless his people with peace" (verse 11).

However, notwithstanding these general lessons, we believe (for the reason stated below) that the psalm is more specific than this and relates to the outpouring of God's judgements upon men. Indeed, although it has, in keeping with the nature of Bible prophecy, recurring fulfilments, we suggest that it has particular reference to the judgement of the last day. The connection with Revelation 10 supports this view; but we are confirmed in this opinion by the words of verse 10 already quoted: "The LORD sitteth upon the flood".

The Hebrew word rendered "flood" in this instance occurs only here in Psalm 29 and twelve times in the Genesis record of Noah's flood. The reference to that divine judgement is therefore beyond question. That Noah's flood was accompanied by earthquake and storm with all kinds of natural phenomena is indisputable. With this in mind we might consider whether the references in the psalm to the mountains skipping and the wilderness trembling are not poetic descriptions of the fury of the storm, but indications of actual earthquakes when God literally causes the earth to shake.

Noah's flood stands as a type of God's judgements upon an evil world. If, as it appears, it stands behind this psalm, then the description of God's power and majesty are also intended to convey the picture of God manifest in judgement. This understanding of the central part of the psalm gives us added insight into the opening and closing sections.

Prelude

"Give unto the LORD, O ye mighty, give unto the LORD glory and strength. Give unto the LORD the glory due unto his name; worship the LORD in the beauty of holiness."   (verses 1,2)

Literally the phrase "O ye mighty" should be rendered "O ye sons of God" (RV, margin). Many have thought the reference to be to the angelic host which inhabits God's temple in heaven (see verse 9). Certainly the words could be true of them in the call to give (lit. ascribe, see Deuteronomy 32:3) unto the Lord, glory. But the scriptural associations of the call to worship Him in the beauty of holiness (with the added consideration that the psalm is written for the benefit of men, not angels) points, we suggest, to the fact that the call is to the people of God, the saints, to recognise His power and greatness and to worship Him at this awesome manifestation of His glory in judgement.

The reference to "the beauty of holiness" carries us back to the garments of the high priest, which were to be made "for glory and for beauty", and the RV margin of Psalm 29:2 confirms the connection with its rendering "in holy array", elsewhere translated "in holy attire". It links most beautifully with the words of Psalm 110: "Thy people are freewill offerings in the day of thy power: in holy attire … thy youth are to thee as the dew" (verse 3, RV & margin).

As dew they will rise from the womb of the morning on that resurrection day (see Isaiah 26:19; 2 Samuel 23:4).

Freewill offerings endowed with everlasting youth and clothed in spirit-nature, they will ascribe glory to Him who has covered them with the robe of righteousness.

We note the emphasis upon God's glory in verses 1 and 2 and in its physical manifestation (verse 3). This physical aspect is seen in the language of verses 3-9, but the section closes most beautifully with the multitude of the redeemed, God's spiritual house, for, having exercised His sovereignty over all the earth, "in his temple every thing saith, Glory" (verse 9, RV).

Conclusion

We have already written of the reference to the flood in verse 10; the final sentence asserts God's eternal sovereignty. He is King for ever, and in contrast to the turmoil and storm of the middle section, in this section He gives strength to His people and blesses them with peace (verse 11).

The thoughts of the psalm are caught together in the angels' song at the birth of the Lord Jesus: "Glory to God in the highest, and on earth peace among men in whom he is well pleased" Luke 2:14, RV).

Some final comments on Revelation 10 and the seven thunders – these are connected with the "mighty angel … clothed with a cloud, and a rainbow was upon his head" (verse 1). He stands with his right foot upon the sea and his left foot on the earth, as if to emphasise his sovereignty and authority, and in his hand he holds a little book open in which he would write the seven thunders as they are uttered. The rainbow about his head connects with the similar words of Revelation 4, where all the associations link it with David's throne. The cloud speaks of the divine presence manifest in a host of the redeemed. It is a reflection of the divine countenance in the day of rain after the storm period of the seven thunders has ended.

Brother John Thomas wrote:

"Arching over this symbol, it (the rainbow) signifies that the angel is a company of kings and priests, related to the rainbowed throne – the throne covenanted to David and his seed." (*Eureka* Volume 2, page 540)

The backcloth is before us in Psalm 29, which stands as a word of encouragement, telling us how the grace of God, shining through all the storms associated with mortal sinful life, will eventually bring us to His kingdom, where we shall know perfect peace.

PSALM 30

T HE psalm bears the superscription, "A Psalm and Song at the dedication of the house of David". This, however, is a little misleading and the RV appears to reflect the meaning more closely with its rendering, "A Psalm; a Song at the Dedication of the House; a Psalm of David".

The occasion that led to the composition of the psalm had nothing to do with David's own house, but it was in fact the dedication of the threshing-floor of Ornan the Jebusite, when David was led by God to acknowledge it as the site of that house of God "exceeding magnifical" that Solomon his son should build (1 Chronicles 22:5).

The historical background is contained primarily in 1 Chronicles 21 and 2 Samuel 24. But to confirm that the reference to "the house" is appropriate, we might note that after paying Ornan 600 shekels of gold for the purchase of the land, David built there an altar unto the Lord (as God had commanded) and offered burnt offerings and peace offerings to the Lord, who answered him by fire from heaven (1 Chronicles 21:26). It appears that David subsequently continued to sacrifice there, and not at the tabernacle which Moses had made (verses 28-30). In consequence David declared, "This is the house of the LORD God, and this is the altar of the burnt offering for Israel" (22:1). The rest of this chapter is concerned with David's preparations for building God's house and the instruction and encouragement that he gave to Solomon who was to carry out the work.

Historical Background

The record of 2 Samuel 24 and 1 Chronicles 21 provides us with the background that is reflected in the language and message of the psalm. These chapters record the occasion

180

when Satan (i.e., God, cp. 2 Samuel 24:1 & 1 Chronicles 21:1) moved David to number Israel.

We believe that this episode is misunderstood by many, and a study of the two chapters and other relevant scripture reveals the true circumstances. Notice that God moved David to number Israel because His anger was kindled against Israel. Thus the circumstances that led to the plague coming upon the people already existed before the numbering, and David's action, providentially motivated, was the catalyst that made the sin of the people open and manifest.

To discover just what the sin of the people was, we might ask two questions:

1. Was it a sin to number the people, as Joab seems to suggest? (1 Chronicles 21:3).
2. Why was David so anxious to number Israel, although opposed in this purpose by Joab and all the captains of the host? (2 Samuel 24:4).

As far as the first question is concerned, there seems to be no legitimate reason why the people should not be numbered, as long as it was done in the proper manner (see Numbers 1:2; 26:2; Exodus 30:11-16). The Exodus passage is particularly helpful, for it describes how every man was to give a ransom for his soul, "that there be no plague among them" (verse 12). The prescribed amount was to be half a shekel according to the shekel of the sanctuary; it was to be an "offering of the LORD" (verse 13), and rich and poor alike were to give the same amount, "to make an atonement for (their) souls" (verse 15). The money thus raised was to be used "for the service of the tabernacle of the congregation" (verse 16).

It should also be noted that the figure employed to describe the numbering of the people is that of a shepherd counting his sheep (verses 13,14); a fact to which David referred when in his feeling of remorse, he said, "Lo, I have sinned, and I have done wickedly: but these sheep, what have they done?" (2 Samuel 24:17).

In the precepts recorded in Exodus we have the key to the answer to our second question. David was not motivated by any fleshly desire to glory in numbers, but

181

rather his consuming passion was to build a house for his God. It dominated all his thoughts (see 2 Samuel 7:1-7; Psalm 69:9; 132:3-5). Although God had made it plain that he should not build that house, with his whole heart he prepared for the day when Solomon would do so. His purpose, then, in numbering the people was to involve them in this great work, that through their contributions of the half-shekel (not now for "the service of the tabernacle"), they might assist in financing the building of the house of his God. The problem was that Israel did not share David's enthusiasm. The people in their prosperity had become spiritually lethargic. They had no time for their king's 'foolish' preoccupations.

Joab, of course, was more in touch with the feelings of the people than the king. He knew that their heart was not in this project, and that the half-shekel of the sanctuary would not willingly and readily be offered. Thus, on his own initiative, Joab set about the matter in what to him must have appeared a more prudent course of action. He numbered the fighting men, which was not the king's intention, and he did not even do that properly (1 Chronicles 21:6, see also 1 Chronicles 27:24). The Revised Version for this latter passage reads: "Joab the son of Zeruiah began to number, but finished not; and there came wrath for this upon Israel". So pestilence came on Israel and seventy thousand men fell.

The sequence of events we have already noted in our introduction began when God stayed the hand of the destroying angel over Jerusalem, who was manifest to David and the elders of Israel who were all clothed in sackcloth, standing by the threshing floor of Ornan the Jebusite (1 Chronicles 21:15,16).

What should be noted is that David felt responsible for the plague that had fallen on the people and associated himself with them in their sin, although, if he was guilty, it was only inasmuch as he had failed to recognise the spiritual decline of the people, and had not sought to arrest it or stir up their enthusiasm for the work.

The Structure of the Psalm

The psalm falls broadly into two sections, the first (verses 1-5) referring to recovery from sickness, and praising God for his deliverance from death; and the second (verses 6-12) describes the psalmist's experiences in the midst of his sickness, referring particularly to his prayer and his response to God's answer.

There is an apparent difficulty, for David was not struck down by the plague. Unlike Israel he was not guilty of forgetting God in his prosperity. Yet he recognised that as king, as the representative of the people, there was a corporate guilt that involved the whole nation including himself, and so he could speak on behalf of the people as though he himself had been personally involved in all their waywardness and punishment. In this respect there are strong connections with the Lord Jesus Christ, our representative, who stood for us – on our behalf – though he himself was guiltless.

Verses 1-5

The psalm opens by extolling God for the manner in which He had raised him up (RV) from the depths of despair. In this way his enemies, who would have rejoiced over his calamity, were confounded. He was not made to suffer that added indignity of their malicious delight in his troubles (verse 1). His cry had been unto God who had healed him, for the plague had been stayed, and God had raised him up from 'Sheol'. It was like a resurrection from the dead, for had God not intervened, even David was as good as dead. But he had been restored to life, separated "from among them that go down to the pit" (verses 2,3, RV margin).

In view of this deliverance, the call is made to all God's faithful servants to join in praise to Him: "Sing praise unto the LORD, O ye saints of his, and give thanks to his holy name" (verse 4, RV). The word rendered "saints" is the Hebrew *chasid*. It is from the same root as that word which describes God's loving-kindness, His fidelity to His people in the bonds of His covenant. It has been described as "covenant love", and his saints are those who have been the objects of this loving-kindness and faithfulness. The appreciation of these qualities can produce but one thing – praise to God.

We might say that God demands praise of us because it is His right, but this is only true if we understand the real nature of praise. True praise is voluntary and springs from a recognition of the character of God, of all that He is, of all that He has done for us. It has its roots in the joy that fills the heart. Consequently, it cannot be given grudgingly, or spring out of a spirit of apathy. It is in fact the expression of an overflowing delight in the things that pertain to God's name. It is His name which brings to remembrance what He is, what He has done, and what He has promised to do. The Revised Version reads, "to his holy name"; the AV, "at the remembrance of his holiness". Literally the word rendered "remembrance" is 'memorial', and links, of course, with Exodus 3:15 – hence the translation of the Revised Version.

The psalm continues by saying that God's anger towards them that fear Him is but for a moment, but in His favour there is life. "Weeping may endure for a night, but joy cometh in the morning" (verse 5). The striking figure behind these words is expressed by the Revised Version margin: "Weeping may come in to lodge at even", just like a passing wayfarer, but joy comes in the morning. It is the recurring message of scripture. The night of sorrow gives place to the dawn of the perfect day. It is the hope that sustains men of faith in every generation.

Verses 6-12
Having considered the gracious outcome of his experience, the answer that he had received to his prayers, the psalmist turns again to consider the detail of his 'brush with death': "In my prosperity I said, I shall never be moved" (verse 6).

The word rendered "prosperity" carries the idea of ease and carefree security – always a dangerous spirit for those who seek to please God (see Deuteronomy 8:10-14). It is so easy to forget our frailty and mortality and, because we prosper, to forget also how much we depend upon God. This was the condition of the people of Israel prior to the numbering initiated by David, and the whole series of events was a most chastening experience to teach them the folly of resting in their own strength and confidence.

By His favour God made His mountain strong (verse 7 – see RV). His mountain was undoubtedly Zion – a fortress by its geographical position, but by God's covenant established as a symbol of the reality of David's kingdom that would eventually stand for ever. Yet through the events we have considered, God had hidden His face and the light of His countenance had no longer shone on His people. They had been "troubled", a word expressing confusion and terror. David, however, made his prayer and supplication unto God (verse 8) and the substance of his prayer is contained in verses 9 and 10:

"What profit is there in my blood, when I go down to the pit? Shall the dust praise thee? shall it declare thy truth? Hear, O LORD, and have mercy upon me: LORD, be thou my helper."

What profit? Death is the cessation of being – the end of life where the body returns to dust. In death there was no opportunity to praise God or to rejoice in His faithfulness. It is truly amazing how men, blinded by human philosophy, fail to see the reality of death as it was expressed by faithful men in the word of God. Hezekiah's example comes readily to mind (Isaiah 38:18,19). But The Book of Psalms itself, with its similar insight into the hearts of men, reiterates the message on several occasions (Psalms 6:5; 39:6; 49:10; 88:12; 89:48; 146:4).

God did hear; the Lord was his helper, for his mourning was turned into dancing, the plague was stayed, the site identified. Sackcloth could be put away (1 Chronicles 21:16) and replaced with the garments of gladness (Psalm 30:11). Most translators use "soul" instead of "glory" in verse 12; but we see no real grounds for this. Surely his "glory" was his joy and gladness that recognised that his royal dignity came not of himself, but from God who had caused him to sit on the throne of the Lord over Israel.

It was in the confidence of God's fidelity to His covenant that he could close his song with the words, "O LORD my God, I will give thanks unto thee for ever". Such was his assurance of eternal joy in God's kingdom.

Conclusion

The words of the psalm are an expression of the thoughts of David on the historical circumstances of 1 Chronicles 21 and 22, and 2 Samuel 24. The association of the threshing-floor of Ornan the Jebusite with the site of Solomon's temple is particularly instructive. It helps through the psalm to identify the manner in which God would be known among His people, the place where He would be pleased to dwell among them and extend His favour and loving-kindness towards them when they prayed towards that place. There the plague was stayed, there He showed forgiveness and deliverance – all of which was caught up in the refrain that runs through Solomon's prayer of dedication when the temple was completed:

"When they shall pray towards this place ... hear thou in heaven thy dwelling place: and when thou hearest, forgive." (1 Kings 8:30)

PSALM 31

IT is difficult to imagine when David wrote some of the psalms that bear his name. We can, perhaps, identify a particular historical background. But if the association is with a time of great peril, flight from his enemies, constant moving from place to place, then it is not easy to think of David writing his psalms as he moved swiftly with his fighting men, or as he rode upon his ass pursued by his enemies. Moved by the Holy Spirit, he would have written some psalms in the midst of the circumstances they reflect. Others he would write later, still recording the state of his heart and mind at the time of the incidents, but composed as he looked back and recalled the difficulties and dangers and the way in which he had reacted to them.

It is this fact that helps us to understand the startling changes of tone that occur in some psalms, leading many to assume, wrongly, that the songs are compilations from the hands of different authors brought together at a later date. We have such an example in the psalm we are considering. In verses 1 to 8 we have a statement of calm, assured faith. In verses 9 to 18 we have what might be described as a crisis of faith. David is in the midst of trouble and turmoil, faced by the duplicity and malice of men who sought to do him harm. Finally, at the conclusion of the psalm, there is a return to the note of confidence as David recognises that God once again has delivered him from his enemies.

An interesting feature of this psalm is its verbal links with Psalm 28 in the first section (verses 1-8) and also in the concluding section (verses 19-24). Some of these are set out as follows:

187

PSALM 28	PSALM 31
"Unto thee will I cry, O LORD my rock (verse 1) ... The LORD is my strength and my shield." (verse 7)	"Be thou my strong rock, for an house of defence to save me. For thou art my rock and my fortress ... thou art my strength." (verses 2-4)
"Blessed be the LORD, because he hath heard the voice of my supplications." (verse 6)	"Blessed be the LORD: for he hath shewed me his marvellous kindness ... nevertheless thou heardest the voice of my supplications when I cried unto thee." (verses 21,22)

In our introduction to Psalm 28 we indicated that, although its background is concerned with the time of Absalom's rebellion, much of the language and figures of speech (e.g., the rock, the shield) are drawn from David's early life. He is recalling his earlier experiences, remembering how God had proved faithful and protected him, and in this knowledge is confident that God would sustain him as once more he fled into the wilderness.

We have a similar situation here. In verses 1 to 8 David expresses his calm, assured faith built on the earlier experiences of his life. In verses 9 to 18 he tells of the crisis of faith that assailed him and of the urgency of his prayers as, through the rebellion of Absalom, his kingdom was threatened. Finally, vindicated by God's righteousness, he reaffirms his faith in God and rejoices in His faithfulness towards him in once more delivering him from the hand of his enemies.

Verses 1-8

"In thee, O LORD, do I put my trust; let me never be ashamed: deliver me in thy righteousness." (verse 1)

The idea of shame in such contexts as this arises from the concept of misplaced trust. Those who put their faith in God will not be disappointed. Their hope will not be confounded. They will never know the shame of exposure as men who have trusted in something that is vain and empty. David's plea is that God would be his "strong rock", a "house of defence". The first phrase indicates a rock that is unmoveable, embedded, as it were, into the very fabric of the mountain. The RV margin renders the next phrase "house of fortresses". In other words, David beseeches God to be his place of refuge and security, for he continues, "Thou art my rock (lit. cliff) and my fortress". It was a prayer for God to manifest Himself as that which David believed Him to be – his rock and his stronghold – and in this confidence he pleaded with God to shew Himself, once more, as a defence and a fortress.

"Therefore for thy name's sake lead me, and guide me. Pull me out of the net that they have laid privily for me: for thou art my strength."   (verses 3,4)

For His name's sake God will do these things. He will show himself to be everything that He has declared concerning Himself. The words "lead me, and guide me" imply gentleness, and are a reference to the figure of the shepherd caring for the flock. (See in this connection our earlier comment on Psalm 23:2,3). His enemies were like hunters, laying traps for him into which they hoped he might fall unsuspectingly; but he knew that God would pull him out of their net, for He was his stronghold (RV).

"Into thine hand I commit my spirit: thou hast redeemed me, O LORD God of truth" (verse 5). These words are, beyond doubt, the focal point around which all other thoughts in this opening section revolve. David was committing his life into God's keeping. The "breath of life" was given and sustained by God. In faith, David gladly placed himself in God's hands, for, once again, he knew by past experience that God would deliver him. "Thou hast redeemed me, O LORD, thou God of truth" (RV) is a reference initially to God's work of deliverance on so many occasions in David's life. Note also that the words, "God of truth" in this context are not just emphasising the truth of God's words as opposed to error, but show that because God's words are true and have inherent within them the power to perform, He can be trusted implicitly. He is the faithful God.

The words, however, go far beyond David's experiences, and the spirit of Christ in the psalms emerges powerfully at this point; for these are the words quoted by the Lord Jesus in his dying breath, the last words spoken by him in his mortal life. "Father, into thy hands I commend my

189

spirit: and having said thus, he gave up the spirit" (Luke 23:46). Before considering these words, it is helpful to reflect upon one of the temptations of Jesus in the wilderness. He was taken up to the pinnacle of the temple:

"If thou be the Son of God, cast thyself down from hence: for it is written, He shall give his angels charge over thee ... Jesus answering said unto him, It is said, Thou shalt not tempt the Lord thy God."

(Luke 4:9,10,12)

This temptation is often misunderstood. Many think it was a challenge to give to the people of Israel one decisive and indisputable sign that he was the Son of God. The temptation, however, was more subtle than this, and its true nature is revealed in the Old Testament scripture quoted by Jesus to combat the suggestion. The quotation is from Deuteronomy 6: "Ye shall not tempt the LORD your God, as ye tempted him in Massah" (verse 16). The reference here is to the events recorded in Exodus 17. There was no water to drink, and the people chided with Moses, and said, "Give us water that we may drink". Moses responded with the words, "Wherefore do ye tempt the LORD?" But they could not be placated and accused Moses of bringing them out so that they, their children and their cattle should perish in the wilderness (verses 1-3).

In this they tempted the Lord. How? Because they doubted God's word and His power; they asked the question, "Is the LORD amongst us, or not?" (verse 7). They sought to put God to the proof. In effect, they said, 'Show us that you are among us. Prove that you can be trusted, give us evidence, visible and tangible, that you are able to sustain us in this wilderness'.

So the Lord Jesus knew that before him there was the cross and the coldness of the tomb. In his death he would be as still and unknowing as any man. He would be completely in the hand of God, totally dependent on His faithfulness to raise him up on the third day. So the temptation was, 'Put God to the proof; cast yourself down; see if His angels do bear you up. Let God show in some visible and tangible way that His word can be trusted and that He will raise you from the dead if you give yourself as a sacrifice for sin'. The Lord Jesus responded in calm assurance of faith, "Thou shalt not tempt the Lord thy God".

This faith sustained him throughout his ministry and in his final moments on the cross. He committed his spirit unto God. It was an act of supreme faith, a declaration of his total dependence upon his Father, a quiet confidence that God was faithful, and that He would fulfil His word and deliver him out of death. So in a truly remarkable way, the words of Psalm 31 become the last words spoken by the Lord Jesus in his mortal life. "Father, into thy hands I commend my spirit", and the next phrase of the psalm becomes the Lord's next conscious thought when raised up by the power of God: "Thou hast redeemed me, O LORD God of truth."

This application of the words of the psalm to the Lord Jesus has an extension into the life of the believer. Stephen, of course, quoted these words when he saw the Lord Jesus standing by the right hand of God; but there is also a most illuminating quotation of the psalm in Peter's First Epistle that confirms the foregoing interpretation: "Wherefore let them that suffer according to the will of God commit the keeping of their souls to him in well doing, as unto a faithful Creator" (4:19).

So, returning to David in the psalm, he can say in the confidence of his trust in the faithful God, "I hate them that regard lying vanities: but I trust in the LORD" (verse 6, RV). "Vanities" is a word meaning 'false gods', those that are no-gods, empty and worthless. Unlike the living God who is faithful, they delude and deceive those who have regard to them (i.e., pay respect to them in worship). All such, David hates, and dissociates himself from them. He will have no fellowship with them, for God in whom he trusted had proved Himself faithful. "I will be glad and rejoice in thy mercy: for thou hast seen my affliction; thou hast known my soul in adversities: and thou hast not shut me up into the hand of the enemy" (verses 7,8, RV). He had not surrendered to the power of the enemy, just as his greater Son was similarly delivered out of the hand of death, the great enemy.

The section closes with David's acknowledgement, "Thou hast set my feet in a large place" (verse 8, RV – see

Psalm 18:19). The idea is of a wide place where David could move unhindered and unrestricted, freed from the limitations placed on him when persecuted by his enemies. It speaks to us of the freedom from sin and the release from the limitations of our mortal nature, when God will change our vile bodies and fashion them like unto the glorious body of His Son (Philippians 3:21).

To recapitulate briefly: we have shown how verses 1 to 8 form an expression of David's calm assurance, built on the experiences of his early life when he was hunted as a vagabond by Saul. We have indicated how the change of mood in verses 9-18 is a reflection of a new crisis of faith which arose at the time of Absalom's rebellion. Finally (verses 19-24), having been delivered out of his troubles, he reaffirms his faith in God and rejoices in His faithfulness.

Verses 9-18

Once again, in the face of dire calamity, David was called upon to fight the good fight of faith. Once again he was plunged into the midst of the most dreadful adversity and tribulation that was to lead (albeit briefly) to a further period of exile, David recounts the events leading to his flight and tells how he turned to God for his comfort and deliverance.

There is, however, a difference in tone in these verses from that found in the psalms of David's youth. At the time of his flight from Saul, David had rested confidently in the knowledge that he was the Lord's anointed and that God in His faithfulness would, in due time, exalt him to the throne of Israel. There is a freshness, a sense of joy in his fellowship with God, that characterises the psalms of that period – a confidence that enabled David to face all the tribulations and adversity that came upon him with a decisiveness of thought and action that springs out of a life unsullied by iniquity and transgression and the shame and guilt it brings. The matter of Bathsheba and Uriah had changed all that. David knew that God had put away his sin; but it does appear, as we read the psalms that David wrote after this time, that he never really forgave himself. There is a dark and sombre tone to them and we begin to appreciate that the shame and the guilt, and the realisation of what he had done, remained with him and changed the whole character and tenor of his life. We know that mental anguish can cause physical illness and there seems little doubt that, in the period between his sin and Absalom's rebellion, David was a sick man (see for example Psalms 38 and 41).

It has been suggested that David actually suffered from a form of leprosy. We examine this particular idea when considering Psalm 38. Whether this is so or not, there was no doubt that, whatever form his affliction took, David associated it with his sin. The words of verses 9 and 10 reflect this very personal experience that he endured:

"Have mercy upon me, O LORD, for I am in distress: mine eye wasteth away with grief, yea, my soul and my body. For my life is spent with sorrow, and my years with sighing: my strength faileth because of mine iniquity, and my bones are wasted away." (RV)

There is a close resemblance to the language of Psalm 6 (see verses 6,7), which is the first of the so-called "seven penitential Psalms". And this, perhaps, confirms the point about David's sin and the effect it had upon him.

Because of his preoccupation with the effect of his sin upon his life, together with his failing health, David lost something of the vigour and decisiveness characteristic of his early years, and it was this that allowed his enemies to flourish, to plot and to scheme against him, and for Absalom to take advantage of every opportunity to ingratiate himself with the people.

David was aware of their treachery. It was a source of great sorrow to him; but he appears to have resigned himself to such things, acknowledging them in part as a consequence of his sin, and placing his trust in God to deliver him from their wicked devices. For, "My times are in thy hand: deliver me from the hand of mine enemies, and from them that persecute me" (verse 15).

In verses 11 and 12 we have a remarkable insight into human nature:

"Because of all mine adversaries I am become a reproach, yea, unto my neighbours exceedingly, and a fear to mine acquaintance: they that did see me without fled from me." (verse 11, RV)

In other words, because of the powerful forces ranged against him, those who might have been his friends, who perhaps in their hearts were convinced of the righteousness of his cause and who would have supported him in different circumstances, now sought to dissociate themselves from him. *Because* of his adversaries – they were the cause of his plight – he was a reproach to his neighbours. His acquaintances, fearful of being thought his friends, passed, as it were, on the other side of the street, lest they be seen, even in some small way, to be lending comfort and support to this man against whom were arraigned some of the greatest and most powerful men in the land:

"I am forgotten as a dead man out of mind: I am like a broken vessel." (verse 12)

Just as the dead are soon forgotten by all except those who hold them most dear, so he was "forgotten" by them. As far as they were concerned, it was as if he had ceased to exist – like a broken vessel, no longer required, no longer considered useful, but thrust aside to find its place with the refuse.

It is a reflection of how the world operates, of how men will turn away from the weak, suppressing conscience and better instincts, to support the strong and influential, so that their own interests should not be prejudiced; lest, perhaps, they should be numbered with those to whom they show sympathy, and suffer with them the wrath and indignation of those who appear to hold the reins of power. Those who have through their work seen large world organisations operate, in business, industrial and political spheres, will almost certainly recognise this situation described by David.

The question for us is, Can these disturbing traits of human nature manifest themselves (perhaps in a less virulent form) in such a community as ours? Sadly, the answer must be, Yes. Our pioneer brethren warned of the danger of extra-ecclesial committees and societies, because they saw the danger of such assuming an authority that was not theirs.

Individuals must have a strong and independent faith based upon the authority of scripture. We should be particularly careful not to run with the stream automatically. The word of God is our only guide in such matters. Scripture has many examples of this kind of human behaviour. David suffered from it; and centuries later, in a like situation, Jeremiah remembered the words of these psalms and thought upon them for his comfort and consolation:

"For I have heard the defaming of many (RV), fear was on every side: while they took counsel together against me, they devised to take away my life."

(verse 13)

These words were quoted by Jeremiah when he was made a derision daily, mocked and made a reproach because of the word of God that he preached (Jeremiah 20:8). God's word was in his heart, and within his bones as a burning fire, so that he could not stay. Here is an example of inspiration at work. The word within him compelled him to speak:

"For I heard the defaming of many, fear on every side. Report, say they, and we will report it. All my familiars watched for my halting, saying, Peradventure he will be enticed, and we shall prevail against him, and we shall take our revenge on him."   (Jeremiah 20:10)

Jeremiah, like David, had heard the slanderous words spoken against him by his enemies. "Report", they said – tell the authorities about him – and "We will report it", was the response of those who were party to the persecution of God's servant. The word "familiars" means literally 'the men of my peace', those whom he might have expected to stand with him and protect him, but who instead watched him that they might prevail against him.

Such things were true in the lives of David and Jeremiah, but, of course, they were preeminently true in the experience of the Lord Jesus – and we have already noted the Messianic character of the psalm. It is not unreasonable to suppose, in view of the Lord's quotation of these words, that the whole of this psalm was part of his meditation in the face of his enemies.

195

Returning now to David – in the following verses he looks to God for his salvation, repeating in part the prayer of verse 1:

> "But I trusted in thee, O LORD: I said, Thou art my God ... Make thy face to shine upon thy servant: save me for thy mercies' sake. Let me not be ashamed, O LORD; for I have called upon thee: let the wicked be ashamed, and let them be silent in the grave. Let the lying lips be put to silence; which speak grievous things proudly and contemptuously against the righteous."
> (verses 14-18)

Verses 19-24: Conclusion

The point made in our opening comments on this psalm is emphasised by this closing section. It is clearly written after the events had taken place. The threatening clouds (verses 9-18) have passed, and David is able to rejoice in the faithfulness of God who had delivered him out of his troubles:

> "Oh how great is thy goodness, which thou hast laid up for them that fear thee, which thou hast wrought for them that put their trust in thee, before the sons of men!"
> (verse 19, RV)

The Revised Version is almost identical to the AV, except in one small particular that might so easily be missed. It places a comma after the words "them that put their trust in thee", and thereby emphasises the true sense of the text – that what God had wrought for His servants had been done before the sons of men.

In David's case, God had publicly vindicated him. Jeremiah was likewise shown to be faithful by the fulfilment of his prophecies, to the shame of those who opposed him. The Lord Jesus was declared to be the Son of God "by the resurrection from the dead" (Romans 1:4).

Thus all God's servants will be vindicated. In some cases they are "faithful even unto death" and men appear to have triumphed over them. But God's goodness is "laid up", kept in store, as it were, until the time when in His wisdom He manifests it. It is not always shown openly in this life, but it is sure, and "(those) that fear him" will experience it ultimately in their own resurrection and exaltation in God's kingdom.

"Thou shalt hide them in the secret of thy presence from the pride of man: thou shalt keep them secretly in a pavilion from the strife of tongues."   (verse 20)

It is inevitable that themes in the psalms will recur, and we have already commented on the very similar language used in Psalm 27 (verse 5), to which readers are referred. It is perhaps enough to add that the words "secret" and "secretly" in this context mean literally 'something hidden', hence 'a hiding place', a place of security. This thought is continued in the words that follow: "Blessed be the LORD: for he hath shewed me his marvellous kindness in a strong city" (verse 21). The words refer back to the thoughts of the opening words of the psalm, when David had described God as "a house of defence" and "a fortress". As in his earlier life God had delivered him from Saul, so once more God had proved Himself to be faithful, building, as it were, a wall about him which the lying lips that had spoken grievous things proudly and contemptuously against him (verse 18) could not penetrate.

"As for me, I said in mine haste, I am cut off from before thine eyes."   (verse 22, RV)

One's first impression is that the word "haste" refers to a hastiness of spirit which led David, in a mood of impatience, to doubt God's care. A quick look at the concordance, however, dispels this impression, for we find that the word is never used in this sense, but always refers to haste of movement or speedy removal from one place to another (see, for example, Exodus 12:11; Deuteronomy 16:3; 1 Samuel 23:26; 2 Samuel 4:4; 2 Kings 7:15, etc.). Forced to flee, like Israel in her Passover haste, David's response as he fled from the land was, "I am cut off from before thine eyes". We suggest that it is a statement of fact rather than an expression of doubt. As the Lord Jesus was "cut off out of the land of the living" (Isaiah 53:8), so David was removed from his throne, and this was done before God's "eyes" which were ever upon the land, the city and the throne. But David made his prayer to God:

197

"Nevertheless thou heardest the voice of my supplications when I cried unto thee."   (verse 22)

As a result of his experiences, his personal knowledge of the goodness of God, David is able finally to give counsel and exhortation to his fellow believers:

"O love the LORD, all ye his saints: for the LORD preserveth the faithful, and plentifully rewardeth the proud doer. Be of good courage, and he shall strengthen your heart, all ye that hope in the LORD." (verses 23,24)

PSALM 32

THIS psalm is the second of the so-called penitential psalms, and with Psalm 51 gives us the most graphic insight into the innermost thoughts of David in the greatest spiritual crisis of his life when, following his sin in the matter of Bathsheba and Uriah, he went through an agony of spirit that can only be appreciated by those who in some measure have trodden the same path.

Psalm 51 contains David's confession and prayer for forgiveness, and seems therefore to have been composed at the very heart of the crisis, when David was finally convicted of the enormity of his sin. Interestingly, following this confession and plea for forgiveness, David says, "Then will I teach transgressors thy ways; and sinners shall be converted unto thee" (Psalm 51:13).

Psalm 32 appears to have been written sometime after the incident. While the first five verses contain David's reflections upon his experiences at that time, the remainder of the psalm is directed to instructing others how they might learn from his sin and God's forgiveness. Thus Psalm 32 is the first of thirteen psalms that carry the inscription "Maschil", literally, 'for instruction'; verse 8 of the psalm should be noted, where the root of the Hebrew word occurs: "I will *instruct* thee and teach thee in the way which thou shalt go."

As a background to both psalms, Nathan's dialogue with David is most illuminating: "Thou art the man"; "I have sinned"; "the LORD hath put away thy sin." It might be noted also that Psalm 32 is the second psalm to begin with the word "Blessed" – literally, 'Oh, the happiness of the man'. The first is Psalm 1, and the two psalms complement each other in a most marvellous way, for the first speaks of the happiness of the perfect man – *The Man*, the Lord Jesus Christ – who "walketh not in the

199

counsel of the ungodly, nor standeth in the way of sinners, nor sitteth in the seat of the scornful" (verse 1), and who consequently knows no shame or guilt, but delights continually in the law of the Lord (verse 2).

Psalm 32, however, takes us into the very shame and degradation of the sinner. It then emphasises the joy that can be his also through the grace and mercy of God, who, because of the sinner's contrition and confession, takes away his sin, so that he too might experience the happiness that belongs essentially to the man who has unbroken fellowship with God. It is here, by implication, that we catch the Messianic significance of the psalm; for the non-imputation of sin, or, put positively, the imputation of righteousness, is one of the great scriptural themes connected with the salvation of men, and the Apostle Paul quotes these words of David in his Epistle to the Romans:

"For what saith the scripture? Abraham believed God, and it was counted unto him for righteousness. Now to him that worketh is the reward not reckoned of grace, but of debt. But to him that worketh not, but believeth on him that justifieth the ungodly, his faith is counted for righteousness. Even as David also describeth the blessedness of the man, unto whom God imputeth righteousness without works, saying, Blessed are they whose iniquities are forgiven, and whose sins are covered. Blessed is the man to whom the Lord will not impute sin." (Romans 4:3-8)

We have commented before on the connection of the word "blessed" with God's covenant with Abraham. The connection is established in a most emphatic way in the verses from Romans, and the working out of the principles involved in relation to the Lord Jesus Christ are seen in the latter part of the chapter:

"Now it was not written for his sake alone, that it was imputed to him; but for us also ... if we believe on him that raised up Jesus our Lord from the dead; who was delivered for our offences, and was raised again for our justification." (verses 23-25)

The contrast between Psalm 1 and Psalm 32 can be seen further in the manner in which the Perfect Man is likened to a "tree planted by the rivers of water, that bringeth forth his fruit in his season; his leaf also shall not wither; and whatsoever he doeth shall prosper" (verse 3). Whereas David, shutting up his sin within, seeking to hide the shame and guilt, first speaks of the psychological and physical effects this had upon him: "My bones waxed old through my roaring all the day long. For day and night thy hand was heavy upon me", and then, with a change of figure, "My moisture (lit. 'my sap') is turned into the drought of summer" (verses 3 and 4). He was like a tree deprived of the rivers of water, his life-giving juices dried up by the scorching heat of the summer sun.

David uses three words to describe the ways in which men break God's law: transgression, sin and iniquity. They are evidently meant to encompass every kind of human wickedness. The Hebrew words mean literally:

transgression –	rebellion, to take away from
sin –	'a coming short of the mark', i.e., a deflection from an aim, not doing that which ought to be done (see use of the word in a different sense in Judges 20:16)
iniquity –	depravity or moral perversity

As there are three words for sin, so also there are three descriptions of God's response:

Transgressions are forgiven, and the word means literally 'to lift up and take away' (Kay, *Psalms with Notes*). It is interesting to note that the very same word is used to describe the scapegoat in Leviticus 16: "and the goat shall bear upon him all their iniquities" (verse 22). Thus the word carries all the associations of atonement.

Sins are *covered*, and though the basic meaning of the word is 'to hide', we must avoid thinking of the sins as remaining under the cover. When God forgives, the sins are as though they had never been. In reality the covering is righteousness imputed by God, and this truth is described in the third instance.

"The LORD *imputeth not iniquity*". We have already commented upon the quotation of these words in

201

Romans 4. It is important to remember, however, that the grounds upon which righteousness is imputed, whereby a man is not reckoned by God to be a sinner, although manifestly he is – is by faith. Abraham *believed* God, and it was counted to him for righteousness (Genesis 15:5,6).

Thus an important principle emerges in relation to the forgiveness of sin. "If we confess our sins, he is faithful and just to forgive us our sins, and to cleanse us from all unrighteousness" (1 John 1:9). But we must ask in faith; we must believe that God is faithful and that He will forgive us: there is no room for doubt, but through our Lord Jesus Christ we must "come boldly unto the throne of grace" (Hebrews 4:16). There must, of course, be no presumption on our part, and David shows how this is excluded from the heart of the man who knows the happiness of forgiveness, for "in (his) spirit there is no guile" (verse 2). He comes with a disposition that is frank and open. There is no attempt to hide his sin or excuse himself, but there is an absolute sincerity. He does not seek to deceive himself or God.

In David's experience there had been a period of approximately eight months when this spirit had been absent. He had kept silent about his sin, with devastating consequences for himself (verses 3,4). But following Nathan's confrontation, and with his heart and mind surely already prepared, he says,

"I acknowledged my sin unto thee, and mine iniquity have I not hid. I said, I will confess my transgressions unto the LORD; and thou forgavest the iniquity of my sin." (verse 5)

Once again great truths are emphasised. There is a remarkable paradox, for in the Hebrew the verb translated "I have not hid" is the same as that rendered "covered" in verse 1. In other words, when we seek to hide our sins there is no escape from the shame and guilt that assails our conscience. Yet when we acknowledge our sins and come with open and contrite heart before God, then He hides it and takes it away.

In David's experience the result of his confession was "*Thou* forgavest". In the Hebrew text there is a tremendous emphasis upon the word 'thou' that cannot be conveyed by the translation. To demonstrate the emphasis, some have suggested that the word should be repeated: "Thou – thou forgavest", thus indicating the sense of wonder and awe that David felt that God should have forgiven *his* sin which had been so great. This sense of wonder is something that should be a part of the common experience of us all when we contemplate what God in His love has done for us through the Lord Jesus Christ.

Before leaving this section of the psalm, we might note that the three words for sin used by David are drawn from the declaration of God's name in Exodus 34:

"Keeping mercy for thousands, forgiving iniquity and transgression and sin." (verse 7)

It is a further indication of David's understanding of all that was involved in the name of God, and how the outworking of all that name stood for had resulted in this happiness that he now knew, for God had restored unto him the joy of His salvation (Psalm 51:12).

David now turns to the application of his experience to others. "For this (cause) shall every one that is godly pray unto thee in a time when thou mayest be found" (verse 6). There is an ambiguity about the Hebrew in the final phrase that is reflected in the margin of the AV, which says "in a time of finding". Perhaps there is design in the ambiguity, for in the experience of David the time of finding, when God discovered and laid bare his sin, was also, because of his ready response, the time when for him God could be found. Everyone who is godly will appreciate this truth, for it is when we are convicted in our hearts because of our waywardness, when in our distress we turn to God, seeking for grace, that God is closest to us. It is the time when He may be found, and it behoves us all "to seek the LORD while he may be found, call upon him while he is near" (Isaiah 55:6).

The Hebrew for "godly" is the word *chasid*. It has been pointed out that its primary meaning is 'faithfulness to the covenant', or again it has been described as 'covenant love'. This is the fidelity that God looks for in those who are brought into covenant relationship with Him. Later in the psalm the same word occurs in a slightly variant form – *chesed*, translated "mercy" in verse 10. This time, while retaining the same essential meaning, it describes God's love and faithfulness to man, for those who come within the bonds of the covenant will find that He will never fail them, but His "mercy shall compass him about".

The man who seeks God while He may be found, who is true to his covenant relationship with God, will find that "surely in the floods of great waters they shall not come nigh unto him" (verse 6). The reference is to the summer storms which fall with such ferocity that the deluge can turn every dried-up river into a raging torrent that can sweep all before it. It was this figure that was behind the Lord's parable of the houses built upon sand and rock (Matthew 7:24-28). The godly will not fall in the day of calamity, for God will lift him up as upon a rock, so that the waters will not come nigh him. So David, appropriating the language of verse 6, addresses his prayer to God, in which he recognises, in one of the recurring themes of the psalm, that "thou art my hiding place; thou shalt preserve me from trouble; thou shalt compass me about with songs of deliverance" (verse 7).

There is some doubt in verse 8 as to whether the words are spoken by David in fulfilment of Psalm 51:13, or by God Himself. Certainly the words seem more applicable to the voice of God; but we must remember that David was a prophet and could well have spoken these words on God's behalf:

> "I will instruct thee and teach thee in the way which thou shalt go: I will counsel thee with mine eye upon thee." (verse 8, RV)

The reference is to one of the principal methods by which God instructs and teaches. It is through the circumstances of life, for always God's eye is upon His servants, His providential care surrounds them. The next psalm (33) takes up the theme: "Behold, the eye of the LORD is upon them that fear him, upon them that hope in his mercy" (verse 18). We are taught through the hand of God in our lives, operating in conjunction with His word.

The psalm has been concerned with sin and its forgiveness. Spiritual calamities like that which overtook

David can be used by God to deepen our understanding of His character. "All things work together for good to them that love God, to them who are the called according to his purpose" (Romans 8:28).

In this knowledge we are exhorted: "Be ye not as the horse, or as the mule, which have no understanding: whose mouth must be held in with bit and bridle, lest they come near unto thee" (verse 9). Animals have no reason, but must be controlled by bit and bridle. They must learn by force to submit to man's will. In the spirit of God's guidance and instruction the godly must willingly and freely submit to His control. Not to do so is to become like the beasts; those who refuse to submit willingly will be forced ultimately to recognise the supremacy of God and the inevitability of His judgement on those who turn away from Him, for "many sorrows shall be to the wicked: but he that trusteth in the LORD, mercy shall compass him about" (verse 10).

We have commented already on the loving-kindness of the Lord towards the righteous. As for the wicked, they will experience many sorrows. The word rendered "sorrow" is a strong word in the Hebrew. It does not convey the idea of grief or tears alone, but means 'pain', 'suffering'. In fact, this was the meaning of the old English word 'sorrows'.

This is the ultimate fate of the disobedient, the unrepentant sinner who finds pleasure in transgression, sin and iniquity. For the righteous, however, who have known God's grace, there is the joy of sins forgiven, the gladness of fellowship with God and the assurance that, encircled by His love, He will bring them at last into His kingdom. Therefore:

"Be glad in the LORD, and rejoice, ye righteous: and shout for joy, all ye that are upright in heart."

(verse 11)

PSALM 33

IN what is commonly regarded as the First Book of the Psalms (1-41), only Psalms 1 and 33 are not specifically attributed to David. We are confident, however, that both were written by the "Sweet Psalmist of Israel" and, in the psalm under consideration, this is manifest by the close link which it has with the preceding psalm.

It will be recalled that Psalm 32 was connected historically with David's sin in the matter of Bathsheba and Uriah the Hittite, but the use made of the psalm by the Apostle Paul in the Epistle to the Romans (4:6-8) is an indication that the psalm transcends David's personal experience and goes to the heart of God's work of salvation among men. It speaks of justification by faith, and it is to those who have been brought into a covenant relationship with God by this means that Psalm 33 speaks.

The connection between the two psalms is established by a comparison of the last verse of Psalm 32 with the first verse of Psalm 33:

"Be glad in the LORD, and rejoice, ye righteous: and shout for joy, all ye that are upright in heart."   (32:11)

"Rejoice in the LORD, O ye righteous: for praise is comely for the upright."   (33:1)

Note that the same Hebrew word is translated "shout for joy" in Psalm 32 and "rejoice" in Psalm 33; and the repetition of the language is an indication that Psalm 33 begins at that point where Psalm 32 ended.

To understand the connection better, and the way in which the message is developed, a brief consideration of the structure of Psalm 33 is necessary, noting in particular that the call to praise the Lord in verses 1-3 is directed to the "righteous" and the "upright", that is, to those who stand in a special relationship with God because they have followed the principles emphasised in Psalm 32. As there is an introductory call to praise the Lord (verses 1-3), so also there is a concluding declaration of faith and trust and a call to God to fulfil His word by bringing all the hopes of the righteous to fruition (verses 20-22).

The central section of the psalm is divided into two parts, separated by what is perhaps the key that unlocks the significance of the song as a whole:

> "Blessed is the nation whose God is the LORD; and the people whom he hath chosen for his own inheritance."
>
> (verse 12)

David's meditation revolves round this fact, and the two sections it divides may be summarised as follows. In verses 4 to 11 there is a declaration of God's moral excellence and of the faithfulness of His word (verses 4,5), followed by a demonstration of the power of that word seen in God's creative acts (verses 6-9) which stand as an indication of His sovereignty and power over all nations (verses 10,11). In the second section, this insight into the nature and character of God is then brought to bear in a practical way upon the manner in which His providential care is exercised on behalf of His people (verses 13-19).

Praise the Lord

To rejoice in the Lord in response to the exhortation of David is something that only those who have known the blessedness (lit. 'happiness') of forgiveness can do, for praise is only "comely" (lit. 'seemly') for the upright (verse 1). Although it is an essential aspect of the spiritual life of the righteous, it must nevertheless be a spontaneous reaction, springing from an appreciation of all that God has done.

Their call was to:

> "Give thanks unto the LORD with harp: sing praises unto him with the psaltery of ten strings."
>
> (verse 2, RV)

The reference to musical instruments is a reminder to us of the prominent place that music and singing had in the worship of Israel (see 1 Chronicles 23:5; 25:1-8). There is in the human spirit that which responds most readily to this faculty God has given us, and we are to use it, as indeed every aspect of our personality, in praise and

207

worship. The Apostle Paul comments: "Speaking to yourselves in psalms and hymns and spiritual songs, singing and making melody in your heart to the Lord" (Ephesians 5:19). Notice that our singing is not only praise directly to God, but it also involves "speaking to ourselves", that is, singing of those things that God has done and will do, that by the remembrance of them in song and melody we might find encouragement and have hearts that are full of "joy in the Lord".

The exhortation to "sing unto (the LORD) a new song" (verse 3) is an indication that it is a song of redemption (see Psalm 40:3; 96:1; Revelation 5:9 etc.), and befits the connection with the forgiveness of sin which is the theme of Psalm 32.

Faithfulness, Omnipotence and Sovereignty of God

For all these attributes God is worthy to be praised. In the moral sphere His word is "right" (from a root meaning 'straight' or 'direct'). In other words, it is sure and steadfast; there is nothing variable or uncertain about it, for it is totally reliable. Because of the trustworthy nature of His word, "all his work is done in faithfulness" (verse 4, RV). The words of the psalm are drawn from the book of Deuteronomy (32:4), and the close connection between the word of God and the work of God first emphasised here should be noted, for it recurs in the psalm on two occasions (verses 6,9).

There is an echo of this same connection in the next words of the psalm: "He loveth righteousness and judgment" (verse 5), for righteousness is, as it were, the expression of the principles which underlie all God's works, whereas judgement is the manifestation of that righteousness in actions. Through these qualities, "the earth is full of the goodness of the LORD" or the "steadfast love of the LORD" (RSV). It is the Hebrew word *chesed*, on which we have previously commented (see chapter on Psalm 32). The same word is used again in verses 18 and 22 of Psalm 33, where it is rendered "mercy", and the suggested meaning of 'covenant love' adds force to the connection between this and the previous psalm.

These moral qualities in which the righteous rejoice have emphasised the link between God's word and His work. This thought is now extended and illustrated by the hand of God in creation:

"By the word of the LORD were the heavens made; and all the host of them by the breath of his mouth. He gathereth the waters of the sea together as an heap: he layeth up the depth (RV, deeps) in storehouses. Let all the earth fear the LORD: let all the inhabitants of the world stand in awe of him. For he spake, and it was done; he commanded, and it stood fast."   (verses 6-9)

The words are a commentary on the record of Genesis 1, when "the Spirit (*ruach*) of God moved upon the face of the waters. And God said, Let there be light: and there was light" (verses 2,3). God uttered His voice, and it was done. His word was with power. Again, there is another association of words that is helpful in our understanding of scripture, for "all the host of them (were made) by the breath (*ruach*) of his mouth". The connection between the word of God and the Spirit of God is important, for when God utters His voice that Spirit goes forth with power to accomplish His purpose. Later, scripture develops the association in its relationship to the written word of God.

"All scripture is given by inspiration of God" (2 Timothy 3:16). Literally, this means 'all scripture is God-breathed'. (See David's words in 2 Samuel 23:1-3 for an illustration of inspiration in action.) Such examples of the use of these words in scripture give credence and authority to the use of the expression 'Spirit Word', to which some who wish to promulgate false views about the work of the Spirit have taken exception.

Verse 7 presents us with further examples of the way in which God utters His voice and it is done: "He gathereth the waters of the sea together as an heap" is a clear reference to two of God's redemptive acts: first, the dividing of the sea for Israel to pass over, and secondly, the parting of the River Jordan for a similar purpose. Strong's Concordance indicates that the Hebrew word rendered "heaps" means 'a heap in the sense of piling up like a great wave', and the only other occurrences of the word are in Exodus 15:8 and Psalm 78:13 in relation to the dividing of the sea, and Joshua 3:13,16 in connection with the parting of the Jordan. The passage in Exodus is particularly interesting as it refers to this act being performed by the breath (*ruach*) of God's nostrils.

The latter half of verse 7, however, presents us with a further example of the power of God's word, for "he layeth up the depth in storehouses", and this surely is a reference to Noah's flood when "all the fountains of the great deep were broken up" (Genesis 7:11). It seems that these words of Psalm 33 form the basis for Peter's message in his second epistle:

"For this they willingly are ignorant of, that *by the word of God* the heavens were of old, and the earth standing out of the water and in the water (creation): *whereby* (i.e. by the word of God) the world that then was, being overflowed with water, perished (the flood): but the heavens and the earth, which are now, *by the same word* are kept in store, reserved unto fire against the day of judgment and perdition of ungodly men."

(2 Peter 3:5-7)

Note also the emphasis on the faithfulness of God who is "not slack concerning his promise" (verse 9).

There is good reason, then, for the earth to fear and all the inhabitants of the world to "stand in awe of him. For *he* spake, and it was done; *he* commanded, and it stood fast" (Psalm 33:8,9). In Hebrew the word "he" is emphatic, to emphasise the supremacy and sovereignty of God, which is now demonstrated by the manner in which He rules in the kingdom of men:

"The LORD bringeth the counsel of the heathen to nought: he maketh the devices of the people of none effect. The counsel of the LORD standeth for ever, the thoughts of his heart to all generations." (verses 10,11)

The AV partly obscures the parallelism between verses 10 and 11, where the counsels of the nations and the thoughts of the people are contrasted with the counsels of Yahweh and the thoughts of His heart.

Like His work in creation, God's counsel, His purpose, stands fast. Nothing that man can do can frustrate it or prevent its fulfilment. Throughout history, men have

210

sought to thwart the purpose of God. The words are reminiscent of Psalm 2:

"Why do the heathen rage, and the people imagine a vain thing? The kings of the earth set themselves, and the rulers take counsel together, against the LORD, and against his anointed … He that sitteth in the heavens shall laugh: the LORD shall have them in derision."
(verses 1,2,4)

The psalm has a recurring fulfilment. Written first when men sought to prevent Solomon ascending the throne, quoted by Hezekiah (Isaiah 37:22,28,29) when faced by the host of Sennacherib, and by the apostles when they thought how men had conspired to frustrate the purpose of God in crucifying His Son, but had done only what His hand and counsel had determined before to be done (Acts 4:25-28). There remain further fulfilments of the words in the day of the Lord's coming and in the final rebellion at the end of the Millennium.

Israel's Privileged Position

"Blessed is the nation whose God is the LORD; and the people whom he hath chosen for his own inheritance." (verse 12)

In our introductory remarks we described this verse as the key to our understanding of the psalm. We have demonstrated in the previous verses the power of God's word, the utter inability of man to frustrate His purpose and consequently the faithfulness of the words He has spoken. These things are a source of great encouragement to those who put their trust in Him. They fill the hearts of those who are privileged to call Him their God with great joy.

In verses 10 and 11 the psalmist's thoughts were directed to God's sovereignty over the nations, for He reigns in the kingdom of men and these are the thoughts that lead to the declaration of verse 12. The only nation which could say that Yahweh was their God was Israel. So the unchanging nature of God's counsel and His control over the nations of the earth is seen to revolve around Israel, the people whom He chose for His inheritance.

This is declared most clearly in Deuteronomy 32:

211

"When the most High divided to the nations their inheritance, when he separated the sons of Adam, he set the bounds of the people according to the number of the children of Israel."   (verse 8)

In other words, everything that God did in His work amongst the nations was done with Israel in mind. They were to be His witnesses (Isaiah 43:10), for it was through them that God would carry out His purpose in the earth to its ultimate completion. The fact that Israel were God's chosen people is often misunderstood, and sometimes its implications not always appreciated, even by some who have espoused "the hope of Israel".

Up to the time when God called Abram, God had dealt with men on an individual basis. There were rules of worship to be observed, principles to be acknowledged, both intellectually and practically, by those who would seek God – but there were no national barriers. During this epoch of human history, however, men twice proved themselves to be unworthy of this privilege. The Flood and the events surrounding the Tower of Babel demonstrate how, but for God's intervention, the light of the Truth could have been extinguished in the earth. Thus God determined to change the manner of His dealings with men. No longer would He deal with men on an individual basis, but He would choose one nation through which He would reveal Himself and in which He would carry forward His purpose in the earth. Where was such a nation to be found? There was none, so God made one. He created the nation of Israel (Isaiah 43:1) by a series of miraculous events (e.g., the birth of Isaac), the working of His providential hand (e.g., Joseph carried into Egypt) and the manifestation in power and great might of His outstretched arm to deliver.

As witnesses, Israel were intended to be "a kingdom of priests, and an holy nation" (Exodus 19:6). A priest is one who shows God to men and brings men to God, and this should have been Israel's role in the midst of the nations. An insight into one aspect of their responsibility in this direction is seen in Deuteronomy 4:

"Behold, I have taught you statutes and judgments … Keep therefore and do them; for this is your wisdom and

212

your understanding in the sight of the nations, which shall hear all these statutes, and say, Surely this great nation is a wise and understanding people. For what nation is there so great, who hath God so nigh unto them, as the LORD our God is in all things that we call upon him for?" (verses 5-7)

Interestingly, the next verse in Deuteronomy 32 (following the emphasis upon the manner in which all God's work amongst the nations had Israel in mind) says, "For the LORD's portion is his people; Jacob is the lot of his inheritance" (verse 9).

There are passages that speak of God as the inheritance of His people (see Psalm 16:5,6; Lamentations 3:22-24; Psalm 73:26). In other words, God was their supreme joy, their possession, valued above all else that life had to offer. The relationship was, however, reciprocal, for God's purpose in His people made them His own possession (see also Deuteronomy 4:20; 9:29). The figure of the inheritance described the relationship between them, and the ultimate joy that both parties will find in union in the ultimate fulfilment of God's purpose, when God will be all in all (1 Corinthians 15:28).

The prophet Jeremiah brings both aspects together:

"The portion of Jacob is not like them: for he is the former of all things; and Israel is the rod of his inheritance: the LORD of hosts is his name." (10:16)

This is not the place to follow the outworking of God's purpose with Israel; but we know her place in that purpose remains secure, for the gifts and calling of God are without repentance.

For the moment, God has cast away His people; but this has been the means of salvation being offered to the Gentiles. Thus the Old Testament ideas associated with inheritance are applied to those who believe in the Lord Jesus Christ, for we too in Christ have been made a heritage of God: "In whom also we have obtained an inheritance, being predestinated according to the purpose of him who worketh all things after the counsel of his own will" (Ephesians 1:11). Significantly, the Revised Version reads: "In whom also we were made a heritage." So the possibility of either interpretation is present in the words.

213

Could there be an intentional ambiguity, in order to embrace both aspects of the relationship?

God's Care for His People

The sovereignty and supremacy of God mentioned in verses 8 to 11 is now emphasised more particularly, showing how God is in absolute control of all human activity and is able, through His providential hand, to fashion human hearts and to override all men's decisions and intentions (verse 13-15). Strong's Concordance indicates that the word rendered "fashioneth" means 'to mould; to squeeze into shape'. It is particularly associated with the work of the potter, and is thus related to other passages of scripture that use the potter's craft to describe how God works with men (see Isaiah 29:16; Jeremiah 18:1-6; 19:1,11; Romans 9:20-23 etc.).

Many find difficulty with this concept, imagining that God compels men to act against their will, or fashions them according to His will so that they cannot be held responsible for what they are. This, of course, is contrary to the way in which God works in the lives of men. God does not compel men to do evil or to act in ways that are inconsistent with their own characters. The classic example is Israel in the passage in Jeremiah 18 referred to above. It is clear that the fault lies in the clay, for Israel had said, "We will walk after our own devices, and we will every one do the imagination of his evil heart" (verse 12). As the potter moulds the clay, so God, who knows the hearts of all men, can bring pressures to bear, subtle influences in the interplay of human relationships that will cause the real man to show himself, causing him to act in the manner for which God raised him up and brought him to a particular moment in time or place in history, that he might do what God's hand and counsel determined before to be done.

The impotence of man to save himself is emphasised:

"There is no king saved by the multitude of an host: a mighty man is not delivered by much strength. An horse is a vain thing for safety: neither shall he deliver any by his great strength."　　　　(Psalm 33:16,17)

214

Perhaps the reference here is drawn from the destruction of Pharaoh's host in the Red Sea, referred to earlier (verse 7). In any event, if one wished to express the symbol of human might and power in those days, then the horse was representative of it. In military terms, it spoke of cavalry and chariots which struck fear into the hearts of those who faced them in battle. But those who put their trust in God would know that, contrasted with His power, these symbols of human might and greatness were in reality illusory. They were a vain thing – empty, a delusion – no strength or power at all when compared with the might of Israel's God; for though "the horse (be) prepared against the day of battle ... safety is of the LORD" (Proverbs 21:31).

So Elisha could say of Elijah, through whom God's power had been manifested: "My father, my father, the chariot of Israel, and the horsemen thereof" (2 Kings 2:12), for the eye of the Lord was upon them that feared Him, and that hoped in His mercy to deliver them even from death and famine (Psalm 33:18,19).

Conclusion

As the psalm opened with a call to praise God, so now, having considered the work of God and His fidelity towards those who put their trust in Him, there is a final declaration of faith and a further call upon Yahweh to extend His mercy towards His people:

"Our soul waiteth for the LORD: he is our help and our shield. For our heart shall rejoice in him, because we have trusted in his holy name. Let thy mercy, O LORD, be upon us, according as we hope in thee."

(verses 20-22)

In these words is expressed the hope of faithful men in all ages. They wait for the Lord. Their spirit is exemplified in the words of Jacob as he blessed his sons shortly before his death: "I have waited for thy salvation, O LORD" (Genesis 49:18). All such can rejoice in Him, for they have known His name and put their trust in those things that were encompassed within it. This is the only true and lasting joy. It surpasses all human forms of happiness, which are at best fleeting and transitory, for 'all to death in this world hasteth, riches vanish, beauty wasteth'.

The final thought of the psalm expresses a great truth and contains a solemn warning. Our relationship with God is reciprocal. It is those who hunger and thirst after righteousness who will be filled. It is those who wait for God who will receive His salvation. He will respond in like measure to that which we long and hope for. His mercy (i.e., loving-kindness, covenant love) will be extended unto us *according* to the manner in which we hope in Him.

If we do not desire God's salvation and truly long for His kingdom to come, then there is no waiting to be satisfied, there is no hope to be fulfilled, for we already have our reward in this life.

PSALM 34

I T seems appropriate at this juncture in our study of the psalms to recapitulate on the question of alphabetical psalms. We have already offered some comments in our study of Psalms 9, 10 and 25. In the case of this last psalm, we drew attention to certain peculiarities that it had in common with Psalm 34, and deferred consideration until such time as we reached that psalm. We have now done so; hence the need to consider again this feature of a number of the psalms.

Alphabetical Psalms

Alphabetical psalms are structured upon the twenty-two letters of the Hebrew alphabet. That is, each stanza or section of the psalm begins with a letter of the Hebrew alphabet, in succession. The most perfect example is Psalm 119. Other examples have certain peculiarities, such as breaks in the sequence (see Psalms 9 and 10) and the omission of a letter or letters, and sometimes the repetition of another letter to make up the total to twenty-two.

As we have shown in our consideration of Psalm 25, that psalm, together with Psalm 34, falls into this latter category.

Most commentators on the psalms assume that the use of the alphabet is intended as an aid to memory. This may have some truth in it; but it does not account for the irregular use of the alphabet discussed when dealing with Psalms 9 and 10, the omission of the sixth letter, *vau*, and the repetition of another letter, *pe*, at the conclusion both of Psalm 25 and 34.

As a general comment, we would point out that the letters of the Hebrew alphabet are the basis of the language through which, under the old covenant, God was

217

pleased to make Himself and His purpose known to men. Herein, we suggest, lies the key to understanding this feature of the psalms, and variations from the perfect symmetry (of Psalm 119, for example) must have some relevance to this fact. When considering Psalms 9 and 10, we offered some suggestions regarding the break in the alphabetical sequence in those cases. Whether we came to the right conclusion or not, readers must judge for themselves. But of this we are confident: there is purpose and design behind the variations and if we cannot discover what that is, it is due to our own lack of spiritual perception and not confusion on the part of the writer, or copyists' errors – which is another of the possibilities commentators blindly trot out. Psalms 25 and 34, having the same variations, are in fact strong evidence for design; and we now turn to consider the question in relation to those two songs.

First of all, it should be noticed that both psalms have the same theme, for they speak of the providential hand of God at work in the life of His servants. This has been shown in our study of Psalm 25, and will become evident as we progress in our consideration of Psalm 34.

Another important factor is that each letter of the Hebrew alphabet has its own meaning. Thus the first two letters, *aleph* and *beth*, mean 'an ox' and 'a house' respectively. The sixth letter, *vau*, which is omitted from this sequence, "denotes 'a nail' ... to this even the modern form of the letter (ו) bears a resemblance" (Gesenius, Hebrew-Chaldee Lexicon). When we think of the Lord Jesus Christ and his crucifixion, the idea of a nail takes on an immediate significance. Perhaps we could look at the section of Psalm 119 which appears under this letter, to reinforce this point. It contains words which are particularly relevant to one who was obedient even unto the death of the cross:

> "Let thy mercies come also unto me, O LORD, even thy salvation, according to thy word ... My hands also will I lift up unto thy commandments, which I have loved."
>
> (verses 41,48)

The repetition of the letter *pe* in the last section of Psalms 25 and 34 might lead us to look at the meaning of that letter for a solution. It means 'mouth', but we believe that this meaning does not give the real answer to the problem. What emerges upon further investigation is that the last stanzas in the two psalms start not only with the same letter, but with the same word. That word is 'redeem', and this, linked with the 'nail' and crucifixion, must surely present us with the most exciting possibilities.

How then can we apply these facts? The alphabetical symmetry of the psalms speaks of the perfection of God's work in the lives of the believers. Providentially, He works for their salvation. All His acts are the result of the divine fiat. He utters His voice, and it is done. The providential work of God is only effective, however, because of the open and manifest way in which, through His Son, He has destroyed the power of sin. Thus the breaking of the sequence by the omission of the letter *vau* demonstrates that providence alone was not enough, for it needed the redemptive act of sacrifice for sin.

Historical Background

The historical information at the head of the psalm states: "A Psalm of David, when he changed his behaviour before Abimelech; who drove him away, and he departed." The margin of the AV substitutes the name Achish for Abimelech, and we have little difficulty in identifying the event referred to, for it is the occasion when David feigned madness before the Philistine king of Gath (1 Samuel 21:10-15). The problem which many find is the use of the name Abimelech instead of Achish, and what they perceive to be the totally unrelated nature of the historical information to the substance of the psalm.

First, with regard to the use of Abimelech, it is almost certainly a title and not a proper name. The word means literally 'king-father', and one can appreciate how a ruler would delight in such a designation describing his relationship to his people (see also Genesis 20:2; 21:22; 26:1). Gesenius (Hebrew-Chaldee Lexicon) draws attention to a similar practice among the Persians, who called their kings Padishah (father, king).

219

As far as the context of the psalm is concerned, we need to look more closely at the events leading up to David's flight to Gath and the outcome of it. The chapter already referred to (1 Samuel 21) contains the clue to the solution. David came to Abimelech the priest at Nob. Abimelech gave to David of the shewbread to appease his hunger, and when David enquired if there were weapons available, the priest also gave him the sword of Goliath of Gath. The key to the sad chain of events which arose out of this incident is in verse 7:

> "Now a certain man of the servants of Saul was there that day, detained before the LORD; and his name was Doeg, an Edomite, the chiefest of the herdmen that belonged to Saul."

Now at this juncture we are told no more, but the information is clearly given as an indication of why David arose and fled that day (verse 10).

This is verified by the subsequent record in the 22nd chapter, for Doeg reported the events at Nob to Saul, and when the king's servants refused to slay the priests of the Lord, Doeg willingly complied with the king's request and slew eighty-five men who wore the linen ephod (verses 17,18). His cruelty did not stop there, for he also smote Nob, the city of the priests, killing men, women and children (verse 19). Note that the key figure is Doeg an Edomite, for a close examination of the context of Psalm 34 reveals that David's meditation had revolved around the history of Jacob and his brother Esau, the father of the Edomites.

If the psalm is read with Jacob in mind, one can readily appreciate how true the language is of his experiences also. But there are, of course, verbal links that establish the point:

1. "The angel of the LORD encampeth round about them that fear him, and delivereth them" (verse 7). This is a clear reference to the occasion when Jacob, returning from Padan Aram, in fear of his brother Esau, was met by the angels of God. When Jacob saw them he said, "This is God's host: and he called the name of that place Mahanaim" (Genesis 32:1,2). The word "Mahanaim" means 'the two camps', for there

was Jacob's camp, and encircling them, protecting them, encamped around them, were the angels of God.

2. Jacob is probably the best example in scripture of the angels of God working in the life of a believer. When he blessed the sons of Joseph, he said, "God, before whom my fathers Abraham and Isaac did walk, the God which fed me all my life long unto this day, the Angel which redeemed me from all evil, bless the lads" (Genesis 48:15,16). Psalm 34 reflects the thoughts, for verse 8 continues, "O taste and see that the LORD is good".

3. When Jacob reminded God of the promises that He had made to him (Genesis 28:13-15), he said, "... and thou saidst, I will surely do thee good, and make thy seed as the sand of the sea" (Genesis 32:12). So David writes, "What man is he that desireth life, and loveth many days, that he may see good? Keep thy tongue from evil, and thy lips from speaking guile" (verses 12,13). Almost without exception, references to speaking guile in the psalms are references to the life of Jacob. There is confirmation in the words of the Lord himself, spoken concerning Nathanael: "Behold an Israelite indeed, in whom is no guile!" (John 1:47).

4. When Jacob wrestled with the angel, he "called the name of the place Peniel: for I have seen God face to face, and my life is preserved" (Genesis 32:30). Also, he halted upon his thigh, for the angel touched the hollow of Jacob's thigh and his thigh was out of joint (verse 25). There are several references to the face of God in Psalm 34: "They looked unto him, and were lightened (RSV, 'radiant'): and their faces were not ashamed" (verse 5); "The face of the LORD is against them that do evil" (verse 16). Perhaps on a more tenuous level we might wonder whether the words of verse 20 are a contrast to the injury to Jacob's thigh: "He keepeth all his bones: not one of them is broken".

5. Finally, the words of verse 14 are an accurate reflection of Jacob's approach to Esau on his return to the promised land: "Depart from evil, and do good; seek peace, and pursue it."

221

If there be any remaining doubt about the references in the psalm to Jacob, the New Testament provides final confirmation, for it quotes Psalm 34 in a section of Hebrews 12 where we have a sustained emphasis upon Jacob and Esau:

"Wherefore lift up the hands which hang down, and the feeble knees (Jacob wrestling with the angel!); and make straight paths for your feet, lest that which is lame be turned out of the way (Jacob halted on his thigh); but let it rather be healed. Follow peace with all men (cited from Psalm 34:14), and holiness, without which no man shall see the Lord ('I have seen God face to face' – Genesis 32:30) … lest there be any fornicator, or profane person, as Esau, who for one morsel of meat sold his birthright." (verses 12-16)

A final thought from the historical record: when Esau came to meet Jacob he was accompanied by 400 men (Genesis 33:1). When David went to the priests at Nob he was alone (1 Samuel 21:1). When, after he fled from Achish, David came at last to the cave of Adullam, his father's house and all his brethren came to meet him, together with everyone that was in distress, in debt and discontented; and there were with him about 400 men (1 Samuel 22:1,2). Coincidence or design?

We have discussed the alphabetical structure of the psalm in its historical background with particular reference to the way in which David's meditations revolved around the lives of Jacob and Esau. We must now turn to consider the substance of the psalm, and in particular its relevance to our daily lives. Before this, however, we point out a feature of the psalms relating to the order in which they are collated. This is evident in a number of cases, and the group Psalms 32 to 35 give us an example of the thoughts of one psalm being taken up in the next.

We have already demonstrated the connection between Psalms 32 and 33 and drawn attention to the manner in which God's providential care on behalf of His people is emphasised (Psalm 33:13-19). We have shown that Psalm 34 is an extension of this topic of God's care, and the link is forged not only by the theme, but also by the language.

Compare, "Behold, the eye of the LORD is upon them that fear him" (33:18) with "The eyes of the LORD are upon the righteous" (34:15). Similarly, the "angel of the LORD encampeth ..." (34:7) is reflected in the language of Psalm 35 (see the reference to "the angel of the LORD", verses 5,6. These are the only psalms that make use of this particular phrase).

There are other examples, but we do not labour the point. Surely, however, there is a lesson that emerges from the First Book of Psalms (1–41) (which are, without question, all psalms of David), that is very relevant to our lives today and particularly pertinent to the controversy about the work of the Holy Spirit in our lives. In those psalms we have what is perhaps the most sustained emphasis in scripture upon the work of God in the life of the believer (David). It reveals in all its intricacy and wonder the providential hand of God. This is the work of the Spirit of God, and the absence of any reference to the direct operation of that Spirit upon the heart of the individual, not just in these psalms, but in the Old Testament itself, is not given sufficient emphasis in the doctrinal controversy surrounding this issue. God does not change; the manner of His working in the lives of faithful men in Old Testament times is no different from the manner of His working in our lives now.

Even without taking into account the acrostic nature of the psalm, it is difficult to divide it into specific sections. It is, as it were, all of a piece. One feature that should be noted, however, is that David refers first to his own experiences and then invites other faithful men to join him in his worship or to learn from him by following his example. Thus:

"I will bless the LORD at all times: his praise shall continually be in my mouth. My soul shall make her boast in the LORD: the humble shall hear thereof, and be glad. O magnify the LORD with me, and let us exalt his name together." (verses 1-3)

And again,

"This poor man cried, and the LORD heard him, and saved him out of all his troubles ... O taste and see that the LORD is good." (verses 6-8)

223

Here is an important insight into what our fellowship with one another should mean. Our enthusiasm for the Truth should be infectious for, by our continuous praise in word and deed, others should be encouraged to join in our worship. The steadfastness of our faith in adversity should serve as an example to others of how they can share the same experiences in times of trouble, when they commit their way unto the Lord. We magnify the Lord when we make Him great in our lives, when we recognise His power and authority. We exalt His name when we embrace the purpose encompassed within it and strive to exhibit the qualities of God's character in our lives.

A Psalm of Deliverance

God's care for His people in their affliction is the primary theme of the psalm. It is a song of deliverance (see verses 7,17,19 and 22 particularly). When we remember the historical circumstances, we can only wonder at the depth of the faith of the man David. If, for instance, the psalm was written in the cave of Adullam, it follows one of the most difficult and perilous periods of David's exile, a time when his life was in such danger that he had even turned to his most implacable foes, the Philistines, in preference to facing the continued hatred of Saul. There he had been compelled to "change his behaviour", that is, "feign madness" by concealing his intellect and hiding his reason. And when driven away all alone, not knowing whither he went, he came eventually to this cave where God encouraged him by assembling around him first his family and then a company of those who were distressed and in debt – the very kind of people, in fact, who needed the encouragement that David was able to give in the verses (1-3) that we have considered.

Surely verse 5 of this psalm is referring to this motley company who had come to David, for, in response to his plea, "they looked unto him, and were lightened: and their faces were not ashamed". In other words, their lives were brightened; God made His face to shine upon them, and they reflected in their lives the light of His goodness. They looked expectantly and were not ashamed, for God did not disappoint them; their trust was not displaced and there

224

was no cause for them to feel shame or to be "confounded" (RV).

The Angel of the LORD

We have already considered the link between the words of verse 7 and the experience of Jacob as he returned from Padan Aram (Genesis 32:1-3). Another graphic illustration of the words is to be found in the experience of Elisha and his servant at Dothan (2 Kings 6). The king of Syria sent a great host, both with horsemen and chariots, to encompass the city to take Elisha, of whom it had been said that he told the king of Israel the words that were spoken in the king of Syria's bedchamber (verse 12).

When Elisha's servant saw the Syrian army, he was filled with dismay: "Alas, my master! how shall we do?" (verse 15). Elisha's answer should inspire faith in the heart of everyone who seeks to serve God: "Fear not: for they that be with us are more than they that be with them" (verse 16). So Elisha prayed, "Open his eyes, that he may see"; and when the Lord opened the eyes of the young man, he beheld the mountain "full of horses and chariots of fire round about Elisha" (verse 17).

There is a great lesson there for us. We have the Lord's assurance "that in heaven (our) angels do always behold the face of (his) Father which is in heaven" (Matthew 18:10). Yet possibly there is nothing we forget more easily: there is nothing that we are less aware of than those guardian angels into whose care and keeping we have been committed. If we were asked, 'Have you ever seen an angel?', almost instinctively we would answer 'No'. Yet would we know if we saw an angel? The exhortation remains as real for us as it was for the Hebrews: "Be not forgetful to entertain strangers: for thereby some have entertained angels unawares" (13:2).

Psalm 34 and 1 Peter

Interestingly, our psalm is quoted twice in the First Epistle of Peter:

"Wherefore laying aside all malice, and *all guile*, and hypocrisies, and envies, and all evil speakings, as newborn babes, desire the sincere milk of the word, that ye may grow thereby: *if so be ye have tasted that the Lord is gracious.*" (1 Peter 2:1-3)

"For he that will love life, and see good days, let him refrain his tongue from evil, and his lips that they speak no guile: let him eschew evil, and do good; let him seek peace, and ensue it. For the eyes of the Lord are over the righteous, and his ears are open unto their prayers: but the face of the Lord is against them that do evil." (3:10-12; cited from Psalm 34:12-16)

Why is the psalm quoted in this way? Surely it is yet another insight into its Jacob background, for Peter writes "to the strangers scattered throughout Pontus, Galatia, Cappadocia, Asia and Bithynia" (1:1). He addresses his epistle to the believing Jews of the Dispersion, and one of his purposes is to convince them that although the Commonwealth of Judah was about to be swept away by the might of Rome, God's promises remained inviolate, His purpose could not be frustrated and they, with all who believed the Gospel, were still the Israel of God. So the epistle alludes to them as:

1. "Elect according to the foreknowledge of God" (1:2).
2. Begotten unto a living hope (1:3).
3. The heirs of "an inheritance incorruptible, and undefiled, and that fadeth not away" (1:4).
4. "Not redeemed with corruptible things, as silver and gold ... but with the precious blood of Christ, as of a lamb without blemish and without spot" (1:18,19).
5. Living stones in a spiritual house (2:5, recalling Jacob at Bethel, the first mention of the house of God in scripture).
6. "A chosen generation, a royal priesthood, an holy nation, a peculiar people" (2:9).
7. Sojourners (1:17), "strangers and pilgrims" (2:11).

So the aptness of the quotations from David's recollections, through the Spirit, of Jacob's experiences becomes clear – Jacob, who became "Israel" – a 'prince with God'.

The quotation from 1 Peter 2 in particular gives us an insight into the psalm that we must notice. The exhortation is to "desire the sincere milk of the word, that ye may grow thereby"; and the basis of the exhortation is that the readers already had experience of this process, for, quoting the Psalm, Peter says, "if so be ye have tasted that the Lord is gracious" (1 Peter 2:3, Psalm 34:8). In other words, he says, 'You have already found God's word to be true for you; let this, then, be the ground of your confidence, the root of your desire'.

When David therefore exhorts his companions to "taste and see that the LORD is good", he is in fact urging them to heed the word of God, to imbibe it, believe it and find for themselves that, because He is faithful, the Lord is indeed good.

What Man is He?

In Psalm 25 we observed that the song revolved around the question, "What man is he that feareth the LORD?" (verse 12). Significantly, Psalm 34 not only has the same alphabetical structure and peculiarities, but also poses a similar question: "What man is he that desireth life, and loveth many days, that he may see good?" (verse 12). An enlightening answer to the question is obtained by listing the descriptions of the godly man contained within the psalm:

>He is humble (verse 2);
>
>poor in spirit (verse 6);
>
>one that fears God (verse 7);
>
>and trusts in Him (verse 8).
>
>He is numbered amongst God's saints ('holy ones'); for he seeks God (verses 9,10);
>
>and is of childlike disposition (verse 11).
>
>His desire is for life (verse 12);
>
>he is numbered amongst the righteous (verse 15),
>
>who are of a broken heart and a contrite spirit (verse 18);
>
>for he is a servant of the Lord (verse 22).

It is a sobering experience to compare ourselves with this description, to measure ourselves by this standard. But this nevertheless is a fitting description of the man David, and also, remembering that his meditation is based upon the experiences of Jacob, an insight that we might not always have appreciated into the character of that patriarch. Above all, remembering that the psalm is Messianic, it is a description of the perfect man, the Lord Jesus Christ.

The Messianic Significance

That the psalm does speak of the Lord Jesus Christ is beyond question, for the words of verse 20, "he keepeth all his bones: not one of them is broken", looks back to the events of the passover (Exodus 12:46) and is quoted in John 19 as fulfilled in the experience of the Lord Jesus on the cross (verse 36).

The circumstances surrounding the command to break the prisoners' legs are strange. Not only was this contrary to Roman custom, but the argument of the Jews (verse 31) seems to lack validity. It is hard to escape the conclusion that it was a deliberate attempt by the Jews to invalidate the claims of Jesus to be the Messiah – to contrive a situation that would contradict the word of prophecy. One example would have been sufficient; but they could not frustrate the word of God and so the soldier when he came to Jesus, seeing that he was already dead, thrust his spear into his side. These things were done, says John, "that the scripture should be fulfilled, A bone of him shall not be broken. And again another scripture saith, They shall look on him whom they pierced" (verses 36,37). The attempt to invalidate one word of prophecy in relation to the Lord Jesus not only failed, but led directly to the fulfilment of another.

The words of the psalm, however, have a further important symbolic significance, for the preservation of the body of the Lord Jesus was representative of the manner in which God would keep all those who were incorporated into the multitudinous body. That body is indivisible; it is secure in the Father's keeping, for of those whom God gives him he will lose none.

Conclusion

Psalm 34 presents us, then, with a description of those qualities of the man who "desires life"; but for our comfort and consolation, describes also the care and goodness that God exercises on their behalf. We have not followed a verse-by-verse exposition, but we have sought to point the way to an understanding of the background and theme that runs through the song.

One of the primary messages for us is that the Truth is not a kind of insurance policy, for "many are the afflictions of the righteous" (verse 19). We cannot escape adversity and tribulation, but ultimately God will deliver us out of them all, for His eyes are always upon the righteous (verse 15). When we cry, the Lord hears (verse 17); He is ever nigh unto us, if we are of a contrite spirit (verse 18). Ultimately, right will prevail over evil (verse 21), for "the LORD redeemeth the soul of his servants: and none of them that trust in him shall be desolate" (verse 22).

PSALM 35

HAVING regard to the connections between Psalms 34 and 35 pointed out in the previous chapter, there can be little, if any doubt as to the period in David's life to which this psalm refers. It is covered broadly by the historical record contained in the chapters 18 to 26 of 1 Samuel, and reveals the heart of David as he reflected upon his experiences in the court of King Saul and his subsequent exile. This fact is amply borne out by the substance of the psalm itself, which, in its general theme, has many points of contact with Psalm 7 (see earlier chapter).

Imprecatory Psalms

Many find difficulty with the so-called imprecatory psalms, that is, psalms that call down God's judgements and curses upon the enemies of the writer. They suggest that the spirit of these psalms is incompatible with the spirit of the Lord Jesus Christ and that required of those who seek to follow him. For those, however, who accept the inspiration and authority of scripture, there can be no question of thinking of these psalms as in any way contradictory to New Testament teaching. Indeed, we have seen time and again that the spirit of Christ is reflected in the psalms and, in fact, the Lord Jesus, as we shall see, actually quoted from Psalm 35 in relation to his own experience.

It is important to appreciate that David was the Lord's anointed. It was known that he was God's choice to replace Saul when the time came. Consequently those who plotted against him and sought to destroy him were, in fact, fighting against God; they were seeking to frustrate His declared will and purpose. There is nothing personal about David's reactions to the intrigue and hatred of his enemies. They were beyond doubt the enemies of the Lord, and for that reason David could plead with God to manifest Himself on his behalf and could speak of their ultimate destruction in a way that would not have been possible if personal offences only had been involved. Thus, the sentiments expressed in the psalm are in fact compatible with the spirit of the Lord Jesus Christ, and, however difficult we might find it to accept, there is a very real sense in which we too can and must enter into the sentiments of the psalm. The attitude is, in fact, to be found in the New Testament as well. To quote but two examples: "How long, O Lord, holy and true, dost thou not judge and avenge our blood on them that dwell on the earth?" (Revelation 6:10); "Alexander the coppersmith did me much evil: the Lord reward him according to his works: of whom be thou ware also; for he hath greatly withstood our words" (2 Timothy 4:14,15).

Structure

The psalm can be divided into three sections, each of them concluding with a call to ascribe praise and thanksgiving to God:

    (a) Verses 1 to 10

    (b) Verses 11 to 18

    (c) Verses 19 to 28

The three sections, though closely related in their substance, each have a different emphasis. They describe: (a) the virility of David's enemies, (b) their subtlety and (c) their malice.

Underlying all three sections is the figure of the judgement seat – not a place where criminal proceedings were held, but the civil court where the oppressed could plead their cause before the judge and beseech him to vindicate them before those who sought their hurt. Thus, David says to Saul, when God had delivered him into his hand but he had refused to lift up his hand against the Lord's anointed:

"The LORD judge between me and thee, and the LORD avenge me of thee: but mine hand shall not be upon thee ... The LORD therefore be judge, and judge between me and thee, and see, and plead my cause, and deliver me out of thine hand." (1 Samuel 24:12,15)

The word rendered "plead" is the same as that used in verse 1 of the psalm: "Plead my cause, O LORD, with them that strive with me."

Verses 1-10

Although the figure is of the judgement seat (verse 1), faced with the vigour with which they pursued their aim, David changes the scene dramatically as he envisages the seat of judgement as the battlefield, with God going forth to champion his cause:

> "Fight against them that fight against me. Take hold of shield and buckler, and stand up for mine help. Draw out also the spear, and stop the way against them that persecute me: say unto my soul, I am thy salvation."
>
> (verse 1-3)

Here is a remarkable insight into David's faith, for these weapons were those that he used to fight against his enemies. His plea was, however, that God would join in the conflict, fighting, as it were, by his side and thus assuring him of victory. The graphic description of the way they are confounded and brought to confusion as the angel of the Lord pursues them and persecutes them (verses 4-6) seems to recall God's deliverance from Pharaoh's host (Exodus 14,15).

It will be recalled that the angel of the Lord who went before the camp of Israel (Exodus 14:19) "took off their chariot wheels, that they drave them heavily" (verse 25), for Moses had assured them, "The LORD shall fight for you" (verse 14); and when Moses sang his song of victory (chapter 15) he said, "The LORD is a man of war: the LORD is his name" (verse 3). Note that in the psalm the RV renders "them that persecute me" as "them that pursue me" (verse 3), and this links appropriately with the historical record in 1 Samuel 24:14.

The reason for David's plea is that his enemies, although they had no cause to hate him, had laid traps for him as though he were a wild beast (Psalm 35:7). So he prays, "Let ruin come upon them unawares! And let the net which they hid ensnare them; let them fall therein to ruin!" (verse 8, RSV). It is a principle that runs through scripture, that when men moved by malice and envy seek

232

to bring evil upon a righteous man, they suffer the fate they thought to inflict upon their fellow. The law of malicious witness (Deuteronomy 19:16-21) demonstrates the principle:

"If the witness be a false witness, and hath testified falsely against his brother; then shall ye do unto him, as he had thought to do unto his brother."

(verses 18,19, RV)

It was an unrelenting struggle. Their purpose was David's death, thus frustrating the purpose of God. There could be no compromise with them whilst they maintained that purpose. The wicked must be ensnared in their own trap. Ultimately, "the sinners (must) be consumed out of the earth, and let the wicked be no more" (Psalm 104:35). If God should so deliver him, then David would have cause to be joyful in the Lord and to rejoice in His salvation (Psalm 35:9). "All my bones shall say, LORD, who is like unto thee, which deliverest the poor from him that is too strong for him, yea, the poor and needy from him that spoileth him?" (verse 10). As the bones feel pain and sorrow (Psalm 6:2), so also the bodily frame feels the thrill and excitement of joy and rejoicing. We have noted the deeper significance of the bones in Psalm 34 (verse 20), involving the completeness of the "Christ Body". If we think of the spirit of Christ in this psalm, then might not the reference be to all the members of his body rejoicing in the victory wrought by God in him? It should not be missed that the phrase "LORD, who is like unto thee?" is yet another quotation from Exodus 15 (verse 11), thus substantiating the background referred to above.

The subtlety of David's enemies is vividly revealed. Once more, the language is of the court of judgement; not, of course, that David was actually on trial, but these evil men bring against him accusations of which he had no knowledge at all. What these accusations were is perhaps evident from 1 Samuel:

"And David said to Saul, Wherefore hearest thou men's words, saying, Behold, David seeketh thy hurt?"

(24:9)

What made it particularly hard for David to bear was the fact that they were rewarding him evil for good. The effect

233

upon David was devastating. They did it, he said, "to the bereaving of my soul" (Psalm 35:12, RV). They left him friendless and alone, like one who had lost his nearest and dearest.

Their sin was all the more abhorrent because they were returning evil for good. When they had been sick, David had prayed and fasted for them. He had behaved towards them as though they had been friends or brothers. He had mourned for them as one might mourn for his mother (verses 13,14). But, says David, "my prayer returned into mine own bosom" (verse 13). Although they had rejected his kindness and recompensed him evil for good, David's prayer was rewarded, and it brought blessing to him as it returned into his bosom, giving him a peace and satisfaction that was beyond their understanding.

For all this love and consideration that David had shown towards them, they, like wild beasts ready to tear and rend, were watching for him to fall into adversity, that they might rejoice and gather themselves about him to destroy him:

"Yea, the abjects gathered themselves together against me, and I knew it not; they did tear me, and ceased not."
(verse 15)

The word rendered "abjects" presents some difficulty. This is the only occurrence of the word in the Old Testament, so comparisons cannot be made. It appears to speak of those who could best be described as 'rabble', the dregs of society; men who, like the modern day hooligans, would for the sheer joy of it set upon the poor and afflicted, particularly if they knew that those in authority would turn a blind eye or even encourage them.

In similar vein, the reference "with hypocritical mockers in feasts, they gnashed upon me with their teeth" (verse 16) is a little obscure. Elsewhere, the word rendered "mockers" is translated "cakes" (1 Kings 17:12). It is suggested that the word means 'mockers for a cake', that is, clowns of the worst type who, for the price of a meal, provide entertainment of the lowest kind by scurrilous and slanderous jesting about the butt of their humour.

So David cries, "How long wilt thou look on? Rescue my soul from their destructions, my darling (RSV, 'life') from the lions" (verse 17). Then, vindicated by all the people, he will give thanks in the congregation, and sing God's praises among a mighty people (verse 18, RV margin). The point, of course, is the public nature of these declarations, the open way in which he is now recognised and acknowledged – no longer vilified and slandered, but accepted as the Lord's anointed.

Verses 19-28
These malicious men who had made themselves his enemies without cause, who had built their curse upon untruths, winked with the eye (verse 19). We all know the attitude: the sly wink, the quiet nudge as men give their signals to their confederates to indicate how they will take advantage or show that the words they speak are intended, to deceive and to lull into false security. David says:

"They speak not peace: but they devise deceitful matters against them that are quiet in the land. Yea, they opened their mouth wide against me, and said, Aha, aha, our eye hath seen it." (verses 20,21)

In effect, they accused the quiet of being "breakers of the peace", of being that sort "who troubled Israel". "Our eye hath seen it", they said, as they falsely accused him. "This thou hast seen, O Lord: keep not silence: O Lord, be not far from me" (verse 22), responded David as he made his plea before God. He brings his prayer to a conclusion with a sustained cry unto God to stir and awake to bring forth judgement. "Judge me", he says, "according to thy righteousness", confident of his faithfulness to God and of his innocence before those who would have "swallowed him up" (verses 23-25).

The thoughts of verse 4 that God would bring his enemies to shame and confusion are repeated: "Let them be clothed with shame and dishonour that magnify themselves against me" (verse 26). In contrast, David says:

"Let them shout for joy, and be glad, that favour my righteous cause: yea, let them say continually, Let the Lord be magnified, which hath pleasure in the prosperity of his servant." (verse 27)

235

God delights in the peace of His servant. He will vindicate him, He will never allow his enemies to triumph over him. So, says David, "my tongue shall speak of thy righteousness and of thy praise all the day long" (verse 28). God's holiness and faithfulness would ever be the subject of his conversation. His meditations upon the goodness of the Lord would be manifest in constant praise.

Conclusion

The psalm reveals human nature at its worst. When men in positions of power have mental aberrations causing unjustified resentment and hatred against another, they will always find themselves surrounded by dishonourable men who will pander to their delusions, who will lie and cheat to ingratiate themselves and to further their own careers – men who will descend to low humour in an attempt to be seen as what we would describe today as "fellow travellers".

David's experiences foreshadowed those of the Lord Jesus. The spirit of Christ pervades the psalm and if we have any doubt of this, the scriptures themselves provide the proof, for, quoting the 19th verse of the psalm, it is recorded: "But this cometh to pass, that the word might be fulfilled that is written in their law, They hated me without a cause" (John 15:25).

236

PSALM 36

THE superscription at the head of the psalm, "A Psalm of David the servant of the LORD", is rendered by some, "A Psalm of the servant of the LORD, of David". If this is accepted, then this means that it is a psalm about the Servant of the Lord which was written by David; the effect of this rendering is that the phrase becomes a direct affirmation that the contents of the psalm are Messianic in character. Nevertheless, whether or not the alternative rendering is justified, the psalm remains just that, a reflection of the mind of the Lord Jesus, for David the servant of the Lord would, through the Spirit, be expressing the thoughts of him who was pre-eminently *the* Servant of the Lord.

As far as the content of the psalm is concerned, it does not appear to have any direct historical background, yet there seems to be a certain appropriateness in its inclusion at this point in the Psalter. It is an assessment by David of his experiences in life. In earlier psalms, Psalm 35 for example, we have seen the malice and hatred of evil men directed at David in their endeavour to destroy him. His words have, as it were, been poured out in the midst of his affliction, forged in the furnace of adversity in which he found himself as he pleaded his cause before God. In this psalm, however, that sense of urgency is not apparent. There is a calmness of expression, as though David is placing on record the lessons he had learned through all the tribulations he had experienced.

The substance of the psalm is concerned firstly with an insight into the hearts of the wicked who, by a deliberate act of will, abandon themselves to a life apart from God with no feeling of remorse or guilt (verses 1-4). Turning from this contemplation of the godless, David next draws comfort from a consideration of the goodness and faithfulness of God (verse 5-9) and concludes with words of supplication that God would continue to bless him and to deliver him from such wicked men, for whom, ultimately, he recognises there can be no future (verses 10-12).

In view of the theme of the next psalm, which, at some length, contrasts the fate of the wicked with the reward of the righteous, and the words of the concluding verse in Psalm 36, which are echoed throughout Psalm 37, it might be worth considering whether Psalm 36 is included at this juncture not only for the reasons stated above, but also as an introduction to that theme which is to be taken up in the psalm that follows.

The Way of the Wicked

That men have found difficulty with the Hebrew text of verses 1 and 2 is evident from a comparison of the various translations. Without the benefit of first-hand knowledge of Hebrew, it can be difficult for the English reader to determine the precise significance of the words. Nevertheless, a careful consideration leads, we believe, to a conviction that the real meaning of the text is best expressed by the RV with margin. We give below the translation of the RV with amendments suggested by the marginal renderings:

'Transgression uttereth its oracle to the wicked within his heart. There is no fear of God before his eyes. For he flattereth him in his eyes, until his iniquity be found out and be hated.'   (verses 1,2)

The RV presents us with a remarkable personification of transgression that rules and deceives in the heart of the wicked. In its own way, it is a remarkable precursor to the personification of sin as a king who reigns unto death (Romans 6), and the New Testament presentation of the Devil as the personification of human wickedness in its various manifestations.

Literally, the word rendered "transgression" means 'rebellion'. The phrase "uttereth its oracle" represents a word that is usually used of divine utterances such as "saith the LORD", and its use here in connection with the rebellious spirit that rules in the hearts of transgressors is significant. It is an indication that the "transgressor"

238

regards the thoughts of his heart as of equal authority to the word of God. The deceitfulness of sin has so beguiled him that his way of life, his transgression, has become his god. Such is the nature of his self-deception that it has become "a lying spirit" within his heart. The result is that there is no fear of God. He has no regard for Him, no dread of His judgements, for he has said in his heart, "I shall not be moved ... God hath forgotten ... He will never see it ... Thou wilt not require it" (Psalm 10:6,11,13). He has come to think of God as such an one as himself. The self-delusion is so deep-rooted, the confidence in his own way so overpowering, that (continuing the personification) "he (i.e., transgression) flattereth him in his eyes"; that is, it is as if he whispered in his own ear smooth words to lull himself into a state of complacency, until his self-deceit is shattered by the exposure of his sin, his iniquity is revealed and his way of life recognised for the hateful and abhorrent thing that it is.

In elaboration of this picture of the transgressor, David continues:

"The words of his mouth are iniquity and deceit: he hath left off to be wise, and to do good. He deviseth mischief upon his bed; he setteth himself in a way that is not good; he abhorreth not evil."   (verses 3,4)

Part of the opening phrase of verse 3 is quoted by the Apostle Paul in his Epistle to the Romans (chapter 3) as he brings a series of Old Testament quotations together to prove that both Jew and Gentile are all under sin (see verse 9): "Their throat is an open sepulchre; with their tongues they have used deceit" (verse 13). The latter part of verse 3 is referred to by the prophet Jeremiah:

"For my people is foolish, they have not known me; they are sottish children, and they have none understanding: they are wise to do evil, but to do good they have no knowledge."   (4:22)

What a dreadful outcome is this practical atheism practised by the rebellious! Characterised by lies and deceit, they have consciously chosen to abandon the wisdom that produces goodness. Instead, those abilities that should have been used to learn of God are devoted to the pursuit of evil. They apply their mental faculties to

239

devise how they might bring their wicked designs to fruition.

"He deviseth (lit. meditateth) mischief upon his bed." What an insight into human experience and behaviour! For so often it is when we relax in our beds, or perhaps when we have bouts of sleeplessness, that our heart dwells upon those things it desires most. It is then that the mind ranges over the field of human activity and plans how to achieve the ambitions and desires that burn within. So often, with the shackles of daily care thrown off, it is then that the real man appears. So the transgressor meditates mischief upon his bed and "setteth" himself, that is, by a conscious act of will decides to walk in a way that is not good, for "he abhorreth not evil". That is a test for any man – how does he regard evil? Although we are all sinners, through the influence of God's word we can come to hate sin. Our attitude towards wrongdoing is a yardstick of our standing in the sight of God:

"Horror hath taken hold upon me because of the wicked that forsake thy law." (Psalm 119:53)

"Rivers of waters run down mine eyes, because they keep not thy law." (verse 136)

"I beheld the transgressors, and was grieved; because they kept not thy word." (verse 158)

To summarise the four verses: There is 1) the sin of their heart; 2) the sin of their lips; and 3) the sin of their hands – in other words, the whole gamut of human sin, in thought, word and deed.

The Goodness and the Faithfulness of God

In contrast to the wickedness of men, David turns now to a contemplation of the character of God:

"Thy lovingkindness, O LORD, is in the heavens; thy faithfulness reacheth unto the skies." (verse 5, RV)

There is a particular emphasis upon the word "lovingkindness" (Hebrew, *chesed*) which is used three times in the course of verses 5 to 10. We have commented upon this word several times in earlier psalms, demonstrating that it represents the love that God has for His people in the bonds of the covenant. It is thus linked in these verses with God's faithfulness and righteousness,

240

and it is in these qualities that David now finds comfort and security in the face of the wickedness of men that fills the earth. Words cannot adequately describe the loving-kindness and faithfulness of God. They are boundless and measureless, stretching to heaven's height and the expanse of the skies. The language of verse 5, however, could be a reference to the rainbow. God said to Noah, "And the bow shall be in the cloud; and I will look upon it, that I may remember the everlasting covenant between God and every living creature" (Genesis 9:16; see also verses 9,11,12,13 and 15).

That the reference is to the rainbow is substantiated to some extent by the next verse:

"Thy righteousness is like the mountains of God; thy judgements are a great deep. O LORD, thou preservest man and beast." (verse 6, RV)

The inclusion of the beasts would appear to be out of context, but the reference to the rainbow and the everlasting covenant between God and every living creature provides the background for the inclusion of both man and beast in this context.

Accepting the allusion to the rainbow, it becomes clear that David, having thought of the wickedness of rebellious men, now acknowledges that God's faithfulness to His covenant remains steadfast. Nothing could frustrate His purpose, for human wickedness would not prevail. Faithful men were secure in God's love, from whence none could snatch them, if they remained true to Him.

God's righteousness was like the mountains of God, that is, the mountains that were of Him. They had their origin in Him and thus were a reflection of His greatness, immoveable and unchanging. So also His judgements are a great deep, fathomless, beyond the fleshly mind to comprehend or understand; they could never be confounded by human wisdom, for always in human affairs, whatever their personal motives, men did what His hand and counsel had determined to be done. In all these thoughts, there is a wonderful consolation for the man of faith. So, in his joy at this knowledge, David breaks forth into an exclamation of praise and exultation:

241

"How precious is thy lovingkindness, O God! And the children of men take refuge under the shadow of thy wings." (verse 7, RV)

To David, God's covenant love was precious: it was like a treasure, to be valued far above all earthly attachments. Under the shadow of God's wings the children of men could take refuge, committing themselves to His care with the utmost confidence. (For further examples of the beautiful figure of the mother bird protecting her young, see Deuteronomy 32:10-12; Matthew 23:37.) But God is not merely a protector; He is also a host, a provider of good things for those who abide under the shadow of His wings:

"They shall be abundantly satisfied with the fatness of thy house; and thou shalt make them drink of the river of thy pleasures." (verse 8)

This is a description of fellowship. Here is a sacrificial meal, for the thought is of the guest sitting at God's table, eating, as it were, "the flesh of the sacrifice of his peace offerings" (Leviticus 7:15), that their soul might be satiated with fatness (Jeremiah 31:14). The word rendered "pleasures" means literally 'delights', and is from the same root as the word 'Eden'. The allusion again carries the thoughts to sins forgiven, to the blessings of fellowship that belong to those with whom God has made a covenant by sacrifice (Psalm 50:5).

The expectations of blessings expressed in verse 8 is no vain dream, for, says David, "with thee is the fountain of life: in thy light shall we see light" (verse 9). Only God possesses life inherently. All other life is derived from Him and sustained by Him. That is, of course, true of natural mortal life and the spiritual life we seek to live in God's kingdom. Through Jeremiah, God indicted Israel because "they have forsaken me the fountain of living waters, and hewed them out cisterns, broken cisterns, that can hold no water" (2:13).

John's Gospel reflects the language of the psalm: "In him was life; and the life was the light of men" (John 1:4). The RV and others suggest alternative renderings in John, particularly in relation to the punctuation, but the AV is sufficient to illustrate the message. Without light, there can be no life. So John emphasises that the life God gives to men is synonymous with light. This, of course, is particularly true of the life God offers through the Lord Jesus Christ. But there is also one aspect of this truth that applies to all human life. Life for man is on a higher level, he is made in the image of God, he can relate to God in a manner that is beyond the ability of the lower orders of creation. So life in man was also to be associated with light – not that there was light in man inherently; there is no inner light; we are not born with an innate sense of right and wrong and an instinctive understanding of the God who sustains us in life. On the contrary, we walked "in the vanity of (our) mind, having the understanding darkened, being alienated from the life of God through the ignorance that is in (us)" (Ephesians 4:17,18). What we do possess, however, is a desire to seek after God, a conscience that can be educated to discern between right and wrong and the ability to receive the light of God's truth, whereby the darkness that fills us by nature can be dispersed.

Thus the psalmist writes, "in thy light shall we see light". The divine illumination must shine into our hearts, "to give the light of the knowledge of the glory of God in the face of Jesus Christ" (2 Corinthians 4:6).

A Prayer for Deliverance

Verse 10 is a prayer for God to maintain His loving-kindness. This is the third occasion that David uses the word in this latter part of the psalm, and again it is connected with God's righteousness. David, having experienced the mercy of God through all his trials and afflictions, was conscious of the need for His continuing care, for his enemies were still there, still determined to discredit and destroy him. So he prays, "Let not the foot of pride come against me, and let not the hand of the wicked remove me" (verse 11). Those described in verses 1 to 4 still plotted his hurt. Their desire was to trample him underfoot, to "drive (him) away" into exile (RV). They would make him a wanderer and a vagabond, but, as if in the contemplation of all that has gone before, David realises the futility of all their evil and malicious thoughts. Abruptly, as if suddenly in his mind's eye he can see the ultimate end of the wicked, he exclaims, "There are the workers of iniquity fallen: they are cast down, and shall not be able to rise" (verse 12).

Such is the end of all wicked and rebellious men. They have no future; their fate is sealed. The eye of faith that looks for the day when God's glory will fill the earth can envisage their fate; there they fall and are cast down, they shall not rise up again. For "the sinners (shall) be consumed out of the earth, and ... the wicked (shall) be no more" (Psalm 104:35).

PSALM 37

THE closing words of Psalm 36, "There are the workers of iniquity fallen: they are cast down, and shall not be able to rise" (verse 12), serve as a fitting introduction to this psalm which contrasts the fate of the wicked with the reward of the righteous. In Psalm 37 we have another alphabetical psalm with twenty-two stanzas (usually of two verses), each introduced by the appropriate letter of the Hebrew alphabet. Once again, however, we have this characteristic that the sequence is broken in one instance: at verse 29, where one would expect to have the letter *Ain*, it is missing. Notwithstanding the efforts of commentators who suggest copying errors, probable alternative readings (all guess work) etc., it does seem, having regard to the other examples we have already noted, that there is design in the omission. While the use of the alphabet would emphasise that the respective destiny of the righteous and wicked was based upon their attitude to the word of God, perhaps the omission of the letter *Ain* was intended to bring to the readers' attention all the more powerfully, through the interruption in the sequence, the words which were spoken that certainly sum up in a most succinct manner the whole message of the psalm: "The righteous shall inherit the land, and dwell therein for ever" (verse 29).

Regarding this theme of the psalm, we can be in no doubt that its basis is the covenant that God made with Abraham. "Dwelling in" and "inheriting the land" are phrases that occur eight times (verses 3,9,11,18,22, 27,29,34). The word translated in some cases "land" and in others "earth" primarily means 'the land'. It was the land which was promised to Abraham and his seed for ever (Genesis 13:14-17 etc.). The promise was not limited, however, to the land alone, for "in thy seed shall all the nations of the earth be blessed" (Genesis 22:18). This

245

universal application of the covenant is seen when the Lord Jesus quotes the psalm (verse 11): "Blessed are the meek: for they shall inherit the earth" (Matthew 5:5) and by the Apostle Paul when he writes: "For the promise, that he should be the heir of the world, was not to Abraham, or to his seed, through the law, but through the righteousness of faith" (Romans 4:13).

א *aleph* (verses 1,2)

"Fret not thyself ... neither be thou envious." The word rendered "fret" occurs in this form on only four occasions in the Old Testament – in verses 1, 7 and 8 of Psalm 37 and in Proverbs 24:19, which has many points of contact with the theme of this psalm. The word means literally 'to be hot or incensed' and it describes that burning jealousy that can fill the hearts of men when they see the prosperity of others, and they themselves are in adverse circumstances. Similarly, the word rendered "envious" comes from a root meaning 'to be red', and carries the idea of heat. We speak of being 'green with envy', but the idea in Hebrew is of the redness that suffuses the face of the man who lets anger burn within because of the prosperity of others. Of course, the warning of the psalm is directed towards those who seek to please God and must ever be exposed to the danger of contrasting their circumstances with the prosperity of the wicked.

"All flesh is grass, and all the goodliness thereof is as the flower of the field" (Isaiah 40:6). Human life at its best is fleeting and transient, like the grass and the flower of the field, so soon to wither and be burned up by the scorching heat of the sun. For the wicked, however much they appear to prosper, that was their end. The word of God, however, stands for ever (Isaiah 40:8); and for those who were led by that word, who took it into their hearts and espoused its promises, there remained that eternal treasure that they would inherit in the land.

ב *beth* (verses 3,4)

The answer to the murmuring and envious heart was to "trust in the LORD, and do good". The RV renders the next phrase "Dwell in the land", thus altering the sense, for it is no longer a consequence of trust, but a command to demonstrate trust by remaining in the land which God

246

had promised. In difficult times many might have been tempted to move to foreign lands that appeared to offer so much more in material terms; but "so shalt thou dwell in the land, and verily thou shalt be fed" was the divine assurance. We can draw the lesson for ourselves. The Ecclesia is both God's heritage, and our inheritance. We must not be drawn away from it. We must remain in the congregation of the saints and we shall be fed, for they that hunger and thirst after righteousness shall be filled. If we delight ourselves in the Lord, then He will give us the desires of our heart. The first sentence qualifies the second. We are not meant to assume that God will give us anything we set our hearts on, but there are some things we can be certain He will provide. Thus if we delight ourselves in Him, make His thoughts our thoughts, desire the spiritual blessings that come from an understanding of His word and long for His kingdom and glory, then we can be sure that God will grant us all the desires of our hearts.

‫ג‬ *gimel* (verses 5,6)

The thoughts of the previous stanza are developed in this and the following section. "Roll thy way upon the LORD" (RV margin) conveys the sense of the word rendered "commit". Some have suggested that, more accurately, it should be 'roll back'. In other words, recognise that God is in control. Whether in prosperity or in adversity, it is all of God, and He desires nothing more than that we should roll back onto Him the burdens He has given us to bear. Peter writes of, "casting all your care upon him; for he careth for you" (1 Peter 5:7). With dramatic emphasis the Hebrew says, 'and He will do', i.e., all that is necessary for our well-being.

The result of this work of God is that we will walk in light, for He will "bring forth thy righteousness as the light, and thy judgment as the noonday". It is true of our life in this dispensation, but it has its ultimate fulfilment when God will vindicate His servants and exalt them in the glory of His kingdom.

‫ד‬ *daleth* (verse 7)

In this knowledge the true man of faith is still (or silent) before the Lord (RV margin). He communes with his own

heart and is still (Psalm 4:4). It is the quietness of faith –
no hot angry murmuring; no fretful anxiety because of the
wicked who prospers in his way. Instead he waits
patiently for the Lord. The word "wait" in this instance
has the primary meaning of twisting or binding as of a
rope, hence to be strong. Thus to wait for God is the
remedy to face all the evil devices and machinations of
men.

ה *he* (verses 8,9)

The exhortation is repeated, to cease from anger and
forsake wrath: "Fret not thyself, it tendeth only to evil-
doing" (RV). To fret is not only a useless exercise, it is also
dangerous. It can lead to a godless anger, and cause a man
to cast in his lot with the wicked. Evildoers will be cut off,
as God had cut off the nations before Israel when they had
entered the land (Deuteronomy 12:29,30). The wicked in
Israel were no better than the Canaanites whom God had
cut off before them. There could be no inheritance in the
land for them either; it was those whose hope was in the
Lord and who waited expectantly for Him who should
dwell in the land for ever (see Psalm 25:13).

ו *waw* (verses 10,11)

The phrase "for yet a little while" is picked up and quoted
by the Spirit in Hebrews 10: "For yet a little while, and he
that shall come will come, and will not tarry" (verse 37).
The time when the wicked shall not be, when their power
will be broken in the earth, is when the Lord Jesus Christ
returns. Then the sinners shall be consumed out of the
earth and the wicked shall be no more (Psalm 104:35).
Then the meek, those that are teachable and amenable to
the influence of the word of God, will inherit the earth and
enjoy abundance of peace.

ז *zayin* (verses 12 and 13)

The rage and anger of the wicked is vanity. Ultimately
they have no power to continue to prosper. They show
their opposition to the righteous, behaving like wild
beasts, they gnash with their teeth. It is interesting to
reflect that this imagery occurs from time to time in the
psalms (see Psalm 3:7; 22:20,21; 35:16,17; 57:3,4; 58:6;
112:10). The passages form a background that helps to

explain the language of the New Testament: "Your adversary the devil, as a roaring lion, walketh about, seeking whom he may devour" (1 Peter 5:8).

The ultimate folly, when the heathen rage and the people imagine a vain thing, is when the nations are confederate together against the Lord and against His anointed. He that sitteth in the heavens shall laugh (Psalm 2). So in this context God laughs at the wicked, for He seeth the day of their destruction coming.

ח *heth* (verses 14,15)

Eventually the evil that the wicked seek to do will recoil upon them. Sword and bow are, on occasions, spoken of literally, as weapons to slay the righteous; but they are also spoken of figuratively, of the words wicked men speak – slander, malice, character assassination, to cast down the poor and needy and those whose way of life (conversation) has been conducted in an upright manner.

Truly in the context of this psalm, which speaks of the righteous inheriting the earth, we can echo the words of the Lord Jesus: "Blessed are they which are persecuted for righteousness' sake: for theirs is the kingdom of heaven" (Matthew 5:10).

ט *teth* (verses 16,17)

If we are to learn not to be envious of the worldly success of the wicked, then we must come to appreciate the nature of true riches. If we can do that, we will know that however little the righteous have, it is to be preferred to the "abundance" (RV) of the wicked. The word rendered 'abundance' carries the idea of tumult, of noisy, riotous opulence (Cambridge Bible).

Thus the arms of the wicked, the symbols of his power, will be broken, for God will at all times uphold the righteous and keep him from falling.

י *yod* (verses 18,19)

The knowledge that God will uphold His servants in their daily lives is emphasised in this stanza, for the Lord knoweth their days (cp. Psalm 1:6) – literally, it means 'He keeps His eye upon them', 'He takes note of them', 'He cares for them'. In other words, He is intimately associated with the lives of the righteous, and because of this they will never be ashamed, never have cause to regret putting their trust in God, for "their inheritance shall be for ever"; and until that day God will sustain them in all life's difficulties. He will always satisfy them with good.

‏כ‎ *kaph* (verse 20)

In contrast, the wicked shall perish. They are described as the enemies of the Lord, for our enemies are His enemies. There is some difficulty over the text of verse 20. The RV renders "(they) shall be as the excellency of the pastures". The figure then would be as in verse 2, a picture of the gay profusion of flowers blooming in the meadow, representing the wicked in their prosperity, but so soon to vanish in the heat of the sun. The reference to them being consumed away as smoke might then find a counterpart in the words of the Lord Jesus when he speaks of all as "the grass of the field, which to day is, and to morrow is cast into the oven" (Matthew 6:30).

If the reading of the AV is retained, however, likening the wicked to the fat of lambs that shall consume away as smoke, perhaps the reference is to a sin offering which was totally consumed on the altar in token of the destruction of sin; and the smoke which ascended was not for a sweet-smelling savour, as with the burnt and peace offerings, so it would be swept away, to indicate the ultimate destiny of the wicked.

‏ל‎ *lamed* (verses 21,22)

The law in Deuteronomy 15 laid down stringent rules as to how the poor were to be cared for, and how men were to dispose of their wealth (verses 1-11). Here we have a contrast between the differing attitudes of the wicked and the righteous, which explains why they are described as either blessed or cursed of God. Men's ultimate destiny depends on this assessment – either inheritance of the earth, or to be cut off. The language is taken up by the Lord Jesus in the parable of judgement, the sheep and the goats: "Come, ye blessed of my Father, inherit the kingdom prepared for you from the foundation of the world" (Matthew 25:34); "Depart from me, ye cursed, into everlasting fire, prepared for the devil and his angels" (verse 41).

מ *mem* (verses 23,24)

The RV renders verse 23: "A man's goings are established of the LORD; and he delighteth in his way". It is an affirmation of the providential control of the life of the righteous and of the delight that God takes in the way he walks. Because of this, although he might fall, he will not be utterly cast down, but God will hold him with His hand. Proverbs 24 is relevant: "For a just man falleth seven times, and riseth up again: but the wicked shall fall into mischief (RV, "are overcome by calamity")" (verse 16).

The godly man never accepts defeat in the battle against sin. It doesn't matter that on occasions he might fall. He has those enduring, tenacious qualities that will never let go of those eternal things to which he has become related, and because of this God will always work with him in his life to uphold him and to lift him up again (see Isaiah 41:10).

נ *nun* (verses 25,26)

In confirmation of what has gone before, the psalmist looks back on his own experiences of life: "I have been young, and now am old", and can say with confidence that he has never seen the righteous utterly destitute or forsaken. Not only so, but when he is blessed with an abundance, he knows how to use it, for "he is ever merciful, and lendeth".

ס *samech* (verses 27,28)

The first line of verse 27 repeats the words of Psalm 34:14. That psalm contained David's meditations upon events in the life of Jacob. In his reflections now upon the covenant that God made with Abraham, Isaac and Jacob, it is appropriate, as he dwells also on the providential care of God, that his thoughts should once more rest upon Jacob. "Depart from evil, and do good; and dwell for evermore". If men seek to do their part, God will not fail them: "For the LORD loveth judgment, and forsaketh not his saints". The Hebrew word *chasid*, rendered 'saint', is derived from the word for mercy and loving-kindness, sometimes rendered "covenant love". The saint is one who has experienced that loving-kindness that God extends to those who have made a covenant with Him by sacrifice and has reciprocated that love in the bonds of the covenant, both in his fidelity to God and in the mercy which he shows towards his fellow men. Thus the rewards of the righteous and the fate of the wicked are re-iterated.

ע *ain*? (verse 29)

See comments in introduction (page 245).

פ *pe* (verses 30,31)

The secret of that security which the righteous know is revealed. His mouth speaketh (lit. meditateth) wisdom and his tongue talketh of judgement – in other words, his conversation is moulded by the word of God. God's law is supreme in his life. It is in his heart, therefore none of his steps shall slide. Psalm 119 reflects the same thoughts: "Thy word have I hid (lit. treasured) in mine heart, that I might not sin against thee" (verse 11). Because of his love for God's word, his feet shall not slide, but he will be characterised by sure-footedness as he follows the path of righteousness.

צ *tzade* (verses 32,33)

The words of this stanza have an exact fulfilment in the experience of the Lord Jesus Christ. "The wicked watcheth the righteous, and seeketh to slay him", so when Jesus healed the man with the withered hand on the sabbath day (Mark 3), "they watched him" (verse 2) and finally "took counsel ... how they might destroy him" (verse 6). Thus although they condemned him falsely, he committed himself to Him that judgeth righteously, and God delivered him out of their hands – He raised him from the dead, and thus overturned the judgement of the wicked and gave to all men an assurance that one day he would rule the world in righteousness (Acts 17:31).

ק *qoph* (verse 34)

The reward of the righteous and the fate of the wicked are reiterated against the background of the malice of evil men discussed in the last stanza. Therefore wait upon the Lord, and when the power of the wicked is finally broken in the earth, the righteous shall see it and rejoice.

ר *resh* (verses 35,36)

Here is another reflection upon the apparent prosperity of the wicked and their ultimate destiny. The psalmist has seen the wicked "in great power" (lit. terribleness) oppressing the poor and righteous. They had been "like a green tree in its native soil" (RV), like some deep-rooted giants of the forest spreading themselves, appearing as though they were established for ever. But in simple brevity, the psalmist says, "but one passed by, and, lo, he was not: yea, I sought him, but he could not be found" (RV).

ש *shin* (verses 37,38)

In contrast to the wicked who, like the green tree, flourished only to pass away, we are exhorted to "mark the perfect man, and behold the upright: for the end of that man is peace". "Mark" means literally 'observe him', and we can think in this context of the Lord Jesus Christ, who in his moral excellence demonstrates to us the way in which we should walk. For him and for those who follow in his footsteps, in contrast to the wicked, "there is a reward (or future) for the man of peace" (RV margin).

ת *taw* (verses 39,40)

The final thought of the psalm is that God will remain faithful to those who are His. He is "the strong hold" (RV) in time of trouble. He will deliver the righteous out of the hands of the wicked, because they trust in Him.

Conclusion

The psalm has established repeatedly what is the reward of the righteous and the fate of the wicked. It has contrasted the qualities and characteristics of them both. It has exhorted the righteous to develop the meek and quiet spirit that will never be deceived by the fleeting prosperity of the wicked. So we can say in conclusion, "Here is the patience of the saints" (Revelation 14:12) and "Remember the glory! remember the land!" (Hymn 337).

PSALM 38

IT is the writer's opinion that nowhere in the psalms is the weight of sin more keenly felt, and the torment of heart and mind that is experienced by the man convicted of wrongdoing more powerfully expressed, than in Psalm 38. It is not just agony of soul that is described; but bodily sickness, and we have a terrible and awesome insight into the effect of sin upon the whole man. Guilt and shame produce physical consequences. There are references in the psalm where beyond question the writer uses the language of leprosy; and some have thought that he was indeed suffering from this dreadful plague. However, in the conviction that David was the author of the psalm, we find it difficult to reconcile such a view with the historical records. We believe, therefore, that although his inner turmoil produced sickness, the references to leprosy are of a spiritual rather than a literal nature. Leprosy in scripture is used almost as a synonym for sin, and the psalmist clearly thought it appropriate to describe his sufferings because of sin in the language of leprosy.

Accepting that David is the author of the psalm, then almost beyond doubt we must associate it with his sin in the matter of Bathsheba and Uriah the Hittite. It must remain a matter of conjecture as to when precisely the words were penned and to what period in that series of events they refer; but noting the emphasis on the attitude provoked in friends, relatives and enemies, it seems appropriate to associate it with the time after David had been confronted by Nathan the prophet. Might it be that it describes David's experiences during the time after he took Bathsheba to wife, until the death of the child that was born to them as a result of their sin?

The psalm bears the title: "to bring to remembrance". Surely there is an allusion to the meal offering (Leviticus

2:1,2), a portion of which was burned upon the altar for a memorial and for a sweet-smelling savour unto the Lord. At first it seems inappropriate that this offering, which spoke of a man devoting his substance to the Lord, should be connected with sin, which is the principal topic of Psalm 38. However, we remember that, associated with that part of the offering that was burned upon the altar, was the frankincense with which it was anointed, which was one of the ingredients that produced the sweet-smelling savour (Leviticus 2:15,16). Now incense speaks to us of the prayers of the saints (Revelation 8:3,4), and our psalm is most certainly the prayer of a man convicted by his conscience of sin and indicted also by God – a man nevertheless whose desire was to cast his burden on the Lord in his desire for his sin to be forgiven. Consequently, it is possible to regard his prayer as producing a sweet-smelling savour, whereas his sin would give God no pleasure at all.

"Lord, remember me!" must be the cry that is uppermost in the heart of every man who feels the burden of guilt and the depravity of his own heart; for unless God is merciful (Luke 18:13), we are without hope. Yet such a prayer, when it springs from a faithful heart, can be uttered in absolute confidence, knowing that when God remembers, then God acts (see Genesis 30:22; Exodus 2:24,25; 1 Samuel 1:19; Luke 1:72). So David's desire to know the salvation of God expressed itself in a cry to God to remember him, and so it must ever be for those who seek the Lord with all their hearts.

The psalm falls easily into three divisions, each of them beginning with a plea to God. There is, though, a marked difference in emphasis in the three sections; but they have one thing in common, in that they reveal the psalmist as a man with a deep consciousness of God. He knew what could be the awful consequences of God's anger; he was aware of the opportunity his sin gave to men to ridicule and revile him, and through him to blaspheme the God he worshipped; yet all this was balanced by an appreciation of the faithfulness of God who he was confident would not forsake him, for He was near to help, and in Him lay his salvation.

255

"LORD, rebuke me not in thy wrath" (verses 1-8)

It is in this opening section that David dwells particularly upon his inner turmoil and the physical symptoms it had produced. The opening words of the psalm are a repetition of the beginning of Psalm 6:

> "O LORD, rebuke me not in thy wrath: neither chasten me in thy hot displeasure."   (verse 1)

We demonstrated in our consideration of Psalm 6 that it was entirely Messianic in its meaning and significance, dwelling upon the manner in which the Lord Jesus bore our nature and entered into our experiences, that he might become a sin offering for us. We now suggest another aspect of the way in which some psalms reflect the work of the Saviour. Psalm 6 and Psalm 38 open with the same words because they complement each other. There is no confession of personal sin or individual guilt in Psalm 6. It describes the experiences of a man who shared the condemnation of all Adam's posterity, though he himself was blameless. Psalm 38 takes us into the mind and experience of one who not only shared Adam's condemnation, but was himself a sinner, worthy of God's anger and knowing in his heart all the shame and guilt that sin brings when it is recognised. Through the experiences of David, faithful men of all ages can recognise their need for the salvation of God and can wonder at the love of God who provided a sinless bearer of our nature who was saved out of death, in that he feared (see Psalm 6:4,5, with Hebrews 5:7).

Although David speaks of God's wrath and displeasure, there is, behind the words, a tacit recognition that if the agony of soul he now endured was of the Lord (for it was "thy wrath ... thy hot displeasure ... thine arrows ... thy hand ... thine anger" (verses 1-3)), then God could also deliver him from that burden. He does not blame God for his suffering, for although there was no soundness in his flesh because of God's anger, the reason he knew no peace (AV margin) was "because of (his) sin" (verse 3).

As one who had been enveloped by deep waters, the waters having passed over his head (see Psalm 69:2 etc.), David cries, "For mine iniquities are gone over mine head: as an heavy burden they are too heavy for me" (verse 4).

256

In his book *Everyday Life in the Holy Land*, James Neil describes how many towns and villages would have a burden-carrier, one who would carry upon his shoulders tremendous weights of goods or possessions to transport them from one place to another. He describes it as a dangerous occupation, for the weight had to be finely balanced, lest a false step or a slip should cause him to stumble and fall, with disastrous consequences. So David uses the figure as he speaks of himself as one burdened beyond measure with his iniquities, crushed by them, in danger of being destroyed by them, and all because of his foolishness (verse 5). How deceitful sin is! How easily we are led astray by the attractions of the flesh! It is only in repentance and contrition that we appreciate that "the foolishness of man perverteth his way" (Proverbs 19:3).

The physical consequences of his sin, divine confirmation that internal turmoil and worry can produce sickness of the body, is described in graphic terms:

"My wounds (lit. bruises) stink and are corrupt (lit. petrified)." (verse 5)

"I am pained and bowed down greatly." (verse 6, RV)

"My loins are filled with burning (i.e., fever) and there is no soundness in my flesh." (verse 7, RV)

"LORD, all my desire is before thee" (verses 9-14)

In the midst of all his suffering, both mental and physical, David clung to the knowledge that there was One who knew his heart, before whom all his desire was known and who had heard his groaning, and was consequently aware that here was a man who had truly repented of his sin (verse 9):

"My heart panteth (RV, throbbeth, i.e., palpitations) ... as for the light of mine eyes, it also is gone from me (through weeping and weakness)." (verse 10)

There follows a significant change in emphasis in the psalm, for David now turns his attention to the reaction of others to his plight. His sin was known and men were not unaware of the depth of despair to which he had sunk. Remember the words of Nathan, "Howbeit, because by this deed thou hast given great occasion to the enemies of the LORD to blaspheme ..." (2 Samuel 12:14). Not all those who turned away from David came into the category of those described by Nathan. Nevertheless, even those who were closest to him treated him as if he were a leper:

> "My lovers and my friends stand aloof from my sore (lit. my plague – see Leviticus 13:3 etc.); and my kinsmen stand afar off."   (verse 11)

There were those, however, who sought to take advantage of his sorry plight:

> "They also that seek after my life lay snares for me: and they that seek my hurt speak mischievous things, and imagine deceits all the day long."   (verse 12)

It is one of the greatest burdens that a godly man can face. When he acts out of character, when he departs from the general tenor of his life and falls into sin, there will always be those who delight in wickedness, who will accuse him of hypocrisy – who will taunt and revile him and through him blaspheme the God he serves. In David's case it seems to have run deeper than mere words, for there were those who sought his life, who laid snares and sought to discredit him so that they might bring mischief or destruction upon him.

The way in which David reacted in this situation is an example that remains for all men of God; and in the manner of his bearing he truly foreshadowed the spirit of the Lord Jesus Christ himself. He was a deaf man who heard not; he was a dumb man who could not speak (verse 13). He maintained a dignified silence. He made no attempt to enter into debate with them, for he knew his guilt; there was no answer to his sin. To have defended himself would only have been to aggravate the situation. "Yea, I am as a man that heareth not, and in whose mouth are no arguments" (verse 14, RV with margin). No attempt was made at self-vindication, no argument, but silence – not just before them, but before the Lord in humble recognition of his guilt.

In the same way the Lord Jesus, a sinless man, displayed this spirit before his accusers:

> "As a sheep before her shearers is dumb, so he openeth not his mouth."   (Isaiah 53:7)

258

"Who, when he was reviled, reviled not again; when he suffered, he threatened not; but committed himself to him that judgeth righteously." (1 Peter 2:23)

So he "held his peace" before the high priest (Matthew 26:62,63) and when questioned by Pilate, "gave him no answer" (John 19:9).

"For in thee, O LORD, do I hope" (verses 15-20)

David, like the Lord Jesus Christ, committed himself to Him that judgeth righteously: "For in thee, O LORD, do I hope: thou wilt answer, O Lord my God" (verse 15, RV). The pronoun "thou" is emphatic; as in other instances, it can best be expressed by repetition: 'Thou, Thou wilt answer'. In contrast to the reviling of his adversaries, before whom he maintained a dignified silence, he looked to God to answer for him, to refute all the taunts and unjust allegations of his enemies:

"For I said, Lest they rejoice over me: when my foot slippeth, they magnify themselves against me."

(verse 16, RV)

He committed himself to God and left Him to answer, lest in seeking to justify himself he should give his enemies cause to find occasion against him, lest in magnifying themselves against him they should blaspheme the God he served.

As far as he was concerned, his one desire was to be at peace with his God:

"For I am ready to halt, and my sorrow is continually before me. For I will declare mine iniquity; I will be sorry for my sin." (verse 17,18)

It is a perfect description of the process of repentance through which all who seek reconciliation to God must pass. We have an illustration of the process in the experience of Peter after he had denied the Lord. Mark records:

"And the second time the cock crew. And Peter called to mind the word that Jesus said unto him, Before the cock crow twice, thou shalt deny me thrice. And when he thought thereon, he wept." (14:72)

In contrast to his own weakness, the depths to which he had sunk both mentally and physically, his enemies remained strong and active; and, most difficult of all to bear, although he had done them good and sought their welfare, they, with base ingratitude, sought only his hurt (verses 19,20). His trust in God, however, remained unshaken. He despaired of himself, but never did he despair of God. So the closing words of the psalm describe the longing of his heart:

"Forsake me not, O LORD; O my God, be not far from me. Make haste to help me, O Lord my salvation."

(verses 21,22)

PSALM 39

THE inscription "To the Chief Musician, even to Jeduthun" at the head of this psalm could belong to Psalm 38 or 39, depending on whether or not one follows the suggestion of Thirtle in his book *The Titles of the Psalms*. For reasons that will become apparent, it is not an issue of any real consequence in this instance. David appointed Levites to form groups of singers and players of instruments for worship in the tabernacle (and afterwards in the temple). Three are mentioned specifically, in 1 Chronicles 15:16-22 (Asaph, Heman and Ethan). Ethan is not mentioned again, unless he is identified with Ethan the Ezrahite whose name appears at the head of Psalm 89. Jeduthun, however, is linked with the other two (see 16:41 and 25:1).

In chapter 25:3 it is recorded of Jeduthun and his sons that they "prophesied with a harp, to give thanks and to praise the LORD".

All three choirs and orchestras were for the service of God, but no doubt each had special functions to fulfil. Thirtle points out that in the Hebrew text both the name "Jeduthun" and the words "to give thanks" come from the same root, which means 'to give thanks, confess, praise'.

There is therefore a connection between thanks and praise to God arising out of confession and forgiveness of sin. This, of course, was the theme of Psalm 38; but Psalm 39 is a continuation of the theme, for both psalms are closely connected, and thus both of them would be appropriate to bear the title "to Jeduthun".

The similarity in thought and expression of the two psalms should be noted:

261

PSALM 38	PSALM 39
"I was as a dumb man that openeth not his mouth ... in whose mouth are no reproofs" (verses 13,14).	"I was dumb with silence, I held my peace" (verse 2). "I was dumb, I opened not my mouth" (verse 9).
"For in thee, O LORD, do I hope" (verse 15).	"And now, Lord, what wait I for? my hope is in thee" (verse 7).
"lest otherwise they should rejoice over me ... (lest) they magnify themselves against me" (verse 16).	"make me not the reproach of the foolish" (verse 8).
"O LORD, rebuke me not in thy wrath: neither chasten me in thy hot displeasure" (verse 1). "My lovers and my friends stand aloof from my sore" (Hebrew, stroke)" (verse 11).	"Remove thy stroke away from me: I am consumed by the blow of thine hand. When thou with rebukes dost correct man for iniquity, thou makest his beauty to consume away" (verses 10,11).

Psalm 39 is a sequel to its predecessor. It has the same historical background and refers to the same events in David's life. There is, however, a difference in emphasis, for whereas Psalm 38 takes us into David's deepest emotions at the time of his agony of soul and bodily suffering as the whole man was affected by sin, Psalm 39 is written as the crisis is passing and is a reflection on the lessons to be learned from his experience.

The first three verses clearly form a preface to the psalm as a whole. If we then follow the divisions of the psalm indicated by the word "Selah", the remainder of the song will be seen to fall into three parts, comprising of:

(1) verses 4,5

(2) verses 6-11

(3) verses 12,13

The Preface (verses 1-3)

In Psalm 38 David had maintained a dignified silence before those who accused him. He had not tried to justify himself, nor argue his case, for he was conscious of his sin. He knew his guilt, and he would give no cause to men to blaspheme the God he served (verses 12-14). These thoughts are reiterated in the first three verses of Psalm 39, but with the intention of leading to a different conclusion. David resolved to take heed to his ways, that he might not sin with his tongue. Indeed, while the wicked were before him, he would behave as though he had a bridle or a muzzle over his mouth. Under no circumstances would he give men cause to imagine that he was murmuring and expressing bitterness towards God. Like a dumb man, he held his peace, although he had no comfort (verse 2, RV margin).

While maintaining this discreet silence before men, David nevertheless experienced a deep desire to express what was in his heart, for, he says, "my sorrow was stirred"; there was an inward agitation, expressed more definitely in the words of verse 3: "My heart was hot within me, while I was musing the fire burned". The heat of his inner turmoil was kindled into a flame (see RV) so that he could no longer restrain himself from speaking forth – not, however, before men, but in the pouring forth of his meditations on his experience to the Lord his God.

"Then spake I with my tongue" (verses 4,5)

Consciousness of sin brings with it a realisation that death is the just desert of all men. It was around this fact that David's thoughts revolved. It was these truths that produced the agitation of spirit and smouldering of heart and mind that finally caused him to speak forth. The inward struggle, however, caused the words of his mouth to be directed towards God. Not in complaint, but in a desire to be taught of Him the lessons that were to be learned from the salutary experience of his sin and contrition:

> "LORD, make me to know mine end, and the measure of my days, what it is; that I may know how frail I am. Behold, thou hast made my days as an handbreadth; and mine age is as nothing before thee: verily every man at his best state is altogether vanity." (verses 4,5)

This is one of the hardest of all lessons for men to learn. It is something that we can all recognise theoretically as a matter of fact. We know it to be true, for we see it happen to others, but somehow we still manage to live as if it could never happen to us. The worldly man usually behaves as if his life is never going to end; so often even those who seek to serve God are influenced by the same spirit, and (with David) we need God, through the interaction of the circumstances of our lives with the teaching of His word, to bring home to us the realities of our situation. Compared with the life of God, who is from everlasting to everlasting, man's transient and brief life is like a hand breadth, one of the shortest of all measures. Man's frailty, even in his very best estate (lit. "when standing fast" – that is, however firmly established he seems to be in human terms), is likened to vanity, a breath, nothing but a puff of wind; in the words of James, "For what is your life? It is even a vapour, that appeareth for a little time, and then vanisheth away" (4:14).

The use of terms of measurement to describe human life is interesting, for it has been suggested that Jesus was alluding to this passage when he said, "Which of you by taking thought can add one cubit unto his stature?" (Matthew 6:27). In other words, which of you by worrying about it can add even a day to your life? In fact, to be always anxious about life is more likely to shorten it than to prolong it. The point is, that learning the lesson of the brevity of life, we should not spend our time in profitless anxiety about our mortal state, but, recognising the reality of the situation, we should put our trust in God and seek eternal things.

The Vanity of Human Endeavour (verses 6-11)

Having emphasised the brevity and transience of human life, David puts into context the futility of all human endeavour apart from God:

> "Surely every man walketh as a shadow: surely they are disquieted for vanity; he heapeth up riches, and knoweth not who shall gather them."
>
> (verse 6, RV with margin)

Man's life is like a shadow. Apart from God there is no substance to it. All his efforts produce no enduring result, and although he be filled with anxiety (i.e., disquiet) to achieve his ambitions, they are but vanity, empty and meaningless. All the riches he gathers in do him no lasting or eternal good, for he dies and knows not who profits from his labours. The Lord's parable of the rich fool is, of course, particularly appropriate:

"Thou fool, this night thy soul shall be required of thee: then whose shall those things be, which thou hast provided? So is he that layeth up treasure for himself, and is not rich toward God." (Luke 12:20,21)

Realising the transience and worthlessness of human life, David turns to consider the abiding nature of God in the confidence that in Him is to be found the answer to the emptiness of human existence lived as an end in itself: "And now ... what wait I for?" The question could be regarded as rhetorical. It introduces the inevitable conclusion of the previous verse, "My hope is in thee" (verse 7). The implication of the question is that there could not possibly be any other answer. Therefore, "deliver me from all my transgressions: make me not the reproach of the foolish" (verse 8). The consciousness of his great sin opened David's eyes to the true nature of human behaviour. As God had forgiven him this sin, so he recognised that only by putting his hope in God could he be delivered from all his transgressions and thus be saved from the reproaches of those foolish men who had no place for God in their lives. They poured scorn and derision on the godly man when he suffered, as if the affliction was a mark of the wrath and disapproval of the God he claimed to serve. In their eyes, it showed the futility and inconsistency of worshipping such a God.

Yet before such men, as David has emphasised, both in this and the preceding psalm, he was dumb and opened not his mouth. He would give them no cause to cast scorn upon his God, for he knew that "thou didst it" (verse 9). He was silent before the taunts of the foolish because of his resignation to the will of God. Thus he prays, "Remove thy stroke away from me: I am consumed by the blow of thine hand" (verse 10). The word rendered "stroke" is the same as that translated "plague" in Psalm 38:11 (RV), and we have already noted its connection with leprosy. If God were to turn His hand against him, he would be utterly consumed; he would be without hope. When God rebukes man for his iniquity, then, like the attack of a moth on a

265

garment, man's beauty wastes away. Again, all men are shown to be but vanity (verse 11). God's judgement is likened to the moth that destroys goodly raiment, and a similar figure occurs in Hosea 5:12: "Therefore will I be unto Ephraim as a moth, and to the house of Judah as rottenness".

A Stranger and a Pilgrim (verses 12,13)

"Hear my prayer, O LORD, and give ear unto my cry; hold not thy peace at my tears: for I am a stranger with thee, and a sojourner, as all my fathers were."

Note the progression in the Psalmist's cry to God to hear him in his distress: "Prayer ... cry ... tears". The words are reminiscent of Psalm 6:6-9, which is quoted in relation to the experiences of the Lord Jesus Christ in the Epistle to the Hebrews:

"Who in the days of his flesh, when he had offered up *prayers* and supplications with strong *crying* and *tears* ... and was heard in that he feared." (5:7)

David's prayer is a lesson to us all, that we can never take our relationship with God casually. We cannot react to sin as if it were of little importance; but from the very depths of our being we must express with earnestness our overwhelming desire for God's blessing, if need be with "strong crying and tears". Of course the Lord Jesus knew no sin, but nonetheless he shared our human condition, and through his observations of his fellow-men came to know something of that utter helplessness in which all men found themselves because of sin. He associated himself with us – he took upon himself the sin of the world, knowing that if he failed, then there was no life for any man. So he, too, prayed and cried with tears, learning obedience by the things that he suffered.

"Hear me!", cries David, "for I am a stranger with thee"; we suggest that in these words we come to the heart of the message of the psalm for us. Here is the answer to the transience and frailty of human life. Here is the substance, in contrast to the emptiness and frustration that is associated with all human endeavour apart from God.

The words "stranger" and "sojourner" are an obvious link with the covenants of promise and the lives of Abraham, Isaac and Jacob, who in the midst of this world of change and decay "looked for a city which hath foundations, whose builder and maker is God" (Hebrews 11:10).

"I am a stranger", says David, "with thee"; and so must all those be, who seek the eternal inheritance that God has promised. It is a call to separation; it is a recognition that this life is not an end in itself, but the pilgrim who journeys to the kingdom is an alien, a man with no permanent abode, for in this life he has no abiding inheritance, and with the men of this world no real affinity. His association, his fellowship, is with God; and in this sense he becomes a stranger with God, Who in the eyes of men is regarded as an alien in His own world, in which He should rightfully be recognised and acknowledged as Sovereign (see also Leviticus 25:23; 1 Chronicles 29:15).

So this most beautiful and touching of songs ends with the words, "O spare me, that I may recover strength, before I go hence, and be no more" (verse 13) – more exactly, "look away from me", in the sense of "turn away thy wrath from me, that I may recover strength", that is, be restored to spiritual health and vitality. It was an essential experience, for without it there would be no hope. "Grant therefore my prayer", says David, "before I go hence and be no more".

Addendum
The teaching of this psalm concerning the ephemeral nature of human life and the reality of death, in which man ceases to have conscious existence (for he is "no more"), is something that is very characteristic of the psalms (see also 6:5; 30:9; 49:10,19; 88:12; 89:48; 146:4 etc.). This is the truth concerning our human condition and destiny apart from the saving work of God. It is interesting to note that many non-Christadelphian writers freely acknowledge this teaching of the Psalms, but then immediately seek to minimise the force by asserting that it is non-christian. It is, they assert, part of the progressive nature of revelation. Whereas the

Psalmist could not appreciate the reality of the future life, except perhaps in glimpses, this becomes more apparent in the later books of the Old Testament before its final revelation in the New.

We mention these things as a word of warning, particularly to our younger brethren and sisters, for if we would venture at all into pages penned by those who have not come to an understanding of "the whole counsel of God", then we need first to be thoroughly grounded in the foundation truths which bind us together. The Faith once for all delivered to the saints must ever remain inviolate.

PSALM 40

W E have reflected in Psalms 38 and 39 on the manner in which David was affected by his sin in the matter of Bathsheba and Uriah. It involved the whole man; we entered into David's agony of soul and body and we had an insight into the manner in which his suffering was intensified by the hatred of his enemies, who sought his destruction. Psalm 39 concluded with a prayer: "O spare me, that I may recover strength, before I go hence, and be no more" (verse 13).

Psalm 40 is a continuation of the theme. In verses 1-3 David tells how he waited for God's answer to his cry, and how, when it came, he sang a new song to the Lord. The song is contained in the words of verses 4-10, and describes David's realisation of what God required of him. But though the burden of his sin was lifted and David was able to rejoice in God's mercy in restoring him to spiritual health and soundness, he still suffered from the consequences of his sin. He was not relieved from the attentions of those who hated him and wished him harm. So the latter part of the psalm (verses 11-17) returns to his concern regarding his enemies and his prayer that God would deliver him from their evil intentions.

Prayer Answered (verses 1-3)

"I waited patiently for the LORD; and he inclined unto me, and heard my cry." (verse 1)

The AV margin says, "in waiting I waited", and perhaps colloquially it could be rendered, "I waited and waited". The words express David's perseverance and endurance. Nothing could divert his attention from this desire for God to answer his prayer. The intensity of his feeling is indicated by the Hebrew word rendered "waited". It means literally 'to gather together by waiting' (Strong's), hence 'a cord'; and it aptly described the tension that David

269

experienced in watching and waiting for God's deliverance. In the New Testament we can think of Simeon "waiting for the consolation of Israel" (Luke 2:25) and Joseph of Arimathea "which also waited for the kingdom of God" (Mark 15:43); and it reminds us of the attitude we should have as we look and pray for the coming of the Lord Jesus, and wait for the day when we will be able to cry, "Lo, this is our God; we have waited for him, and he will save us: this is the LORD; we have waited for him, we will be glad and rejoice in his salvation" (Isaiah 25:9).

David did not wait in vain, for God inclined unto him, and heard his cry. Perhaps there is a play upon the words of verse 13 of Psalm 39. There the cry was, "O spare me" (literally, 'look away from me' in the sense of 'turn away thy wrath from me'). Now in deliverance God inclines to him, that is, bends down towards him that He may listen to and answer his prayer:

"He brought me up also out of the pit of destruction (RV margin), out of the miry clay, and set my feet upon a rock, and established my goings."   (verse 2)

Figuratively, David likens the trouble he had experienced to a morass into which he had fallen, sinking like a man floundering in quicksand. But God had lifted him out and placed him upon a rock, a figure of security and stability. But this safety was no temporary refuge, for looking to the way ahead, God had established his goings. The word "established" means literally 'to be erect, to stand perpendicular'; and that rendered "goings" is from a root meaning 'to be straight or level', hence 'goings' or 'steps'. Not only had he been made secure, but the way before him had been made firm. Spiritually, God had restored him, and David had real cause to rejoice, for "he hath put a new song in my mouth, even praise unto our God" (verse 3).

New songs are always associated in scripture with God's works of salvation and redemption (see Psalm 33:3 etc.). Notice also the change of pronouns as David speaks of "our God". Evidently surrounded as he was by enemies who sought his hurt, there were still faithful men to whom he could relate and have fellowship. Some of these come to the fore in the record of Absalom's rebellion, when they showed their faithfulness to the king.

Because God had blessed him in this way, David says, "Many shall see it, and fear, and shall trust in the LORD" (verse 3). One of the great lessons that we all need to learn is that when God blesses His servants, others see it and sometimes recognise the work of God in our lives. The result is that they are moved to fear God. This fear is not fright, but reverence; and this awe of God leads to them putting their trust in Him.

A New Song (verses 4-10)

It may be considered conjecture on our part, but we believe, nevertheless, that the substance of this new song that God had put into David's mouth is contained in the verses indicated:

> "Blessed is the man that maketh the LORD his trust, and respecteth not the proud, nor such as turn aside to lies."   (verse 4, RV)

Happy indeed is the man who makes the Lord his trust! The word "trust" implies a place of refuge and security. It carries the thought of assurance that will be experienced by the man who puts his faith in God. The word rendered "man" is also interesting, for its root meaning is 'to be strong', hence a valiant man or a warrior. The Spirit through David has used a word which conveys the idea of a man who might have relied on his own resources, standing firm in his own strength and ability – but who realises the futility of trusting in the arm of flesh, and looks instead to God.

The word rendered "respecteth" means literally 'to turn' (Strong's) and is used frequently to describe those who turn from the true God to the worship of idols (see Leviticus 19:4; Deuteronomy 29:18 etc.). Thus having made Yahweh his trust, he does not turn away to associate with the proud (lit. arrogant, insolent) or those that turn aside to lies. The word translated "turn aside" comes from a root which means 'derelict'. Inherent in this verb, which describes those who practise falsehood, is the idea of paucity of spirit. If we might put it into modern terms, those who practise falsehood are the spiritual 'drop outs' among God's people; we need to remember that the psalm

271

is not speaking of the godless nations that surrounded Israel, but of men of Israel who had failed to appreciate the real character of their calling.

David's heart is full to overflowing as he dwells on the wonder of all that God has done for him. It passes human comprehension:

> "Many, O LORD my God, are thy wonderful works which thou hast done, and thy thoughts which are to us-ward: they cannot be reckoned up in order unto thee: if I would declare and speak of them, they are more than can be numbered." (verse 5)

The declaration that God's works and thoughts towards men are beyond number recalls similar expressions. God promised Abraham that his seed should be like the stars that could not be numbered (Genesis 15:5). Similarly, Jeremiah writes:

> "As the host of heaven cannot be numbered, neither the sand of the sea measured: so will I multiply the seed of David my servant, and the Levites that minister unto me." (33:22)

It is a fact that the stars cannot be numbered, nor the sand of the sea measured – but surely it is not true literally that the seed of Abraham, David and the Levites are not capable of being numbered! Another example occurs in the New Testament:

> "And there are also many other things which Jesus did, the which, if they should be written every one, I suppose that even the world itself could not contain the books that should be written." (John 21:25)

Surely we are dealing with colloquial language, figures of speech which are intended to express those works of God in relation to man which baffle the human intelligence to comprehend their wonder fully. We cannot number; therefore we cannot fully know.

Thus David delighted in the wonder of God's grace in delivering him from the bondage of sin, restoring him to spiritual health, so that once more he knew the joy that springs up in the hearts of men who have experienced God's works of salvation.

It was this overflowing of his heart in praise and thanksgiving that resulted in his expressing the realisation of his responsibilities before God in words that demonstrate that true service is to be found not in formal worship, but in obedience to the will of God:

"Sacrifice and offering thou didst not desire; mine ears hast thou opened: burnt offering and sin offering hast thou not required. Then said I, Lo, I come: in the volume of the book it is written of me, I delight to do thy will, O my God: yea, thy law is within my heart."
(verses 6-8)

If we might paraphrase these verses – David is asking, What can I give to God in return for all His manifold goodness? Once, the answer might have been to offer sacrifices prescribed by the Law of Moses, seeing these as a proper and adequate acknowledgement of God's kindness towards him. Now, however, David had come to realise how inadequate these were, that the formal outward show of worship was not nearly enough. Through the circumstances of life God had taught him this lesson. He had opened his ears so that David knew that above all things God desired a willing and obedient heart that delighted in His law.

Sacrifice and offering, burnt offering and sin offering were the four great sacrifices of the law: peace, meal, burnt and sin offerings. In contrast to these, what God required was a willing response to His law. This truth runs like a golden thread through the pages of scripture (see Psalm 50:8-15; 51:16,17; 1 Samuel 15:22; Hosea 6:6 etc.).

Although the allusion is not certain (the reference to "ears" rather than "ear" does not lend itself to the idea), it is possible that the words of verse 6, "mine ears hast thou digged" (AV margin), are taking us back to the provision under the law whereby a bondservant could voluntarily commit himself to the service of another for life. The custom is described in Exodus 21:2-6 and closes with the words: "his master shall bore his ear through with an aul; and he shall serve him for ever".

Whether or not the allusion is correct, however, the meaning of the words remains the same. The words

273

convey the idea of a life of service and obedience as prescribed in the word of God. Note that the RV margin renders the words "written of me" as "prescribed to me", and the exact Hebrew construction recurs in 2 Kings 22:13, where it is rendered in connection with the discovery of the Book of the Law in the days of Josiah, "to do according unto all *that which is written concerning us*". David is not claiming that there was a special revelation concerning himself in the volume of the book, but rather that the will of God prescribed for him to obey was found there. In response to this, he says in the words of the bondservant, "Lo, I come" – in answer, as it were, to his master's call. The reply is similar to that of Isaiah in response to his vision of the glory of God: "Here am I" (Isaiah 6:8).

These words (verses 6-8) are quoted in the Epistle to the Hebrews in relation to the Lord Jesus Christ (10:5-10). Some find difficulty in this quotation because of an apparent variation in the text from that which appears in the psalm. It is claimed that the quotation is from the Septuagint and also that there may have been corruptions or amendments in the texts. We do not feel it necessary to get involved in these questions. The answer to the variations is that the Spirit is its own interpreter.

We cannot question the right of God, in quoting His own word, to vary the text as a means of expanding the meaning of the Hebrew. The Apostle writes, "Wherefore (because the blood of bulls and goats could not take away sin) when he cometh into the world (i.e., commenced his ministry), he saith, Sacrifice and offering thou wouldest not, but a body hast thou prepared me". Though the words are different, the meaning is precisely the same. "Mine ears hast thou digged" is peculiarly Hebrew, describing the bondservant who devoted himself to his master's service for life. "A body hast thou prepared me" is peculiarly Greek, for the term "body" was used to describe a slave who was owned by a master and was bound to him for life. The Spirit is therefore its own exponent of the meaning of the psalm.

The word "prepared" means "to render fit, sound or complete". So Jesus was perfectly fitted for the task God had given him to perform. We, too, follow in his footsteps, for later in this same epistle, three key words from this quotation are brought together:

"Now the God of peace, that brought again from the dead our Lord Jesus, that great shepherd of the sheep, through the blood of the everlasting covenant, make you perfect (i.e. prepared) in every good work to do his *will*, working in you that which is *wellpleasing* in his sight, through Jesus Christ."   (13:20,21)

In relation to the Lord Jesus, it should be noted that the words "in the volume of the book it is written (prescribed) of me" take on a deeper significance than with David. There in the word of God, the Lord Jesus could read, as no other, the will of God for him – not just in the commandments he was to keep, but in the very path his steps should lead him through life. So he "took upon (himself) the form of a servant ... and became obedient unto death, even the death of the cross" (Philippians 2:7,8).

The argument in Hebrews develops and expands the words of the psalm, for "He taketh away the first (that is, sacrifice and offering), that he may establish the second (that is, the will of God). By the which will we are sanctified through the offering of the body of Jesus Christ once for all" (10:9,10).

This great truth which David had learned – what the Lord required of him – was not something that he could keep to himself. He felt the need to demonstrate his praise and thanksgiving by telling others also "the glad tidings" (verse 9, RV margin) of what God had done for him. Therefore:

"I have preached righteousness in the great congregation: lo, I have not refrained my lips, O LORD, thou knowest. I have not hid thy righteousness within my heart; I have declared thy faithfulness and thy salvation: I have not concealed thy lovingkindness and thy truth from the great congregation." (Psalm 40:9,10)

David's heart "burned within him". Words were piled upon words as he declared his eagerness to witness for God: "I have preached"; "I have not refrained"; "I have not hid"; "I have declared"; "I have not concealed". Before all

275

the people he became a living testimony of God's righteousness, faithfulness, salvation and loving-kindness.

David's Enemies (verses 11-27)

It is difficult sometimes to understand why men who were close to David should have hated him so much. In the days of his exile from the court of Saul we can appreciate how some would have tried to ingratiate themselves with the king, to further their own ambitions, and so have allied themselves with Saul against David. But now David was the king; yet so often the psalms reveal the malice that men had towards him and the hypocrisy by which they hid their real feelings. Men knew he was the Lord's anointed; yet still they desired to have him removed from the throne. It is hard to escape the conclusion that for most of them, their hatred was rooted in their antagonism to the way in which David lived his life. They did not share his love for God or the manner in which he pursued spiritual aims in his rule over the kingdom. These things had become more than just irksome to them; they had become a positive hindrance to the pursuit of their own fleshly ambitions. Thus they would not have this man to reign over them.

It is ever so with human nature, and we should not be surprised that persecution arises for righteousness' sake. The Lord Jesus Christ was the most lovely (and therefore the most lovable) character who has ever lived; yet he was despised and rejected of men: he was taken by wicked hands and crucified.

So it was that although David had been relieved of the burden of his sin, he was still surrounded by enemies; and in this latter part of the psalm he makes his plea to God to deliver him out of their hands, to show the same mercy towards him in respect of them that He had shown in taking away his personal agony of body and spirit. Thus the words of verse 11 repeat the language of verse 10:

"Withhold not thou thy tender mercies from me, O LORD: let thy lovingkindness and thy truth continually preserve me."

Why? Because innumerable evils had compassed him about. His iniquities had taken hold upon him so that he was not able to look up (verse 12).

Once again we have this idiomatic use of language. This time he speaks of evils beyond number, perhaps indicating David's inability to comprehend why men should be so antagonistic to him. He continues by describing his iniquities as being more than the hairs of his head. We can, possibly, equate the innumerable evils with the iniquities that had taken hold of him. If this is so, then the evils and iniquities are used to describe the effects of his sin rather than the sin itself; and we know that David readily accepted that the troubles that had come upon him were the results of his sin. In fact, in his mind the two could not be separated, so that he could readily put the cause for the effect.

If this line of reasoning is correct, then it helps us to appreciate how these words could apply to the Lord Jesus Christ, for the psalm is undoubtedly Messianic. He shared our nature; he partook of all the effects of Adam's transgression, although he himself was sinless. He died as a representative of sinful men. He freely and willingly associated himself with them and recognised the justice of God's sentence by accepting with all men the condemnation that Adam's transgression brought. In short, he shared our common heritage, and with David could say, "Thou art my help and my deliverer" (verse 17).

The last five verses of the psalm (13-17) reappear later, with some variations, as Psalm 70. We do not consider it appropriate to consider this fact here. There are also verbal links between these five verses and Psalm 35. Compare particularly 40:14 with 35:26. Psalm 35 was written against the background of David's exile from the court of Saul. Psalm 40 is concerned with those events that followed David's sin in the matter of Bathsheba and Uriah, leading to Absalom's rebellion.

There is nothing strange about the differing backgrounds, however, for they both deal with men who hated David and sought to destroy him. It was therefore appropriate that as David recalled God's deliverance so many years before, he should recall the words of the song he had written then and repeat them in these new but similar circumstances.

David's trust that God would hear him and deliver him is finally emphasised in the last verse:

"But I am poor and needy; yet the Lord thinketh upon me: thou art my help and my deliverer; make no tarrying, O my God."

We, too, can enter into the spirit of David's prayer when we cry, "Even so, come, Lord Jesus" (Revelation 22:20).

PSALM 41

THERE can be little (if any) doubt that this psalm is connected historically with the time of Absalom's rebellion. It has much in common with Psalm 38, as it presents King David as a sick man who is confined to his bed, unable to take positive action, yet totally aware of the hypocrisy of those who presented themselves as his close friends and associates. They visited to sympathise and offer condolence; yet in their hearts they rejoiced at the calamity that had overtaken him, and anxiously waited for the day of his death, which they anticipated with malicious satisfaction.

There is, of course, no record of David being afflicted in this way in the historical books; but the fact that such was his experience helps to explain how Absalom's rebellion was able to develop and be carried out effectively, with David apparently helpless to prevent it. Thus Absalom was able to take the initiative and steal the hearts of the men of Israel by offering to act as judge in his father's stead when men came to seek the king's counsel (2 Samuel 15:1-6).

Similarly, the plotting of such as Ahithophel and those who supported Absalom was able to prosper unhindered, without interference from the king; and when at last Absalom made his move, we can appreciate the lack of decisiveness, and note the contrast between the attitude of the bold, courageous warrior of earlier years and the apparent weakness and lack of initiative of David at this time (see 2 Samuel 17:1-4).

"Blessed are the merciful"

The first three verses of the psalm exemplify the spirit that David had shown so often, not only to his friends, but also towards those that hated him. They could be summed up in the Lord's words, "Blessed are the merciful: for they shall obtain mercy" (Matthew 5:7); and David's introduction of these thoughts at the beginning of the psalm seems intended as a direct contrast to the attitude of his false friends in verses 4-10. There is real happiness to be found in showing consideration for the poor (note that the word means literally, 'weak', thus incorporating the sick as well as the deprived). Of course, men do not always respond positively to the goodness shown, for David himself is an example of one who was rendered evil for good. The heart of the matter lies in our faith in God. He will reward the compassionate for their concern for the poor, for in words that the Lord alluded to in the quotation from Matthew 5, David had written in an earlier psalm, "With the merciful thou wilt show thyself merciful" (18:25). Thus Psalm 41 emphasises this truth: "the LORD will deliver him" (verse 1); "the LORD will preserve him" (verse 2); "the LORD will strengthen him" (verse 3).

David is confident that God will deliver him from his enemies, bless him upon the earth and comfort him when human weakness brings him down upon his "bed in his sickness" (verses 1-3). He is undoubtedly looking back upon his experiences and remembering those who, in contrast to his false friends, had shown real sympathy and concern for him – men, no doubt, like Ziba and Barzillai, who came to his aid when he fled from Absalom (see 2 Samuel 16:1-4; 19:31-33).

David's Reflection on his Time of Sickness

The opening words of verse 4, "I said ...", are a clear indication that what follows is David's recollection of what happened at that time. In his distress his plea had been for God to show mercy to him in healing his soul, for he had sinned against Him. Once again David acknowledges that the circumstances in which he finds himself are the consequence of his sin, and recognises that the healing he requires encompasses both his bodily and spiritual ailments (verse 4). The words that follow are a terrible insight into, and indictment of, human nature at its worst. The spirit shown by the false friends reflects something of the spirit of Psalm 109, which we believe to be substantially the curse with which Shimei cursed David – compare, for instance, "When shall he die, and his name perish?" (verse 5) with "Let his posterity be cut off" (Psalm 109:13).

It is interesting to conjecture as to what motivated Absalom in his rebellion. He was, of course, the eldest son, having been born before David was enthroned in Zion. No doubt therefore he felt that he had a right to the throne, and felt resentment at the implications of the covenant that God had made with David whereby Solomon had been chosen to be king. Verse 6 seems to apply to a particular individual ("... and if he come to see me") who was to the fore amongst those who wished for David's name to perish. If this was in fact Absalom, then perhaps we get a deeper insight into the heart of an embittered man. He had no son, no posterity who would preserve his name on the throne of David, for that privilege had been promised to Solomon. Note that Absalom did have sons (see 2 Samuel 14:27). He built a pillar to perpetuate his name in the earth (2 Samuel 18:18). How then must the thought of his father David and the prospect of his line being assured through Solomon have eaten him up with jealousy and a brooding conviction that God had defrauded him of what was rightfully his!

So when he visited David, his words of solace were empty words. When he left the bedchamber, he gathered about him those who shared his hatred, and they "whispered together" (verse 7), plotting David's destruction. No doubt they could find excuses to justify their actions. Human nature always can: "An evil disease, say they, cleaveth (lit. 'is soldered') fast unto him: and now that he lieth he shall rise up no more" (verse 8). They saw his affliction as a punishment for sin; perhaps they had convinced themselves that because he was a sinner, God had revoked the covenant. At such times true friends are made manifest, and sometimes those with whom we have had long association and whom we hold dear in our affection show themselves to be false. Thus it was for David:

"Mine own familiar friend, in whom I trusted, which did eat of my bread, hath lifted up his heel against me."
(verse 9)

281

Almost certainly this is a reference to Ahithophel, for so many years David's counsellor and friend, who had eaten at the royal table and shared fellowship with David (see also Psalm 55:12-14). We say almost certainly, because of an element of doubt in the writer's mind that does not seem to be shared by others. The margin (AV) renders "mine own familiar friend" as "the man of my peace". Absalom's name means 'father of peace'. Could therefore the reference be a play upon his name, and in this instance (though not in Psalm 55) could he be the individual referred to? It is not a matter of great consequence, for the two men shared a common purpose, and the words indicate the motivation of the "friend", and lend credence to the suggestion above. "Hath lifted up his heel against me" is a description of the customary way of trampling upon a serpent. With Genesis 3:15 in mind, it could be said of both men that they regarded David as "serpent seed". In destroying him they thought they did God service.

The initial plan was to wait for him to die; but David recovered. Perhaps by then they had gone too far in their preparations for the succession; there was no alternative to open rebellion. In this way God answered David's prayer: "But thou, O LORD, be merciful unto me, and raise me up, that I may requite them" (verse 10).

Perhaps then the seed of doubt was sown in Ahithophel's mind. When Absalom heeded the counsel of Hushai rather than his own carefully planned strategy (2 Samuel 17:1-14), he knew that all was lost; the Lord was still with David; he went and hanged himself (2 Samuel 17:23). This verse is quoted, of course, in John (13:18) in respect of Judas Iscariot, who played a part in the life of the Lord Jesus like that played by Ahithophel in David's life – and shared Ahithophel's end. It should be noted that the words quoted omit reference to the "familiar friend, in whom I trusted", for Jesus knew from the beginning who it was that should betray him; and while the words were appropriate to David, they were not true of the Lord Jesus, although Jesus always treated Judas as though he was a friend. He made no distinction between Judas and the other disciples, and Judas was not condemned until he had actually performed his treacherous deed.

David's Confidence

It was because of these circumstances, and the manner in which God had delivered him from the hand of his enemies, that David knew he had found favour in God's sight (verse 11). He knew his future was assured, for he maintained his integrity before God, and ultimately it would be his joy to stand in the presence of God and to behold His face for ever (verse 12).

Perhaps there could be no more fitting end to what is commonly regarded as the first of the five books of the psalms. Every psalm was written by David. It is an impressive testimony to his God-consciousness, to his delight in those things that belonged to God's purpose and the work of God in his life to bring these things to fulfilment. The concluding verse, whether written by David himself or by some later compiler of the psalms (e.g., Hezekiah) is an eloquent testimony to the greatness of the God who had worked with His servant David, a man after His own heart, to such marvellous effect.

> "Blessed be the LORD God of Israel from everlasting, and to everlasting. Amen, and Amen." (verse 13)

A wonderful paean of praise!

PSALMS 42,43

AS we begin what is generally known as the Second Book of the Psalms (Psalms 42 to 72), we come in Psalms 42 and 43 to two songs which are, in the writer's opinion, the first that are not from the pen of David, "the sweet Psalmist of Israel".

They are the first of a series of psalms that bear the title "For the sons of Korah". These number twelve in total, or eleven if we regard Psalms 42 and 43 as one song. This is that Korah who perished with Dathan and Abiram in the rebellion in the wilderness. The record tells us, however, that "notwithstanding the children of Korah died not" (Numbers 26:11); and among some of the illustrious descendants of this rebellious priest was Samuel, the prophet of the Lord (1 Chronicles 6:22,28).

It is apparent that the Levites described as the sons of Korah were of the family of the Kohathites, and prominent amongst those who "ministered before the dwelling place of the tabernacle of the congregation with singing" were members of this family (1 Chronicles 6:32,33). Mentioned particularly is Heman, a singer (verse 33). Apparently he had fourteen sons and three daughters, and "all these were under the hands of their father for song in the house of the LORD, with cymbals, psalteries, and harps, for the service of the house of God" (25:5,6). Two of the house of Heman were prominent in helping Hezekiah to cleanse the house of the Lord (2 Chronicles 29:14). It appears that Korah's descendants had a talent for music and singing that was first recognised in the days of David, and passed through subsequent generations to members of Korah's family in the times of Hezekiah. We make this point particularly, because we believe that taken collectively the psalms for the sons of Korah contain

284

strong internal evidence to link them with the reign of Hezekiah.

Some of these psalms, if they stood alone, might appear to be so general in character that they could refer to many historical circumstances (undoubtedly Psalms 42 and 43 fall into this category). But most bear unmistakable links with Hezekiah's times, and in the circumstances it seems reasonable to suppose that all the psalms bearing this title belong to the same period in Judah's history.

We do not know who was the author of Psalms 42 and 43, but we do know his circumstances, for he was cut off from Jerusalem with its temple worship for which he longed so much. We do know precisely the geographical location in which he found himself, almost in the northernmost borders of the land of Israel – the mountains of the Hermonites on the other side of Jordan. Whoever the author was, he seems to have been a person of some distinction, perhaps a priest; and although cut off from the temple service at Jerusalem, he did not anticipate that his plight would continue indefinitely, but longed for the day when he could return.

We can well imagine a servant of God in the reign of Hezekiah finding himself in such a situation. The Assyrian had wrought havoc in the land – remember Samaria was besieged for three years, and only Jerusalem remained secure; yet the host of Sennacherib had laid siege to it and there was no way to go up to the city. The psalmist, knowing the words of the prophet Isaiah and putting his trust in them, knew that the city would not fall, and that ultimately God would deliver it. Nevertheless, living as he did on the east of the Jordan, and with the temple services undoubtedly disrupted, it would be impossible for him to attend the feasts "to appear before God". No doubt he felt this all the more keenly because he would recall the great festival of joy and thanksgiving that Hezekiah had initiated, and in which he would have participated (2 Chronicles 30). Note also the similarity of expression between the words of the psalm, "Where is thy God?" (42:3) and the arrogant taunts of the servants of Sennacherib (2 Chronicles 32:14-17).

That the two psalms constitute one song seems evident from the similarity of language and, in particular, the refrain that closes each section of the two psalms: "Why art thou cast down, O my soul? and why art thou disquieted in me? hope thou in God: for I shall yet praise him for the help of his countenance" (Psalm 42:5,11; 43:5).

The psalms fall into three sections, which might be summarised as follows:

1. The Psalmist's yearning for God (42:1-5)

2. His perplexity in distress (42:6-11)

3. His prayer for deliverance (43)

It can be noted also that there is a regular poetic metre throughout both psalms. It has been described as a halting 3:2 rhythm particularly suitable for lamentations (Dr. N Snaith).

Yearning for God

"As the hart panteth after the water brooks, so panteth my soul after thee, O God. My soul thirsteth for God, for the living God: when shall I come and appear before God?"   (42:1,2)

The familiar figure of the hart 'heated in the chase' is not the simile employed by the Psalmist. It is, in fact, the picture of wild animals affected by a long period of drought. As one writer expressed it: "It is impossible for anyone to understand the depth of meaning in this metaphor who has not lived in a drought-ridden country of seasonal rains". And yet while this must be true, there is also a sense in which it is not, for it represents the writer's intense desire for God; and anyone who has had a like experience knows the reality of this representation. Consequently, although we may not understand the desire of the wild creature as he panted at the scent of water in a dry and arid land, we can enter into the experiences of the Psalmist and share his yearning for God. How great a longing is seen in the expressions that he uses, the way in which God dominated all his thoughts. He is "the living God" (verse 2), "the God of my life" (verse 8), "God my exceeding joy", "O God my God" (43:4). There is a progression of thought running through the words.

286

The living God for whom he thirsts stands in contrast to the gods of the nations, and indeed all material and transient things, as the ultimate reality. He is "the fountain of living waters" (Jeremiah 17:13), "the fountain of life" (Psalm 36:9). Apart from Him, life has no real meaning; in Him is found the life that is life indeed. So the Psalmist describes Him as "the God of my life". It is this preoccupation with God who dominates and motivates his life that causes the Psalmist to describe Him as his "exceeding joy", a treasure far surpassing anything that human life apart from God has to offer. So he says, recognising the intimacy of his fellowship and association, He is "God my God". These thoughts present us with an interesting reflection. We know that nothing can separate us from the love of God – that wherever the godly man might be, his fellowship with Him cannot be affected by location or external circumstances. Yet here the Psalmist's desire, his longing for God, is expressed in his yearning to go up to Jerusalem "to appear before God". This, of course, is the phrase used in regard to the three great feasts: "Three times in the year all thy males shall appear before the Lord GOD" (Exodus 23:17; see also Psalm 84:7). And his recollections of happier times are of "leading" the multitude to the house of God with the voice of joy and praise on holy day (Psalm 42:4). It is generally agreed that the verb "I had gone with" carries the idea of leading – hence the conclusion that the Psalmist was a person of some eminence.

The lesson would appear to be that all the feasts of the Lord, all His holy ordinances, had their part to play in bringing man nearer to God. Our fellowship with God, although it cannot be broken by location or external circumstances, can become far more difficult to maintain if we are separated for any length of time from the place where He has chosen to meet with His people, and if, in particular, we are denied the company of those who are like-minded, who share our love for God and faith in His promises.

The festivals that Israel celebrated were an integral part of their relationship with God. To be denied these opportunities of celebrating God's work on behalf of His people was to be deprived of some of the greatest delights in spiritual experience. No man who had truly known the joy of these occasions would willingly absent himself from them; he would yearn for them, for they spoke to him of that ultimate spiritual joy to be experienced in God's kingdom, when His purposes would be consummated in the earth.

We have to appreciate that nothing has changed. We meet to break bread and drink wine and should feel the same longing and yearning for these occasions. Our ecclesias are spiritual oases in the desert. We should never forsake the assembling of ourselves together, for all these occasions have been provided as part of our spiritual experience to bring us nearer to God. Once the joy of these experiences has been appreciated, the yearning is created. Nothing should be able to keep us away.

Denied such opportunities, the Psalmist had lost all appetite for natural food. Overwhelmed by grief, tears had been his meat day and night. In his extremity the cry of the enemy had been, "Where is thy God?" It was the bitterest of all taunts to suggest that his God was powerless to help, that He was indifferent to his situation or impotent to act.

In this situation, the Psalmist expresses the conflict within in the words of the refrain that closes each section of the psalm: "Why art thou cast down, O my soul?" – "cast down" is literally "bowed down", and the word carries the idea of mourning. "Why art thou disquieted within me?" (RV) – "disquieted" is used elsewhere of the raging of the sea, and expresses the turbulence and agitation that he felt within. Yet for all the tribulation and adversity that enveloped him, he knew the answer: "Hope thou in God", trust that He would ultimately deliver; "for I shall yet praise him for the help (lit. salvations, i.e., many deliverances) of his countenance".

Perplexity and Distress

In this second stanza (verses 6-11) the Psalmist tells us where he is in the land, for he remembers his God from "the land of Jordan, and of the Hermonites, from the hill Mizar" (verse 6). While remaining in the land of Israel, he

288

is almost as far away from Jerusalem as it was possible to get. He would not have been far from the Caesarea Philippi of the New Testament, where the Jordan rises from the foothills of the Hermon range. It is not possible to identify the hill Mizar. It means literally 'the little mountain' and perhaps serves as a conscious contrast with the stronghold of Zion for which he longed.

The nature of the countryside, the terrain in which he found himself, furnished the imagery for the inner turmoil that he was experiencing. When the snows melted, the rocky defiles would become filled with torrents of water. The wild and rugged countryside would be filled with the noise of the rushing torrents as "deep called unto deep" at the noise of the waterspouts (lit. cataracts or waterfalls). So the Psalmist recognised that all he suffered was of the Lord: "all thy waves and thy billows are gone over me." His suffering, his agonising, his intense longing had engulfed him like many waters; perhaps like the waves on the sea shore, of which the mountain torrents would remind him. "Yet the LORD will command his lovingkindness in the daytime, and in the night his song shall be with me" (verse 8).

It is significant that whereas God has been described by the word 'Elohim' in every other instance, here the covenant name of God is used: Yahweh will command His loving-kindness. The reason for this use of the name is obvious. We have already commented on several occasions upon the Hebrew *chesed*, rendered "lovingkindness", or more appropriately, "covenant love". God's loving-kindness is a ray of hope that shines upon the Psalmist in his despondency and perplexity, and because of this he is comforted by his song in the night. These have been his experiences in the past, and he calls upon them to find strength for the present. So, in the light of these past mercies, he will say to God his Rock (lit. crag, i.e., place of safety), "Why hast thou forgotten me? why go I mourning because of the oppression of the enemy?" One of the greatest tests of faith to come upon the servant of God is the feeling, through the circumstances of life, that God has left him. Psalm 10 speaks eloquently of this: "Why standest thou afar off, O LORD? why hidest thou thyself in

289

times of trouble?" (verse 1). It is not, of course, that God abandons the sufferer in his distress. It only appears so to the individual, so that in these circumstances men of faith may show their true quality. They emerge with their faith made richer by the experience.

Nevertheless, the sadness and mourning that the Psalmist knew were very real. The experience was like a sword thrust into his bones as his enemies reproached him with the taunt, "Where is thy God?" It was not just a passing jibe; daily they cast their insults upon him and the God upon whom he waited.

Prayer for Deliverance

Psalm 43, which we have subtitled: 'A prayer for deliverance', reproduces much of the thought and language already considered in Psalm 42. The emphasis is different, for it is primarily a prayer for God to act on the writer's behalf. Thus he cries, "Judge me, O God, and plead my cause against an ungodly nation: O deliver me from the deceitful and unjust man" (verse 1). The word rendered "ungodly" is the Hebrew *chasid* with a prefix added. This lends weight to the suggestion that the enemy was not of the covenant people, but was the Assyrian invader to which we have already made reference. We feel, however, that the deceitful and unjust man of whom the writer speaks could well allude to those men of Israel and Judah, of whom there were many, who threw in their lot with the Assyrian and worked for the destruction of their own people.

Verse 2 is a repetition in a more emphatic form of the expostulation made in verse 9 of Psalm 42, and on which we have already commented. This time, however, faith asserts itself more strongly and prayer ascends in confident tones as the writer pleads with God: "O send out thy light and thy truth: let them lead me; let them bring me unto thy holy hill, and to thy tabernacles" (verse 3). Possibly "light" and "truth" are an allusion to Urim and Thummim, the stones which were kept within the breastplate of the high priest, and were the medium by which God spoke to His people. They represented the presence of God dwelling in the midst of His people, leading and directing them, and all these thoughts are inherent in the Psalmist's prayer. By these he will be brought again to God's holy hill and to His tabernacles (dwelling places – note the plural, no doubt referring to the temple buildings, a point reiterated in the New Testament:

"In whom each several building, fitly framed together, groweth into a holy temple in the Lord"

(Ephesians 2:21, RV)

Then once more he will go to the altar of God. Here is the answer to the question in Psalm 42: "When shall I come?" (verse 2). Coming to God his exceeding joy, he cries, "Yea, upon the harp will I praise thee, O God my God" (Psalm 43:4). It raises an interesting speculation, that not only was the psalm for the sons of Korah, but it was actually penned by one of that company who showed such skill in the playing of musical instruments, and would, perhaps, in that capacity have led the throng to worship (Psalm 42:4).

The Lord Jesus Christ

We turn now to the Messianic significance of the psalms, and, taking as understood the manner in which the spirit of the Psalmist would have reflected the Lord's own language and yearnings, we turn in particular to a specific period in his ministry and a definite event that seems to have been prefigured by the words of this psalm.

We know that the Lord Jesus was driven by his enemies from the city and temple that he described as his Father's house. He came unto his own (inheritance) and his own (people) received him not. As his ministry progressed it became more dangerous for him to present himself at Jerusalem for the feasts, and each time the fact of the nation's rejection became more apparent. How closely would he associate himself with the feelings of the Psalmist! There came therefore a time when Jesus came into the very area (geographically) from which the Psalmist had looked so longingly to Jerusalem.

It was at Caesarea Philippi (to which we have already made reference) that Jesus asked his disciples, "Whom do men say that I the Son of man am?" (Matthew 16:13). The answers given were such that it was evident the people

291

THE PRAISES OF ISRAEL (PSALMS 1-72)

had rejected him as the Christ: "John the Baptist; but some say, Elias; and others say, that one of the old prophets is risen again" (Luke 9:19). It is hard to believe the credulity of men. They could believe he was John the Baptist or one of the prophets risen from the dead, but accept him as the Christ, the Son of the living God? Never! They would believe anything, grasp at any straw rather than face up to the responsibilities such a recognition would have placed upon them. Human nature has not changed at all. It is just the same today.

This was the turning point in the ministry of Jesus. All the Gospels make clear that it marked a change in the attitude of the people towards him, and he himself began to prepare his disciples for the things he must suffer at Jerusalem. But Jesus also needed preparation. All three synoptic Gospels tell how at this time Jesus was transfigured before his disciples. Knowing that before him lay the agony of Gethsemane and the shame of the cross, he would have found the words of Psalm 42 particularly appropriate: "Deep calleth unto deep at the noise of thy waterspouts: all thy waves and all thy billows are gone over me" (verse 7). So he went up into a high mountain – surely one of the Hermon range. Remember the reference to the snows of Hermon and Peter's personal reminiscence through Mark: "And his raiment became shining, exceeding white as snow" (9:3).

It is Luke, however, who tells us the details of the conversation that he had with Moses and Elijah. They "spake of his decease (lit. exodus) which he should accomplish at Jerusalem" (9:31). They strengthened him for the task ahead, and the result was that "he stedfastly set his face to go to Jerusalem" (verse 51). So from "the land of Jordan and of the Hermonites" he set his face to become obedient even unto the death of the cross. How beautifully the thought is reflected in the last stanza of the song:

"O send out thy light and thy truth: let them lead me; let them bring me unto thy holy hill, and to thy tabernacles. Then will I go unto the altar of God."

(Psalm 43:3,4)

He steadfastly set his face and came to offer himself for the sin of the world, knowing that beyond the cross there was the joy set before him; for through his exodus, his coming out, he would go to the Father, to God his exceeding joy; for at His right hand there were pleasures for evermore – perfect, never-ending fellowship (Psalm 16:11).

PSALM 44

THOSE acquainted with J. W. Thirtle's book *The Titles of the Psalms* will be aware of the thesis proposed there regarding the musical and literary information appended to the psalms. Briefly, this information can be broken down into five separate headings:

(1) Authorship

(2) Historical Background

(3) Literary Features

(4) Liturgical Use

(5) Musical Directions

Thirtle's argument, based on examples such as the third chapter of Habakkuk, is that all literary information is placed at the head of the psalm, whereas musical directions and information as to how and when the psalm was to be sung in the temple services is given at the end of the song. This leads to the proposition that in some instances information which appertains to the preceding psalm has been included mistakenly in compilation at the head of the psalm following. One feels that the suggestion has much to commend it, Psalm 8 being a notable example, where the evidence is very strong in supporting Thirtle's argument.

There are a few examples where evidence seems less convincing, but Psalm 44 is undoubtedly amongst those where the weight of evidence seems to support Thirtle's thesis. Thus the information, "To the chief musician, upon Shoshannim", which appears between Psalms 44 and 45, belongs in fact to Psalm 44. The preposition rendered "upon" can also be rendered "concerning" or "relating to"; hence the meaning of the word "Shoshannim" becomes of primary importance. Strong's Concordance indicates that the meaning of the word is "lilies", and Thirtle includes the word with a small group that have to do with the season of the year (e.g., *Gitteth,* winepress). Thus he concludes that lilies, which speak of spring and the time of Passover, indicate that the psalm was to be sung at that festival.

The associations of the lily in scripture lend themselves to this interpretation. Lilies figured prominently in the ornamentation of the temple and its furniture (1 Kings 7:19; 2 Chronicles 4:5; Exodus 25:31-34 – LXX, supported by the *Targum*, renders "flowers" as lilies). Secondly, on the high priest's robes (Exodus 28:33,34) the golden bells and pomegranates on the hem were understood by the rabbis as lilies and pomegranates (i.e., the golden bells were shaped like the cup of a lily), supported by the association between the two in Solomon's temple. Thirdly, the lily figures prominently in the Song of Solomon (2:1,2,16; 4:5; 5:13; 6:2,3; 7:2). It thus comes to be regarded as a symbol of the redeemed people of Israel in the bonds of their covenant relationship with God (see also Hosea 14:5,6 in this connection).

How then does this apply to Psalm 44? We notice first that verses 1-3 speak of the events of the Exodus, of how God in the days of old delivered the people and planted them in the Promised Land, emphasising that Israel had possessed the land, not by their own sword or power, but by God's strength and through the light of His countenance shining upon them. Secondly (see paragraph following), the psalm is set in the days of Hezekiah, when a Passover was proclaimed in the second month (2 Chronicles 30; see Numbers 9:9-14) as Hezekiah swept away the idolatrous practices of his father Ahaz, and reconstituted the true worship of the Lord his God. Indeed, it can be concluded that the destruction of Sennacherib's host was in fact a Passover deliverance, for writing of these events Isaiah said, "As birds flying, so will the LORD of hosts defend Jerusalem; defending also he will deliver it; and passing over he will preserve it" (31:5; see Exodus 12:12, 2 Kings 19:33-35). The angel of the Lord passed through the midst of the Assyrian camp.

Historical Background

In our consideration of Psalms 42 and 43 we indicated that all the psalms bearing the inscription "to the sons of Korah" belong to the reign of King Hezekiah, and this has already been referred to in connection with Psalm 44 in our introduction. We can, perhaps, elaborate a little upon this historical background. The psalm can be divided into four parts:

1. In the past God had established His people in the land, and through Him had come all the success in which they rejoiced (verse 1-8).

2. In contrast with past mercies, they had now been delivered into the hand of their enemies (verses 9-16).

3. However, this was not because of their wickedness, for the Psalmist was able to write of their faithfulness to the Covenant (verses 17-22).

4. The psalm concludes with a prayer to God to rise and redeem them for His mercies' sake (verses 23-26).

In relation to sections 1 to 3 we draw attention to the following connections in the historical books:

1. Note the similarity in language between the first section of the psalm and the words of encouragement spoken to Hezekiah by the prophet Isaiah (2 Kings 19). Both recall God's work in the days of old (Psalm 44:1; 2 Kings 19:25); the psalm emphasises that Israel were established in their land not by their own strength, but by God's power (Psalm 44:2-8). Isaiah reproaches the Assyrians because they thought that it was by their power that they had overcome their enemies, and conquered many nations, whereas it was the God of Israel who reigned in the kingdom of men (2 Kings 19:23-26).

2. The psalm speaks of the people of God being made a reproach, a scorn and a derision to their enemies. To reproach and deride them was, of course, to speak against their God. So God says to the Assyrian, "Whom hast thou reproached and

blasphemed? and against whom hast thou exalted thy voice, and lifted up thine eyes on high? even against the Holy One of Israel ... thy rage against me and thy tumult is come up into mine ears" (2 Kings 19:22,28). Notice that the words "reproacheth and blasphemeth" (Psalm 44:16) are only associated together elsewhere in the words of Sennacherib's defiance of Israel's God (2 Kings 19:6,22).

3. The plea that they had not sinned against God is particularly relevant when considered against the reforms initiated by Hezekiah and supported by the people (read 2 Chronicles 29-31).

Scriptural Background

Turning from the historical background, there is also a scriptural background worthy of note, which reflects the feelings of Hezekiah and the faithful remnant in Judah. Running through the psalm there is an underlying play upon the events recorded in the First Book of Samuel, when the ark was taken by the Philistines. Notice the plaintive cry of verse 9: "But thou hast cast off, and ... goest not forth with our armies", recalling vividly the way in which the Israelites had carried the ark forth, mistakenly believing that thus they could be assured that God went forth with their armies. It is perhaps of significance also that the title "LORD of hosts" or "Yahweh of armies" occurs first in the scriptures in the record in Samuel (see 1 Samuel 1:11; 4:4; 17:45).

After the ark was recovered from the Philistines and came to rest at Kirjath-jearim, it is recorded that "the time was long ... and all the house of Israel lamented (RV margin, 'was drawn together') after the LORD" (1 Samuel 7:2). Commenting on these events, and the consequence of Israel through this period of testing and trial turning again to their God, the Psalmist writes:

"He forsook the tabernacle of Shiloh, the tent which he placed among men; and delivered his strength into captivity, and his glory into the enemy's hand. He gave his people over also unto the sword; and was wroth with his inheritance." (Psalm 78:60-62)

297

But the time came when "the Lord awaked as one out of sleep, and like a mighty man that shouteth by reason of wine" (verse 65).

The prayer of the Psalmist was, "Awake, why sleepest thou, O Lord? Arise, cast us not off for ever" (Psalm 44:23). The plea to arise recalls the words when the ark went forth: "Rise up, LORD, and let thine enemies be scattered; and let them that hate thee flee before thee" (Numbers 10:35; see Psalm 68:1).

Verses 1-8

We have already commented upon the substance of this opening section of the psalm, and it remains to draw attention to a number of salient points within these verses. The recollection of God's work in the days of old is something that His servants should find a continual source of comfort. Hezekiah and the faithful in Judah cried, "We have heard with our ears, O God, our fathers have told us" (verse 1). Thus is emphasised for us the responsibility laid upon us to instruct the generation to come, to instil into their hearts a reverence for the word of God and an understanding of the work of God in past ages, for the principles upon which God acts remain the same in our day as in all previous generations. We have a responsibility to teach sound doctrine, for "faith cometh by hearing, and hearing by the word of God" (Romans 10:17).

In verse 3 the reference to the light of God's countenance is another direct link with the events of the Exodus. Literally, the word "countenance" means 'presence'. So God told Moses:

"My presence shall go with thee, and I will give thee rest. And he said unto him, If thy presence go not with me, carry us not up hence. For wherein shall it be known here that I and thy people have found grace in thy sight? is it not in that thou goest with us? so shall we be separated, I and thy people, from all the people that are upon the face of the earth." (Exodus 33:14-16)

We also read:

"The LORD went before them by day in a pillar of a cloud, to lead them the way; and by night in a pillar of

298

fire, to give them light; to go by day and night."
(Exodus 13:21)

Similarly, the words of verse 4, "Command deliverances for Jacob", are strikingly illustrated by the events of the Exodus. The dividing of the Red Sea (Exodus 14:13-30) is a most impressive example of how God commanded the wind and the sea to effect deliverance for His people.

Note also the figure of "pushing" in Psalm 44:5. Literally it means pushing as with a horn, as an ox or a bull does. The use of the word in Exodus (21:29) illustrates the meaning (see also Deuteronomy 33:17). As always, it is "through thy name" that Israel treads underfoot the enemy. Their strength lay in all that God had revealed Himself to be, both in word and action; and all this, of course, was summed up in the name of God in which was enshrined His purpose, character and attributes.

Verses 9-16
We have already intimated the circumstances to which these verses refer. They find their fulfilment in Hezekiah's reaction to the invasion of Sennacherib and his host, and the success of his military adventure that saw all the fenced cities of Judah fall before his might, until only Jerusalem remained out of his hands. In his pride, the Assyrian wrote on his inscriptions, "Hezekiah have I shut up like a bird in a cage".

Verses 17-22
Undoubtedly these words are the reflection of the faithful remnant who, with Hezekiah, put their trust in God and hearkened to the words of the prophet Isaiah. We have spoken of the spiritual revival which Hezekiah initiated, and of the manner in which the people responded in sweeping away all the abominations of his father Ahaz. It is nevertheless clear from a careful reading of the historical records and Isaiah's prophecy, that for the majority it was not a complete repentance; it did not encompass their hearts, but in many respects it was concerned with the externals of their religion. Also, as the threat from the Assyrian grew more ominous, there were all kinds of factions appearing among the princes and rulers. Some were seeking peace with Assyria, some were

299

speaking of an alliance with Egypt; few, in fact, kept faith with Hezekiah.

If this was the attitude of the princes, there can be no doubt that it was a reflection of the attitude of the people at large. God was testing the people, and the result of this fiery trial of their faith was that Hezekiah and a faithful remnant alone came through it.

Again, this lesson is timeless. The time of trial came on all alike. Amongst the righteous in Judah there were those who for God's sake were killed all the day long. They were counted as sheep for the slaughter. Like martyrs, they died in their faithfulness. There was no discrimination; their faith was not like an insurance policy, but they all suffered in the general affliction that overtook the nation. There was of course for them as individuals a greater issue that went far beyond the deliverance from the Assyrian, concerned with their eternal destiny.

In the same way we in our day partake of all human nature's weakness, and suffer with all men the things to which the flesh is heir. We have no guarantee as far as this life is concerned. Sickness and disease affect us, as with all men, and in the time of calamity, epidemics, war, insurrection, terrorist activity and natural disaster, we can have no absolute assurance that we shall escape. But we must live our lives faithfully and rest always in the knowledge that this life is not an end in itself, but a pilgrimage to God's kingdom, for we are related to things that are eternal.

It is against these thoughts that the Apostle Paul quotes the words of the psalm in the Epistle to the Romans:

Who shall separate us from the love of Christ? shall tribulation, or distress, or persecution, or famine, or nakedness, or peril, or sword? As it is written, For thy sake we are killed all the day long; we are accounted as sheep for the slaughter. Nay, in all these things we are more than conquerors through him that loved us."

(8:35-37)

We are more than conquerors because we are secure in His love, which by God's grace will secure us a place in the kingdom of our Lord Jesus Christ.

Verses 23-26
Nevertheless, from Judah's point of view and the unfolding purpose of God, the nation as a whole had to find deliverance in their God. Their prayer contained in these closing verses was heard. The taunts and reproaches of the Assyrian came up into the ears of the Lord of hosts, for He who keeps Israel neither slumbers nor sleeps. The night of trial and affliction passed. God rose up as in the days of old. Not for ever did He appear to hide His face and forget their oppression, for in one night the angel of the Lord went forth and slew the host of Assyria. Jerusalem was delivered, and as a result "many brought gifts unto the LORD to Jerusalem, and presents to Hezekiah king of Judah: so that he was magnified in the sight of all nations from thenceforth" (2 Chronicles 32:23).

Thus was Yahweh of Armies, sanctified in the eyes of all nations.

Addendum
Hezekiah, as we shall see more clearly as we proceed through the Psalms associated with his reign, was a wonderful type of the Lord Jesus Christ. It seems reasonable to look for a recurring fulfilment of these events in Psalm 44 at the time of the second coming of the Lord. Indeed, we have scriptural evidence, for Micah's prophecy, surely based initially on the life of Hezekiah, speaks of the one who should come forth out of Bethlehem to be ruler in Israel (Micah 5:2); "and this man", says Micah, "shall be the peace when the Assyrian shall come into (the) land" (verse 5).

How do we understand this? Could it be that the refining of Israel will cover more than one phase, and as with Hezekiah's day, so with that of the Lord Jesus – the initial repentance will for many be no more than a superficial and external thing? Will the latter-day Assyrian come down upon the land and the plaintive verses 17-22 have a recurring fulfilment – a judgement as

301

wheat is sorted from chaff? If so, the end is sure, for the Lord will awake as one out of sleep, with disastrous consequences for the invader and oppressor of His people. In this context, the words of Micah find their fulfilment – for he that is to be ruler in Israel will be the peace when the Assyrian comes into the land.

PSALM 45

THIS psalm is described in the inscription that heads it as "A song of loves", and is clearly written to celebrate the marriage of a king, almost certainly to a foreign bride. Speculation as to the precise occasion that caused the writing of this psalm ranges over a wide variety of possibilities, the most commonly preferred being the marriage of Solomon to one of his foreign wives. Perhaps among the more bizarre is the suggestion that it was the marriage of Jehoram to Athaliah, daughter of Ahab and Jezebel.

It is the writer's conviction, however, that it was written to celebrate Hezekiah's wedding to Hephzibah, the mother of Manasseh (2 Kings 21:1). We are led to this conclusion by the fact that the psalm is amongst that group of songs that are stated to be "for the sons of Korah", which we have previously indicated (see Psalms 42 and 43) to be associated with the times and reign of Hezekiah. In addition, attention should also be paid to verse 10: "Forget also thine own people, and thy father's house". There is a clear allusion here to the command given to Israel regarding a wife taken from amongst the captives of war, recorded in the book of Deuteronomy. She was to be permitted to bewail her father and her mother a full month (21:13) and if, subsequently, the captor had "no delight in her", he was to permit her to go whither she would (verse 14).

Not only is there a connection between the words of Deuteronomy and the exhortation to 'forget … thy father's house', but the name Hephzibah means 'my delight is in her' (see Isaiah 62:4, AV margin). This also seems to be a conscious play upon the words of Deuteronomy, perhaps indicating that Hephzibah was, if not a captive bride, a Gentile princess who was given her name at the time of her union with Hezekiah. Perhaps it should also be noted that she named her son "Manasseh", which means 'forgotten', indicating that in the joy of the birth of her son she had truly forgotten all those things that pertained to her earlier life.

The psalm has strong similarities in thought and expression to the Song of Solomon, and the language far transcends the historical circumstances as it speaks unerringly of the marriage supper of the Lamb, when he who is "altogether lovely" (Song 5:16) will be made one with his redeemed bride, of whom he can say, "Thou art all fair, my love; there is no spot in thee" (4:7).

With such an exalted theme, it is understandable that the writer of the psalm (possibly Isaiah) should be moved by the Spirit to describe the reaction in the hearts of all those who delight in this wondrous theme:

"My heart is inditing a good matter: I speak of the things which I have made touching the king: my tongue is the pen of a ready writer." (verse 1)

Literally the first sentence is: "My heart bubbleth over with a good matter". The figure is drawn either from boiling water, or from a fountain bubbling up from its source. In either case, it dramatically describes the way in which the hearts of faithful men "burn within them" or overflow with zeal and spiritual excitement when they contemplate the consummation of God's purpose in His Son and those that are his. They are unable to contain themselves, for when they speak and write they can think only of him who fills their thoughts and is the object of their deepest longings and desires – he of whom Hezekiah was but a shadow – *The* King. Many say the better rendering is "a king"; but the noun rendered "king" is used without the article in verses 13, 15 and 16, for instance, although it is definite in these cases, as in verses 5 and 11 where "the" does appear.

The King in His beauty

"Thou art fairer than the children of men (lit. Adam): grace is poured into thy lips: therefore God hath blessed thee for ever." (verse 2)

304

Thus is described the beauty of the king. Throughout scripture we find in the case of special individuals raised up by God to perform His work descriptions that, at face value, seem to be limited to personal beauty, but which, upon reflection, are seen to apply to deeper intrinsic qualities that mark them out as unique among their contemporaries. Thus Moses is described as "a goodly child" (Exodus 2:2); David was "ruddy, and withal of a beautiful countenance, and goodly to look to" (1 Samuel 16:12); even Saul was described when chosen as king as "a choice young man, and a goodly" (9:2).

The Lord Jesus Christ, of whom the psalm speaks preeminently, is unique amongst all the sons of Adam. He is fairer than all, for grace is poured into his lips. The Gospel records bear witness to the fact, for "never man spake like this man" (John 7:46); he "taught them as one having authority" (Matthew 7:29); "And all bare him witness, and wondered at the gracious words which proceeded out of his mouth" (Luke 4:22); or, as the prophet testified, "The Lord GOD hath given me the tongue of the learned, that I should know how to speak a word in season to him that is weary" (Isaiah 50:4).

Those who would "see the king in his beauty" (Isaiah 33:17) must strive to be like him, for Isaiah describes the quality of the lives of such in words that are reminiscent of Psalms 15 and 24:

"He that walketh righteously, and speaketh uprightly; he that despiseth the gain of oppressions, that shaketh his hands from holding of bribes, that stoppeth his ears from hearing of blood, and shutteth his eyes from evil."   (verse 15)

The book of Proverbs sums up the necessity of emulating the characteristics of the Lord Jesus in our lives: "He that loveth pureness of heart, and hath grace in his lips (AV margin), the king shall be his friend" (Proverbs 22:11). Those who do so will, with him, be blessed for ever. Thus is emphasised once again the perpetuity and everlasting stability of the throne and kingdom of David.

Because of these things, the Psalmist beseeches the king to manifest himself in strength and power. His gracious character is the basis for the work that God will ultimately send him forth to perform in the earth:

> "Gird thy sword upon thy thigh, O most mighty, with thy glory and thy majesty. And in thy majesty ride prosperously because of truth and meekness and righteousness; and thy right hand shall teach thee terrible things. Thine arrows are sharp in the heart of the king's enemies; whereby the people fall under thee."
>
> (verses 3-5)

To return briefly to the historical background, it might seem strange to think of Hezekiah in terms of these words, and certainly they can only have a precise fulfilment in the Lord Jesus Christ. However, it is worth noting that after the destruction of the host of Sennacherib and Hezekiah's recovery from his sickness, Hezekiah received gifts:

> "And many brought gifts unto the LORD to Jerusalem, and presents to Hezekiah king of Judah: so that he was magnified in the sight of all nations from thenceforth."
>
> (2 Chronicles 32:23)

The way in which the life of Hezekiah forms a background to Isaiah's prophecy might also be considered. This is not a theme we can pursue in the context of our psalm. But if we accept that the words of Isaiah 9: "Unto us a child is born, unto us a son is given: and the government shall be upon his shoulder: and his name shall be called Wonderful, Counsellor, The mighty God, The everlasting Father, The Prince of Peace" (verse 6) were occasioned by the birth of Hezekiah, and in some senses, albeit shadowy and partial, received a fulfilment in him, then we note also that the word *Gibbor* used in Isaiah of "The mighty God" is used also in the psalm of the Warrior Bridegroom – "O most mighty".

The prayer of the Psalmist for the king to manifest himself as a warrior in all his power against his enemies is reflected in the believers' prayer, "Even so, come, Lord Jesus" (Revelation 22:20). The purpose of this display of his military prowess is, however, totally different from that which motivates the nations of the world when they wage war upon each other. He girds his sword and goes forth in glory and majesty, that is, displaying divine qualities, for the sake of (RV margin, in behalf of) truth and meekness and righteousness. It is in order to uphold and assert these qualities in the earth, to show the highest and noblest aspirations of kingship, and to stamp himself unquestionably as God's representative on earth, that the king girds on his sword.

Isaiah 11:1-5 speaks of this same manifestation of might and power on behalf of the poor and meek of the earth. The words of verse 4 form a link between the psalm and the words of the Apocalypse. Revelation 19:11-16 has close links with Isaiah 11: "And he shall smite the earth with the rod of his mouth, and with the breath of his lips shall he slay the wicked" (verse 4). It describes the Lord Jesus symbolically represented as going forth on a white horse. He is called Faithful and True, and in righteousness he judges and makes war; out of his mouth goes a sharp sword to smite the nations. On his vesture and on his thigh he has a name written, "King of kings, and Lord of lords". The sword is not girded on the thigh, but comes from his mouth, relating to Isaiah 11:4. But the thigh is also mentioned in Revelation 19 (verse 16). It is inscribed with the name of God; and in the words of Brother Thomas, "he goes forth as the expression of the Eternal Spirit". We are clearly in the realm of God-manifestation. The king is God's representative upon earth, and this is of particular importance when we come to consider verses 6 and 7 of our psalm. The connection of Revelation 19 with this psalm is, however, even more apparent when we read the earlier part of the chapter, for it describes that with which the theme of the psalm is primarily concerned:

"Let us be glad and rejoice, and give honour to him; for the marriage of the Lamb is come, and his wife hath made herself ready."   (verse 7; see also verses 8,9)

Returning to the psalm, it is further recorded of the warrior king that his "right hand shall teach thee terrible things". The words recall similar expressions used when God had manifested Himself on behalf of His people, particularly in delivering them from bondage in Egypt (see Deuteronomy 10:21; 2 Samuel 7:23; Isaiah 64:3 etc.). His right hand, that is, his strength and power, teach or show him these "terrible things", in the sense that as he

307

succeeds in battle he comes by experience to appreciate fully the divine energy with which he has been endowed. So his arrows are sharp in the heart of the king's enemies (see Psalm 7:11-13), and so the wicked fall before him.

"Thy throne, O God, is for ever and ever: the sceptre of thy kingdom is a right sceptre. Thou lovest righteousness, and hatest wickedness: therefore God, thy God, hath anointed thee with the oil of gladness above thy fellows." (verses 6,7)

Orthodox commentators show the futility of turning to their writings for a proper understanding of the foundation truths of God's revelation by their handling of these particular verses. The key, of course, lies (as already intimated) in an appreciation of the scriptural teaching on God-manifestation. It is in the understanding of this that we have the answer to so many passages of scripture that have been distorted and wrested by Trinitarians in an endeavour to establish their teaching.

Various expedients have been resorted to in an effort to remove the force of the expression "Thy throne, O God"; but almost all seem to the writer not just to be grammatically unsound, but generally awkward and unconvincing in their construction. It seems to have been recognised by the orthodox commentators that, far from supporting the doctrine of the Trinity, the AV translation presents a difficulty. This difficulty is readily understood in terms of God-manifestation, but cannot be allowed by those who are committed to a view of progressive revelation that moves beyond Biblical teaching to the authority of the Church and to the eventual evolution in its fullness of the doctrine of the Trinity. As one writer expressed it, "It is impossible to suppose that the mystery of the incarnation was distinctly revealed, and clearly understood, under the Old Testament dispensation. God does not thus make haste with men".

Scriptural usage must be our guide. We know, for instance, that the judges of Israel were called "gods" (see Exodus 21:6; 22:8,28, RV). Particularly relevant is the use of the word *elohim* in relation to the judges of Israel in Psalm 82, for this psalm was used by the Lord Jesus to defend his claim to be the Son of God:

308

"Jesus answered them, Is it not written in your law, I said, Ye are gods? If he called them gods, unto whom the word of God came, and the scripture cannot be broken; say ye of him, whom the Father hath sanctified, and sent into the world, Thou blasphemest; because I said, I am the Son of God?" (John 10:34-36)

"If he called them *elohim* to whom the word of *elohim* came" – because they spoke the word of God – they were God's representatives upon earth. His word came through them; how much more so was God manifest in His Son?

The reference in the psalm, however, is broader in its application, for it is founded on the covenant that God made with David: "I will be his father, and he shall be my son" (2 Samuel 7:14). Of course this declaration was implicit in the words used by the Lord Jesus in John 10; but David's throne was "the throne of the kingdom of the LORD over Israel" (1 Chronicles 28:5). Those who sat on it did not rule in their own right, but were God's representatives on His throne over Israel. In this sense the words were true of all faithful sons of David, particularly so of Hezekiah, of whom it is recorded:

"He trusted in the LORD God of Israel; so that after him was none like him among all the kings of Judah, nor any that were before him. For he clave to the LORD, and departed not from following him, but kept his commandments, which the LORD commanded Moses." (2 Kings 18:5,6)

In this sense the words, "thou lovest righteousness and hatest wickedness", have an incipient fulfilment in Hezekiah, although, like the rest of the psalm, they are finally and fully realised in the Lord Jesus Christ.

The words then reaffirm the everlasting stability of the throne of David when the Lord Jesus reigns on his Father's behalf over all the earth. The sceptre, the symbol of his royal authority, is exercised in righteousness and justice, and because of his love of righteousness and hatred of iniquity God has anointed him with the oil of gladness above his fellows. This anointing is not the coronation anointing of the king, but the festive joy of the marriage feast. It is linked with the Lord's victory over sin, for his bride has been redeemed through his

309

righteousness and sacrifice. His fellows in this context are surely those who have preceded him upon the throne of David.

"Thou lovest righteousness, and hatest wickedness": we do well in considering the relationship between the Lord Jesus Christ and his Father to avoid unnecessary speculation. We know he was truly man and also the only begotten Son of God. That his unique relationship with God enabled him to conquer sin is without question. But to seek too precise definitions of what it was that Jesus inherited from God that made his victory possible, can lead us to go beyond what is written. In this area we do well to be guided rigidly by what God has been pleased to reveal. The words before us help us to say with confidence that one of the key factors in his relationship with God that enabled him to remain sinless was this unique love of righteousness and hatred of wickedness, inherited from his Father, that dwelt in him as in no other man, and in this respect gave him an advantage that other men had not possessed. It should be noted that as far as his human nature was concerned, the Lord Jesus had no advantage, but shared the same disabilities that condemnation in Adam had imposed upon the whole human race.

Before leaving our consideration of these particular verses, it should be noted that they are quoted in the Epistle to the Hebrews (chapter 1) as part of the argument to demonstrate that the Lord Jesus was superior to the angels. To demonstrate this truth, the writer is guided to collate a series of Old Testament quotations, all of which show that God "hath in these last days spoken ... by his Son" (verse 2), and all are drawn from contexts that deal with the covenant that God made with David:

"Thou art my Son, this day have I begotten thee."
(Hebrews 1:5; see Psalm 2:7)

"I will be to him a Father, and he shall be to me a Son." (Hebrews 1:5; see 2 Samuel 7:14)

"Let all the angels of God worship him."
(Hebrews 1:6; see Psalm 97:7)

"Thy throne, O God, is for ever and ever."
(Hebrews 1:8; see Psalm 45:6)

"Sit on my right hand, until I make thine enemies thy footstool." (Hebrews 1:13; see Psalm 110:1) The superiority of the Lord Jesus Christ has its basis in the covenant that God made with David, for implicit in it was the truth that God would manifest Himself in His Son. It is an indictment of those who espouse the doctrine of the Trinity, for what basis would there be for these words of the Spirit if Jesus was in fact 'God the Son'? His superiority over the angels would then undisputably have rested upon this fact.

"All thy garments smell of myrrh, and aloes, and cassia, out of the ivory palaces, whereby they have made thee glad. Kings' daughters were among thy honourable women: upon thy right hand did stand the queen in gold of Ophir." (Psalm 45:8,9) As a result of the anointing, which in the case of the original historical background would have been a literal pouring forth of costly perfume, the sweetness of the odour is described. The "oil of joy" was in contrast to mourning, i.e., "the garments of praise for the spirit of heaviness" (Isaiah 61:3). Such joy was written concerning Solomon:

"Go forth, O ye daughters of Zion, and behold king Solomon ... in the day of his espousals, and in the day of the gladness of his heart." (Song 3:11) Myrrh, aloes, cassia and fragrant spices speak to us of the pleasure that "the king in his beauty" gives to all those who share his joy. It is instructive to note that this odour of the Royal Bridegroom is something that other scriptures associate also with the bride. "Thou art all fair, my love; there is no spot in thee ... better is thy love than wine! and the smell of thine ointments than all spices!" (Song 4:7,10). She is likened to a garden, and amongst her pleasant fruits are "myrrh and aloes, with all the chief spices" (verses 12-14). (In this context see also Hosea 14:4-7, which speaks of Israel restored to her bridal status after the depths to which she had descended described in the enacted parable of chapters 1 to 3.)

The importance of this imagery is that it emphasises the unity that exists between the king and his bride. They share the glory and beauty, and his righteousness envelops and thus characterises the bride. It is a wonderful thought that without the Ecclesia, his bride, the Lord Jesus, like Adam without Eve, is incomplete. In the purpose of God it was never intended that the Lord Jesus should enter into glory alone. He was the first-begotten from the dead; through him the Father was bringing many sons unto glory. In the words of Paul, writing to the Ephesians, God "hath put all things under his feet, and gave him to be the head over all things to the church, which is his body, the fulness of him that filleth all in all" (1:22,23).

The joy of the occasion is emphasised by the voice of praise, for "out of the ivory palaces stringed instruments have made thee glad" (Psalm 45:8, RV). So the splendour of the occasion is brought to a conclusion with the introduction of the bride. All nations will be blessed in him in that day; thus kings' daughters, the representatives of Gentile nations, will be in attendance when the queen stands on his right hand in gold of Ophir. It is said that the very finest gold came from Ophir, which was probably situated in Southern Arabia, from where it carried on trade with India. Spiritually, of course, the fine gold represents a tried faith, which is the essential characteristic of the bride.

Exhortation to the bride (verses 10-12)

Verses 10-12 are addressed to the bride:

"Hearken, O daughter, and consider, and incline thine ear; forget also thine own people, and thy father's house; so shall the king greatly desire thy beauty: for he is thy Lord; and worship thou him. And the daughter of Tyre shall be there with a gift; even the rich among the people shall intreat thy favour."

The thought developed in the introduction to the psalm, that the bride was in fact a Gentile, gives a deeper, more urgent significance to the words of exhortation. It was necessary for her to break her ties with the past, to forget all her former associations, so that she might give her devotion and loyalty to her husband. The words are reminiscent of other women who left their fathers' houses to join themselves, not only to their husbands, but also to their God.

Rebekah was asked, when Abraham's servant came seeking a bride for Isaac, "Wilt thou go with this man? And she said, I will go" (Genesis 24:58). The simplicity of her resolve, the determination to forget her father's house and to go to Isaac are, as with the words of the psalm, a true reflection of the spirit of all those who would be constituents of the Bride of Christ.

Our father's house is our heritage "in Adam" and all that is associated with it. When we commit ourselves to the Lord Jesus Christ we sever all our former connections with this present evil world and come to him in the spirit of Ruth:

"Intreat me not to leave thee, or to return from following after thee: for whither thou goest, I will go; and where thou lodgest, I will lodge: thy people shall be my people, and thy God my God." (Ruth 1:16)

It is in this spirit that the Lord delights, for it is intrinsically a part of that beauty which rejoices his heart. When so many prefer their own people, and their father's house, it is a consolation to him to know that there are still those who with all their hearts will respond, "Lord, to whom shall we go? Thou hast the words of eternal life".

"The daughter of Tyre", like the "daughter of Zion", is a personification of the people of that nation who, at the "wedding supper of the Lamb" at the inauguration of the Millennial age, will be among the rich of the peoples of the earth who will bring gifts and entreat the favour of the bride in her beauty.

"The bride hath made herself ready" (verses 13-15)

The Psalmist's attention is now turned to the beauty of the bride. The words "all glorious" are often misconstrued to be a reference to the purity of heart of those who constitute the Bride of Christ. While this quality is undoubtedly one of her characteristics, it is not the meaning of the words in the psalm. Rather, the reference is to the bride, having made herself ready, waiting in her chamber to be conducted into the presence of the king for the celebration of the wedding ceremony. She is nevertheless "all glorious", literally "all glory". Such is the splendour in the day of their exaltation of those who have been covered by the blood of the Lamb! Her clothing is described as being of "wrought gold", or "gold-woven robes" (RSV) – once again the symbol of a tried and perfected faith (see 1 Peter 1:7; Lamentations 4:2). She is brought to the king in "raiment of needlework", literally a garment embroidered in many colours. Surely this is the result of many hours of loving work! It is different from the "fine linen, clean and white", which is "the righteousness of saints" (Revelation 19:8), for that was "granted to her", and is the righteousness which is imputed through faith. The emphasis in the psalm, however, is upon the willing and joyful endeavours of the bride to prepare herself for her Lord. We do well to remember that although we cannot be saved by our own efforts alone, and that but for the grace of God we would all perish, yet it remains true that "to them who by patient continuance in well doing seek for glory and honour and immortality, (God's gift will be) eternal life" (Romans 2:7).

Conclusion (verses 16,17)

Once again the king is addressed: "Instead of thy fathers shall be thy children." The message seems to be giving an assurance that although perhaps his ancestry gives no reason for rejoicing, he will be more than compensated by his posterity, for they will be better to him than his fathers. It is difficult to see a precise fulfilment in the experience of Hezekiah (or indeed of any other of David's sons). It is only in the Lord Jesus Christ that we see a real fulfilment. The covenant that God made with David is consummated in him who preeminently loved righteousness and hated wickedness. For this reason "the children whom God hath given (him)" will, through him, become princes in the earth. He will see of the travail of his soul and be satisfied, in that day when God's perfect representative will sit on the throne of his father David for ever. His name will be remembered in all generations. We remember that when God made His name known to Moses, he was told that "this is my name for ever, and this is my memorial unto all generations" (Exodus 3:15). So God's name is manifest in His Son, and the consequence is that he is the object of perpetual praise.

The subscription of the psalm, to be found at the conclusion and not at its head, reads, "A song upon Alamoth". The word "Alamoth" means 'maidens'. It would appear therefore to have been intended for a female choir (Thirtle).

This "marriage ode", "a song of loves", takes us to the heart of the consummation of the unity that is to exist between the Lord Jesus Christ and his bride. In our understanding of it, the manner in which we are able to enter into its spirit, we shall find comfort and consolation in the knowledge that "Blessed are they which are called unto the marriage supper of the Lamb" (Revelation 19:9).

315

PSALM 46

W E continue our consideration of the nine psalms for the sons of Korah which we have previously shown to be associated with the life and times of Hezekiah. Psalm 46 is particularly clear in its allusions to the historical records and to the prophecy of Isaiah. These will become apparent as we consider the words of the song; but it seems appropriate to relate the history of Sennacherib's incursions into the land, for this provides the historical background to this psalm, which could have been written by Isaiah, or Hezekiah himself.

The early years of Hezekiah's reign were peaceful and in the main prosperous. Nevertheless, the continuing threat of Assyrian military power was an ever-present anxiety. Some preparations were made for a future siege of the city by the ingenious feat of engineering, whereby the "upper pool", the main source of water for the city, was covered in completely, and the underground flow of water that fed the pool diverted by means of a tunnel into the pool of Siloam, thus providing a continuous supply for the city and, at the same time, cutting off the main source of water for any besieging army (see 2 Chronicles 32:4).

The anticipated invasion eventually came. It appears that Sennacherib had two separate armies at his command. One moved against Lachish, intent, after capturing the fortress, on moving against Egypt. The other devastated the land of Judah, attacking the fortress cities that Hezekiah had set up, with the ultimate intention of challenging Jerusalem itself.

The Biblical records make it clear that, faced by the might of the Assyrians, the morale of the people disintegrated. Their faith in Israel's God collapsed. A deputation under Shebna was sent to mediate with the Assyrians and they, in contradiction to the spirit of

316

Hezekiah, accepted the most shameful and humiliating terms for peace. Their rejoicing in the apparent deliverance of the city was, however, shortlived. It is clear that these princes of Judah had no intention of keeping the agreement they had made. It was a subterfuge on their part, intended to buy time (see Isaiah 28:15,18-20); and while outwardly friendly to the Assyrian, they were frantically seeking to make an alliance with Egypt.

Whether it was because Sennacherib discovered these underhand diplomatic moves, or because he himself treacherously disregarded the treaty, we do not know; but he moved his army against Jerusalem. The army was led by several of his generals and senior officers, amongst them Rabshakeh, who played such a major role in trying to intimidate and strike fear into the hearts of the defenders of the city. All seemed lost; delegations were sent to conduct negotiations, but Rabshakeh treated them with disdain, seeking to influence the common people on the walls of the city by shouting to them of the might of Assyria and her gods, the poverty of their feeble defences and the inability of Israel's God to deliver them.

He must, however, have been disturbed by the failure of his bullying tactics, for the people "held their peace, and answered him not a word: for the king's commandment was, saying, Answer him not" (2 Kings 18:36). Clearly, Hezekiah was still in control and retained the allegiance of the people. Rabshakeh varied his tactics, attacking the king and his God in particular, but leaning upon the prophet Isaiah and putting his faith in God, Hezekiah was assured that God would deliver the city. Yet it appeared hopeless, for all the fenced cities had fallen and vast numbers of the people had been carried off as captives to Assyria. Jerusalem only remained to Hezekiah and the faithful remnant.

No more negotiations took place, but, moved by frustration, Sennacherib now composed a letter in which he attacked Israel's God (19:10-13). Moved by this letter, and confident in Isaiah's assurance that God would save the city, Hezekiah took the letter and spread it out before the Lord in the house of the Lord. He concluded his prayer with the words, "Now therefore, O LORD our God, I beseech thee, save thou us out of his hand, that all the kingdoms of the earth may know that thou art the LORD God, even thou only" (verse 19). God's reply was this:

"He shall not come into this city, nor shoot an arrow there, nor come before it with shield, nor cast a bank against it ... For I will defend this city, to save it, for mine own sake, and for my servant David's sake. And it came to pass that night, that the angel of the LORD went out, and smote in the camp of the Assyrians an hundred fourscore and five thousand: and when they arose early in the morning, behold, they were all dead corpses."
(verses 32-35)

Structure

The psalm consists of three stanzas, each concluded by the word "Selah". The second two end with the same refrain, "The LORD of hosts is with us; the God of Jacob is our refuge" (verses 7 and 11). In the first stanza the God of Israel is presented as the refuge of His people in the midst of their recent distress. The second stanza (verses 4-7) illustrates this truth by alluding to recent events, and the third (verses 8-11) regards the events of which the psalm speaks as an earnest of God's final triumph over all nations.

Verses 1-3

In their extremity, when all hope seemed lost, God had proved Himself by His deliverance from Sennacherib's host. He had responded to the prayer:

"O LORD, be gracious unto us; we have waited for thee: be thou their arm every morning, our salvation also in the time of trouble."
(Isaiah 33:2)

So the Psalmist could respond,

"God is our refuge and strength, a very present help in trouble."
(verse 1)

The word translated "refuge" is different from the word used in verses 7 and 11. Literally it means 'shelter, hope, place to flee for protection'. God had proved Himself their hope and confidence, for, concerning their treaty with the Assyrian, Shebna and his associates had said, "We have made lies our refuge"; and God had responded, "I will ...

318

sweep away the refuge of lies" (Isaiah 28:15,17), here using the same word as in verse 1 of our psalm.

He is a "very present help in trouble". The RSV margin says, "a well proved help" (for they had known it in their own experience). Literally the Hebrew says, "A help in trouble He is very surely found".

"Therefore will not we fear, though the earth be removed, and though the mountains be carried into the midst of the sea; though the waters thereof roar and be troubled, though the mountains shake with the swelling thereof." (verses 2,3)

The scriptures testify that "the earth abideth for ever". The RV gives the sense "though the earth do change". The verses describe a scene of catastrophic upheaval – the utter confusion without being contrasted with the quiet security of those who dwell in Zion. The language is not, of course, intended to describe just the literal upheaval of the earth, but is symbolic of the raging of the nations, the verse standing in apposition to verse 6:

"The heathen raged, the kingdoms were moved: he uttered his voice, the earth melted."

This symbolic aspect of the language is seen more clearly when we remember that the roaring of the waters find a counterpart in the language of the prophet used to describe the Assyrian invasion:

"... the waters of the river, strong and many ... and he shall come up over all his channels, and go over all his banks ... he shall overflow and go over, he shall reach even to the neck." (Isaiah 8:7,8)

Again the word rendered "swelling" is normally translated "pride", the swelling of the waters being a fitting description for the arrogance of the Assyrian monarch.

Verses 4-7

As a result of God's activity on behalf of His people, they experience peace and assurance because He is their refuge. This second stanza describes the security that is theirs in Zion, the city of their God:

"There is a river, the streams whereof shall make glad the city of God, the holy place of the tabernacles of the most High. God is in the midst of her; she shall not

319

THE PRAISES OF ISRAEL (PSALMS 1–72)

be moved: God shall help her, and that right early."

(verses 4,5)

The reference to the river which made glad the city is a clear allusion to the conduit constructed by Hezekiah. But of course the allusion goes beyond the literal application, for the pool of Siloam was contrasted to the River Euphrates in the passage already referred to:

"Forasmuch as this people refuseth the waters of Shiloah that go softly ... behold, the Lord bringeth up upon them the waters of the river."   (Isaiah 8:6,7)

The waters of Shiloah represented the authority of God, the quiet, sweet influences of the word of God. It is representative of the presence of God which dwelt in the city, for it is "the holy habitation of the Most High" (RSV). The title "Most High" is particularly appropriate, for it indicates the supremacy of the God of Israel over all the so-called gods of the nations. He alone was exalted above all.

"God is in the midst of her" recalls again the words of Isaiah (see 12:6), and because God dwells in the midst of His people they will, unlike the mountains (and nations they represent), never be moved (lit. slip, shake or fall).

"God shall help her, and that right early" (AV margin, "when the morning appeareth") brings to mind the destruction of Sennacherib's host: "In the morning, behold, they were all dead corpses." Again, of course, the psalm looks forward to that morning without clouds when "there shall be a fountain opened to the house of David and to the inhabitants of Jerusalem for sin and for uncleanness" (Zechariah 13:1).

We have already intimated that verse 6 is parallel to verses 2 and 3, but there is also a most interesting connection with Psalm 2 and Isaiah's prophecy. Psalm 2 deals with the antagonism of the kings of the earth towards Zion's king: "Why do the heathen rage ...?" (verse 1) – and tells of the futility of their efforts to frustrate God's purpose:

"He that sitteth in the heavens shall laugh: the LORD shall have them in derision ... Yet have I set my king upon my holy hill of Zion."   (verses 4,6)

320

Whenever men rise up and seek to overthrow the throne of David and to frustrate God's purpose His response is always the same. The psalm has a recurring fulfilment, and the quotation of this earlier psalm in Psalm 46 is clear, when we look at the raging and blasphemy of Sennacherib.

After Hezekiah had received the letter and laid it before the Lord, Isaiah responded with words of comfort and encouragement. God's reply to Sennacherib was constructed in part around the words of Psalm 2:

"The virgin, the daughter of Zion, hath despised thee, and laughed thee to scorn ... But I know ... thy rage against me. Because thy rage against me, and thy tumult, is come up into mine ears ..."

(Isaiah 37:22,28,29)

Perhaps extending the thought a little further – there was another fulfilment when the apostles quoted Psalm 2 in connection with the crucifixion of the Lord Jesus Christ (Acts 4). Again, men sought to frustrate the purpose of God, but to no avail. For He will yet set His King upon His holy hill of Zion. What is particularly interesting is that the apostles preface their quotation from the psalm with the words: "Lord, thou art God, which hast made heaven, and earth, and the sea, and all that in them is" (Acts 4:24). Surely this is a reference to the prayer of Hezekiah when he laid the letter before the Lord, as recorded in Isaiah 37 (see verse 16).

The section in Psalm 46 concludes :

"The LORD of hosts is with us; the God of Jacob is our refuge." (verse 7)

Yet again the link is with Isaiah's prophecy and Immanuel – God with us (see 7:14; 8:8 etc.) – a clear indication of the historical background to the psalm. Perhaps the reference to the God of Jacob in this and the last verse arises out of the fact that there is some evidence that the Edomites (i.e., Esau) were confederate with the Assyrians (see Isaiah 21:11). On another level, however, the angel of the Lord had encamped about Jacob (Genesis 32:2) and this had also been true of Israel's experience in the destruction of the Assyrian.

Verses 8-11

The closing stanza is based upon the previous two. It is a call to recognise that He who is a refuge to those who put their trust in Him, who so recently had manifested His might and power in their experience by destroying the armies of a haughty and arrogant foe, was the God who ruled in the kingdom of men. Before Him all men's power was futile, for none could frustrate His will. So, "Come, behold the works of the LORD". See how He brings to desolation the most mighty of human forces, for He makes wars to cease; He breaks the bow, cuts the spear and burns the chariot.

The destruction of Sennacherib is a lesson to all generations. It is a type of God's ultimate victory over those who oppose Him.

The final exhortation is to all who will heed the warning: "Be still (lit. cease, i.e., drop the hands, stop your vain opposition), and know that I am God." Ultimately, at the appointed time, God will fulfil His purpose:

"I will be exalted among the heathen, I will be exalted in the earth."

In this confidence, what a consolation it is for those who seek to emulate the faith of Hezekiah to know that "The LORD of hosts is with us; the God of Jacob is our refuge (lit. 'strong tower').

PSALM 47

PSALMS 46 to 48 form a trilogy of songs concerned with the same historical events. This, as we have seen in our consideration of Psalm 46, was the destruction by the Lord of the host of Sennacherib. The close connection between Psalms 46 and 47 is evident in the insertion of a "Selah" at the conclusion of Psalm 46, indicating the need for a pause for reflection. It demonstrates that there is a link in thought with what has gone before, and consequently a need to prepare the mind for that which is to follow. Bearing this in mind, it is not difficult to see that Psalm 47 in its entirety is a fulfilment of the thought of verse 10 in Psalm 46: "I will be exalted among the heathen, I will be exalted in the earth."

In this respect the psalm, although its composition arose out of events current at the time it was written, is totally prophetic, and describes God's ultimate triumph over all nations in the consummation of His purpose in the earth, when all nations recognise and acknowledge His sovereignty as a result of His victory through the Lord Jesus Christ over all human opposition. Israel is then exalted among the nations. Of these things, of course, the destruction of the Assyrian and the recognition of Hezekiah by the nations, was a type (2 Kings 19:19: 2 Chronicles 32:27-33).

It is worth noting that in the worship of the synagogue, this psalm was associated with the New Year, because of its reference to "the sound of a trumpet" (verse 5). Apparently it was recited seven times before the sounding of the trumpet amongst some Jews, and only once amongst others. Much more interesting, however, is the fact that the trumpet in this instance is a translation of the Hebrew *Shofar*, according to Strong 'a trumpet of horn'. It has to be distinguished from the silver trumpets

323

which Moses was commanded to make for a whole variety
of uses, described in Numbers 10:1-10, and in particular
for a memorial over Israel's burnt offerings and peace
offerings and on their new moons and solemn days (verse
10). The significant point is that the ceremonial
distinction between the *shofar* and the silver trumpets
had a notable exception, for the *shofar* was used on the
day of Jubilee; it was "the trumpet of the jubile" (Leviticus
25:9), and it was to sound throughout all the land,
proclaiming the year of liberty. The Jubilee was
preeminently a new beginning and spoke of God's
deliverance, looking forward to that glorious future era in
which the nation would fulfil its destiny and all nations
would be gathered in to share the blessing contained in
the covenant that God made with Abraham (Psalm 47:9).

In structure the psalm falls into two closely related
parts:

(a) Verses 1-4 – a call to the nations to acknowledge
God's sovereignty
(b) Verses 5-9 – a recognition that this sovereignty
has been established through the manifestation of
God's power in the earth.

Verses 1-4

"O clap your hands, all ye peoples; shout unto God
with the voice of triumph." (verse 1, RV)

Note the change of "people" in the AV for "peoples" in the
RV, indicating that all the nations of the earth are
encompassed within the word. Consistently similar
renderings occur in verses 3 and 9. The references to
clapping and shouting are, in scripture, associated with
the accession of a king to his throne. Thus when Josiah
was proclaimed king "they clapped their hands, and said,
God save the king" (2 Kings 11:12), and when Samuel
announced regarding Saul, "See ye whom the LORD hath
chosen", it is recorded that "all the people shouted" (1
Samuel 10:24).

The prophecy of Balaam is particularly relevant:

"He hath not beheld iniquity in Jacob, neither hath
he seen perverseness in Israel: the LORD his God is with

him, and the shout of a king is among them."

(Numbers 23:21)

Here the "shout of a king" in their midst is the token that God was with them, and this directs our thoughts to Psalm 46 (verses 5,7,11) and the Immanuel prophecies of Isaiah previously considered. Strong states that the word "triumph" means 'a shout of gladness', from a word variously translated in the AV as "gladness", "joy", "proclamation", "rejoicing", "shouting" and "singing".

The sense, then, of the opening words of the Psalm is clear. God (in Christ) is enthroned as King over all the earth and all nations are called to rejoice in his accession to the throne. Verse 2 emphasises this fact:

"For the LORD most high is terrible; he is a great King over all the earth."

Inherent in the word rendered "terrible" is the idea of one to be held in awe or revered, although the conventional idea of fear is not absent. Looking at the background of the destruction of the Assyrian host, we can well understand how both ideas come together – and that will certainly be true in the future, after God's judgements have been manifest in the earth. The title "Great King" had been arrogantly assumed by Sennacherib (Isaiah 36:4) when he reproached the God of Israel through the words of Rabshakeh. Now He to whom the title truly belongs is recognised and acknowledged for His universal sovereignty, for "he (subdued) the peoples under us, and the nations under our feet. He (chose) our inheritance for us, the excellency of Jacob whom he loved" (Psalm 47:4, RV). Readers who investigate the text will find some confusion amongst translators over the tense of the verbs in these verses. Because we regard the psalm as a prophecy of the kingdom, we feel that the past tense, thus indicating what God has accomplished, is most appropriate. Of course, there is a recurring sense in which the words can be understood, for they describe accurately the way in which God led His people out of Egypt, through the wilderness and into the land of Canaan, their promised inheritance. He subdued the nations before them, in fulfilment of His promise to Abraham:

"Unto thy seed have I given this land, from the river of Egypt unto the great river, the river Euphrates."

(Genesis 15:18)

He established them in the land. This, of course, was proof of His universal sovereignty, for His promises to Israel were linked inseparably to His purpose for the earth at large:

"Now therefore, if ye will obey my voice indeed, and keep my covenant, then ye shall be a peculiar treasure unto me above all people: *for all the earth is mine.*"

(Exodus 19:5)

The destruction of Sennacherib's army was itself a token of the truth of these things. In destroying the Gentile host and blessing Hezekiah and the faithful remnant that supported him, God showed His fidelity and His love for this people. Again, these events were but a shadow of that deliverance yet to come, when God will bring His purpose to fruition in the earth, and Israel will be the first among the nations.

All this God has done, and will do, not because of any inherent worth in Israel, but because of His love for them and for the fathers of the nation (see Deuteronomy 4:37; 7:8; Malachi 1:2 etc.). In His eyes they have a unique position. "The excellency of Jacob" describes their privilege, and is summed up in the words of Exodus 19:5 referred to above (see also Psalm 135:4).

Verses 5-9

Although the theme remains the same, the emphasis now is upon the actions of God that have brought about the state of affairs described in the first part of the psalm. Thus we read:

"God is gone up with a shout, the LORD with the sound of a trumpet." (verse 5)

We have already commented on the sounding of the trumpet; but the expression "God is gone up" is rich in meaning and other scriptural association. At the time of the Exodus God saw the affliction of His people and heard their cry. The result was that God came down to deliver them out of the hand of the Egyptians and to bring them up out of that land unto a good land, a land flowing with milk and honey (see Exodus 3:7,8).

God came down to deliver. He was manifest in the earth through the Angel of His Presence and through Moses and Aaron. When that deliverance was complete and the work of salvation finished, then God (in the language of God-manifestation) went back up to His throne in heaven. Psalm 68 uses the language of the Exodus in a most striking manner, clearly illustrating the scriptural idiom we have described:

Thou hast ascended on high, thou hast led captivity captive: thou hast received gifts for men; yea, for the rebellious also, that the LORD God might dwell among them." (Psalm 68:18)

These words are, of course, quoted by the Apostle Paul in the Epistle to the Ephesians and applied to the deliverance wrought by God through the Lord Jesus Christ. Especially significant are the added inspired comments of the apostle that establish the significance of the language we have been considering:

"Wherefore he saith, When he ascended up on high, he led captivity captive, and gave gifts unto men. (Now that he ascended, what is it but that he also descended first into the lower parts of the earth?)" (Ephesians 4:8,9)

We must remember that we are dealing with the language of God-manifestation. It does not mean that the Lord Jesus literally came down from heaven, but as at the Exodus, God was manifested in the earth to save – although in the case of the Lord Jesus, when the work was complete he did literally ascend into the heavens.

Thus the psalm looks forward to the establishment of God's kingdom, when the anti-typical year of Jubilee will come; then with the work completed, God will, as in the days of old, go up with a shout, with the sound of a trumpet. In looking forward to this ultimate triumph, we should not forget the historical background, for God came down and destroyed the host of Sennacherib. With the deliverance completed, He ascended up on high, having demonstrated His sovereignty over all the earth.

327

There is a further connection that must not be overlooked. The ark of the covenant was the symbol of God's presence in the midst of His people. It was His throne upon earth, from whence He reigned and exercised His dominion. Thus, when the ark went forth, Moses declared, "Rise up, LORD, and let thine enemies be scattered"; when it rested he said, "Return, O LORD, unto the many thousands of Israel" (Numbers 10:35,36; Psalm 68:1). Clearly the ark going forth and returning to its rest was a parallel with God coming down and ascending up on high after manifesting Himself for the deliverance of His people. Remember also that the ark was referred to as "the ark of the covenant of the Lord of all the earth" (Joshua 3:11,13). Here is yet another demonstration of the sovereignty of God. These thoughts were drawn together when David, with great rejoicing, brought the ark to Zion:

"So David and all the house of Israel brought up the ark of the LORD with shouting, and with the sound of the trumpet."   (2 Samuel 6:15)

In God's victory there is cause for great rejoicing:

"Sing praises to God, sing praises: sing praises unto our King, sing praises. For God is the King of all the earth: sing ye praises with understanding."
(Psalm 47:6,7)

The verb rendered "sing" means literally 'to make music accompanied by the voice; hence to celebrate in song and music' (Strong's). It appears that music played a greater part in the worship of Israel in the past than perhaps we allow for in our meetings today. It is not, however, music for its own sake, for this singing with music is to be "with understanding". It is in the knowledge and understanding of God and His purpose that true praise has its foundation. There is more than one aspect to this praise in song. We can ascribe praise directly to God, recognising His greatness and thanking Him for all He provides. But it is also possible to praise in another way, as Paul writes:

"… speaking to *yourselves* in psalms and hymns and spiritual songs, singing and *making melody in your heart* to the Lord."   (Ephesians 5:19)

Note that we can "speak to ourselves" through our singing. In other words, our hymns need not be directly spoken to

God as prayers of thankfulness and praise, but can be a means of reminding one another of the wonderful promises God has made, of rejoicing together and encouraging one another in the things most surely believed amongst us.

The apostle emphasises also "making melody in (the) heart". Perhaps our appreciation of music, a God-given gift, was intended on suitable occasions to bring us to a state of heart and mind in which we could more readily contemplate the things that are eternal and meditate more deeply upon the word of God. We do not know the type of music that was common in ancient Israel, but we remember that Saul was soothed by David's playing of the harp and the scriptures testify that there were those such as the sons of Asaph, Heman and Jeduthun who prophesied with harps, psalteries and cymbals (1 Chronicles 25:1-3).

If the purpose of music is as we suggest, how careful we have to be! So much that passes for music evokes not peaceful contemplation, or the spirit rejoicing in God, but rather, like "sounding brass, or a tinkling cymbal" (1 Corinthians 13:1), is empty of all meaning and appeals only to the flesh – often in its baser manifestations.

The last two verses (8 and 9) present us with a final picture of the kingdom age. God reigns over the nations. Literally:

"He has become (i.e., recognised as) King. He has sat down upon the throne of his holiness."   (verse 8)

His sovereignty is now universally acknowledged:

"The princes of the peoples are gathered together unto the people of the God of Abraham."

(verse 9, RV & margin)

The desire expressed in the exhortation of verse 1 is now seen to be fulfilled, for the leaders of the Gentile nations are gathered to Jerusalem to pay homage to the Great King, the Lord of all the earth, manifest in His Son, the Lord Jesus Christ. They are gathered unto the people of the God of Abraham, and the exaltation of Israel amongst the nations is emphasised, chosen to be a witness, that they might show forth among the nations the light of His

329

glory; their destiny is finally fulfilled, as the scriptures testify (Isaiah 2:2; 11:12; 56:6,7; 60:3; Zechariah 8:21-23; 14:16). Here is the ultimate fulfilment of the promises made to Abram: "In thee shall all families of the earth be blessed" (Genesis 12:3).

The psalm closes with the words: "For the shields of the earth belong unto God: he is greatly exalted." Shields are for protection and defence. Princes are the protectors and defenders of their people. Now they all belong to God, who declared to Abram, "I am thy shield, and thy exceeding great reward" (Genesis 15:1). All nations now recognise His sovereignty and dwell under His protection, for "he is greatly exalted" and "The kingdoms of this world are become the kingdoms of our Lord, and of his Christ; and he shall reign for ever and ever" (Revelation 11:15).

PSALM 48

PSALM 48 is the last of the trilogy of songs concerned with the destruction of Sennacherib's host. Psalm 46 spoke of the presence of God in the midst of the city to defend it from the Assyrian and of the subsequent deliverance wrought by God. Psalm 47 called on all the nations of the earth to rejoice in God's victory and recognise His sovereignty, whereas this final hymn of praise rejoices in the exaltation of Zion and the joy that ensues from its glory. As we have seen, however, the destruction of the Assyrian was typical of God's ultimate triumph through the Lord Jesus Christ over all human opposition and Psalm 48, while clearly having the same historical background as the other two psalms, contains language that can only find fulfilment in the future outworking of the purpose of God. The psalm can be conveniently divided into three parts:

    (a) The glory and security of Zion (verses 1-3)
    (b) Reflections on the defeat of the Assyrians (verses 4-8)
    (c) The joy of Zion's citizens (verses 9-14)

The glory and security of Zion
In Psalm 46 the presence of God had been the guarantee of her security; here in Psalm 48 that security, which was the result of His presence, is one of the main underlying themes. God had proved Himself to be "a very present help in trouble" (Psalm 46:1). He had destroyed the host of Sennacherib in token of His ultimate victory over the kingdom of men. Because of this He was worthy of all praise from the faithful remnant in Judah; yet how much more so of those who will be citizens of Zion in the day of her future glory!

331

"Great is the LORD, and highly (RV) to be praised in the city of our God, in the mountain of his holiness. Beautiful in elevation (RV), the joy of the whole earth, is mount Zion, on the sides of the north, the city of the great King. God is known in her palaces for a refuge."

(Psalm 48:1-3)

It is because Jerusalem is the city of God, His holy mountain, that it will surpass all other cities in beauty. It will be glorious in that day when God consummates His purpose, because His glory will reside there. From that city God's sovereignty will be exercised over all the earth, and because of the beneficence of that rule, it will be "the joy of the whole earth". It is described as "beautiful in elevation" and as being on the sides of the north. This topographical information has caused some confusion, for while the city is certainly elevated, at the present time it could not be described with accuracy as being "on the sides of the north". The language belongs, however, to the future, and scripture provides the key:

"And his feet shall stand in that day upon the mount of Olives, which is before Jerusalem on the east, and the mount of Olives shall cleave in the midst thereof toward the east and toward the west, and there shall be a very great valley; and half of the mountain shall remove toward the north, and half of it toward the south."

(Zechariah 14:4)

Brother Henry Sulley writes,*

"Since the Olivet earthquake is to form a 'very great valley', it is not unreasonable to suppose that this valley will be wide enough to extend from Jerusalem northward as far as Geba. This supposition is confirmed by a prophecy contained in (Psalm 48:1,2). This Psalm must be a prophecy, not only because Jerusalem is not now on 'the sides of the north', but also because of the distinct reference to the immensity of its palaces and towers (verses 12,13). Situated on the ends of a ravine, on the southern side of the new valley, after the site of the Temple has been prepared by the earthquake,

---

* H Sulley, *The Temple of Ezekiel's Prophecy*, "Coming Physical Changes" – page 152.

'Mount Zion' will be *on the sides of the north,* or literally at the 'extreme limit of the northern side.'"

The earthquake will also have the effect of further elevating the site of the Lord's house. The familiar words of Isaiah testify to this fact:

"The mountain of the LORD's house shall be established in the top of the mountains, and shall be exalted above the hills; and all nations shall flow unto it." (Isaiah 2:2)

It will then have become in truth the city of the great King. It is interesting to reflect upon the fact that the throne of the Lord Jesus is in fact synonymous with the house of the Lord. It is not a case of a temple and a royal palace – although, as Psalm 48:13 makes clear, there will be palaces, no doubt for the use of those in Israel who will administer the affairs of the kingdom. In these palaces, because of His work of deliverance, God will be known for a refuge.

Because of these things, God is "highly to be praised". Praise involves worship, thanksgiving, confession. It is not confined to words, but involves the human spirit (our attitude of heart and mind) and the works we do. We must "shew forth the praises of him who hath called (us) out of darkness into his marvellous light" (1 Peter 2:9). In other words, we best praise God when we show in our lives those characteristics of the divine character that are worthy of our praise.

Reflections on the defeat of the Assyrian

Verses 4 to 8 of Psalm 48 describe in dramatic form the advance and destruction of the Assyrian army: "For, lo, the kings were assembled, they passed by together" (verse 4). The King of Assyria with his vassal kings gathered together to invade the land. They passed over the border into Judah. "They saw it, and so they marvelled; they were troubled, and hasted away" (verse 5). They saw the holy city. There is here great emphasis in the original text, as if to stress their hostility and its ultimate effect. They were overtaken by astonishment; dismay filled their hearts and they fled in panic.

So, if we might summarise – the Gentile kings assembled themselves together, they marched into the holy land. They saw the city Jerusalem, but they proceeded no further, for they were thrown into confusion and fled in terror. Their fear and the suddenness of their destruction is further described in the following two verses:

"Fear took hold upon them there, and pain, as of a woman in travail. Thou breakest the ships of Tarshish with an east wind." (verses 6,7)

Their confusion and terror is portrayed by two figures. Firstly, there is the figure so common in both Old and New Testaments of a woman in travail. Secondly, there is the destruction of a fleet of ships by the east wind sent by God.

It is, of course, believed by many that the reference to the ships of Tarshish is a prophecy of a specific event at the time of the end. We suggest, however, that it is difficult to see the relevance of such a prophecy in this context; and the sense of the Hebrew suggested by some seems more appropriate, i.e., "Thou, O God, breakest them as thou breakest the ships of Tarshish with an east wind". In other words, God's might is irresistible, and as great ships are broken in the storm, so God broke the Assyrian in His land (Isaiah 14:25).

Thus the Psalmist concludes this section with the words:

"As we have heard, so have we seen in the city of the LORD of hosts, in the city of our God: God will establish it for ever." (Psalm 48:8)

As they had heard of God's wondrous works on behalf of His people, so now they had experienced them, and seen with their own eyes. God had shown them that He would both defend and deliver His city, and in this confidence they would be assured that God would establish His city and David's throne for ever.

The joy of Zion's citizens

The "Selah" at the end of verse 8 indicates that there is a need for the reader to pause and reflect on that which has gone before, that the mind might be prepared for that which follows:

"We have thought of thy lovingkindness, O God, in the midst of thy temple. According to thy name, O God, so is thy praise unto the ends of the earth: thy right hand is full of righteousness."   (verses 9,10)

Now delivered and redeemed from the hand of the enemy, God's people ponder His faithfulness and consider the wonder of all that He has accomplished. It was in the courts of the temple particularly that they felt most keenly the wonder of God's salvation, for it was there that His glory dwelt between the cherubim. It is a lesson that we all need to learn. We must draw near to God and develop our God-consciousness. It is then that we shall appreciate more fully the things that God has done for us in the Lord Jesus Christ. As it was in the temple that the Israelite consciousness of God was heightened, so also it is in our ecclesial life that we should find strength and encouragement. In the company of those who share the same beliefs and spiritual values, we should be strengthened and our appreciation of divine things sharpened. These experiences should not be forgotten, but we must carry them with us into the world in which we live, so that even when we are alone, our minds are actively contemplating the love of God and the wonder of all that He has done for us.

By His name God was known. That name, of course, encompasses everything that God is and has shown Himself to be by His acts. He was known and praised, not only in Israel, but "unto the ends of the earth". Of course this is a prophecy of the ultimate recognition of God's authority and sovereignty when He establishes His kingdom, but there was also a limited fulfilment in Hezekiah's days, for there must have been many nations who rejoiced in the destruction of the Assyrian. We have already referred in other psalms to the way in which God blessed Hezekiah amongst the nations after this victory (see 2 Kings 19:19; 2 Chronicles 32:22,23).

That God's right hand is full of righteousness (Psalm 48:10) might seem self-evident. Against the same historical background Isaiah wrote:

"The LORD is exalted; for he dwelleth on high: he hath filled Zion with judgment and righteousness."   (33:5)

335

Can we not see here, however, a reference to the Lord Jesus Christ, the man of His right hand, the Son of man whom He made strong for Himself (Psalm 80:17; see also Psalm 110:1,2; Acts 7:56)? Truly he was one who was full of righteousness, and through whom God will manifest Himself in righteousness before all nations.

So the cry goes forth:

> "Let mount Zion rejoice, let the daughters of Judah be glad, because of thy judgments." (Psalm 48:11)

In this context the daughters of Judah are the cities and towns that had fallen before Sennacherib and suffered from the cruelty of the Assyrian (see Isaiah 36:1 – the *Cambridge Bible* points out that in Numbers 21:25 and Joshua 17:11,16, the words rendered "villages" and "towns" mean literally 'daughters', for that was their relationship as country towns to their capital city).

The horrors of the invasion are now at an end, the siege of Jerusalem, when they had been "shut up like birds in a cage", raised and the enemy vanquished. In this new-found freedom, how they must have rejoiced in Jerusalem, and gone forth freely and joyfully to walk about Zion and go round about her, to count the towers and mark her bulwarks, to consider in wonder her palaces! That which they saw was but a pale shadow of what will be the greatest 'sightseeing' tour of all times in the day of Zion's future glory (verses 11,12).

But viewing and rejoicing in the material and physical glory is not an end in itself. They do so that they may tell the generations to come that the wonder of this city is not of man's origin. It is not human ingenuity and power that has produced it, but the hand of God:

> "For this God is our God for ever and ever: he will be our guide even unto death." (verse 14)

The truth of the last phrase and its meaning for every disciple cannot be doubted. But that it seems a little out of context, and incompatible with the general theme, is also evident. Without great conviction that such is the case, we feel we ought to record the fact that some regard the phrase as belonging to the next psalm, as a heading or title giving its literary content. As such, it would certainly

336

fit Psalm 49, as the sentence "God will redeem my soul from the power of the grave" (verse 15) shows.

Addendum

It is interesting to note that the Rabbinical commentators refer the psalm to the time of Messiah and the struggle with Gog and Magog (Ezekiel 38). If this is so, the events of Hezekiah's day foreshadow those events in a remarkable way and give added insight to Micah's prophecy that "This man shall be the peace, when the Assyrian shall come into our land" (5:5).

PSALM 49

THIS is the last of the group of eight psalms that bears the inscription "for the sons of Korah". As we have seen, all the others had clear historical links with the times of Hezekiah, and some of them at least were written by that righteous king. Psalm 49 is different in character, however, as it appears to have no discernible historical background and is general in approach, dealing with the vanity of riches and the inevitable end of those who put their trust in them. Nevertheless, it would seem reasonable to suppose that this psalm belongs to the same period. Perhaps its place at the conclusion of this group of psalms has a relevance, in that it is a reflection of the attitude of heart and mind, both in Judah and Israel, that led to God bringing down the Assyrian in judgement upon His land and His people.

If this can be shown to be the case, then not only does it stand as a testimony for all subsequent generations, but it is of particular relevance for us who live in these momentous times that will culminate in God's final judgements on a world that, as in the days of Noah, has put its trust in material things.

We need to look, then, not at Hezekiah's days specifically, but at the times of his predecessors, and in this connection the prophecies of Isaiah (who prophesied in the days of Uzziah, Jotham, Ahaz and Hezekiah) and Amos (who prophesied in the days of Jeroboam II of Israel and Uzziah of Judah) are particularly relevant.

The psalm speaks of those "that trust in their wealth, and boast themselves in the multitude of their riches" (verse 6). Again, "their inward thought is, that their houses shall continue for ever, and their dwelling places to all generations; they call their lands after their own names" (verse 11). The exhortation of the Psalmist is, "Be

338

not thou afraid when one is made rich, when the glory of his house is increased" (verse 16). These words can be compared with the following passages from Isaiah and Amos:

"Woe unto them that join house to house, that lay field to field, till there be no place." (Isaiah 5:8)

"And I will smite the winter house with the summer house; and the houses of ivory shall perish, and the great houses shall have an end, saith the LORD."

(Amos 3:15)

"Woe to them that are at ease in Zion, and trust in the mountain of Samaria ... that lie upon beds of ivory, and stretch themselves upon their couches, and eat the lambs out of the flock, and the calves out of the midst of the stall; that chant to the sound of the viol, and invent to themselves instruments of musick, like David."

(Amos 6:1,4,5)

There seems to be a definite emphasis upon the riches and prosperity that was enjoyed by the people in the days of the kings Jeroboam II of Israel and Uzziah of Judah, and this was no doubt perpetuated through the reigns of their successors.

In the relative luxury of our Western civilisation there are many parallels. The "summer houses" and "winter houses" remind us of how common the second house, the holiday home, has become, even for those who are only moderately successful in this life. And while we may not have "houses of ivory", the luxury in which we live would have staggered our forbears of just a generation or so ago. "Lambs out of the flock, and calves out of the midst of the stall" remind us of the richness of our diet, and with television and Hi-fi we are well able to "chant to the sound of the viol", and invent "instruments of musick" in filling our houses with sound and enjoying every form of comfort and pleasure the world has to offer. The danger from riches has never been so real, or the possibility of failing to appreciate the peril to our spiritual well-being of material possessions.

THE PRAISES OF ISRAEL (PSALMS 1–72)

Structure

The psalm falls simply into three sections. The first, by way of introduction, is a call to all people of the earth to keep the words of the Psalmist, which have been given to him by inspiration (verses 1-4). The introduction is followed by the main section of the psalm, which is divided into two, each part ending with a similar refrain (verses 12,20). The first of these two parts (verses 5-12) emphasises the foolishness of men who trust in riches, imagining they can obtain for them some kind of immortality, although they are utterly incapable of saving either themselves or their brother. The second part speaks of the consolation of the righteous, in contrast to the hopelessness of the worldly (verses 13-20).

In considering the psalm, one can well envisage that the words could have been spoken by the Lord Jesus Christ; and we see here in the sentiments expressed the spirit of Christ in the psalms.

Verses 1-4

"Hear this, all ye people; give ear, all ye inhabitants of the world: both low and high, rich and poor, together."

(verses 1,2)

The theme of the psalm is not restricted to the covenant people of God, but is one that embraces all the inhabitants of the earth. It is a matter of universal concern that touches all humankind.

The word rendered "world" appears in this form only in one other place, and conveys the idea of that which is transitory, fleeting and passing. The all embracing nature of the message is seen by the call to low (lit. sons of Adam) and high (lit. sons of Ish) – in other words, the common mass of humanity and those who individually stand out, and are thereby distinguished from their fellows. They are further identified as "rich and poor together". The rich need to learn the vanity of seeking earthly glory, whereas the poor also need to recognise this truth and to be content with their lot in life.

"My mouth shall speak of wisdom; and the meditation of my heart shall be of understanding. I will

340

incline mine ear to a parable: I will open my dark saying upon the harp."   (verses 3,4)

The words for "wisdom" and "understanding" are both plural in form in the Hebrew text, probably to denote manifold wisdom and profound insight (*Cambridge Bible*). The references to "parables" and "dark sayings" are not easy to understand, as the message of the psalm, far from being enigmatic, is clear and forthright. However, we may see the answer in the fact that the word translated "parable" has a wide range of meanings and can simply carry the idea of a teaching or a comparison, to which the contents of the psalm certainly correspond. The "dark saying" is more difficult; but if we regard the problem to which the psalm addresses itself as the enigma, i.e., the prosperity of the wicked, then the words become clear, for the writer's purpose is "to open" the dark saying – in other words, to make the matter plain. The reference to the harp indicates that the words of the psalm were sung to the accompaniment of this instrument.

Verses 5-12

"Wherefore should I fear in the days of evil, when iniquity at my heels compasseth me about?"

(verse 5, RV)

The reference to fear is repeated in the next stanza of the psalm:

"Be not thou afraid when one is made rich." (verse 16)

It is interesting to note that the psalm does not accuse the rich of oppressing the poor or of obtaining their wealth by fraud. The emphasis is upon the folly of trusting in riches. The references to "fear" may therefore not be to the persecution of the poor by the rich, but to the anxiety and fear for personal security that can arise when others prosper and we, perhaps, have to struggle to make ends meet. In keeping with this thought the next phrase (an obvious allusion to the words of Genesis 3:15, "it shall bruise thy head, and thou shalt bruise his heel") indicates the danger of sin (the serpent's bite) taking advantage of such a state of worry and concern to produce envy and jealousy in the hearts of the poor.

THE PRAISES OF ISRAEL (PSALMS 1–72)

There is, of course, no need to fear, for it is all a matter of seeing things in proper perspective, for:

"They that trust in their wealth, and boast themselves in the multitude of their riches; none of them can by any means redeem his brother, nor give to God a ransom for him: (for the redemption of their soul is precious, and it ceaseth for ever:) that he should still live for ever, and not see corruption."   (verses 6-9)

Man cannot buy salvation. In this world money will buy almost anything; but the remorseless hand of death none can escape. It is the great leveller between rich and poor alike.

It is probable that the language of these verses alludes to the Exodus 21. The words "ransom" and "'redemption of their soul (life)" occur together in verse 30 (RV), and the second phrase occurs nowhere else in the Old Testament. The record in Exodus is dealing with the man who failed to take proper care to restrain a dangerous animal (i.e., an ox). If the ox was to kill a man or woman, then the owner's life was to be forfeit. It was possible, however, for him to redeem his life by paying to the relatives an agreed sum of money. One can imagine that this was the most likely outcome of such an event, particularly where the owner of the animal was a rich man.

The contrast, however, between the case in Exodus and the psalm is most marked. Where his personal salvation, or his brother's, is concerned, there is nothing that a man can pay to God to ransom his life. There is undoubtedly an irony lying behind the thought that the rich man would give all his wealth to God to save his soul from death. But there was no escape. "Therefore it ceaseth for ever", or, idiomatically, "the question should never be raised" – it must be left alone.

Of course, underlying the words there is the great truth that salvation can only be obtained by "the precious blood of Christ, as of a lamb without blemish and without spot" (1 Peter 1:18,19). This truth serves to emphasise the utter futility of trusting in wealth or seeking fulfilment and satisfaction in this world's goods.

342

Verse 9 is a continuation of verse 7, the intervening words being a parenthesis. To follow the thread of thought we should read:

"None of them can by any means redeem his brother, nor give to God a ransom for him ... that he should continue to live on for ever, and never see the Pit."
(verse 7, AV; verse 9, RSV)

However, such a man deludes himself that he can somehow keep on eluding death, and shuts his mind to the reality of his human condition. Experience must teach him that whether men be wise, foolish, or behave no better than an animal (brutish person), they are all doomed to perish "and leave their wealth to others" (verse 10). Literally the word "leave" means 'to abandon', for the emphasis is upon the fact that all must surrender their wealth, that cannot save them from death, and which they are unable to take with them. While they live they console themselves with the thought that their names will be perpetuated by their works and remembered through their riches, in the houses and lands they have acquired:

"Their inward thought is, that their houses shall continue for ever, and their dwelling places to all generations; they call their lands after their own names."
(verse 11)

Such thinking motivated Cain who called the city that he built after the name of his son Enoch (Genesis 4:17). But all who go in the way of Cain will find it to no avail; for although men might hold them in esteem and admire them because of their wealth and riches, "man being in honour abideth not: he is like the beasts that perish" (verse 12).

Verses 13-19

This final stanza introduces the hope of the righteous in contrast to the hopelessness of those who put their trust in riches. The opening words are a summary of what has gone before. In particular, they pick up the theme of verse 11:

"This their way is their folly; yet their posterity approve their sayings. Selah." (verse 13)

343

The manner of their living is not foolish in the simple sense of the word; the original Hebrew denoted 'a stupid security or a presumptuous confidence'. It is self-will serving itself in arrogance in which their folly is seen and, even though they die, those who follow them adopt the same standards and live by the same false values. Of course, this is ever the way of the world. One has translated the verse:

"This is the way of those who have folly, and of those after them who delight to speak in like manner."

The word "Selah" indicates the need at this point to pause and reflect on what has gone before. And then in the realisation of the utter folly of those who put their confidence in riches, the Psalmist exclaims:

"Like sheep they are laid in the grave; death shall feed on (lit. shepherd) them; and the upright shall have dominion over them in the morning; and their beauty shall consume in the grave from their dwelling."

(verse 14)

Death shepherds them, and in the morning of deliverance the upright will have dominion over them, putting their feet, as it were, upon their necks – the seed of the woman trampling the seed of the serpent underfoot; not, of course, those who have perished like the beasts in the grave, but those of the same type who dominate the earth at this present time, and will continue to do so until the day dawn and the shadows flee away. In that day the righteous who sleep in the dust, but not perpetually, will be redeemed from the grave and will participate in the victory, for He will receive them to Himself (verse15).

Once again there is a pause (Selah) for reflection. The fact of the resurrection from the dead should have an effect upon the attitude of all godly men towards the world in which they live. The godly man is not envious of the foolish; he is not affected by unnecessary anxieties when he sees the prosperity of the wicked, for he knows that "when he dieth he shall carry nothing away: his glory shall not descend after him" (verse 17).

It is in this confidence that the Psalmist exhorts his fellows with a solemn reminder of the futility of human life apart from God:

"Though while he lived he blessed his soul: and men will praise thee, when thou doest well to thyself. He shall go to the generation of his fathers; they shall never see light. Man that is in honour, and understandeth not, is like the beasts that perish."

(verses 18-20)

The rich man no doubt gets a certain satisfaction from his riches. He blesses his soul, that is, he counts himself happy. It is a sorry fact that worldly men cannot appreciate what they are missing in turning their back upon spiritual treasures. They feel they have real fulfilment in what the world offers, and it is often only in advancing years, when bodily weakness and approaching death bring home the reality of the human condition, that they realise how futile and empty human life is apart from God.

We remember the parable of the rich fool. Like the rich men in the psalm, whose inward thought was that their houses should continue for ever, he too thought within himself: "Soul, thou hast much goods laid up for many years" (Luke 12:17-19). He knew not that very night his life should be required of him, for he would die. And if we are deceived by riches then men will, by their attitude, confirm us in that way. They will praise us, for they believe that a man's life consists in the abundance of the things that he possesses. They measure a man's worth not by the quality of his life, but by the quantity of his possessions. If we get on in the world we shall never be lacking in admirers, although how sincere their flattery will be a matter of doubt. But all to no avail, for they will go to the generation of their fathers, never again to see light – only oblivion, perpetual darkness, nothing but the coldness and stillness of the tomb.

The second stanza finishes with the repetition of the words of verse 13, but with a significant variation: "Man that is in honour, and understandeth not, is like the beasts that perish." The man who dies held in honour and reputation because of his riches is bankrupt if he is unable to discern the difference between false and true riches. If he has no understanding of God and His purpose, he is no better than the beasts that perish. It may not have been

345

the main thrust of the Psalmist's argument, but nevertheless this verse (20) stands as an indication that it is knowledge that brings responsibility before God and brings man to a condition of accountability before His throne of judgement.

The lesson of the psalm is for all generations, and never more necessary than for those of us living in the affluent society of the West. Though we be the richest men on earth, if we die without hope and without God in the world we are spiritual paupers, and no better than the beasts of the field.

PSALM 50

THERE are twelve psalms which bear the inscription "A Psalm of Asaph". Eleven of these occur together (Psalms 73-83); and one, Psalm 50, stands in isolation.

Asaph was, together with Heman and Ethan (also known as Jeduthun), one of the three singers chosen to lead the music when the ark of God was brought up from the house of Obed-edom to the tabernacle David had prepared at Jerusalem (1 Chronicles 15:16-19). In the tabernacle he was appointed to minister before the ark continually (16:37), whereas Heman and Jeduthun ministered in the tabernacle at Gibeon (verses 39-42). Later, in the days of Hezekiah, he was referred to as Asaph the seer: the Levites were commanded to sing praises to the Lord with "the words of David and Asaph the seer" (2 Chronicles 29:30).

Clearly, then, Asaph was responsible for the writing of psalms. An examination, however, of the psalms that bear his name indicates that some of them belong to a much later date than that of David and his contemporary, Asaph. What then is the answer? It appears to lie in the fact that Asaph was the founder of what has been termed "a guild of singers and musicians" who continued to use his name. References are made to these singers or musicians in the days of Jehoshaphat (2 Chronicles 20:14), Hezekiah (29:13) and Josiah (35:15). After the captivity reference is again made to the singers of the sons of Asaph (Ezra 2:41).

To these singers and musicians who bore the name of their illustrious forbear, psalms were committed for their keeping and performance. In fact, at the time of the bringing up of the ark, it is recorded that David committed a psalm into the hands of Asaph and his brethren (1

347

Chronicles 16:7). The psalm is a combination of parts of Psalms 96, 105 and 106. All such psalms would come to be regarded as "Psalms of Asaph", whether actually written by him or not. It must be said therefore that whether Psalm 50 was written by Asaph or by some other author, is a matter of conjecture. The theme of judgement, which is strong in this group of psalms, is nevertheless very evident in Psalm 50.

Introduction (verses 1-6)

The psalm is divided into three sections. The first, introducing the theme of judgement which dominates the song, speaks of the coming of God as Judge in terms that are reminiscent of God's manifestation of Himself at Sinai when the law was first given. He is manifest in fire and storm and cloud, bursting forth with dazzling brightness, not now from Sinai, but from Zion "the perfection of beauty", the place which He had chosen to set His name:

"The mighty God, even the LORD, hath spoken, and called the earth from the rising of the sun unto the going down thereof. Out of Zion, the perfection of beauty, God hath shined. Our God shall come, and shall not keep silence: a fire shall devour before him, and it shall be very tempestuous round about him." (verses 1-3)

The opening words of the psalm, "El Elohim Yahweh", occur only on one other occasion (Joshua 22:24).

The various translations show a manifest lack of understanding of the significance of the name and titles of God. "El" speaks of Him as the source of supreme power and strength. "Elohim" reminds us of that strength and power manifest in a host of mighty ones, and is particularly relevant in this context, calling to mind the God of creation who sustains all life in being. "Yahweh", of course, is the covenant name of God, the name of purpose which relates to the outworking of His will and counsel in human affairs. The threefold combination embraces all the might and majesty of the God with whom Israel had to deal. He had uttered His voice and called heaven and earth to witness this solemn act of judgement.

The phrase "Zion, the perfection of beauty" is linked with the words of Psalm 48, "the joy of the whole earth" (verse 2) in Lamentations 2:15, indicating beyond any doubt that both psalms belong to a period before the overthrow of the kingdom, as the prophet compares Zion's former glory with the desolation and destruction that had fallen upon it. As God had spoken in Sinai, so now His voice goes forth in Zion from between the Cherubim where He now dwells. From thence His glory shines, as at Sinai of old, when "He shined forth from mount Paran, and he came with ten thousands of saints" (Deuteronomy 33:2).

As at Sinai, all the tokens of the divine presence are associated with this manifestation, and all creation is called to witness this act of judgement:

"He shall call to the heavens from above, and to the earth, that he may judge his people. Gather my saints together unto me; those that have made a covenant with me by sacrifice. And the heavens shall declare his righteousness: for God is judge himself." (verses 4-6)

The word "saints" translates the Hebrew word *chasid*, related to the word *chesed*, which, as we have previously shown, relates to God's love and faithfulness towards His people. They in turn are God's covenant people who have known His loving, saving power and should therefore be His faithful ones. These are they who have made a covenant by sacrifice.

Initially, of course, the covenant was that made at Sinai, when the people declared, "All the words which the LORD hath said will we do" (Exodus 24:3). Moses wrote all the words of that covenant in a book and read it in the audience of the people before ratifying it by sacrifice through "the blood of the covenant" (verses 4-8). It encompasses also, of course, all those of subsequent generations who entered into that covenant, and the principles involved run through into the New Covenant and have relevance for the people of God today. Our special relationship with God is dependent on, and arises out of, the sacrifice of the Lord Jesus Christ.

These first six verses should be compared with the first six verses of Psalm 97: there is a close correspondence between the two psalms.

349

"Sacrifice and offering thou didst not desire" (verses 7-13)

God is both Accuser and Judge of His people:

"Hear, O my people, and I will speak; O Israel, and I will testify unto thee: I am God, even thy God. I will not reprove thee for thy sacrifices; and thy burnt offerings are continually before me." (verses 7,8, RV)

It is important to grasp the point emphasised in these verses. God does not condemn them because of their offerings. Indeed, God had given command concerning them and they had no authority to disregard this. The people had not neglected these externals of their religion. They had not forgotten to bring the sacrifices prescribed by the law, but their failure lay in the fact that they brought them as though they were an end in themselves – as if their real meaning and the spirit in which they were brought was of no consequence. They had failed to appreciate that what God delighted in was obedience, the spirit of praise and the thankful heart.

The prophets testify to the truth of the psalm's teaching:

"To what purpose is the multitude of your sacrifices unto me? saith the LORD: I am full of the burnt offerings of rams, and the fat of fed beasts; and I delight not in the blood of bullocks, or of lambs, or of he goats." (Isaiah 1:11)

"Will the LORD be pleased with thousands of rams, or with ten thousands of rivers of oil? ... He hath shewed thee, O man, what is good; and what doth the LORD require of thee, but to do justly, and to love mercy, and to walk humbly with thy God?" (Micah 6:7,8)
(see also 1 Samuel 15:22,23; Psalm 40:6-8)

In the material sense there was nothing they could give God, the possessor of heaven and earth; and in most majestic terms, with more than a touch of irony that need no words of ours to elucidate, God speaks:

"I will take no bullock out of thy house, nor he goats out of thy folds. For every beast of the forest is mine, and the cattle upon a thousand hills. I know all the fowls of the mountains: and the wild beasts of the field

350

are mine. If I were hungry, I would not tell thee: for the world is mine, and the fulness thereof. Will I eat the flesh of bulls, or drink the blood of goats? Offer unto God thanksgiving; and pay thy vows unto the most High: and call upon me in the day of trouble: I will deliver thee, and thou shalt glorify me."

(Psalm 50:9-15)

There was a need for the offerer to recognise the holiness of God and to acknowledge that he was a sinner. It is only in appreciating that "the sacrifices of God are a broken spirit: a broken and a contrite heart, O God, thou wilt not despise" (Psalm 51:17) – that we can truly know the wonder of God's love and the debt of thankfulness we owe Him.

It is a difficult thing to try to dissect the human emotions and perhaps analyse which of the things that commend a man to God, like faith and thankfulness, come first in human experience. We know that "faith cometh by hearing, and hearing by the word of God", but surely it is true also that real faith and thankfulness are born together in the human heart. It is the appreciation of all that God has done for us, both in relation to this life and the life to come, that brings also the realisation that we owe Him a debt of gratitude we can never hope to repay adequately. Yet, though that is true from our human perspective, it is surely an inducement to even more thankfulness and praise to know that God is pleased to accept the efforts that we make, feeble though they may be.

If we offer (i.e., sacrifice) the offering of thanksgiving, if we call upon God in the day of trouble, we are in effect giving to Him the only thing we can – our hearts. Thus in our willing recognition of His love and faithfulness, our acknowledgement of His greatness and holiness, we glorify Him. The fact that a man can keep the externals of his religion and yet fail to offer the sacrifice of thankfulness and praise, is a solemn warning for us today. In effect we can give our money and our time; we can do the daily readings and play a full part in ecclesial life – all absolutely vital aspects of life in Christ – and yet still have failed to give God our heart. The question to which we

351

need to address ourselves is, 'Are the sacrifices of thankfulness and praise something that is lacking from our public and private worship?'

God's verdict upon the hypocrites (verses 14-23)

The third and last section of the psalm is God's declaration to the wicked amongst His people. It is not spoken to the man who abandons his religion or openly scorns the way of righteousness. Rather, it is addressed primarily to the man who, while espousing the laws of God, lives in contradiction of them. He says one thing, but does another – in a word, he is a hypocrite:

"But unto the wicked God saith, What hast thou to do to declare my statutes, or that thou shouldest take my covenant in thy mouth? seeing thou hatest instruction, and castest my words behind thee."   (verses 16,17)

Literally the word "declare" means 'to rehearse' in the sense of numbering or counting, as if to affirm one's intention to keep them diligently. They had taken God's covenant in their mouths, but they hated instruction. The Hebrew word means literally 'correction or chastening'. It is the word used in Proverbs: "My son, despise not the chastening of the LORD" (3:11). They had cast God's words behind them – in more graphic terms, they had "flung them aside", thus showing their disdain for the way of God.

It is not difficult to live a lie, to be a play-actor, to build a facade that hides the real person. Nevertheless, each in his heart will know how real God and the Lord Jesus Christ are to him – whether he despises the chastening, or is prepared to submit humbly to God's will, either in the form of instruction from His word or in the circumstances of life. Either His word will be supreme in our lives, or we will choose to ignore it, or at least those parts of it which do not suit us; and to cast even a part away from us is to be as guilty as if we were to abandon it all, for it shows in the last analysis what we really think of God and His word.

"When thou sawest a thief, then thou consentedst with him, and hast been partaker with adulterers."
(Psalm 50:18)

The Hebrew is stronger: "Thou delightedst in him". The fact that a man was a thief or an adulterer was of no consequence to the wicked man. He still accepted their company; they treated him as though he were guiltless. The LXX renders this: "Thou didst run along with him"; in effect he condoned their sins by accepting them into his fellowship. No doubt such a broad-minded outlook, such moderation and refusal to take an extreme stance, is very attractive to the flesh. It teaches us, however, that there is such a thing as "guilt by association", and the principle runs through into the New Testament and is shown to apply to doctrinal issues:

"If there come any unto you, and bring not this doctrine, receive him not into your house, neither bid him God speed: for he that biddeth him God speed is partaker of his evil deeds." (2 John verses 10,11)

We cannot escape the implication by claiming that the words only refer to the doctrine specifically mentioned by John. That would be to assert that while we should not keep company with a thief or adulterer because these are mentioned by the Psalmist, there is no reason why we should not freely mix with fornicators or murderers.

"Thou givest thy mouth to evil, and thy tongue frameth deceit. Thou sittest and speakest against thy brother; thou slanderest thine own mother's son."
(Psalm 50:19,20)

The danger of the tongue is perhaps one of the most potent of evils, and at the same time one of which we are least aware. No doubt we all speak injudiciously at times and say harmful things that we come to regret bitterly. The sin described in the psalm goes beyond this, however, for it is wilful and deliberate, calculated and planned, contriving a whole structure of deliberate falsehood. The verb "to frame" means literally 'to weave', and the fact that the wicked is described as "sitting" again emphasises the deliberate nature of the slander (Psalm 1:1). The implication is that like associates with like. They sit in company and slander those who are linked to them by the closest of ties. They speak against their brother and slander their mother's son. The word rendered "slander" may mean 'to thrust at', or 'settest a stumblingblock for' (see The *Cambridge Bible*). The reference to "mother's son" emphasises the closeness of the tie. Perhaps we can see a spiritual significance as we think of Jerusalem, the mother of us all (Galatians 4:26) and of those who are born in Zion (Psalm 87:4-6). Our thoughts are then carried to our brethren and sisters in Christ and the relationships in our ecclesial life. We might say, 'Surely such deliberate wickedness could never be manifest by those who are in Christ!' Unhappily, scripture testifies of the depths to which human nature can sink, and the fact that the words of the psalm are spoken to those who have made a covenant by sacrifice is a dire warning of the hypocrisy that can infiltrate even into the household of God.

Although they lived by such double standards, because God had not acted but had kept silence, they imagined that His longsuffering was indifference, that God did not care. They thought God was altogether like themselves, having no more regard for sin than they did:

> "These things hast thou done, and I kept silence: thou thoughtest that I was altogether such an one as thyself: but I will reprove thee, and set them in order before thine eyes." (verse 21)

God would cause them to recognise all the sins of which they were guilty, for He would set them in order before them, although, deceived by the deceitfulness of sin, they imagined God did not care. God's warning was, "Consider this, ye that forget God". If they neglected to do so, God would tear them like a lion and none would be able to deliver them (verse 22).

The psalm concludes with words that sum up the lessons of its two main sections. God showers us with blessings, both natural and spiritual. We must ensure that we are not indifferent to His beneficence and return to Him the thanks and praise that is His due. As the wicked and hypocritical man rehearsed or numbered God's commandments (verse 16) in order to give the impression, falsely, that it was his intention to keep them diligently, so God looks also to the man that orders or prepares his way of life in accordance with His precepts, to whom He may reveal His salvation:

"Whoso offereth praise glorifieth me: and to him that ordereth his conversation aright will I show the salvation of God." (verse 23)

PSALM 51

WE have already commented on the close relationship between this psalm and Psalm 32. They are both concerned, as the title to our present psalm indicates, with David's sin in the matter of Bathsheba and Uriah the Hittite. Psalm 51 was undoubtedly written in the very midst of the circumstances surrounding the sin – as the title indicates, "when Nathan the prophet came unto him, after he had gone in to Bathsheba".

The psalm has therefore a sense of urgency, an immediacy that is not apparent in Psalm 32. That song, written some time after the event, is a calm appraisal of the events and David's reaction to them, and was written in part to instruct others, to fulfil the words of Psalm 51:

"Restore unto me the joy of thy salvation; and uphold me with thy free spirit. Then will I teach transgressors thy ways; and sinners shall be converted unto thee."

(verses 12,13)

Psalm 32, significantly, bears the inscription "Maschil" (i.e., 'for instruction'), and in verse 8 of that psalm the root of the same Hebrew word occurs: "I will instruct thee and teach thee in the way which thou shalt go."

It is not always easy to divide a psalm into its various sections, and sometimes it might appear that this is done in an arbitrary fashion. Nevertheless it is helpful to any attempt at exposition, and to the present writer it appears (contrary to most other attempts to identify the stanzas) that the psalm can be divided into four parts:

1. David's plea for forgiveness (verses 1-8)
2. His desire for God to create a right spirit (verses 9-12)

356

3. His resolution in the light of the experience of God's grace (verses 13-17)

4. An epilogue (verses 18,19)

The themes of the first three sections are not, perhaps, so clear-cut, as we have indicated; and there is of necessity a continuation of the main theme (the desire for forgiveness) throughout the psalm.

David's plea for forgiveness (verses 1-8)

In our consideration of Psalm 32 we looked at the three words for "sin", repeated here in verses 1 and 2. "Transgression" (*pesha*) means 'rebellion'; "sin" (*chattath*) means 'to miss the mark' and "iniquity"' (*awan*) means 'perversion or depravity'. The three words occur together for the first time in connection with the manifestation of God's name in Exodus 34:

"And the LORD passed by before him, and proclaimed, The LORD, The LORD God, merciful and gracious, longsuffering, and abundant in goodness and truth, keeping mercy for thousands, forgiving *iniquity* and *transgression* and *sin*, and that will by no means clear the guilty." (verses 6,7)

Although it might appear that on occasions the words are used interchangeably, they are not synonymous, and their meanings are quite separate and distinct.

Notice that the emphasis here in the declaration of God's name is upon His forgiveness. This is important, for, when we examine the law given through Moses, a significant fact emerges. In the law of the offerings for personal sin, only two of these words are used (i.e., *chattath* and *awan*). There would appear to have been no offerings prescribed for transgressions (*pesha*), although it was covered by the ritual of the day of atonement (Leviticus 16).

If, then, David knew that the law could not give him forgiveness, for the punishment for adultery and murder was death, then his only hope was to cast himself on God's mercy, in the belief that what the law could not do the Lord through the qualities revealed in His name might graciously grant.

357

David's plea for forgiveness is therefore based on his understanding of God's revealed character: "Have *mercy* ... according to thy *lovingkindness*: according unto the multitude of thy *tender mercies*" (verse 1). The forgiveness extended by God set aside the legal requirements of the law and recognised the humble and contrite spirit exhibited by David:

"I, even I, am he that blotteth out thy transgressions for mine own sake, and will not remember thy sins."

(Isaiah 43:25)

As there were three words for sin, so also there were three terms to describe the manner in which it could be put away – "blot out", "wash me" and "cleanse me" (verses 1,2). All three are taken from the ritual of the law, but used, of course, in a deeper spiritual sense.

The request to "blot out my transgressions" is interesting, in that the Hebrew word rendered "blot" is used specifically in relation to the "law of jealousies" in Numbers 5. This had to do with the woman who had committed adultery, the very sin of which David had been guilty. The curses which would fall upon the guilty woman were written in a book and then "blotted out" with the bitter water that she was caused to drink (verses 23). So David beseeches God to blot out his transgressions and the curse that he would bear if God would not forgive. Perhaps the dire consequences within the inward parts of the guilty woman (verse 27) were reflected, by contrast, in the words of David: "Behold, thou desirest truth in the inward parts: and in the hidden part thou shalt make me to know wisdom" (Psalm 51:6).

The word "wash" was often used in the law for ceremonial ablutions, in particular for the washing of clothes (Exodus 19:10; Leviticus 11:25; 13:6,54; 14:8,47 etc.). Here it refers to that inner cleansing of which the outward washing was but a type. But realising the gravity of his sin, David feels a need to be washed throughly (lit. 'abundantly') – that is, again and again, as if one cleansing would be insufficient to wash away his sin.

It is worth noting that in Leviticus 13 and 14 the word is used with reference to the law of leprosy, and this thought connects with the third of David's petitions:

"Cleanse me from my sin", for the word rendered "cleanse" was used especially in connection with the law of leprosy (Leviticus 13:6,34 etc.). The connection between sin and leprosy is, of course, a familiar Biblical theme and it serves to emphasise how loathsome and heinous sin is in the sight of God.

David's plea for forgiveness is based upon his recognition of God's mercy and his own humble acknowledgement of his sin:

"For I acknowledge my transgressions: and my sin is ever before me. Against thee, thee only, have I sinned, and done this evil in thy sight." (verses 3,4)

God had known of David's sin from the moment he had conceived this wickedness; but now David himself had come to know (the word carries great emphasis) his sin. There was an inner conviction, and with it a continuous consciousness of what he had done. It was ever before him, or, as one translation has it, "never out of mind".

There are important lessons to be learned in these opening verses of the psalm about sin and its forgiveness. Note that both in verses 1 and 3, David writes in the plural of his "transgressions", for in the very nature of things, one sin can never stand alone, but is like a cancer or a "root of bitterness". Inevitably it spawns other sins, and the repercussions of just one act in its effect upon the human heart can be incalculable.

It is also not enough to know we have sinned. Human nature is adept at accommodating itself to its own shortcomings. Before David was convicted by the words of Nathan – "Thou art the man" – he knew that what he had done was wrong (Psalm 32:3,4). His conscience had troubled him and he had known no inner peace. It had destroyed the joy of his fellowship with God. One can imagine how David could have tried to rationalise the situation. After all, he was the king; think of the consequences if Uriah lived! Why not expose him to extreme danger in the battle, then God could be the judge of what he ought to do? Uriah's death at the hand of the enemy – might it not be a sign from God who would surely have protected him, if He had wanted it otherwise. We speculate, of course – but such is the way in which the thinking of the flesh so often permits a man to live with his sins. Thus to know we have sinned is not enough; there must be a deep sense of sorrow, a recognition of the way in which God views sin and the way in which it separates us from Him. It must be ever before us; we must live in the consciousness of it and its consequences for us, for only then will we produce that sacrifice of a broken spirit, that broken and contrite heart that God will not despise (Psalm 51:17).

That David understood the true nature of sin is evident, for "against thee, thee only, have I sinned", he said. In fact David had sinned against Bathsheba, Uriah and their families. His act had repercussions for his own family and indeed for the nation of Israel; but first and foremost, sin is a breaking of God's law, and there is nothing that man can do to heal the breach created. Men might forgive us for our actions; but it is our relationship with God which is of supreme importance, and it is His forgiveness alone which can ultimately lift the burden of guilt and the shame felt. Thus when David was confronted by Nathan and his sin finally exposed and recognised, his simple response was, "I have sinned against the LORD" (2 Samuel 12:13). It was in God's sight that David had done this evil, and his words recall the record in 2 Samuel:

"The thing that David had done was evil in the eyes of the LORD." (11:27, AV & AV margin)

"Wherefore hast thou despised the commandment of the LORD, to do evil in his sight?" (12:9)

The prayer for forgiveness and the confession of his sin was also a recognition of God's justice and judgement. Just as to seek to justify one's sinful actions would be a challenge to God's authority and to question His judgement, so by his self-condemnation David was recognising that God was right in His condemnation and sentence of death upon sin:

"... that thou mightest be justified when thou speakest, and be clear when thou judgest." (Psalm 51:4)

These words are, of course, quoted by the Apostle Paul in his argument about Israel's unfaithfulness in Romans 3:4, where the passage is prefaced by the words, "Let God be

360

true, but every man a liar". The acknowledgement of our personal sins is, however, only part of what is involved in recognising God's justice and declaring His righteousness, for:

"Behold, I was shapen in iniquity; and in sin did my mother conceive me. Behold, thou desirest truth in the inward parts: and in the hidden part thou shalt make me to know wisdom." (verses 5,6)

The human predicament is emphasised, the root cause of the sins we own laid bare. The problem is hereditary, for we are born, as Brother John Thomas expressed it, "under the constitution of sin". This is not our fault, for we are no more responsible for this situation than for the fact that we are born British or any other nationality. Nevertheless, we bear the consequences of Adam's transgression, and we need in this respect also to acknowledge that God was right in His judgement.

There are those such as Calvin and others who speak of "original sin" and who teach that infants need to be regenerated by the sprinkling of holy water, lest they suffer the torments of hell fire. As Brother Thomas said, the original sin was Adam's. All his progeny, including the Lord Jesus Christ, inherit through him a sin-prone nature justly sentenced by God to die (see *Elpis Israel*, chapter 4 on "The Constitution of Sin").

In verses 5 and 6 the human dilemma is emphasised in a most vivid and powerful way. Twice the word "behold" is used, firstly to describe our predicament as a result of being born in Adam, and secondly to emphasise what God requires of man – truth in the inward parts, wisdom in the hidden parts. Only in the Lord Jesus has the conflict created been satisfactorily resolved. He alone overcame the handicap brought by sin and manifested the qualities in which God delights. For the rest of us, we must identify with Paul and say:

"For I know that in me (that is, in my flesh,) dwelleth no good thing: for to will is present with me; but how to perform that which is good I find not. For the good that I would I do not: but the evil which I would not, that I do … O wretched man that I am! who shall deliver me from the body of this death?" (Romans 7:18-25)

Once again David returns to the language of the law as he renews his plea for forgiveness:

"Purge me with hyssop, and I shall be clean: wash me, and I shall be whiter than snow. Make me to hear joy and gladness; that the bones which thou hast broken may rejoice." (verses 7,8)

The tense of the verbs in these verses is in fact future, and presents us with another interesting development of thought – "Thou wilt purge me ... Thou wilt wash me ... Thou wilt make me ..." We have to remember that God had put away David's sin and had given an assurance that he would not die (2 Samuel 12:13). But such is the complex nature of human emotions and reactions that the scars that sin leaves cannot always be so easily put away. The process of renewal can be a slow and painful experience. Thus David seems to view his reinstatement into full fellowship, with all its joy and gladness, as a continuing experience; and here again there is a lesson to be learned.

We must never take sin lightly. We believe God, that if we confess our sins, He is faithful and just to forgive us our sins (1 John 1:9). Nevertheless, there is no room for apathy or presumption. Forgiveness is not a casual request and a shrug of the shoulders, but a matter of earnest entreaty. David teaches us that sometimes one sin can have the most disastrous effect upon our lives. In one sense, nothing can be the same again. The shame, the guilt, the sorrow can be recurring experiences; they can become a cross we have to carry in life, and yet in the knowledge that God has forgiven us; in the light of His mercy we can come to a deeper appreciation of the love of God than might otherwise have been possible, and find that all things (even our sins) can work together for good for those who love God.

Once again the outward purification is a type of inner cleansing, and the implication of the use of hyssop should be clear. It was used in the Passover to sprinkle the lintels (Exodus 12:21-23); again, it is associated with the ashes of the red heifer (Numbers 19:17-19) and also with the cleansing of the leper (Leviticus 14:4,6). The repetition of the plea for God to wash him has been dealt with earlier. As a consequence of the cleansing he is "whiter than snow" – so completely does God put away the sin of the truly penitent man (see also Isaiah 1:18).

David's desire to be filled with gladness is linked with the thought that the bones which God had broken might yet rejoice. It is an insight into the physical effect that sin can have upon a man. The shame and guilt can manifest themselves in bodily symptoms. It was as if God had crushed the very frame of his body, so that the pain was felt in his broken bones. Once again we recall the Passover. This time the image is of the lamb and the prophecy of the Lord Jesus that not a bone of him should be broken (see Psalm 34:20; John 19:36,37). The perfection of the Lord Jesus, who maintained his wholeness, is contrasted with the sin of David, whose very bones were symbolically broken by his experience.

David's desire for God to create a right spirit (verses 9-12)

That a new stanza starts at verse 9 seems to be indicated by the change from the future tense of the verb seen in verses 7 and 8 to the present tense in verse 9: "Hide thy face from my sins, and blot out all mine iniquities" (verse 9). Usually when God hides His face, it is a sign of His displeasure. However, David may well be recalling the language of Psalm 90 written by Moses concerning that generation that perished in the wilderness, for there it was written:

"For we are consumed by thine anger, and by thy wrath are we troubled. Thou hast set our iniquities before thee, our secret sins in the light of thy countenance." (verses 7,8)

In effect, David says: 'Regard me not as that rebellious generation that perished in the wilderness'. If this was to be the case, there would be a need for a new creation – for God to work in his life in such a way that the spiritual man would be renewed.

It is said that the word translated "create" (Psalm 51:10) means 'to make that which has not existed before'; but a perusal of the concordance would indicate that this is not always the case, and the parallel line, "Renew a right spirit within me" would imply that the creation that

David longed for was the restoration of that which had been lost through his sin. Thus he pleads also that God would "restore unto (him) the joy of (his) salvation" (verse 12).

We can see the analogy in the case of David likening his spiritual condition, as a result of his sin, to the primaeval chaos described in Genesis 1:

> "And the earth was without form, and void; and darkness was upon the face of the deep."   (verse 2)

It was by the word of God that the darkness was scattered and order brought out of chaos. So it is with the hearts of men. It is the influence of the word of God that enlightens and convicts of sin, that converts and transforms, thus creating a new man. It was to this divine activity in his life, in conjunction with God's grace and loving-kindness, that David now submits himself (cp. Paul's words in Ephesians 4:22-24).

What David desires is a clean or pure heart and a right spirit. The word rendered "right" means literally a steadfast or constant spirit. That is an attitude of mind that will maintain its faithfulness in the face of trial and temptation – a heart that is fixed in its allegiance to God:

> "Cast me not away from thy presence; and take not thy holy spirit from me."   (verse 11)

In contrast to David's plea that God would hide His face from his sins (verse 9), David now asks that God would not cast him away from His presence (Hebrew, 'face'). There seems to be a direct allusion here to the words spoken regarding Saul, for when David was anointed by Samuel, "the Spirit of the LORD came upon David from that day forward" (1 Samuel 16:13). The next verse tells us, however, "but the Spirit of the LORD departed from Saul" (verse 14). The Holy Spirit rested upon the king, for he was God's representative. It was the seal of his royal authority; and as God had rejected Saul and taken His Spirit away from him, so David beseeches God that he might not experience a like judgement.

Notwithstanding the above view, we think it right to mention a possible alternative. The Holy Spirit is only mentioned in one other passage in the Old Testament, i.e., Isaiah 63:

> "In all their affliction he was afflicted, and the angel of his presence saved them ... But they rebelled, and vexed his holy Spirit." (verses 9,10)

Note that the "angel of his presence" stands parallel to "his Holy Spirit"; and remembering that "He maketh his angels spirits", it could be that the angel of God's presence is described in Psalm 51 as his "holy spirit". If this is the case, the same parallelism could exist in Psalm 51:

> "Cast me not away from thy presence; and take not thy holy spirit from me."

In other words, David is pleading, 'Do not desert me, do not take thine angel, who encampeth about me, away from me'.

In hoping to continue to enjoy God's favour, his overwhelming desire was to know, as previously he had in all its freshness, "the joy of his salvation". "Uphold me", he pleads, "with a willing spirit" (verse 12, RSV). The idea of the willing spirit is illustrated in the book of Exodus:

> "Take ye from among you an offering unto the LORD; whosoever is of a willing heart"; "as many as were willing hearted ... brought bracelets, and earrings ..." (35:5,22)

An interesting association of the word is a connection with the idea of 'noble' or 'princely':

> "(He) lifteth up the beggar from the dunghill; to set them among princes (same word), and to make them inherit the throne of glory." (1 Samuel 2:8)
> (see also Psalm 47:9; 113:8 etc.)

A vital quality of those whom God will make princes in the earth is that they have a willing spirit, for such an attitude towards God is the mark of true nobility. Lest any should think that in some way those verses imply that God will directly provide a man, by His Spirit, with a willing spirit and a clean heart, let it be noted that in another psalm David writes, "Uphold me *according to thy word*". Whatever the manner of God's work in our lives, it will always be according to His word, and by the way revealed in that word. And although space does not allow an examination of this subject now, we can be assured that God does not provide directly for men that which He looks for in those who would commend themselves to Him.

His resolution (verses 13-17)

It must be the resolve of any who have experienced God's forgiveness in their lives to seek to tell others of what God has done for them – to teach them, that they too might turn unto the Lord:

"Then will I teach transgressors thy ways; and sinners shall be converted unto thee."　　　(verse 13)

We have already commented on the relevance of Psalm 32 to these words. David realised that he was responsible for the death of Uriah. He had not wielded the sword, but he had engineered his death. So he cried,

"Deliver me from blood-guiltiness, O God, thou God of my salvation: and my tongue shall sing aloud of thy righteousness."　　　(verse 14)

David's joy would be in God's righteousness, for it was that which God had promised to impute to those who put their faith in His word. To believe God was to be counted righteous; and the work of God in salvation is ultimately to bestow His righteousness upon those that seek it (Psalm 24:5).

Knowing that God was faithful and just (i.e., righteous) to forgive his sins, David exclaims,

"O Lord, open thou my lips; and my mouth shall shew forth thy praise."　　　(verse 15)

The request that God would open his lips has a special association in scripture. It has the significance of the mouth being opened to utter the word of God, to deliver a message for men to be enlightened. It has, in fact, to do directly with the process of inspiration. The following examples make the point clear:

"I will open my mouth in a parable: I will utter dark sayings of old."　　　(Psalm 78:2)

"And seeing the multitudes, he went up into a mountain: and when he was set, his disciples came unto him: and he opened his mouth, and taught them, saying ..."　　　(Matthew 5:1,2)

"Praying always ... that utterance may be given unto me, that I may open my mouth boldly, to make known the mystery of the gospel." (Ephesians 6:18,19) Holy men open their mouths, and grace is poured into their lips. David's prayer was that God's Spirit might continue to rest on him, so that he might praise God in the composition of psalms and spiritual songs, whereby men might be edified. This resolution to act sprang out of his realisation of the enormity of his sin and the magnitude of God's grace and condescension:

"For thou desirest not sacrifice; else would I give it: thou delightest not in burnt offering. The sacrifices of God are a broken spirit: a broken and a contrite heart, O God, thou wilt not despise." (Psalm 51:16,17)

It has been argued here that David recognises animal sacrifice to be of no avail. It is inferred, further, that in the last two verses we have a later addition to the psalm which seeks to redress the balance by emphasising a time when God would delight in sacrifice, burnt offering and whole burnt offering. We accept that some psalms (e.g., Psalms 14 and 53) were adapted by later writers to suit their particular circumstances, but we see no grounds whatever, other than expediency, for adopting such an argument in this case. A proper understanding of the circumstances holds the key to the language.

The law commanded animal sacrifices; there could be nothing wrong in offering them, provided they were brought in the right spirit and offered in the manner prescribed. It should be noted that the sacrifices mentioned, which God did not desire or delight in *at that time*, were not sin offerings, but thank offerings (as the word in Hebrew clearly indicates) and burnt offerings.

Under the law, before a man could offer thanksgiving and burnt offerings, symbolising the dedication of his life to God, he had first to offer a sin offering; for while sin separated a man from God, there was nothing that a man could do that would be acceptable to God, or in which He could delight. Surely this is the point that David is making. He had first to be reconciled to God through a sin offering presented out of a broken and a contrite heart, for that sacrifice God would not despise. Only then, when he had been forgiven his sin, could he bring his thank offerings and his burnt offerings, for only then would his dedication be accepted by God.

What an important principle this is! It is a first principle of the Truth. Men might in human terms be good men. They might show love and compassion; they might be men of the highest integrity. But nothing can alter the fact that they are sinners, and that because of sin they are separated from God. Nothing that they can offer is acceptable to Him, as far as their salvation is concerned, unless first their sin is put away. They must come to the Lord Jesus Christ – the sin offering. They must associate themselves with his cross through baptism, and only then are they able to offer "in him" works that are acceptable to God.

This is the lesson, and this is the truth, that lies behind the words of David in the psalm.

The epilogue (verses 18,19)

These final words are therefore not a later addition, but very relevant to the substance of the psalm:

"Do good in thy good pleasure unto Zion: build thou the walls of Jerusalem. Then shalt thou be pleased with the sacrifices of righteousness, with burnt offering and whole burnt offering: then shall they offer bullocks upon thine altar." (verses 18,19)

It may be that the walls of Jerusalem were at that time in need of repair. That no mention is made of the fact in the historical books does not prove anything. Be that as it may, however, the point David is making is that by his sin it was as though the walls had been breached, broken down, and Zion placed in great peril. There was need for a work of restoration, a repairing of the breach – for when that was done, when sin had been effectively dealt with and removed, then God would be pleased to accept the sacrifices of righteousness. There is no contradiction: verses 16,17 and 18,19 are in complete harmony.

Perhaps, looking at the Messianic significance of the psalm we can think of those last two verses as expressing the thoughts of the Lord Jesus Christ. He did no sin, he knew no shame or guilt. How much therefore would he have been helped to understand the sinner's plight and to seek to enter into his experiences by such psalms as this! And how much more, as he contemplated the ruin that men brought upon themselves by sin, though they be prospective constituents of the heavenly Jerusalem, could he exclaim as no other, as he thought of God's work of salvation:

"Build thou the walls of Jerusalem!"

For only then would God be pleased to accept "through him" the sacrifices of righteousness.

PSALM 52

PSALMS 51 to 60 inclusive, with two exceptions, have clear historical notes as to the events which formed the background to their composition. Four (52 to 55 inclusive) are described as "Maschil of David" and the following five (56 to 60) bear the inscription "Michtam of David". As previously indicated, the term "maschil" means 'instruction', the primary purpose for which the psalm was written. What precisely is indicated by a "michtam" is a matter of some obscurity, although we find no reason to change the conclusion reached when we considered this term in relation to Psalm 16

Both "michtam" and "maschil" psalms have essentially the same purpose. Originating in David's personal experiences and his reflections arising out of those circumstances, they were intended to teach or to instruct.

As far as Psalm 52 is concerned, the historical information at the head of the song tells us that it is "A Psalm of David, when Doeg the Edomite came and told Saul, and said unto him, David is come to the house of Ahimelech". As is so often the case, most orthodox commentators have difficulty in reconciling this historical information with the content of the psalm. The emphasis in the first section of the psalm (verses 2-5) is upon a deceitful man who delights in lies as a means of creating mischief. This, they say, is neither true of Doeg or Saul, and they find difficulty also because there is no reference to the barbarous destruction of the priests by Doeg at Saul's command.

The present writer finds it strange that David, not just in this psalm, but in all the records we have, does not condemn Saul for his action. In fact, his words to Abiathar, "I have occasioned the death of all the persons of thy father's house" (1 Samuel 22:22) imply that David himself felt a measure of guilt for what happened. There are two points that we would like to make regarding the historical information and the context of the psalm, both of which, we feel, can help to resolve the doubts raised by many writers.

First of all, it does not necessarily follow that the historical information is the precise substance of the psalm. Rather, it indicates that the psalm was written at that time, and that David's meditation was occasioned by those events. Thus the actions of Doeg, an Edomite, could lead to David writing of the archetypal "profane person", Esau – one who lived for the world and had no place in his life for God. The second half of the psalm speaks of the ultimate fate of the wicked man and the exaltation of the righteous. In keeping with this, the musical information at the end of the psalm reads: "For the Chief Musician; set to Mahalath (meaning 'with dancings' – Thirtle, *Titles of the Psalms*)". Truly this would reflect the rejoicing associated with that day when "the upright shall have dominion over them (the wicked) in the morning" (Psalm 49:14).

Secondly, the fact has already been referred to, that the sins emphasised in the psalm do not appear to reflect the conduct of Doeg. It is worth considering, that sometimes the historical records do not tell us all that was done or said in particular circumstances. The fact that David does not openly condemn Saul for his undoubted barbarous act can, perhaps, be understood if in fact Saul was deceived. It does not excuse his hatred of David or his violent reaction but, if Doeg had falsely reported what had happened, retaining the simple facts but embellishing them with falsehood as to the motives and intentions of the priests, then Saul's unreasonable reactions to Ahimelech' s protestations of ignorance of the real circumstances behind David's visit to Nob are more easily understood (see 1 Samuel 22:9-16).

Doeg had devised mischief with his tongue, and the words of the psalm are seen to be appropriate to the type of man he was.

Structure

The psalm falls naturally into two parts, with the first verse serving as a kind of preface describing the theme to be developed:

"Why boasteth thou thyself in mischief, O mighty man? The goodness of God endureth continually."

The two halves of the verse correspond with the two sections of the psalm:

1. The unscrupulous evildoer who delights in causing mischief by deceit and lies is described and his ultimate fate foretold (verses 2-5).
2. The righteous, filled with godly fear, contemplate the end of the wicked and rejoice in the security they enjoy as the covenant people of God (verses 6-9).

The manner in which he rejoices in his mischief is now seen as an indication of Doeg's attempt to ingratiate himself with Saul and to further his own ambitions. He is called "O mighty (Hebrew, *gibbor*) man"; and this surely is a term of deep irony. Elsewhere the word carries the idea of 'hero' – and, after all, Doeg was no more than "chief of the herdsmen" who had slaughtered defenceless people. In contrast, "the goodness of God (Hebrew, *El*) endureth continually". Significantly, the singular "El", indicating the source of all power and strength, is set against the empty boast of the man who would finally be brought to acknowledge the One who was stronger than he and would bring judgement upon him for his wicked works.

Verses 2-5

These verses describe not the violent acts of the man, but the way in which by deceit he brought about the destruction of the innocent:

"Thy tongue deviseth mischiefs; like a sharp rasor, working deceitfully. Thou lovest evil more than good; and lying rather than to speak righteousness."

(verses 2,3)

The sins of the tongue are amongst the most dangerous that men have to fear. Falsehood, false witness, slander, gossip, can all bring misery to those who are their victims; yet at the same time they destroy also those who indulge in them, being such clear indications of the envy, jealousy and perversion that characterises human nature.

When the tongue is used in this way it is like a sharp (lit. whetted) razor. It cuts before you are aware. It should always be used with caution. It can be equally dangerous both to the man who speaks without due consideration and to the one at whom the cutting and hurtful words are directed. (Thus the words of the tongue are likened to swords, spears and arrows – see Psalm 55:21, 57:4, etc.)

The danger for us is that we can allow our tongue to rule without realising the peril in which we stand and the damage we do to our brethren and sisters. The man described in the psalm has, however, deliberately and knowingly indulged in this vicious use of the tongue to achieve his ambition and to destroy the righteous. He loved evil, not *more* than good, but *rather* than good. He does not simply have a preference for evil, but he is counted among those "who hate the good, and love the evil" (Micah 3:2). Note also that "lying" is not contrasted with truth, but with "righteousness", for it is not simply false words for which he stands condemned, but false conduct. His actions had been a deliberate act of will. He had chosen the evil rather than the good:

"Thou lovest all devouring words, O thou deceitful tongue. God shall likewise destroy thee for ever, he shall take thee away, and pluck thee out of thy dwelling place, and root thee out of the land of the living."

(Psalm 52:4,5)

Literally the first sentence reads, "Thou lovest words of swallowing up, O thou deceitful tongue". Note that the tongue stands for the individual. There is, of course, an appropriateness about the use of such a figure, for James writes of the tongue in terms which show that often it is not the man who controls his tongue, but the tongue that controls him: "… but the tongue can no man tame; it is an unruly evil, full of deadly poison" (James 3:8). Thus the words that are spoken have for their aim the swallowing up of the righteous and the figure, of course, vividly portrays that end.

Other psalms perpetuate the figure: "Their throat is an open sepulchre (lit. a yawning gulf)" (Psalm 5:9); "Let

373

them not say, We have swallowed him up" (Psalm 35:25). In this the deceitful man delights, for he loves such words, and his "mouth is full of cursing and bitterness" (Romans 3:14), for he eats up (God's) people like bread (Psalm 53:4).

In contrast, he will not escape the righteous judgement of God; for because of his unscrupulous actions, his words of deceit and falsehood, God will treat him as he has treated others: "God shall likewise (i.e., in the same manner) destroy thee for ever." Literally, the word translated "to destroy" means 'to break down' (Strong's); and the term is illustrated by Gideon's words to the men of Penuel, "I will break down this tower" (Judges 8:9).

Whereas the wickedness of men may destroy the righteous, it cannot separate him from the love of God; his trials do not last "for ever", for his place in the purpose of God is secure. When God destroys the wicked, however, there is no reprieve. Their judgement is final and irrevocable. The psalms prefigure the work of the Lord Jesus:

"And fear not them which kill the body, but are not able to kill the soul: but rather fear him which is able to destroy both soul and body in hell (Gehenna)."

(Matthew 10:28)

Although the wicked might dwell in complacency, at ease in his tent, God would pluck him out as a man takes coal from a hearth. Gesenius (*Hebrew / Chaldee Lexicon*) indicates that on every other occasion that the word "pluck" is used, it is connected with fire or burning coals – e.g., "to take fire from the hearth" (Isaiah 30:14).

Although he might spread himself "like a green bay tree (AV margin, 'in his own soil')" (Psalm 37:35), it would be to no avail, for God would root him up out of the land of the living. This was what the men of Anathoth had said regarding Jeremiah:

"Let us destroy the tree with the fruit thereof, and let us cut him off from the land of the living, that his name may be no more remembered."   (Jeremiah 11:19)

As they thought to do to him, in like manner would God do to them.

Verses 6-9

From these judgements upon the wicked others would learn and fear:

"The righteous also shall see, and fear, and shall laugh at him: Lo, this is the man that made not God his strength; but trusted in the abundance of his riches, and strengthened himself in his wickedness."

(Psalm 52:6,7)

The fear which the righteous experience is not terror, but awe and reverence at this demonstration of the righteous anger of God. With that fear is mingled joy in the destruction of the wicked who oppress the "poor in spirit". The laughter spoken of is not derision or vindictive exultation at the wicked man's ruin; it is rather a righteous joy at the manifestation of God's judgements, the overthrow of the oppressor and the justification of the righteous. It is a salutary fact that we must all recognise, that there can be no peace on the earth, no consummation of God's purpose, without the destruction of the wicked. Thus the Psalmist writes:

"Let the sinners be consumed out of the earth, and let the wicked be no more. Bless thou the LORD, O my soul. Praise ye the LORD."   (Psalm 104:35)

In keeping with the words of the psalm, the New Testament also testifies of the fall of "Babylon the Great", "Rejoice over her, thou heaven, and ye holy apostles and prophets; for God hath avenged you on her" (Revelation 18:20).

The man who would please God, however, must learn the reason why these judgements have befallen the wicked: "Lo, this is the man that made not God his strength" (Psalm 52:7). The Hebrew word translated "man" (*geber*) appears to have been used with a touch of irony, for it is akin to *gibbor* or 'hero', the word used in verse 1. The tense of the verb "made" also implies a continuous habit of mind, of a man whose trust was not in God but riches – he "strengthened himself in his substance" (AV margin). In other words, like Esau, he was a profane person who trusted in this present world. He was a worldly-minded man, and because of his trust in material things he had no thought or place for God in his life. This is the lesson the righteous learn from the end of the wicked – do not be deceived, put your trust in God, that you do not suffer a like condemnation.

Verses 8 and 9 turn to the first person singular, as David speaks now of himself. The words, however, must be especially true of the Lord Jesus Christ, whose spirit is reflected through these final verses:

"But I am like a green olive tree in the house of God: I trust in the mercy of God for ever and ever. I will praise thee for ever, because thou hast done it: and I will wait on thy name; for it is good before thy saints."

(verses 8,9)

Here we have a marvellous contrast with the description of the wicked. In verse 5 we were told that the wicked had been rooted out of the land of the living, although, like a green bay tree, they had seemed to prosper. The bay tree is an evergreen, and so, perhaps, it conveys the conviction of the wicked that they will never be moved, determined to live their lives as though they were going to continue for ever. "But as for me, I am like a green olive tree." (RV)

The olive is also an evergreen, and it is said never to die, for it sends forth fresh shoots, even when cut down. It would therefore be a fitting symbol of the righteous, who, though they fall seven times, rise up again (Proverbs 24:16). But the real secret is that the wicked take root in the world, whereas the righteous grow in the house of God. The reference here is not to the literal temple, which had not been built at the time the psalm was composed, and there is no evidence that trees were planted in its courts. We have here God's spiritual house where the righteous flourish, "that they might be called trees of righteousness, the planting of the LORD, that he might be glorified" (Isaiah 61:3).

The righteous man had trusted in the mercy (covenant love) of God and was confident that he should do so for ever and ever, for, with striking emphasis, he says, "Thou hast done it". The works of God are absolute; they can never be frustrated. Therefore "I will give thee thanks" (RV) and "I will wait on thy name, for it is good, in the presence of thy saints" (RV).

To wait on God's name is to rest patiently, in the confidence that He will perform all that is conveyed by that name through which He has revealed Himself in the earth. Ultimately the man will proclaim the goodness of God's name and demonstrate in himself the truth of those things that God had spoken in the presence of His saints (lit. 'His beloved ones'). It is God's *chasidim* who are the objects of His *chesed* (covenant love) and in that we can all take confidence, for as the Lord himself declared, "I will declare thy name unto my brethren, in the midst of the church will I sing praise unto thee" (Hebrews 2:12, quoting Psalm 22:22).

NOTE:
Psalm 53 is considered earlier with Psalm 14

PSALM 54

THE historical information at the head of the psalm tells us that it was written on the occasion "when the Ziphims came and said to Saul, Doth not David hide himself with us?" The record of this event, and those surrounding it, is to be found in 1 Samuel 23 to 26.

We include these four chapters because there are two records describing the Ziphims' betrayal of David to Saul (1 Samuel 23:19-26 and 26:1-4). The accounts are very alike and some have suggested that they are two records of the same event. For that reason we give a brief summary of the contents of these chapters, for we believe that they are two similar, but separate, events and that consequently all that is recorded between them is appropriate to David's meditation in this short psalm.

Chapter 23 opens with an account of the Philistines attacking and oppressing the city of Keilah. After enquiring of the Lord, David encounters the Philistines, defeats them, and saves the inhabitants of Keilah. Saul, however, hears that David is in Keilah and, because it is a city with walls, bars and gates, imagines that God has delivered David into his hand. Again David enquires of the Lord who reveals to him that, notwithstanding the debt they owed him, the men of Keilah would deliver him into the hand of Saul. David and his men being thus warned of God, come down eventually to the wilderness of Ziph. Here, in a wood, Jonathan (Saul's son) meets David and strengthens his hand in the Lord, assuring him of his conviction that one day David would be king over Israel.

It is at this juncture that the Ziphites come to Saul, saying, "Doth not David hide himself with us?" Not only did they report David's whereabouts to Saul, but they assured him of their willingness to deliver him into his hands. David, being warned of Saul's intention, came into the wilderness of Maon, where it would appear he found himself in a desperate plight, for Saul and the men with him surrounded David's company. However, God helped David, for the Philistines invaded the land and Saul was compelled to withdraw to deal with this threat.

David makes his escape to the strongholds of En-gedi, and it is here, after repulsing the Philistines and returning to his relentless search for David, that Saul, while sleeping in a cave, is delivered into the hand of David, who refuses to take advantage of the opportunity, for he would not lift up his hand against the Lord's anointed. Faced by this amazing act of faith and graciousness on David's part, Saul recognises that "thou art more righteous than I", and departs.

At this juncture the death of Samuel is recorded (25:1), and David comes again to Maon, where dwelt Nabal and Abigail. Chapter 25 is a detailed account of David's dealing with that churlish and foolish man and his prudent wife. It is after these events, with David again in the general area in which the events of chapter 23 occurred, that the Ziphites once again report to Saul that David was hidden in the hill of Hachilah which is before Jeshimon. Saul once more comes out to seek David, but again the Lord delivers him into David's hand. Yet again, although urged by Abishai to allow him to smite Saul with his spear, David demurs from raising his hand against him. Once again Saul is compelled to recognise David's integrity and returns to Gibeah. David, however, says in his heart, "I shall now perish one day by the hand of Saul", and departs to dwell among the Philistines. From that time Saul sought him no more (1 Samuel 27:1-4).

One wonders if the death of Samuel had an effect upon David. Perhaps through all this time Samuel had urged restraint upon Saul and those who would help him. Now with his influence gone, David felt that every man's hand would be against him, for the treachery of the Ziphites is the first occasion (not taking Doeg the Edomite into account) that any of the people of the land are recorded as having openly sided with Saul. Thus it was against this background that David penned this short psalm, which in some respects is couched in such general terms that it

379

could apply to many different kinds of crises in life. Nevertheless, with the guidance given, we do know the particular events that occasioned its composition. It falls very easily into two sections:

Part 1, verses 1-3, ending with a "Selah";

Part 2, verses 4-7.

Part 1 (verses 1-3)

"Save me, O God, by thy name, and judge me by thy strength. Hear my prayer, O God; give ear to the words of my mouth. For strangers are risen up against me, and oppressors seek after my soul: they have not set God before them. Selah."

Once again David refers to the name of God, which describes His revealed will and purpose and sums up all the attributes by which He has made Himself known to man. It had for David a relevance to the circumstances in which he found himself, for it was a recognition on his part of the fidelity of God – the fact that nothing could frustrate the word that God had spoken. But for David, that name "Yahweh" – "He who will be" – must also have spoken of the ultimate salvation from sin and death when the purpose enshrined in that name was finally worked out in the experience of men.

"Vindicate me by your strength" (NKJV) is his cry, and therein is the acknowledgement that with God there was not only the will to perform, but also the power (RV, might) to deliver His servant. There is a reflection here of words of David spoken to Saul in 1 Samuel 24:

"The LORD therefore be judge, and judge between me and thee, and see, and plead my cause, and deliver me out of thine hand." (verse 15)

David's desire that God would hear his prayer arose out of the fact that strangers and violent men had risen against him and sought after his life (verse 3, NKJ). This verse is repeated almost verbatim in Psalm 86:14, except that the word "proud" is substituted for "stranger". The *Cambridge Bible* points out that the consonants in the Hebrew words *zarim* (strangers) and *zedim* (proud) are almost identical, and some manuscripts read *zedim*, not *zarem* in Psalm 54.

There is a problem in regarding either the men of Keilah or "the Ziphites" as strangers, for they belonged to the covenant people. The variant reading would remove the difficulty, although there is a suggestion that the men of Keilah were of Canaanite origin, which would make them the strangers referred to. The evidence for this is, however, inconclusive. Once again there is a connection with the historical record, for "David saw that Saul was come out *to seek his life*" (1 Samuel 23:15).

The final words of the section, "they have not set God before them", recall the words of earlier psalms:

"The wicked, through the pride of his countenance, will not seek after God: all his thoughts are, There is no God." (Psalm 10:4, AV with margin)

"The fool hath said in his heart, There is no God." (Psalm 14:1)

The words describe men who, knowing the declared will and counsel of God in regard to David, seek not only to ignore it, but also to frustrate it. Bearing in mind the words of Psalm 10 and Psalm 14, might it not be that numbered amongst them was Nabal? Surely this is the basis for the Lord's parable of the rich fool (Luke 12:16-21).

Part 2 (verses 4-7)

The prayer of the first stanza now gives place to David's acknowledgement of God's work in his life, his recognition of His continuing mercy, and his determination to offer to God the things in which He delighted:

"Behold, God is mine helper: the Lord is with them that uphold my soul. He shall reward evil unto mine enemies: cut them off in thy truth. I will freely sacrifice unto thee: I will praise thy name, O LORD; for it is good. For he hath delivered me out of all trouble: and mine eye hath seen his desire upon mine enemies." (verses 4-7)

God had shown Himself to be David's helper by the manner in which providentially He had caused the Philistines to invade the land, forcing Saul to withdraw when, in human terms, he had David and his men at his mercy. This was but a repetition of many similar events

381

that had strengthened David's conviction that the Lord was on his side. He affirms: "The LORD is of them that uphold my life" (RV with NKJV). It is said to be an idiomatic expression indicating, not that God is counted amongst those that uphold his life, but that He is supremely the one who does so, being as those who sustain David.

But is this all that the phrase teaches us? God is undoubtedly such a one as this interpretation of the Hebrew implies. Nevertheless, God works in manifold ways, and often through human agencies. Thus God used Jonathan "to strengthen David" and sent Abigail to prevent David from needless bloodshed. Both Jonathan and Abigail acted of their own volition, and they were numbered amongst those who sustained David's life. Yet they were, nevertheless, raised up by God to perform their work of comfort and exhortation, for God always has the right man (or woman) in the right place at the right time. So in an added sense, it could be said, by the manner in which He controlled events and used human agencies who were sympathetic to David, that the Lord was of them that sustained his life. The principle is seen reflected in the New Testament also, for Paul writes:

"Nevertheless God, that comforteth those that are cast down, comforted us by the coming of Titus."

(2 Corinthians 7:6)

The NKJV says, "He will repay my enemies for their evil" (Psalm 54:5) – a truth attested to by the fate that befell Nabal. And when God acts in this way, it is "according to his truth", the faithfulness of the word He has spoken, of the promises He has made. For these things, says David:

"I will freely sacrifice unto thee; I will praise thy name, O LORD; for it is good." (verse 6)

There is an important principle involved that stands as a lesson for us today. The sacrifice which David offered was prescribed under the law; it was an obligation laid upon him. But in his joy David saw it not just as a responsibility to be acknowledged, or as a burdensome and onerous task, but as something that he freely and willingly undertook as an expression of his desire to praise and honour God.

So it must ever be for those who would offer to God the sacrifices of praise for His goodness. We have an obligation, a responsibility laid upon us. Nevertheless the Truth must never be a burden grievous to be borne, but freely and willingly, from the fullness of our hearts, we must deny ourselves and rejoice in our walk in the way of salvation. As God had delivered David out of all his troubles and destroyed his enemies (for David had seen with his eyes his desire fulfilled – see NKJV), so we can be assured that we too will experience God's deliverance and the fulfilment of all His promises.

Some might feel that it is difficult to reconcile David's words with the spirit of the Lord's teaching in the Gospel. But we must remember that for David at that time, it was a temporal deliverance. These men sought to slay him and thus frustrate the purpose of God. To deliver him and bring their endeavours to ruin, God destroyed them and David witnessed the salvation of God with his eyes.

We, too, must remember that for us to inherit and enjoy the blessings of the kingdom, God must first consume the sinners out of the earth, that the wicked might be no more (Psalm 104:35). This has nothing to do with seeking redress for personal wrongs committed against us, but is concerned with the fulfilment of the will and purpose of God in the earth.

PSALM 55

IT is significant that in an age when men 'lived by the sword' in a sense that has little in common with our own experience (and David for much of his life was threatened by men who literally sought to kill him), David places less emphasis in his psalms upon these very real physical dangers than he does upon the wounds inflicted by the words of slanderous men, unfaithful friends and the manner in which lies and deceit were used to defame his character:

"For there is no faithfulness in their mouth; their inward part is very wickedness; their throat is an open sepulchre; they flatter with their tongue." (Psalm 5:9)

"His mouth is full of cursing and deceit and fraud: under his tongue is mischief and vanity." (Psalm 10:7)

"Thy tongue deviseth mischiefs; like a sharp razor, working deceitfully." (Psalm 52:2)

Such words, typical of so many of the psalms he wrote, indicate the sense of injury and hurt David felt as a consequence of the smooth speeches and the pretexts by which men sought to cover their true feelings and intentions, and when the time came, to show their loyalties openly, to justify their mischievous and pernicious acts:

"For it was not an enemy that reproached me; then I could have borne it: neither was it he that hated me that did magnify himself against me; then I would have hid myself from him." (Psalm 55:12)

The world is characterised by such men, who manifest a lack of fidelity in their dealings with their fellows and whose "tongues (are) a fire, a world of iniquity" (James 3:6). Public life, industry, and commerce at all levels is riddled with lying and deceitful words designed to slander and destroy the reputations of others. It is "out of the abundance of the heart the mouth speaketh" (Matthew 12:34), and by his words – the use of his tongue – the true quality of the man is revealed. Unhappily our ecclesial life is not free from this particular trait of human nature. Remember that David's deep hurt arose from the fact that these men were not his enemies, but his brethren, as Psalm 55 makes clear.

We would not wish to be misunderstood. There is a responsibility on all brethren and sisters, in keeping with scriptural principles, to speak against un-Christlike behaviour, against worldliness and false teaching. So often those who have embraced error, whether in conduct or teaching, seek to hide themselves from confrontation by accusing their faithful brethren and sisters of "evil speaking". In no sense is what we write to be thought of as offering comfort to such; indeed, it is their infidelity and the manner in which so often they resort to bitter and slanderous accusations, that is more in keeping with those of whom David complained.

It is important that we appreciate that the psalms have a message for us today and that we should not confine them to the experiences of the writers, or, prophetically, of the Lord Jesus Christ.

Psalm 55 relates to the time of Absalom's rebellion. It covered a period of approximately four years, and we know that through illness and shame (see Psalms 38 and 41) David lacked the decisiveness that was so characteristic of his earlier years. It was a time of trouble in Jerusalem, and as the day of the Lord's coming draws near his ecclesia is also passing through times of difficulty. For this reason we may be able to associate ourselves with David in his heartache and, on occasions, with his desire to escape from it all: "Oh that I had wings like a dove! for then would I fly away, and be at rest" (verse 6). This particular verse is indicative of the fact that (according to Thirtle' s *Titles of the Psalms*) the information at the head of Psalm 56 ("Jonath-elem-rechokim") refers to Psalm 55. Literally, it means 'the dove of the far off terebinths' and it reflects beautifully the substance of this psalm ('concerning the silent dove' – *Cambridge Bible*) which presents David as the silent sufferer, patiently enduring the trials in which he found himself and from which he would flee but for that resolute sense of responsibility as the shepherd of God's flock which he always maintained.

The language of the psalm is full of pathos. It is a beautiful expression of the deepest feelings of a man of God, and it can conveniently be divided into three sections, i.e., verses 1-7, 8-19 and 19-23.

David's prayer in distress (verses 1-7)

In the seething unrest, the plotting, the evil speaking of men who were more interested in protecting their own interests than right or wrong, David makes his plea to God:

> "Give ear to my prayer, O God; and hide not thyself from my supplication. Attend unto me, and hear me: I mourn (lit. am 'tossed to and fro', i.e., restless) in my complaint, and make a noise (lit. 'groan'); because of the voice of the enemy, because of the oppression (lit. 'to hem in' or 'to crush') of the wicked: for they cast iniquity upon me, and in wrath they hate me. My heart is sore pained (lit. 'writhes as in travail') within me: and the terrors of death are fallen upon me. Fearfulness and trembling are come upon me, and horror hath over-whelmed me."   (verses 1-5)

Although ultimately they intended to depose David and beyond doubt kill him, this was not something that could be achieved easily. It was first necessary to undermine his position in the eyes of the people. To accomplish this, it was essential to enlist the support of those who were powerful and influential, both in the court of the king and in the country at large. They were preparing the way for Absalom. Thus the city was alive with rumour and innuendo. Slanderous assertions were made, not openly, but by a campaign of whispering and secret plotting.

It is not surprising that, in this atmosphere, with his health broken, the shame of his sin still, perhaps, torturing him from time to time, and not knowing who might be secretly working for those who hated him, David was filled with fearfulness and trembling. He lived with an overwhelming sense of horror which, like a dark cloud, had covered (AV margin) him because of the hypocrisy and perfidious nature of so many of those who presented themselves before him as faithful men.

Sometimes it all seemed too much for him to continue. He felt that he would be overtaken with grief, his heart distraught because of the pressures that bore down upon him, and because of the continuing conspiracy against him. So he cried, feeling a desperate need to escape from the machinations of such evil men:

"Oh that I had wings like a dove! for then would I fly away, and be at rest. Lo, then would I wander far off, and remain in the wilderness. Selah."   (verses 6,7)

No doubt it was in the spirit of the Song of Songs that he uttered these words. The dove was regarded as a symbol of God's people (i.e. the Israel of God), holy, harmless and undefiled. So in the spirit of the bride he would be found "in the clefts of the rock, in the secret places of the stairs", that he might see his countenance, and hear his voice (Song 2:14). The language has unmistakable echoes of Moses' vision of the glory of God (Exodus 33,34) and is an indication of what David really longed for – not escape for its own sake, but fellowship with God without the distractions and burdens imposed upon him by those who sought his hurt.

Inasmuch as the experiences of David foreshadowed the sufferings of the Lord Jesus, who, more than any man, felt the depths of human baseness, cruelty and ingratitude, it is interesting to reflect that it was to the wilderness and the solitary place that, like the dove, he turned for solace in prayer and communion with the Father. The expression "Selah" marks the end of this first section and emphasises, as always, the need to pause and reflect before proceeding to the next part of the psalm.

Wickedness in the city (verses 8-19)

If such an escape were possible – if he could shrug off his responsibilities – then he "would hasten (his) escape from the windy storm and tempest" (verse 8). This, however, could not be so and David, contemplating the wickedness that filled the city and his own impotence to frustrate it, called upon God to confound and destroy the wicked. It is important to realise, however, that it was not his own

387

personal hurt and wounded dignity that caused him to speak in this way, for David was not a vindictive man. He was large-hearted and of a generous spirit, and the real cause of his anger was the way in which these men were denying the truth of God, and seeking to frustrate His purpose in the furtherance of their own desires and ambitions. That this is so is evident in the language that David uses:

"Destroy (lit. 'confound'), O Lord, and divide their tongues: for I have seen violence and strife in the city."
(verse 9)

The language echoes the words of Genesis 11, when men sought to make themselves a name by building a city and a tower. Their intention was to frustrate the purpose of God, and they were prevented by God confounding their speech and scattering or dividing them over the face of the earth.

Similarly, David recalls the rebellion of Korah, Dathan and Abiram:

"Let death seize upon them, and let them go down quick (i.e., alive) into hell: for wickedness is in their dwellings, and among them." (verse 15)

Those men had challenged the authority of Moses and Aaron. They had called in question the will of God and sought to frustrate it. Korah had built an alternative tabernacle from which the people were commended to separate themselves; they were to depart from the tents of those wicked men lest they be consumed in their sins. The earth opened her mouth and swallowed them up, so that all that pertained to them went down alive into the pit (Numbers 16).

In like fashion those who spoke against David trod in the steps of those wicked men, and David knew that God would never permit them to succeed in their evil purposes. He describes their wickedness in verses 10 and 11:

"Day and night they go about it upon the walls thereof: mischief also and sorrow are in the midst of it. Wickedness is in the midst thereof: deceit and guile depart not from her streets."

388

In his contemplation of the evil that filled the city, David's mind eventually focused upon one particular individual, who by his treachery caused him grief and sorrow of heart so deep that he found it almost impossible to bear. In most poignant words David describes the close relationship that had existed between them in the past. Whoever he was, he had behaved himself as a true brother in whose company David found solace and spiritual refreshment:

"For it was not an enemy that reproached me; then I could have borne it: neither was it he that hated me that did magnify himself against me; then I would have hid myself from him: but it was thou, a man mine equal, my guide, and mine acquaintance. We took sweet counsel together, and walked into the house of God in company." (verses 12-14)

It is generally supposed that the individual referred to was Ahithophel, David's counsellor. When Absalom eventually made his attempt to usurp the throne and David was compelled to flee, it is recorded:

"And one told David, saying, Ahithophel is among the conspirators with Absalom." (2 Samuel 15:31)

It might be implied from this that David had no prior knowledge of Ahithophel's treachery. If that were so, he could not be the individual referred to in Psalm 55, which was written in the middle of an intrigue that preceded the rebellion. However, it is recorded also that Absalom sent for Ahithophel to Giloh, the city where he dwelt (2 Samuel 15:12). He was not at Jerusalem when events came to a head, and David would have been unaware of his attitude towards Absalom. It has to be remembered that although David was well aware of the slander spoken and the manner in which he was defamed, it is unlikely that he could bring himself to believe that Absalom, his son, would actually lift up his hand against him. Others might seek to destroy him, but not Absalom. With this background, we can understand how David was aware of Ahithophel's true feeling towards him, but unaware of the stance he had adopted in the particular circumstances of Absalom's rebellion.

No other character of whom we have knowledge fits the circumstances. If it was not Ahithophel, we have to recognise an anonymous brother who proved himself unfaithful.

When the words are extended, however, to the Lord Jesus Christ and the betrayal of Judas Iscariot, it presents us with an interesting thought. If this, as we believe, is the spirit of Christ in the psalms, what was the relationship between the Lord Jesus and Judas in the early days of their acquaintance? Was there a deeper bond between them than we might have considered possible? Was there in fact a spiritual affinity between them that makes the black deed of Judas darker still, when "mine own familiar friend, in whom I trusted ... lifted up his heel against me"? (Psalm 41:9).

In the face of such troubles David had only one recourse:

"As for me, I will call upon God; and the LORD shall save me. Evening, and morning, and at noon, will I pray, and cry aloud: and he shall hear my voice."

(verses 16,17)

"Evening", of course, stands first because the day began at sunset and like Daniel (6:10), David's life was dominated by prayer. After the tensions of the earlier verses, we begin to see again that inner serenity so characteristic of David, that sprang from his consciousness of God. This was David's customary approach to each day of his life. It does not mean that he did not pray at other times also, as the occasion demanded, and it emphasises the exhortation to all who seek to follow the Lord Jesus: "Pray without ceasing" and "continue instant in prayer".

The outcome was sure. God would deliver him in peace, although it might have appeared that the battle was lost. Though there were many against him (RV), God would hear his prayer and humble them (verses 18,19). Why? Because He was supreme; none could withstand His power, "Even he that abideth of old. Selah".

Almost without exception, writers maintain that the "Selah" is a copyist's error; it has somehow become misplaced. Some go further and seek to adjust the order of the verses, placing verses 20 and 21 after verse 14. We believe that it is not wise to meddle with the word of God

390

in this way, unless there is very substantial evidence for so doing. As far as we can discover, there is no evidence for this at all, other than a feeling that the pause for reflection and the verses referred to are not where they ought to be.

The "Selah", although occurring in the middle of verse 19 (no verses were in the original, remember), makes very good sense. Literally the meaning of the Hebrew before the word "Selah" is "for he sitteth enthroned eternally". A contemplation of the sovereignty of God who changeth not was most appropriate in the circumstances in which David found himself, for it showed in greater contrast the folly of the men described in the opening words of the final section.

David's confidence in God (verses 19-23)
The final phrase of verse 19 states: "Because they do not change, therefore they do not fear God" (NKJV). "They" did not recognise the sovereignty of God or acknowledge His power. They did not appreciate that He alone changed not. Consequently, because there was no change in their lives, no break in their prosperity, there was no fear of God. David was undoubtedly speaking of his contemporaries; but there is a lesson for all time. Do not draw conclusions from the circumstances of life alone. Do not imagine that because we prosper in our way and our paths fall into pleasant lines, this is an indication that we have God's blessing. It may be so. However, it could be God's way of testing us; and whatever our circumstances, we must always search our hearts and try our ways by the word of God, for this is the only true guide as to whether we have ordered our lives aright before Him.

It appears that these thoughts regarding mistaken conclusions drawn from unbroken prosperity had at least some allusion to the faithless friend of verses 12-14, for David now returns to his consideration of this man:

"He hath put forth his hands against such as be at peace with him: he hath broken his covenant. The words of his mouth were smoother than butter, but war was in his heart: his words were softer than oil, yet were they drawn swords." (verses 20,21)

The smoothness and softness of his words spoke of his false and hypocritical flattery; but in his heart was hatred, and the false charm and friendliness was, in fact, like a drawn sword that desired to cut to the very heart.

Such reflections once more draw from David his conviction that God will uphold the righteous and destroy the wicked:

> "Cast thy burden upon the LORD, and he shall sustain thee: he shall never suffer the righteous to be moved. But thou, O God, shalt bring them down into the pit of destruction: bloody and deceitful men shall not live out half their days; but I will trust in thee." (verses 22,23)

The word rendered "burden" signifies literally 'that which he hath given thee', and it is a powerful exhortation to us all. We must recognise that God is in control. His providential care will sometimes give us burdens to bear – times of weakness, sickness, loneliness, difficult and adverse circumstances in life. But God does not want us to bear what He has given us alone. He wants us to give it back to Him: "Cast thy burden upon the LORD". For when we do so, He will sustain us. He will not necessarily take the burden away, but He will enable us to bear it, for He will never suffer the righteous to be moved. He will not allow us to fall under the burden of care, if we truly trust in Him and in the power of His word.

As Peter writes, perhaps alluding directly to this psalm, "Casting all your care upon him; for he careth for you" (1 Peter 5:7). Or, as David more tersely expresses it in the final words of the psalm, "I will trust in thee".

PSALM 56

THIS psalm is one of six that carries the title "a Michtam of David" (Psalms 16 and 56-60 inclusive). We have already considered the word in relation to Psalm 16 and repeat here briefly the conclusions reached.

One of the psalms (60) gives an indication of its purpose: "Michtam of David, to teach". All of the psalms are personal meditations or prayers, and the idea of "an inscription" that lies behind the word conveys the thought that the lessons learned from his personal experiences were engraved upon his heart. These lessons, of course, were intended also for others and, no doubt, the psalms were used in public worship.

Psalm 56, however, in common with Psalms 57 and 58, has a subscription. This appears (see Thirtle – *The Titles of the Psalms*) at the conclusion of each of these psalms and binds them together in a way that will be developed as we come to the respective songs. The subscription is "Al-taschith", which means 'destroy not', hence indicating that God's special blessing was sought at a time of intense personal adversity, when life seemed threatened in circumstances of extreme danger. An example of the word elsewhere in scripture is to be found in Deuteronomy:

"I prayed ... unto the LORD, and said, O Lord GOD, destroy not thy people and thine inheritance."   (9:26)

"When the Philistines took him to Gath"

The circumstances in which David wrote Psalm 56 are clearly indicated, for it is a "Michtam of David, when the Philistines took him in Gath". The appropriateness of the language to these circumstances will be considered when we deal with the text of the psalm, but it is helpful to reflect first, in a general way, about David's sojourn amongst the Philistines.

393

The record of David's flight as a solitary fugitive to dwell with the enemies of Israel, is recorded in 1 Samuel 21:10-15. It was a desperate expedient on his part, and in escaping from one danger he was placing himself in what we might imagine to be an even more perilous situation. The record in Samuel is brief. Consequently we have, to some extent, to use imagination, albeit in an intelligent way. It may be that David's intention was to conceal his identity and dwell among them secretly, or he might have hoped that because of the hatred of Saul they would accept him as a fugitive and a possible ally. However, suspicions were soon aroused, for the question was asked:

"Is not this David the king of the land? did they not sing one to another of him in dances, saying, Saul hath slain his thousands, and David his ten thousands?"

(1 Samuel 21:11)

At any event, the result was that taking these things to his heart, David "was sore afraid of Achish the king of Gath" (verse 12). Indeed, his situation became so perilous that he was compelled to feign madness before Achish to make his escape eventually. We cannot be sure, but there is a possibility that once he was recognised, David was confined in some way. Notice that the record states that he feigned himself mad "in their hands" (verse 13), and when he departed from them he *"escaped to the cave of Adullam"*. The historical information at the head of the psalm also says, "when the Philistines took him in Gath". In any event, we can readily understand the suspicion with which he would have been regarded and the manner in which he would have been kept under surveillance, with every move watched and every word listened to and examined critically. He would have lived with them under the most intense pressure and could have felt no sense of security.

As far as structure is concerned, the psalm is composed of two short stanzas, each ending with the same refrain (verses 1-4 and 5-11), followed by a final ascription of praise to God (verses 12 and 13).

394

Verses 1-4

"Be merciful unto me, O God: for man would swallow me up; he fighting daily oppresseth me. Mine enemies would daily swallow me up: for they be many that fight against me, O thou most High." (verses 1,2) The idea of fighting does not readily lend itself to the background of David's sojourn among the Philistines. However, the word has a wider range of meaning and use and comes from a root 'to feed on'. Figuratively it meant 'to consume', and is variously translated as 'to battle, to devour, to eat, to prevail' (Strong's). Clearly then the word is used not in the literal sense of fighting, but in keeping with the context (where his enemies are likened to wild beasts who would swallow him up) the ideas of feeding, consuming, devouring and eating are all appropriate. The unrelenting pressure to which he was subjected is indicated by the repetition of the word "daily". There was no respite, but continuously he was aware of how quickly and easily they could swallow him up. Nevertheless, in making his prayer for God to be merciful unto him, David recognises the weakness of man, for he uses the word *enosh*, which describes the mortality and frailty of man compared with the "most High" to whom he made his request.

"What time I am afraid ..." (verse 3)

The occasion in 1 Samuel 21 which tells us that "David was sore afraid of Achish" is, as far as we can discover, the only instance recorded in the historical books when David was afraid of men. Yet in this most distressing of situations, when anxiety and uncertainty must have filled his heart, David shows his true calibre, for "I (the word is emphatic) will trust in thee". They rested on their own power, but David put his confidence in God.

Some have found it difficult that fear and trust are spoken of as though they coexisted in David's experience, but there is no problem in reconciling the two. To be afraid is a natural reaction to circumstances that can arise in all manner of ways, and because we trust in God, we do not cease to be subject to our human emotions. The mark of true faith is that it conquers fear; it prevails over it –

indeed, in the very midst of fear it hears the voice that says, "Fear not, for I am with thee" (Genesis 26:24; Joshua 1:9, etc.). As one writer has put it, "Each day of peril (was) a discipline of faith" (Kay, *The Psalms with Notes*).

We do well to remember that even the Lord Jesus knew these human emotions. The word 'fear' may not be used, but the experience is clearly implied:

> "Now is my soul troubled; and what shall I say? Father, save me from this hour: but for this cause came I unto this hour. Father, glorify thy name."
>
> (John 12:27,28; note: "troubled", indicates 'to stir or agitate" – Strong's)

When we fear, our faith is exercised, for then we must put our trust in God. It is when we are conscious of our own weakness and inadequacy that we are best motivated to put our hope in Him.

> "In God I will praise his word, in God I have put my trust; I will not fear what flesh can do unto me."
>
> (verse 4)

These words conclude the first stanza, as similar words bring the second stanza to an end in verse 11. There are significant differences, however, for here "Elohim", the source of all strength and might, is contrasted with "Enosh" – mortal man who is but "flesh" – a frail and corruptible being. In verse 11 a different word is used for man, and the name of God (Yahweh) is introduced.

David's trust in God arose from his knowledge of God's word, for he had found that word to be true for him in his experiences in life. God's promises were sure, therefore fear would not prevail but he would triumph over it, even in this most distressing plight in which he found himself.

Verses 5-11

> "Every day they wrest my words: all their thoughts are against me for evil. They gather themselves together, they hide themselves, they mark my steps, when they wait for my soul."
>
> (verses 5,6)

The historical background helps the words to come alive. We can see how the Philistines would in their suspicions of him wrest his words; that is, twist them, misrepresent him to seek to discredit him. All their thoughts were against him for evil. How could they show Achish that the man David, whom they described as Israel's king, was a threat to them? They were determined to be rid of him; they hid themselves as they watched him, marking his steps as they waited for an opportunity to destroy him.

Once again the continuous danger in which he stood is emphasised, as the phrase "every day" is repeated. The words "steps" means literally 'heels', and almost certainly the words are meant to describe them as like serpents lying in wait to strike at the heel; and our thoughts are directed to the seed of the woman and the seed of the serpent in Genesis 3:15.

These words remind us also of the experiences of the Lord Jesus during his ministry, for the words of the psalm express precisely the attitude of those who sought his life. "They watched him" (Mark 3:2) and they gathered themselves together:

"The Pharisees went forth, and straightway took counsel with the Herodians ... how they might destroy him."   (verse 6)

Normally implacable opponents with nothing in common, they were united in a common purpose – to destroy the Lord Jesus Christ. As with David, so with the Lord, it was a daily experience: unrelenting pressure as they tried to catch him in his words, to twist them, to misrepresent him and to discredit him in the eyes of the people or to find cause to accuse him before Rome. In effect, they were behaving towards him like Philistines.

Perhaps we can extend the thought a little more. We have to remember that the Romans were an occupying power, and though it is not mentioned explicitly in the Gospels, is it not probable that they too were watching him and listening to his words? We remember the excitement caused amongst the common people by the Lord's preaching, and how the multitudes thronged him. Is it likely that the Roman authorities would have ignored such things? Almost certainly not. They, too, would have had their investigators, their spies, watching and listening to ensure that he posed no threat to Rome. It explains why on so many occasions the Lord spoke in an enigmatic form and did not openly declare himself to be the Christ. No doubt when the Lord Jesus was asked such questions as: "Is it lawful to give tribute to Caesar, or not", it was because the representatives of Rome were present, listening, and the twisted minds of the Jews thought the Lord had no way out – either he discredited himself before the people or he aroused the wrath of Rome. They had not allowed for the divine wisdom that resided in him and his answer confounded them all.

In similar circumstances, David cries,

"Shall they escape by iniquity? in thine anger cast down the people, O God."   (Psalm 56:7)

The translation is awkward, but the sense is clear. Would their evil plotting enable them to escape the judgement of God? David's response is that God would bring them down in His anger. The "people" were the Philistines, but are a type for all peoples of the earth who stood against the Lord's anointed:

"He that sitteth in the heavens (would) laugh; the LORD (would) have them in derision."   (Psalm 2:4)

Having reflected upon God's certain anger coming upon the iniquity of the nations, David turns again to a contemplation of the wonder of his relationship with God:

"Thou tellest my wanderings: put thou my tears into thy bottle: are they not in thy book? When I cry unto thee, then shall mine enemies turn back: this I know; for God is for me."   (verses 8,9)

The word rendered "wanderings", is singular. It stands therefore for the whole of David's life which he lived, like all God's servants, as a pilgrim and a stranger. David was able to put all his experiences into this context, for they were not an end in themselves. Even the throne that God had promised him pertained only to his pilgrimage. He looked for the security of eternal fellowship with God, to the consummation of His purpose in the earth. To that end he knew that God had counted the steps of his pilgrimage; every one of them was known to Him. What need then to fear the Philistine who watched his steps to destroy him? For, set against the wonder of God's work of salvation, all their efforts were utterly futile. Every deed, every thought and desire, all the motives of our hearts are known to God

– registered, as it were, in His memory. Knowing this, in a touching and moving figure, David pleads with God to put his tears into His bottle, to store them up and record them in His "Book of Remembrance" (Malachi 3:16) for those who fear the Lord and think upon His name. It is a wonderful thought that everything is known to Him before whom all hearts are open and manifest.

If we love Him, then He will have counted our steps, stored our tears, written them in His book. He will treasure us and the faith we have shown in His memory. We shall not be forgotten, but, like Abraham, Isaac and Jacob – even though we sleep in the dust of the earth – we will live unto Him.

All these things David knew, for God was for him and he, with us, could have no greater consolation. So he concludes the second stanza in similar fashion to the first:

"In God will I praise his word: in the LORD will I praise his word. In God have I put my trust: I will not be afraid what man can do unto me."   (verses 10,11)

The repetition of thought is obvious and the ideas expressed are similar, but there are significant changes. For now, in the light of his reflections in verses 8 and 9 he introduces God's name of purpose – Yahweh, the covenant name, the family name, the name of salvation. For now he looks beyond his deliverance from the Philistines to God's ultimate deliverance of him from sin and death. For this reason he will not fear what man can do unto him, and this time he uses the word *adam* for man, as if to encompass the whole human race, which, because it was flesh and blood, could not inherit the kingdom of God. His trust in God, however, enabled him to look beyond the promise of His word, and therein find peace in the midst of his fear.

Verses 12,13

David concludes his song with an ascription of praise to the God who had done so much for him:

"Thy vows are upon me, O God: I will render praises unto thee. For thou hast delivered my soul from death: wilt not thou deliver my feet from falling, that I may walk before God in the light of the living?"

399

In the earlier verses the word translated "praise" was *halel*. In verse 12 it is a word of wider compass (*todah*, meaning 'to adore, to offer thanks, to make confession'), for he had made his vows to God and he would fulfil them in the prescribed manner. Although David played his part – feigned madness before Achish – God used those circumstances to deliver him from what must have appeared at the height of the crisis to be certain death.

David sees this as a type of his ultimate deliverance from sin and death, for he pleads that God would keep him from stumbling, to the end that he might walk to and fro (literal meaning) before God in the light of the living. There can be no life without light. We have entered into life that is "life indeed", because God has shined into our hearts to give the light of the knowledge of His glory in the face of Jesus Christ (2 Corinthians 4:6).

With God is the fountain of life. In His light shall we see light (Psalm 36:9). To this end He has manifested Himself in His Son, who could say:

"I am the light of the world: he that followeth me shall not walk in darkness, but shall have the light of life." (John 8:12)

Some final reflections

It is worth remembering that when David became king in Hebron, he was thirty years of age. He was therefore at the time of his flight from Saul and his sojourn among the Philistines a young man in his twenties (we cannot be sure of his precise age). He was young in years, but not in experience. He was a leader of men and a shepherd in Israel. When we reflect upon the psalms that this young man wrote, his depth of knowledge of the word of God, his trust and faith in God learned from the experience of life, then only do we begin to appreciate what a spiritual giant he was and why he should be called by God "a man after mine own heart".

We wonder how David felt about the tribulations he endured. We have read of his fear before Achish and we have read of his tears that he asked God to store in His bottle. Yet in this respect he was like the Lord Jesus, who with strong crying and tears made his request to Him who was able to save him from death. It gives us an added insight into the suffering that David endured, the pain he felt because of his situation – not just physical pain, but anguish of heart that moved him to tears.

It is a lesson to all brethren and sisters. We must not be ashamed of our emotions, for the Truth touches the deepest reaches of our hearts, the depths of our being. It would be unusual if we too are not, on occasion moved to tears in our striving against sin, in our endeavours to be numbered amongst those who will be counted worthy to enter into the joy of their Lord.

PSALM 57

T HIS is the second of the three psalms that bear the inscription "Al-taschith" ('destroy not') and also the second of the group of five "Michtam" ('engraved upon the heart') psalms that conclude with Psalm 60. As previously indicated (in connection with Psalm 56), the subscription would seem to refer to a time of extreme and exceptional danger in the life of David, a man who in this period of life was never free from danger of one sort or another.

In considering Psalm 56 we saw that the event that formed the background to that song was David's sojourn among the Philistines. The historical information at the head of Psalm 57 tells us that it was written when "he fled from Saul in the cave". There are two occasions when David is recorded as dwelling in a cave. The first is following his escape from the Philistines, when he came to the cave of Adullam (1 Samuel 22:1-5) and the second is the occasion when God delivered Saul into his hand when he was in the cave of En-gedi (1 Samuel 24:1-8). In our judgement, given the historical sequence with Psalm 56, the time when David came to the cave of Adullam is more appropriate, for it was a time of continuing peril for him. Notice that it was at this time that David was constrained to take his father and mother away from the danger in which he felt they stood and bring them to the King of Moab to ensure their safety (1 Samuel 22:3,4).

If we continue the historical sequence, then the third of the "Al-taschith" psalms (58) would refer to the treachery of Doeg and the Ziphites (of which we have already written when dealing with Psalm 54). We might just note in this connection the words of 1 Samuel 23:

"And Saul went on this side of the mountain, and David and his men on that side of the mountain: and

David made haste to get away for fear of Saul; for Saul and his men compassed David and his men round about to take them." (verse 26)

The three psalms are, then, bound together historically and refer to a time of extreme danger in David's exile, surpassing in their sense of imminent destruction the peril in which he stood continuously.

There are verbal and structural links between Psalms 56 and 57 which establish their close association. These will be noted as we consider the substance of the psalm; but we draw attention particularly to the manner in which David likens his enemies to wild beasts who would swallow him up, in both Psalm 56 (verses 1,2) and Psalm 57 (verses 3,4). Again, in structure each psalm falls into two parts, each ending with a similar refrain:

"In God I will praise his word, in God I have put my trust; I will not fear what flesh can do unto me." (Psalm 56:4,11)

"Be thou exalted, O God, above the heavens; let thy glory be above all the earth." (Psalm 57:5,11)

There is nevertheless a difference in tone; for Psalm 56 describes the dangers and reveals quiet confidence, whereas Psalm 57 bursts forth in exultant joy at the deliverance of God.

Part 1 (verses 1-5)

The opening words of the psalm are identical to those of Psalm 56:

"Be merciful (lit. 'gracious') unto me, O God, be merciful unto me: for my soul trusteth in thee: yea, in the shadow of thy wings will I make my refuge, until these calamities be overpast." (verse 1)

In the face of imminent danger David seeks God's blessing and expresses his trust and confidence. The language used, the illustrations employed, are an indication of the closeness of David's relationship to his God. It is under the shadow of His wings that he finds refuge while these calamities are upon him. The word rendered "calamities" carries the association of 'mischiefs'. Thus David makes clear that his troubles arise from the plotting and scheming of evil men and not from the everyday problems

403

that confront humankind and which can usually be attributed directly to the providential hand of God. This is not to say, of course, that God does not also use the malice of men to try His servants to enable their faith to grow and mature.

The idea of dwelling under God's wings is a touching and poignant figure of the protection given by a parent bird to its young and occurs several times in the pages of the Old Testament (see Deuteronomy 32:11,12; Ruth 2:12; Psalm 17:8, 36:7, 91:4, etc.). In the New Testament the Lord Jesus adopts a similar figure when he mourns the lack of faith which he found in Israel:

"How often would I have gathered thy children together, even as a hen gathereth her chickens under her wings, and ye would not!"   (Matthew 23:37)

Notwithstanding these references, perhaps some thought ought to be given to the possibility that where there is no reference to the bird itself, the allusion might be to the wings of the Cherubim which covered the mercy seat – God's throne in the midst of His people. Hence it would be an acknowledgement of God's sovereignty and His power to protect and save. In this particular psalm the refrain (verses 5,11): "Be thou exalted, O God, above the heavens; let thy glory be above all the earth" would lend itself to this point of view.

However one regards the words, the affinity that existed between God and David should not be minimised. This relationship is unique to the God of the Bible. The gods of the nations were feared and held in awe. Men sought to appease their wrath, and a realisation of this fact should help us to appreciate more deeply the wonder of God's love and the privilege that we enjoy to be called His sons and daughters, dwelling under the shadow of His wings.

Before leaving verse 1 we should also notice how the force and beauty of the words is emphasised by the change in the tense of the verb from the present to the future: "My soul *trusts* in You: and in the shadow of Your wings I will make my refuge" (NKJV). It is a present and continuing experience. What is experienced now is the ground and confidence for the future.

404

These thoughts are reiterated in the next words, for David cries unto "God most high", an acknowledgement of the supremacy and sovereignty of the Almighty, and yet He is one who performs all things for him. Although so great, He had condescended to the needs of His servant and had performed all that was necessary for him. Again it is a wonderful thought, a source of comfort and consolation for us. Weak and frail though we may be, fleeting, transient creatures in our human nature, yet we too are secure in His love, for "God (will) supply all (our) need according to his riches in glory by Christ Jesus" (Philippians 4:19).

How will God deliver? Why, cries David:

"He shall send from heaven, and save me from the reproach of him that would swallow me up. Selah. God shall send forth his mercy and his truth." (Psalm 57:3)

The idea behind the word translated "reproach" is that of 'defaming' or 'slandering'. It reflects the attitude noticed so often in the psalms of David's enemies who sought to discredit him, that, like wild beasts, they might swallow him up. The "Selah" in the middle of the verse, calling for pause and reflection, is unusual. Nevertheless, we remain suspicious of claims about so-called 'copyists' errors' etc. After all, verse numbers and chapter divisions, as we understand them, are not part of the original text.

David says, "He shall send from heaven, and save me ...". The reflection upon this truth brings the expansion of thought that God will send forth His mercy and His truth. We are dealing with the language of God-manifestation. Mercy and Truth are not abstract qualities, but, showing His power to save, God's loving-kindness and faithfulness are seen in the acts He performs. It is by seeing His involvement in David's life that these qualities are appreciated. The language is part of the rich fabric of scripture, helping us to understand the great work of God in saving men, unhindered by the vain philosophies of men.

We remember in this context the language of the Exodus: "I am come down to deliver them out of the hand of the Egyptians" (Exodus 3:8) and the words of John's Gospel regarding the manna and the Lord Jesus:

405

"Our fathers did eat manna in the desert; as it is written, He gave them bread from heaven to eat. Then Jesus said unto them, Verily, verily, I say unto you, Moses gave you not that bread from heaven; but my Father giveth you the true bread from heaven. For the bread of God is he which cometh down from heaven, and giveth life unto the world." (John 6:31-33)

Having expressed his hope and made his prayer, David's thoughts return to the reality, humanly speaking, of the situation in which he found himself:

"My soul is among lions: and I lie even among them that are set on fire, even the sons of men, whose teeth are spears and arrows, and their tongue a sharp sword." (Psalm 57:4)

The Hebrew appears to present difficulty to translators. The various versions we have consulted all retain an element of awkwardness in the phraseology of the English. Nevertheless, the ideas are not difficult to comprehend. David is once again thinking of his enemies as wild beasts. Their teeth and their tongues are like weapons that wound and destroy. Underlying the words is the thought once again of the malicious words that his enemies directed against him.

It might appear that this is a note of despair on David's part; but in keeping with the confident tone of the psalm, it is suggested that the words are in reality an expression of firm resolution and steadfastness – literally, "*I will lie down* ..." How appropriate, then, that David should conclude this section of the psalm by turning from the murderous intentions of men to extol the God who had wrought so wonderfully for him! In his exaltation, in the recognition of His glory, all such men would be blotted out from the earth.

Part 2 (verses 6-11)

In this second section of the psalm, David sees the plotting of his enemies turned back upon them and reasserts his own confidence in God, giving thanks with joy for His goodness towards him:

"They have prepared a net for my steps; my soul is bowed down: they have digged a pit before me, into the

406

midst whereof they are fallen themselves. Selah."
(verse 6)

The metaphors are taken from the hunters' use of nets and pits, whereby animals were trapped. In the same way David's enemies had prepared to ensnare him; but such was God's care, that He had caused them to be caught in their own traps. So in contemplation of His work, David expresses the steadfastness of his faith in God:

"My heart is fixed, O God, my heart is fixed: I will sing and give praise."
(verse 7)

Here was no man "moved by every wind of doctrine", but a man, steadfast and constant in his commitment to God, firm in his desire to please Him, fixed in his determination to obey Him.

This singleness of mind, which characterised his whole life, overflowed in praise, and we get an insight into the part which music and song should play in our worship. The word translated "praise" means literally 'to touch the strings or parts of a musical instrument – hence to play upon it; to make music' (Strong's). It is also the root from which the word translated "psalm" is derived, the meaning then being "words set to music". The thought of worship in song and music is continued:

"Awake up, my glory; awake, psaltery and harp: I myself will awake early. I will praise thee, O Lord, among the people: I will sing unto thee among the nations."
(verses 8,9)

The word "awake" is commonly used as a call to action. David's desire is to stir up his "glory", a word used both of God and man. The basic meaning of the word is 'weight'; but associated with that are the ideas of splendour and copiousness. By his glory David evidently means to describe the totality of all his higher powers – what we might call the spiritual side of his life. He calls for psaltery and harp, two stringed instruments often linked together, that these may be used in the praise of God. Then he uses a bold and beautiful metaphor: "I will awake the dawn" (RV margin). It is usually men who are wakened by morning light; but David speaks vividly of his songs of praise during the night season, awakening the dawn.

407

As a result he will witness in song and praise among the people and before all nations. The words carry us beyond the immediate circumstances of David, for we can think of the praise of all God's people in every age, who by their song in the night will truly awaken the dawn of that perfect day when the Lord shall come. In that day saints will sing the praise of God, their Saviour, before all people and nations.

As we read verses 8 and 9 of this psalm, we can surely hear echoes in the words of Paul written to the Ephesians:

"… speaking to yourselves in psalms and hymns and spiritual songs, singing and making melody in your heart to the Lord." (5:19)

The reason for this paean of praise is that God by His deeds has once again demonstrated His mercy and truth:

"For thy mercy is great unto the heavens, and thy truth unto the clouds." (Psalm 57:10)

The final ascription of praise, a repetition of the words of verse 5, is surely a recognition, not just of David's deliverance from his enemies, but of the ultimate triumph of God, through the Lord Jesus Christ, when all those who oppose His purpose will be rooted out, and all the earth will recognise His sovereignty and supremacy:

"Be thou exalted, O God, above the heavens: let thy glory be above all the earth." (verse 11)

PSALM 58

W E have already indicated the probable historical background to this psalm in our consideration of Psalms 56 and 57. It is the last of the trilogy of psalms that bears the subscription "Al-taschith" ('destroy not'), referring to times of exceptional danger in the life of David. Psalm 56 refers to the time when David was compelled to go down to the Philistines at Gath (1 Samuel 21:10-15); Psalm 57 to the time when he dwelt in the cave of Adullam (1 Samuel 22:1-5); and if we follow the historical sequence, Psalm 58 would be written as David contemplated the hatred of Doeg and the treachery of the Ziphites (1 Samuel 23). We have considered these particular events in detail in our introduction and background to Psalm 54.

This psalm, however, does not have any direct historical allusions in its context, and is a reflection by David on the conduct of those who were judges in Israel at that time. It is an indictment of the manner in which they perverted justice while pretending to uphold it, and a plea to God to confound their evil intentions by manifesting himself as the true Judge. In developing this theme, David uses a number of striking and dramatic images; and it is said that the original Hebrew conveys a sense of nervous tension that would be appropriate to the circumstances out of which all three psalms sprang.

For convenience the psalm can be divided into three parts:

1. The protest against unrighteous judges (verses 1-5).
2. The swift retribution that God will bring upon evil men and for which David prays (verses 6-9).
3. The joy of knowing the ultimate triumph of the righteous over the wicked (verses 10,11).

Unrighteous Judges

It is appropriate as we come to the opening verse of this psalm (and later verses) to consider our general approach to scripture. We believe it is important to emphasise that we do not need to be intellectuals to understand the word of God. While, undoubtedly, an understanding of the original words of both Old and New Testaments will enhance our appreciation of the meaning, it is by no means essential in grasping the general tenor of their teaching. With the English text, it is possible to grasp all the essentials of Bible doctrine and to see clearly the way in which God would have us to live. This is because in the great majority of cases the message is essentially simple and straightforward. So often its teaching only appears difficult when flesh complicates the issues. We need to recognise that this is one of the primary devices to which the human heart resorts in order to evade its responsibilities before God. It is what the scriptures term "the deceitfulness of sin" and "an evil heart of unbelief". It will not be an acceptable excuse to say at the judgement that we were unable to live the Truth acceptably because we were confused by scripture. We make these comments because it seems, on occasions, that study can become an end in itself, and our writing and addresses no different from the commentaries of Orthodoxy, instead of giving proper attention to the application of what we learn to practical living.

These reflections arise out of the opening words of the psalm, because of the quite diverse translations which scholars of Hebrew have produced. Yet at the end of much abstract discussion, nothing destroys or changes in any manner the obvious message of the word of God. The AV, following a twelfth century Jewish Rabbi, renders the words in verse 1: "Do ye indeed speak righteousness, O congregation?" Others render the words: "Do you indeed speak righteousness, you silent ones?" (NKJV); "Do you indeed in silence speak righteousness?" (RV); "Do you indeed, O ye gods, speak righteousness?" (RV with margin).

It seems to be generally agreed that the AV rendering "congregation" cannot be supported and that the basic meaning of the Hebrew word is 'silence'. However, if the vowel points were changed, then the word could properly be rendered 'gods', as for instance in Psalm 82:1,6, words which were quoted by the Lord Jesus when the Jews accused him of blasphemy (John 10:34). The judges of Israel were elohim (gods) because unto them the word of Elohim (God) came. They were His representatives in the midst of His people Israel. But nothing changes the obvious sense of the message, and we accept the idea of silence, remaining (as we have stated previously) suspicious of changes in the text without clear and unmistakable evidence for making them.

So the judges who should have spoken were dumb, maintaining silence in the face of violence and injustice. We can imagine how this was so in the experience of David. It was at the time, as we have indicated, that Samuel had died. No doubt with advancing years and his estrangement from Saul, Samuel's influence in Israel would have waned. Now a greater responsibility rested upon the judges. They should have spoken; but they remained silent. For whatever reason, they felt it more important to ingratiate themselves with Saul than to judge righteous judgement. Indeed, one wonders, bearing in mind how the psalms of David do not appear to indict Saul personally, whether his attitude was fostered by the personal ambitions of those who were powerful and influential in Israel. It would account for the genuine love David had for Saul; and, no doubt, if this were the case, for David's sorrow and anger at the manner in which evil men were casting stumbling blocks in the path of a man who lacked the strength of character to hold fast to the word of God.

David could therefore ask, "Do ye judge uprightly, O ye sons of men?" (Psalm 58:1), reminding the judges that, although they were powerful in the congregation, they were themselves nevertheless but men subject, like all others, to the righteous judgement of God. In their hearts they planned wickedness, and the result was that they "weighed out" (RV) violence openly in the land. There is deep irony in the use of scales, the symbol of justice, to describe the manner in which they "weighed" their actions (verse 2).

The final three verses of this section indicate the true character of these judges in Israel. They were not men who had been misled by others; they were evil men. Even in human nature there are degrees of wickedness, and some men plumb depths of iniquity that horrify even the 'ordinary sinner', if we can use such a term. As one writer put it, there are some "who have more than an ordinary aptitude for wickedness".

"The wicked are estranged from the womb: they go astray as soon as they be born, speaking lies. Their poison is like the poison of a serpent: they are like the deaf adder that stoppeth her ear; which will not hearken to the voice of charmers, charming never so wisely." (verse 3-5)

They were a serpent's brood. We should not use this passage as a general description of human nature, for it is clearly identifying the "wicked" with the corrupt judges. They had pursued throughout their lives a way of unrestrained wickedness, like the adder which was deaf to the enchantment of the snake charmer, so they would not hear the reproofs and warnings of the word of God. Habits formed almost from birth had been nurtured into maturity, and now they were hardened in the way they had chosen to go.

If there is a lesson for us in our ecclesial life from this, it is surely highlighted by the thought of these judges who were silent when they should have spoken, and deaf when they should have listened. We cannot for ever be ignoring the problems of our community, turning a blind eye, saying in our hearts, 'It's nothing to do with me', or, 'Best to ignore it for the sake of peace'. This is especially true in the case of doctrinal error in our midst. If we choose to ignore false teaching, for whatever reason, we need to remember that we are dealing with the issues of life and death. What Gospel is being preached? Into what Gospel might misguided individuals be baptised under the cloak of the name "Christadelphian"?

Divine retribution

Moved by the wickedness of such men, David, reverting to the imagery we have noted in the two previous psalms, calls upon God:

"Break their teeth, O God, in their mouth: break out the great teeth of the young lions, O LORD." (verse 6)

The insidious cunning of the serpent is now replaced by the open ferocity of the lion. The figure of the wild beast is sustained through all three psalms (56:1,2; 57:4). David's prayer is that God would break their teeth (or frustrate their purpose), rendering them impotent to carry out their evil designs towards him – and, indeed, towards all who were righteous in Israel. So he cries, changing the figure of speech in a graphic manner:

"Let them melt away as waters which run continually: when he bendeth his bow to shoot his arrows, let them be as cut in pieces. As a snail which melteth, let everyone of them pass away: like the untimely birth of a woman, that they may not see the sun." (verses 7,8)

The meaning is clear. In the rainy season, or following a sudden storm, the water courses would fill quickly, but the waters would soon vanish away (see Job 6:15). "When he aimeth his arrows" (RV), let them be blunted and broken off so they are unable to wound.

David asks that they may be like a snail that melts. Some render "snail" as "slug", and others refer the melting to the trail of slime left by a snail as it moves. Here is another example of the way scholarly argument leads back to the obvious meaning. Be it snail or slug, any amateur gardener will have seen the effect of drought or heat upon such creatures, an effect seen even more vividly in the more extreme climatic conditions of the land of Israel. All the plans of the wicked would be aborted. They themselves would become like a stillborn child which never saw the light of the sun.

The section ends with yet another vivid symbol which is not so easily understood by those unacquainted with the land:

413

"Before your pots can feel the burning thorns, He shall take them away as with a whirlwind, as in His living and burning wrath." (verse 9, NKJV)

The reference is to the dry thorns that would be burned under the cook-pot by a traveller in the wilderness, yet swept away by a sudden whirlwind before the heat was felt. Even so would God in His wrath sweep away the wicked before they could bring their evil schemes to fruition.

The triumph of the righteous

"The righteous shall rejoice when he seeth the vengeance: he shall wash his feet in the blood of the wicked. So that a man shall say, Verily there is a reward for the righteous: verily he is a God that judgeth in the earth." (verses 10,11)

Here, in conclusion, the Psalmist contemplates the outcome of the judgements so vividly described. The language is such that we might find difficulty in associating with it. It is, however, the kind of language that a warrior like David would have appreciated. No doubt it was the kind of descriptive language that would be used of the victors in the wars of those times. The righteous find joy because they *see the vengeance*. Not only are they delivered, but God, in whom they put their trust, is vindicated. Those who witness the righteous triumph over the wicked acknowledge that ultimately they will be victorious, although the wicked appear to prosper for a time. In that day it will be recognised that, verily – in very truth – although the fact might have been doubted by many, there is a reward (lit. fruit) for the righteous. So "let us not be weary in well doing: for in due season we shall reap, if we faint not" (Galatians 6:9).

In this knowledge, while deploring the unrighteous judges in Israel, David could take confidence; for in very truth, whatever men might think, there was a God who was righteous, who was Judge of all the earth.

PSALM 59

THE historical information at the head of the psalm states: "When Saul sent, and they watched the house to kill him". The narrative is found in 1 Samuel 19:11-17 where Michal, David's wife, was instrumental in effecting David's escape by letting him down through a window. Many writers find it difficult to equate this event with the context of Psalm 59. Firstly, because they feel that the emphasis of the psalm does not lend itself to this one event; and secondly, because of the references to the heathen (verses 5,8) which they feel demands a much later date for the psalm. On both counts, we feel that they show a lack of perception.

In the first instance, we believe it to be important to realise that the historical information tells us the time in David's life when the psalm was composed. It may not be the only or primary subject with which the psalm deals. Events, for instance, can be significant not just for themselves, but because they mark turning points in the writer's life, or the end of a particular train of circumstances. Hence the thoughts of the writer would dwell, not on the one incident, but on the whole range of circumstances that culminated in the event highlighted. We feel this to be the case in this instance, and for this reason we give a brief outline of David's experiences in the court of Saul.

There are two aspects of David's life in the royal household. First, there was his occupation as a musician who soothed Saul with his playing on the harp. Secondly, there was his position as a warrior, first armour-bearer to the king, then as a captain in his own right. Three times in 1 Samuel 18 it is emphasised that David behaved himself wisely (verses 5,15,30); in contrast, we are told

415

three times that Saul was afraid of David (verses 12,15,29).

No doubt by this time Saul knew that David had been anointed by Samuel to be king in his stead. Certainly Jonathan knew, and was prepared to accept the fact that he would never be king (verses 1-3). Saul remonstrated with Jonathan because of his friendship with David, and told him bluntly that he would never be king while David lived (20:30-33). When the women sang, "Saul hath slain his thousands, and David his ten thousands" (18:6,7), the king was smitten with jealousy and was moved to exclaim, "What can he have more but the kingdom? and Saul eyed David from that day and forward" (verses 8,9). Although in his rage, with his heart blinded by jealousy, Saul cast his javelin at David, it seems evident that, because of David's popularity, Saul could not openly command that he be put to death. David conducted himself wisely; he gave no cause for Saul to take action against him, and perceiving that the Lord was with him, Saul was afraid of David. He was torn within, for his jealousy and envy drove him to try to kill David; yet his fear of God and of the people restrained him.

It has to be remembered, however, that there were many in that court who owed their positions to the patronage of Saul. They knew that if David became king, there would be no place for them amongst his councillors and servants (see 22:7). Their ends were served, therefore, by encouraging Saul to destroy David. No doubt they fed his jealousy with slanderous reports, and also by a whispering campaign sought to destroy David's popularity with the people.

It was thus that David's situation became more precarious. Unable to take direct action, Saul tried to destroy him by the hand of the Philistines through the expedience of offering his daughters in marriage. Perhaps also he thought that within his own family he might find some occasion against David. Acting prudently, David extricated himself from the offer of marriage to Saul's eldest daughter Merab, but when Saul perceived that there was a genuine love between David and Michal, he instructed his servants to prepare secretly the ground for

416

the marriage to take place. Although, as a dowry, Saul requested a hundred foreskins of the Philistines, by his valour David provided two hundred, and Saul became David's enemy continually (18:12-29).

The situation gradually changed, until Saul felt that he need no longer restrain himself. So he commanded Jonathan and his servants to kill David (1 Samuel 19:1). No doubt Jonathan was instrumental in protecting David for a while, but his position was becoming untenable. A climax was reached when Saul sent his servants to watch David's house through the night and to kill him in the morning. Michal enabled David to escape, but it was the end of his sojourn in Saul's court. From henceforth he would be a fugitive.

Saul's preoccupation with destroying David could not have been to the advantage of Israel, and it is likely that surrounding nations probing Israel's defences would become aware of inherent weakness and begin to flex their military muscle. The flight of David would have encouraged them further. Perhaps they imagined that the time was ripe to spoil Israel and, in particular, to dispose of David himself, who they were well aware was a greater danger to them than Saul (see 1 Samuel 21:11). All these factors, though not specifically recorded in the historical books, would have weighed on David's mind at the time of the composition of the psalms.

Structure

The psalm seems to fall into easily defined sections. We note first that there are two main parts, each ending with a similar refrain: "Because of his strength will I wait upon thee: for God is my defence" (verse 9). The closing verse of the psalm (verse 17) reiterates these thoughts in similar language, easily identifiable, although having certain variations. These two major sections are both subdivided into two. Verses 1 to 5 end with a "Selah". Verse 6 begins, "They return at evening: they make a noise like a dog". Similarly verses 7 to 13 end with a "Selah" and verse 14 begins, "And at evening let them return; and let them make a noise like a dog". Thus we have:

Verses 1-5:   David's prayer for deliverance from those who sought his life.

Verses 6-9:   His confidence in God and the bewilderment of his foes.

Verses 10-13: God's judgement on his enemies.

Verses 14-17: Reiteration of his faith, and frustration of his adversaries.

David's prayer for deliverance (verses 1-5)

"Deliver me from mine enemies, O my God: defend me from them that rise up against me."   (verse 1)

The Hebrew word rendered "defend" means 'to exalt'. It is the verb from which is derived the epithet "high tower", beloved of David as a description of the manner in which God protected him. Indeed, this idea of the high tower where his enemies could not reach him is a feature of the psalm, for the actual word is used and translated "defence" in verses 9,16,17. Literally it means 'a cliff' or any 'inaccessible place' (Strong's). His confidence sprang out of his relationship with God, who was to him as a place of safety. In Him he was secure from all the machinations of his enemies; and the use of the figure in this psalm is an indication how soon David, a lone fugitive, had to seek refuge in such places.

"Deliver me from the workers of iniquity, and save me from bloodthirsty men."   (verse 2, NKJV)

It is clear from David's language that those who sought his life were not misguided men motivated by a false sense of loyalty to Saul, but, as we shall see, they were wicked men who knew precisely what they were doing. Their overwhelming concern was self-interest, and they would not hesitate to kill to achieve their ends. In the hands of such men, Saul, for all his jealousy and fear of David, was no more than a pawn to be used for their purpose. So, as the superscription to the psalm indicates, they laid in wait and gathered against him, They had plotted secretly; now they moved against him openly.

Their hostility against him, however, was unprovoked. Always he had behaved himself with discretion. There was no transgression, sin or fault to be found in David as far as his behaviour towards them was concerned. He was innocent (verse 3,4). So David pleads with God to awake out of His apparent slumber, for "they run and prepare themselves". Both the words rendered "run" and "prepare" have military associations. It is appropriate therefore that David should ask God "to meet him" (AV margin), for this word also has military associations in its usage, e.g., 'to meet as with an army' (*Cambridge Bible*).

These men were no better than the nations around. They had no thought for God or His purpose. They would have killed His anointed with no more compunction than an uncircumcised Philistine. So David's thoughts revolve around all the enemies of God and His people. Having thought of God coming to his aid as with an army of the angelic messengers encamped around him, so now David declares:

"Thou therefore, O LORD God of hosts, the God of Israel, awake to visit all the heathen: be not merciful to any wicked transgressors."   (verse 5)

We know that Doeg, an Edomite, was prominent among Saul's servants and, further to the comments in our consideration of the historical background, we wonder whether in Saul's entourage there were others of foreign extraction, who were prominent in seeking to destroy David. The psalm would then be supplementing the information contained in the historical books and would give further grounds for David to extend his thoughts to "all the nations". Perhaps, as in the case of Doeg and the priests of Nob, Saul may have had to rely to some extent upon foreign mercenaries to watch David and to carry out his bidding to kill him. In any event, conscious of the danger to Israel from the surrounding nations, and knowing they were watching and waiting as his enemies had done, David could not dissociate his own peril from individuals, from the determination of all worldly motivated peoples to destroy Israel and frustrate the purpose of God.

David's confidence and the bewilderment of his adversaries (verses 8-9)

After the pause (Selah) for meditation and reflection, David's thoughts return to those who watched his house.

David likens those who sought his life to the savage, half-wild dogs that roamed the city:

> "They return at evening: they make a noise like a dog, and go round about the city. Behold, they belch out with their mouth: swords are in their lips: for who, say they, doth hear?" (verses 6,7)

Ceaseless in their hatred, they not only watched through the day, but returned to continue their laying in wait throughout the night. Like the dog howling, hungry for food, so they greedily waited to swallow him up. From their mouths came forth a flood of evil words ("belch" means 'to utter', not just in the sense of ordinary speech, but words that 'gush forth' – Strong's). The words were like swords, cutting and piercing, designed to destroy. There were no misgivings on their part; they scorned even the God of Israel to whom David cried, "For who", they said, "doth hear?" They stand, however, indicted not only for their wickedness, but also for their foolishness:

> "But thou, O LORD, shalt laugh at them; thou shalt have all the heathen in derision." (verse 8)

Nothing could frustrate God who, sitting in the heavens, exercised His sovereignty over all the earth. This, of course, is the ultimate folly of the nations who comprise the kingdom of men; and it is interesting to reflect that these thoughts which through the Spirit filled the mind of David as a young man, were to be expressed again in a wider context about forty years later, when he would write Psalm 2 (see verses 1-4) in connection with the accession of Solomon to the throne. In this confidence David can exclaim:

> "O my strength, unto thee will I watch: for God is my high tower." (verse 9, *Cambridge Bible*)

Like Habakkuk (2:1), David had climbed the high tower of faith, from whence, safe from all the assaults of his foes, he could reflect on the fact that they could do nothing except it were permitted by the God who rules in the kingdom of men and in whom he had put his trust.

God's Judgements (verses 10-13)

"My God of mercy shall come to meet me; God shall let me see my desire on my enemies."

(verse 10, NKJV)

Here is a request that God would answer the prayer of verse 4 and see him victorious over his enemies. His desire, however, is interesting, for initially he does not ask for their destruction, but for the confounding of their purpose, that they, in their shame, might come to realise their folly and that others, beholding the calamity that has come upon them, might appreciate the folly of their way and be deterred from following in their steps.

"Slay them not, lest my people forget: scatter them by thy power; and bring them down, O LORD our shield. For the sin of their mouth and the words of their lips let them even be taken in their pride: and for cursing and lying which they speak."   (verse 11,12)

The presence of the angelic host who watched over him seems to have been very much in David's thoughts in the composition of this psalm. We have seen the idea of 'to meet as with an army' and the emphasis on the Lord God of hosts in earlier verses. Here the word rendered "power" is interesting, for it also means 'an army' (Strong's). It has been variously translated elsewhere as "a band of men", "a company of men" and, indeed, "an army".

The sentiments expressed in these verses show the differing methods God uses in dealing with men. Stubborn rebellion can bring sudden and swift destruction. Sometimes, however, God will bring men to appreciate His power and the utter futility of resisting His will. This principle is seen in the Gospels, when the Lord Jesus told the people of his day:

"I say unto you, That many shall come from the east and west, and shall sit down with Abraham, and Isaac, and Jacob, in the kingdom of heaven. But the children of the kingdom shall be cast out into outer darkness: there shall be weeping and gnashing of teeth."

(Matthew 8:11,12)

Of course, although God may seek to bring man to a recognition of his folly and an acknowledgement of His sovereignty, his ultimate fate remains unchanged.

> "Consume them in thy wrath, consume them, that they may not be: and let them know that God ruleth in Jacob unto the ends of the earth. Selah." (verse 13)

We have written often of David's God-consciousness. This psalm emphasises a particular aspect of it: his awareness of God's sovereignty and dominion over all the earth and the comfort this gave him. Nothing could happen unless God willed it, so everything was under His control. He was not only king in Israel, but also "the governor among the nations" (Psalm 22:28). David's awareness of this truth from an early age is seen in his words to Goliath:

> "This day will the LORD deliver thee into mine hand ... that all the earth may know that there is a God in Israel." (1 Samuel 17:46)

David's faith that God would frustrate his enemies (verses 14-17)

The section opens with a repetition of the figure of verse 6, but with a significant difference. The same words are used, but with a different emphasis:

> "And at evening let them return; and let them make a noise like a dog, and go round about the city. Let them wander up and down for meat and howl (NKJV) if they be not satisfied." (verse 14,15)

Whereas in verse 6 David had likened his enemies to wild dogs, hungry, gathering to lie in wait for their prey, now he describes them as dogs who cry to be satisfied of their hunger, wandering aimlessly in their search. It is the language of irony used to describe these malicious men who had been frustrated in their purpose. So in contrast David describes his own untroubled trust in God:

> "But I will sing of thy power; yea, I will sing aloud of thy mercy in the morning: for thou hast been my defence and refuge in the day of my trouble. Unto thee, O my strength, will I sing: for God is my defence, and the God of my mercy." (verses 16,17)

Clearly David is looking back and reflecting on his experience, "for thou hast been my defence". Here is a repetition of the thoughts and language used in earlier verses; but the dominant word is "sing". It is a reminder to us of the happiness that, in the midst of all life's troubles, should characterise the lives of those who have experienced the goodness of God. The heart overflows in praise to God; for though weeping may endure for a night, joy cometh in the morning.

"Upon Shushan-eduth"

The psalm has a subscription (following Thirtle). Others have suggested an alternate view to Thirtle. We have, however, followed him generally in this series of studies and therefore feel it appropriate to give some evidence that would support his view. The word "Shushan" means 'Lily' and the word "Eduth" 'testimony'. Lilies were associated with the spring when Passover was celebrated, and the word "Eduth" was connected with the law. These two ideas are brought together and illustrated by a passage from *The Temple – Its Ministry and Services* by Edersheim:

"The feast of unleavened bread may be said not to have quite passed until fifty days after its commencement, when it merged in that of Pentecost or 'of weeks'. According to unanimous Jewish tradition, which was universally received at the time of Christ, the day of Pentecost was the anniversary of the giving of the Law on Mt. Sinai, which the feast of weeks was intended to commemorate. Thus as the dedication of the harvest – commencing with the presentation of the first omer on the Passover – was completed in the thank offering of the two wave loaves at Pentecost, so the memorial of Israel's deliverance appropriately terminated in that of the giving of the law." (page 260)

Thirtle believed that the subscriptions were the work of Hezekiah who appended them to indicate the associations of the psalms and when they could most appropriately be used in worship.

What is interesting is the fact that there is clear evidence that Hezekiah and Isaiah had this particular

423

psalm in mind at the time of Sennacherib's invasion and saw in his overthrow the fulfilment of the sentiments expressed by David. Thus we note the following words from Isaiah 37. The allusions to the psalm are self-evident (all are from the NKJV):

"Then Hezekiah prayed to the LORD, saying, O LORD of hosts, God of Israel, the One who dwells between the cherubim. You are God, You alone, of all the kingdoms of the earth." (verses 15,16)

"Now therefore, O LORD our God, save us from his hand, that all the kingdoms of the earth may know that You are the LORD, You alone." (verse 20)

"This is the word which the LORD hath spoken ... The virgin, the daughter of Zion, has despised you, laughed you to scorn." (verse 22)

"Then the angel of the LORD went out ... and when people arose early in the morning, there were the corpses – all dead." (verse 36)

If, as has been suggested, the destruction of the Assyrian host was a "Passover deliverance", the appropriateness of the language of the psalm would account for its selection to celebrate Shushan-Eduth and to be particularly associated by the temple worshippers with that time of the year.

PSALM 60

W E have precise information at the head of this psalm as to when it was written. It is the last of the series of six "Michtam" psalms, and we have commented previously upon the significance of this term. It is said to be a Michtam of David "when he strove with Aram-naharaim and with Aram-zobah, when Joab returned and smote of Edom in the valley of salt twelve thousand". Details of David's military campaigns are given briefly in 2 Samuel 8 and 10. There is no precise information regarding the circumstances described at the head of this psalm, although his victories over both the Syrians and the Edomites are recorded there. It should be appreciated that the record in Samuel is not a chronological sequence of events in the sense that events described in chapter 8 follow those of chapter 7; rather, it is a summary of all David's military conquests whereby he subdued the surrounding nations and brought them under sovereignty to Israel. Indeed, it seems that all the battles of chapter 8 had occurred before God made His covenant with David recorded in chapter 7. Note the words of 2 Samuel 8:13, "and David gat him a name" (i.e., he was a man of renown among the nations), and compare with 2 Samuel 7:9: "And I was with thee whithersoever thou wentest, and have cut off all thine enemies out of thy sight, and have made thee a great name, like unto the name of the great men that are in the earth."

Psalm 60 is significant in that, together with the historical information at its head, it indicates that David's military accomplishments were not all unqualified successes. 2 Samuel 8 records the ultimate victories, but it appears that while engaged in his campaign against the Syrians, the Edomites, always opportunists, attacked the south, even occupying the south of Judah.

425

Although he had achieved remarkable victories, almost doubling the territory under his control, it must have come as a salutary shock to David when the Edomites invaded. Scripture makes clear that although a special relationship should have existed between Israel and Edom, for they were brothers (see Deuteronomy 2:4-8; 23:7,8), Edom bore a perpetual hatred against Israel (Amos 1:11) and was never slow to take advantage of any weakness in Israel (see Joel 3:19; Obadiah verses 10-14).

We propose to develop the historical background from the text of the psalm, but draw attention first to the fact that although David despatched Joab immediately with an expeditionary force (and as the heading indicates, he achieved a notable victory in the Valley of Salt, the ancient border between the two countries), both David and Abishai seem to have also been involved personally (see 2 Samuel 8:13,14; 1 Chronicles 18:12) and the campaign was not brought to a conclusion until some six months at least had elapsed (see 1 Kings 11:15,16). Appreciating that so little is known of the actual sequence of events, we need not be too concerned at the apparent discrepancy which at the head of the psalm mentions 12,000 slain, and 18,000 in the historical books, especially as the 18,000 are particularly connected with David and Abishai.

Structure

The psalm falls into three sections:

1. A recognition that God had brought this calamity upon them (verses 1-4).
2. God's assurance that they had no cause for fear (verses 5-8).
3. A consequent declaration of trust that God would deliver (verses 9-12).

Verses 1-4

It would appear that David recognised the attack from the south with its initial success as an indication of God's displeasure with His people:

"O God, thou hast cast us off, thou hast scattered us, thou hast been displeased; O turn thyself to us again."

(verse 1)

God's anger (RV) was aroused against Israel, and one can only conjecture that it might have been the unparalleled, and perhaps unexpected, success in battle against their neighbours which had produced a sense of complacency, a failure to recognise fully the work of God and a tendency to imagine that in some way they were succeeding by their own power and effort alone (see verse 11).

So it was necessary for Israel (and David in particular) to be put to the test. As with Hezekiah, "God left him, to try him, that he might know all that was in his heart" (2 Chronicles 32:31).

"Thou hast made the land to tremble; thou hast rent it. Heal its breaches thereof; for it shaketh."

(Psalm 60:2, RV)

Some writers say that the calamity that overtook the kingdom was likened to an earthquake. We suggest that there is no reason to believe that it was not an actual earthquake and that, in the ensuing confusion, always quick to take advantage of Israel's calamity, Edom struck. Thus the earthquake emphasised the fact that the danger threatening the nation was an act of God. Notice that seven times in the first three verses the words "thou hast" (referring to God) occur.

"You have shown Your people hard things; You have made us drink the wine of confusion." (verse 3, NKJV)

They had to learn a grievous (Strong's) lesson, and in the circumstances in which they found themselves, they were like drunken men, staggering in their confusion (see Isaiah 51:17,21).

We can imagine David's thoughts at this time. Although Israel had grown strong and had won such famous victories, she was surrounded by implacable foes quick to take advantage at this time of crisis. But David was concerned not only about his hostile neighbours, but the tribal rivalry within Israel (e.g., the envy of Ephraim, Isaiah 11:13) was a continuing source of anxiety. There were always those ready, for personal advantage, to go their own way.

David's response was typical of the man:

427

"Thou hast given a banner to them that fear thee, that it may be displayed because of the truth. Selah."

(Psalm 60:4)

A significant verse in the psalm, it is shrouded in controversy as to its proper meaning. The idea of the "banner" is not in dispute. A selection of instances where the original word occurs is given below:

1. After the victory over the Amalekites Moses built an altar and called the name of it Yahweh-*Nissi* (the Lord my banner) (Exodus 17:15).
2. After the plague of flying serpents the Lord said to Moses, "Make thee a fiery serpent, and set it upon *a pole*" (Numbers 21:8).
3. "And in that day there shall be a root of Jesse, which shall stand for an *ensign* of the people; to it shall the Gentiles seek: and his rest shall be glorious" (Isaiah 11:10; see also verse 12).
4. "Go through, go through the gates; prepare ye the way of the people; cast up, cast up the highway; gather out the stones; lift up a *standard* for the people" (Isaiah 62:10).

It has clear associations prophetically with the Lord Jesus Christ; with God's work of salvation and the outworking of His purpose.

The difficulty revolves around the second part of the verse:

"… that it might be displayed because of the truth."

(AV)

"that they may flee from before the bow."

(RV margin)

"to rally to it from the bow." (RSV)

"Thou hast given those fearing thee an ensign; to be lifted up as an ensign because of truth."

(Young's Literal)

Notice that the two different readings give quite different meanings. In one they flee from the bow of the enemy to find protection under God's banner. In the other, the banner is set up as a rallying point for God's people, that under it they might find encouragement to rout the armies of the enemy – and they can do so because of God's truth,

428

His fidelity, His faithfulness to the things He has promised.

We feel that the second is more in keeping with the spirit of David and although the "Selah" forms a natural break for pause and reflection, verse 4 would then serve as a bridge between the first and second sections of the psalm.

Verses 5-8

"That thy beloved may be delivered; save with thy
right hand, and hear me."   (verse 5)

The word rendered "beloved" is plural in form. It means literally, 'beloved ones', that is, Israel; and David's prayer is on their behalf, that they might be saved out of this catastrophe that had overtaken them. Literally, he cries, 'Answer me', and God speaks in His holiness (verse 6). The word translated "holiness" can quite properly be rendered 'sanctuary'. If this is so, then surely the reference is to a direct message from God delivered through the priest by Urim and Thummim. It was a message which assured him that all his fears were groundless, for, says God:

"I will exult (RV): I will divide Shechem, and mete out
the valley of Succoth."   (verse 6)

The words rendered "divide" and "mete out" recall the division of the land under Joshua, and it is a reassurance to David that Edom would not prevail. These locations are particularly relevant because of the part they played in Jacob's life when he returned from Padan Aram in fear of Esau. It was after crossing the brook Jabbok and prevailing over the angel, wrestling throughout the night, that Jacob, with his name changed to Israel, finally met Esau and the men that were with him. Strengthened by the encounter with the angel, Jacob was received by Esau in peace and, departing from him, came first to Succoth and then to Shechem, where he erected an altar, El-elohe-Israel, God the God of Israel (Genesis 33:20). At Shechem he bought a parcel of land from the sons of Hamor, and before coming to Bethel, where he had met with God when he fled from the wrath of Esau, cleansed his house of all the strange gods that were among them.

As God's angels had encamped around Jacob, so God was in control over David's life, and he had no cause to fear. Gilead and Manasseh, who had settled on the east bank of the Jordan, were His, as was Ephraim with his fretting jealousy. He was the "defence of mine head" (RV), like a warrior's helmet, firm with Judah, to whom belonged the sceptre (RV) in the defence of the nation. God's answer was that David had no cause to fear on Israel's behalf, for they were united in his cause (Psalm 60:7).

Similarly, those nations so recently defeated gave no cause for anxiety:

> "Moab is my washpot; over Edom will I cast out my shoe: Philistia, shout (RV) thou because of me."

(verse 8)

Moab, for all her pride and arrogance, would be like the bowl in which the victorious warrior washed his feet. Haughty Edom, continuing the figure, would be like the lowliest slave who carried away his shoes. And for all its might, Philistia would be able to do nothing but raise its voice in homage to its conqueror.

Verses 9-12

In anticipation of victory, David turns finally to God and asks, "Who will bring me into the strong city? Who will lead me into Edom?" The strong city is presumed to be Petra, situated high in the rocks, and thought to be impregnable because it was approached by a rocky defile a mile-and-a-half long.

Yet God, who had appeared to cast them off, and initially had not come forth with their armies, letting Edom win a notable victory, would give victory over the adversary (verse 11, RV). They had learnt the lesson that all man's help was in vain; there was no strength to be found in flesh. It was through God that they would do valiantly, for He it was who would tread down their enemies (verse 12).

That God responded to David's prayer, not just in the assurance He gave, but also in the manner in which He delivered Edom into David's hand, is the subject of record in the historical books. The lesson we can learn from the

430

psalm is that when things are going well and we seem to be prospering (perhaps materially and spiritually), then is the time to be particularly careful, aware of the wiles of the flesh, lest we imagine that by our own strength and ingenuity we have triumphed and we are in control of the situation.

David, and perhaps more particularly Israel, learned the lesson the hard way, for whom the Lord loves He chastens; and if we exalt ourselves, then (for our good) He will humble us, that finally through the Lord Jesus Christ He might give us the victory.

PSALM 61

THERE is no information at the head of this psalm to indicate in which period of David's life it was written. Nevertheless there are several indications in the text which point with reasonable certainty to the historical circumstances that occasioned the sentiments expressed by David.

We can dismiss the period of exile in the days of Saul for the psalm was clearly written when David was king (verse 6). It was written after David had brought the ark of God to the tabernacle that he had built for it (verse 4) and the tone of the psalm suggests that it was composed after God had made the everlasting covenant with him.

Having regard to these factors and the evident fact that at the time the psalm was penned, David was absent from Jerusalem (verse 2), once more driven away by enemies (verse 3), we have little difficulty in placing it at the time of Absalom's rebellion – probably when he came to Mahanaim and waited there for news of when it might be possible for him to return to Jerusalem.

As far as structure is concerned, the psalm appears to fall into two easily discernible sections. The first, ending with the familiar "Selah" (verses 1-4), is a prayer to God to support him in his trouble and to bring him again to His dwelling place, recalling with confidence past experiences of God's goodness. Verse 5 appears to stand alone: it is the pivot around which the first and second sections of the psalm revolve. It is an expression of David's confidence that God had heard his cries and that because of this the everlasting stability of his throne was assured. Thus the second section of the psalm (verses 6-8) deals with this theme – the blessings laid up for the king, initially David but looking beyond to his greater Son who would reign for ever.

Verses 1-4

"Hear my cry, O God: attend unto my prayer. From the end of the earth will I cry unto thee, when my heart is overwhelmed: lead me to the rock that is higher than I." (verses 1,2)

It is possible when reading the Psalms to become so familiar with words that call upon God to "hear my cry" and "attend unto my prayer" that they cease to make any real impression upon us. We fail to appreciate how deeply the Psalmist felt about those things that he held most dear in life and, in consequence, we in turn fail to appreciate that the Psalmist's words are an exhortation to us as to how we should feel about the Truth.

A simple analysis of verse 1 with the aid of a lexicon helps to bring home the intense emotional stress out of which the words spring. The Hebrew word rendered "hear" means literally 'to hear intelligently'. In other words to comprehend, to understand the significance and meaning of the cry. It is a plea that recognises, for those that put their trust in Him, that God enters into their experiences, understands and appreciates their motives and deepest yearnings. The word rendered "cry" can mean either a cry of joy or a shout of grief. Clearly it is the latter meaning that applies here. His cry to God was that He would understand the anguish of heart that he felt.

Similarly, the word translated "attend", although accurately rendered, has a literal meaning that perhaps sharpens our perception of the Psalmist's desire. Literally it means 'to prick up the ears'. In other words it conveys the idea not just that God attends to the prayers of His servants but that His ear is ever tuned to respond to their deepest needs.

This brief insight into the words used in verse 1 should help us to understand more fully the depth of the Psalmist's feelings: how much his relationship with God meant to him and how dear to his heart was the place where God was pleased to dwell in the midst of His people, and those everlasting promises associated with the outworking of His purpose.

That it was the expression of a deep emotional experience, a yearning and longing for his desires to be fulfilled, a cry of distress springing from an aching heart is emphasised by the words of verse 2:

"From the end of the earth will I cry unto thee, when my heart is overwhelmed."

It should be noted that the word translated "earth" is also translated "land" in relation to the land of Israel. From our consideration of the historical background we know that David had in fact been driven to the very borders of the land, so the phrase could well be understood in this way. If we take it in the larger sense of the earth in its entirety, then clearly the phrase is not to be taken literally but in a metaphorical sense or as it has been expressed, as the use of hyperbole (an exaggerated statement, not to be taken literally, to give emphasis to the point). This could be true whichever meaning we give to the word "earth" for the truth was that wherever David found himself in exile, separated from the City of God he would, spiritually, have felt deeply a sense of being distanced from the sanctuary of God. We give a very simple illustration: if we were prevented from attending the meeting to partake of the bread and wine we should feel the same sense of loss and separation, if we were one mile away or a hundred miles away.

In this situation David says that he will cry (a different word from verse 1 – to call by name) to God when his heart is overwhelmed. Strong's Concordance says of the word translated "overwhelmed" that its root meaning is 'to shroud or to cover', hence the idea of darkness. It is a graphic description of the blackness of despair and despondency that David felt because of his separation from God.

Because of the desperate plight in which he found himself David beseeches God, "Lead me to the rock that is higher than I" (verse 2). Literally, 'Thou wilt lead me to the rock that is too high for me' – that is, too high for me to scale by my own unaided efforts.

However, the thought is not of the rock as an obstacle but as a place of safety. It is an expression of David's confidence that although his enemies might appear to

434

have triumphed, it was God who was in control. He himself might not be able to find refuge from their hatred unaided, but God, his rock, would deliver him from the hand of those who hated him and exalt him once more. Clearly David's thoughts have reverted to the experiences of his early life when he fled from Saul. Then the rock, the cliff, the tower, those places that had been his literal places of safety had come to stand as figures for his God who was his real source of security. So now he draws on his past experiences and as we grow older in the Truth, we too should be able to call upon a rich recollection of the work of God in our lives. David continues:

"For thou hast been a refuge for me, a strong tower from the enemy."   (verse 3, RV)

The concept of God as a refuge, a place of safety, is of course, a common figure in the Psalms. If we were to look for a literal example of a "strong tower", then we have an instance in the history of Abimelech in Judges 9: one example where men's efforts to find security in a tower proved ineffectual (verses 46-49) and another where the strong tower withstood his onslaught and he himself was killed (verses 50-55). We look though to the spiritual significance and Proverbs 18:10 provides us with the key.

"The name of the LORD is a strong tower: the righteous runneth into it, and is safe."

The name of the Lord, of course, encompasses all that He is, all that He has shown Himself to be by the manner in which He has manifested Himself on behalf of His people; all that He has promised and will ultimately fulfil when His purpose is consummated in the earth.

It is important to appreciate that this is not like an insurance policy that protects us from the ills common to all men. In David's case because of the outworking of the purpose of God in his life it meant, on so many occasions, actual physical deliverance from evil, frustrating the intentions of wicked men who sought his life. We do not say that on occasions it might not mean some physical deliverance from evil in our lives, but the reality of that safety to be found in the name of God comes from our covenant relationship with Him – from our knowledge

435

that it is His good pleasure to give us the kingdom and the confidence that He will never leave us nor forsake us.

That through all his troubles it was this deeper, spiritual meaning that David treasured in his heart is apparent from his next words:

"I will abide in thy tabernacle for ever: I will trust (make my refuge, AV margin) in the covert of thy wings. Selah." (verse 4)

The reference is clearly to the tabernacle of David, where the ark of God now resided and the overshadowing wings of the Cherubim spoke of that safety and security that God offered to this people amongst whom He was pleased to dwell.

The words rendered "for ever" are a translation of the Hebrew *olam* – the hidden period, which refers to the kingdom age. It was David's deepest longing to enjoy perpetual fellowship with God and this of course he could only know in all its fullness when God finally fulfilled His word of promise.

It is interesting to note that when Ruth, the Moabitess, came to the God of Israel and entered into the bonds of the covenant, Boaz said to her, using similar language:

"The LORD recompense thy work, and a full reward be given thee of the LORD God of Israel, under whose wings thou art come to trust." (Ruth 2:12)

The "Selah" at the end of verse 4 indicates the need to pause and reflect; verse 5 as we suggested, is the pivot on which the thoughts of the psalm revolve.

Verse 5

"For thou, O God, hast heard my vows: thou hast given me the heritage of those that fear thy name."

The key word in our view is that rendered "heritage". It is variously rendered "inheritance" and "possession" and in each instance has clear reference to the literal inheritance or possession of land. It is used for instance of Israel's inheritance of the land of Canaan (Deuteronomy 2:19; 3:18 etc.). Such phrases as "The LORD is the portion of mine inheritance" (Psalm 16:5) do not come within its scope.

The indication seems to be that, although still separated from God in the manner described in verses 1 to 4, David now knows that Absalom's rebellion has failed. God has heard his prayers and has restored to him and to those who had remained loyal to him, for they feared God's name, the literal inheritance of the kingdom of Israel.

Although the reference is to the literal restoration of the land it is of great spiritual significance, and out of the thoughts expressed the latter section of the psalm grows. The restoration to David of his throne was an assurance to him that God's covenant was sure. His kingdom and throne would be established for ever and through these circumstances he was able to look forward in confidence to the fulfilment of those things that God had promised concerning his Son and Lord.

Verses 6-8

"Thou wilt prolong the king's life: and his years as many generations. He shall abide before God for ever: O prepare mercy and truth, which may preserve him."

(verses 6,7)

Of the word rendered "prolong", Strong's Concordance says 'to add to, to augment, to continue to do a thing'. Thus one writer has rendered it, "to add days to days", that is in the sense of a continuous process. When we see the word in this light we can appreciate how in an initial sense David was taking comfort in the knowledge that God would restore him to his throne and prolong his days, but clearly David was saying much more. His thought extended beyond his own experience to the covenant that God had made with him; to his seed who should sit on his throne for ever.

It was this purpose that was the grounds of David's faith and confidence and nothing men could do could ever frustrate it. So the words carry the significance also of a never ending reign – of a king to whom God would add days to days as a continuous process, hence an everlasting kingdom. The latter phrase in verse 6, "his years as many generations" conveys the same truth – David's thought perhaps initially being of God's promise that his house should continue for he would never want a man to sit upon

437

his throne. Throughout the "generations" this proved true and we could say that David lived on in his sons. But ultimately in the Lord Jesus Christ the promise would find its fulfilment and all those previous generations (good and bad) who sitting on David's throne had maintained the promised line, now met in him who would sit upon the throne for ever – figuratively speaking "as many generations".

In unmistakable terms David says, "He shall abide before God for ever". The word rendered "abide" may also be translated 'sit' when referred to a king. Thus it is translated in this way in Jeremiah's prophecy:

"David shall never want a man to sit upon the throne of the house of Israel."   (33:17)

The promise would finally be fulfilled when God's Son would sit enthroned *before God for ever*. Notice the connections between these words which we have emphasised and the words of David spoken in relation to the covenant in 2 Samuel 7:

"Let the house of thy servant David be established before thee."   (verse 26)

"Therefore now let it please thee to bless the house of thy servant, that it may continue for ever before thee."
(verse 29)

Mercy and truth are of course characteristically associated with the covenant. Mercy, perhaps better rendered loving-kindness, speaks of the love that God bears in the bonds of the covenant to those who are His. Truth speaks of the faithfulness and fidelity of God. It is in these two qualities, His love in it, and faithfulness to it, that makes God's covenant sure. "Prepare them" says David. Strong's renders the word 'to allot, to count'. It is often rendered 'appoint'. So God has appointed or allotted, counted a perfect measure of those necessary qualities that will preserve His king for ever (see also Proverbs 20:28).

Psalm 61 concludes with David's own word of joy and thanksgiving:

"So will I sing praise unto thy name for ever, that I may daily perform my vows."   (verse 8)

In that day when God's purpose would be brought to fruition it was David's confidence that he would be there rejoicing in all that God had done, for "thine house and thy kingdom shall be established for ever before thee: thy throne shall be established for ever" (2 Samuel 7:16).

PSALM 62

THERE is little doubt that as with the preceding psalm, this song also belongs to that period in David's life when Absalom rebelled against him. There is nevertheless a difference in time, for whereas Psalm 61 was written after David had fled from Jerusalem, Psalm 62 refers to the period immediately prior to the rebellion when men, associated with Absalom and his cause, plotted against him. This is evident from the following facts clearly stated in the text of the psalm:

1. Dishonourable and deceitful men were plotting mischief against him to depose him from his seat of dignity (i.e., his excellency; Strong's – elevation in rank – verses 3-4).

2. There was a danger that those who followed him would be seduced by the power of his enemies and the lies that they told (verses 8-10).

3. There are strong verbal links with Psalm 4 which is obviously an extension of Psalm 3 (compare verse 2 with Psalm 4:6) bearing the historical information at its head, "A Psalm of David when he fled from Absalom his son". Compare the language of Psalm 4:2 with Psalm 62:3,4,7,9.

A feature of the psalm is the use of the Hebrew particle *ak* which occurs six times in the twelve verses of the song. Translated "truly" in verse 1, "surely" in verse 9 and "only" in verses 2,4,5,6, it can carry either meaning and its sense has to be determined by context. The *Cambridge Bible* states, "It may be affirmative, 'truly', 'surely' or restrictive, 'only'". It may not necessarily carry the same significance on every occasion in this psalm but it appears to be only verse 9 which demands the affirmative "surely", whereas verses 2,4,5,6, are best understood as translated "only". It is for this reason that we follow the RV rendering of verse

1: "My soul waiteth only upon God" as in keeping with the other instances (with the exception of verse 9). It is a remarkable recognition by David that in God alone, in whom all power resided (verse 11) was help to be found in his troubles. Although in times of crisis men like Jonathan might help him by strengthening his hand in God (1 Samuel 23:16), David recognised that ultimately it was only God who could preserve and keep him for that word covenanted to him could never fail.

The psalm falls into three sections divided by the familiar "Selah" with its instruction to pause and reflect:

1. In God only is his defence (verses 1-4).
2. With slight variations the words of the opening stanza are repeated as David exhorts his supporters to put their trust in God (verses 5-8).
3. David reflects on the truth that compared with God man is but vanity (verses 9-12).

God only is his defence (verses 1-4)

"My soul waiteth only upon God. From him cometh my salvation. He only is my rock and my salvation: He is my high tower; I shall not be greatly moved."

(verses 1,2, RV)

The word rendered "waiteth" means literally 'to be silent'. The idea conveyed by the opening words of this psalm is expressed beautifully by the similar sentiments of Psalm 37: "Be silent to the LORD and wait patiently for him" (verse 7, RV margin).

In the realisation that his help came from God, David showed his longsuffering in the face of all his adversity by keeping silence before God. He did not allow bitterness to destroy his life; he did not let the murmurings of flesh rankle in his heart, but patiently he waited for God to deliver. The symbol of the rock to describe God's strength and unchanging character had been used by others before him: Moses in Deuteronomy 32 (verses 4,15,18,30,31,37); Hannah in 1 Samuel 2 (verse 2). So also for David, like a rock in the midst of a burning wilderness, God alone was his shelter and defence, his means of stability in the midst of all the uncertainty of life's changing scene.

We considered the figure of the "high tower" in dealing with Psalm 61. The repeat of the word "salvation" in these verses is, however, not without significance. Note that in the first instance his *salvation comes from God,* whereas on the second occasion *God is his salvation.* In the circumstances of life God so controlled events that David could say with confidence that his salvation came from Him. However, his relationship with God was even deeper for, ultimately, because he was encompassed by God's love, he would be drawn ever closer in his relationship with Him; finally, considering salvation in the widest sense, he would enter into the life of God and be like Him, a partaker of the divine nature (2 Peter 1:4). As a result of God's care he would not be "greatly moved" (Strong's – 'to slip, to fall'). The thought is summed up by the contrast between the wicked and the righteous recorded in Proverbs:

"For a righteous man falleth seven times, and riseth up again: but the wicked are overthrown by calamity."
(24:16, RV)

With the faith of David we shall never be utterly cast down. The lesson is that we must never be discouraged and never give up for "he that endureth to the end shall be saved."

"How long will ye imagine mischief against a man? Ye shall be slain all of you: as a bowing wall shall ye be, and as a tottering fence." (Psalm 62:3)

This verse presents some difficulty in translation. It requires only a change of vowel points to give an alternative sense to the words and rival Hebrew scholars have differed in their interpretations. The issue is whether the passage is active or passive.

Is it David who is the object of the words spoken, i.e., "How long will ye set upon a man, that ye may slay him, all of you" (RV)? Or, following the AV translation is it the enemies of David who are to be slain because of the mischief they imagine against him? Is it David or those that hated him who are likened to a "bowing wall" and a "tottering fence"? We believe that the indictment of verse 4, "They only consult to cast him down from his excellency: they delight in lies: they bless with their mouth, but they

442

curse inwardly", points to the conclusion that David is the object of the words. They would take away his dignity, his throne. To this end they plotted to kill him. The pressure of their plotting had already taken effect and they saw him like a wall or fence about to collapse. They sensed, vainly, that victory would be theirs for they had put their trust in lies. They believed that God would not preserve David, that His covenant would not stand and in this conviction they resorted to hypocrisy and duplicity, blessing him openly with their mouths, while cursing him in their hearts. Like so many men of God in such circumstances, David was moved to cry plaintively, "How long?" It is a cry that echoes in the heart of all God's servants as they await the day when He will reveal Himself to be their God.

Trust in Him at all times
With minor variations the opening words of the psalm are repeated. It is as though David would find comfort and consolation in the reiterations of these truths in which he had delighted: God his salvation, his rock, his defence, his high tower, his glory, his refuge. In all these things he found continual delight and it is a lesson for us that we can never be reminded too often of what our God should mean to us in our pilgrimage to the kingdom.

However, the repetition of these words was not simply for David's benefit, for the thrust of the psalm turns now to those who were still faithful to David. The pressure upon them must have been tremendous. With rebellion in the air and the hearts of the people with Absalom they would have experienced great doubt and anxiety. Their own future, their very lives appeared to be at risk. It is a remarkable insight into the spirit of David that in this situation he did not appeal to their loyalty to him personally, or indeed to his own standing amongst them, but he exhorted them to put their trust in God. "Trust in him at all times: ye people, pour out your heart before him: God is a refuge for us" (verse 8).

To the faint-hearted who would have turned after Absalom, David says in effect, 'remember the word of God, His covenant cannot be broken'. Trust Him therefore at all times and pour out all your fears and anxieties before

443

Him. In that confidence He will show Himself to be a refuge for us all.

The vanity of men who trust in riches (verse 9-12)

In vivid contrast to that refuge to be found in God, David turns now to the contemplation of those who sought his destruction:

"Surely men of low degree are vanity, and men of high degree are a lie: to be laid in the balance, they are altogether lighter than vanity." (verse 9)

Whether they were common men (low degree) or men of rank (high degree) there was no substance to them; they were empty and transitory. There was no need to be influenced by their apparent strength for it was not real – it was a lie, a deception and before God they were as nothing. If they were to be weighed in the balance they would be lighter than a breath (vanity) – so insubstantial were they, so lacking in real power and strength.

To those who wavered in their allegiance, who were enticed by thoughts of power and riches if Absalom and those associated with him should prove successful, David says:

"Trust not in oppression, and become not vain in robbery: if riches increase, set not your heart upon them." (verse 10)

Oppression and robbery are linked together in scripture. See for example Leviticus 6:2-4. It was in effect a civil war and we have seen in our times the cruelty and injustice that such conflicts cause. It was no different in Israel and those who were tempted to follow Absalom would have coveted the power that wealth would bring and no doubt would have been in real danger of resorting to unscrupulous means to obtain it. To behave in this way was vain. The foolish trust in riches. The word is from the same root as that rendered "vanity" in verse 9. In such behaviour there was no fulfilment; only empty, worthless endeavour which caused them to lose the true riches enjoyed by those who made God their refuge.

It may well be that one of the factors which created the discontent exploited by Absalom was David's desire to build a house for God. He expected all Israel to share his enthusiasm and give generously, as he did himself, in preparation for its construction. Perhaps the whole economy of Israel was directed to that end and the emphasis upon riches in this passage could be a reflection of the social disaffection of the people. David's response to the desire of some to follow Absalom was to remind them:

> "God hath spoken once; twice have I heard this; that power belongeth unto God. Also unto thee, O Lord, belongeth mercy: for thou renderest to every man according to his work."   (verses 11,12)

It could be that the reference to 'once yea twice' is an idiom to express the idea of repeatedly. However, the Septuagint is interesting. It renders the words thus:

> "God hath spoken once, and I have heard these two things, that power is of God; and mercy is thine, O Lord".

In these two qualities and the appreciation that they belonged to God was the answer to all temptation. Power and mercy, the ability to fulfil absolutely and completely the word He had spoken, for He was faithful to His covenant. All men's efforts to subvert His anointed were doomed to fail and because of His fidelity, His unchanging character, judgement belonged to Him and He would render to every man according to his work. Almost certainly these words are quoted by Paul in the Epistle to the Romans and they form a fitting summary of the theme developed in the last section of the psalm:

> "(God) will render to every man according to his deeds: to them who by patient continuance in well doing seek for glory and honour and immortality, eternal life: but unto them that are contentious, and do not obey the truth, but obey unrighteousness, indignation and wrath, tribulation and anguish, upon every soul of man that doeth evil, of the Jew first, and also of the Gentile."
> (Romans 2:6-9)

PSALM 63

THE brief historical information at the head of the psalm tells us that it is "A Psalm of David when he was in the wilderness of Judah". This might lead us to think that it relates to the time when he was a fugitive from Saul. However, in verse 11 in an obvious reference to his own person he describes himself as "the king". Our thoughts are therefore directed to the time of Absalom's rebellion and it has been pointed out by several writers that the wilderness of Judah, although usually associated with the tract of land to the south and east of Jerusalem, would also encompass in its extremities the west bank of the Jordan.

It was here that David halted before the brook Kidron (2 Samuel 15:17-23) before passing over towards the wilderness. A little later he tarried in the wilderness while he waited for news from Jerusalem (verse 28). It was at this time that David, with that special spiritual insight that was so characteristic of him, refused to look upon the ark of the covenant as a talisman – a token of protection in itself – and sent it back with the priests to Jerusalem (verses 24-29). His words at this time are particularly significant in the light of the context of the psalm, for David's appreciation of his association with God was not built upon a superstitious reverence for the ark, important though it was as the symbol of God's presence in the midst of His people:

"Carry back the ark of God into the city: if I shall find favour in the eyes of the LORD, he will bring me again, and shew me both it, and his habitation: but if he thus say, I have no delight in thee; behold, here am I, let him do to me as seemeth good unto him." (verses 15:25,26)

The psalm itself is one of the most beautiful and touching in the Psalter. It is, we believe, impossible for

446

any who seek to serve God not to find the sentiments that David expressed, giving the circumstances in which he found himself, intensely moving and uplifting. Our ability to associate ourselves with David's thoughts about God becomes a most searching exhortation – an indication of our own standing in spiritual things.

It is difficult to divide the psalm into stanzas. It is all of a piece, the outpouring of David's heart in his desire for God in the midst of all his privations. One of the most remarkable features of the psalm is that it contains no petitions, no plea for deliverance, although David could hardly have been in a more difficult situation.

David's longing for God

"O God, thou art my God; early will I seek thee: my soul thirsteth for thee, my flesh longeth for thee in a dry and thirsty land, where no water is." (verse 1)

There can be little doubt that David was suffering physically as he took his flight. He was faint from lack of water (2 Samuel 16:2); Shimei the son of Gera cast stones at him (verse 13); he was hungry, weary and thirsty (17:29). Yet these things were not predominant in his thoughts. The language of verse 1, although reflecting the physical circumstances of his flight, is clearly metaphorical. It tells us how David felt about his relationship with God.

One of the most tremendous thoughts is David's conception of belonging to God. He was as real to him as his closest relatives and friends. His longing to be in God's presence and to have fellowship with Him was David's overwhelming desire. The word rendered "early" is associated with the breaking of the dawn and the concept is of David's earnestness to seek and find the God, not only to whom he belonged, but who belonged to him.

As in a dry and thirsty land where they longed for natural sustenance, so now David had an intense spiritual thirst for the "water of life", a longing and pining for spiritual refreshment.

It was with his whole being, his flesh (i.e., his body) and his soul, that he fainted with desire to be in the presence of his God:

447

"… to see thy power and thy glory, so as I have seen thee in the sanctuary. Because thy lovingkindness is better than life, my lips shall praise thee." (verses 2,3)

The words "power" and "glory" are clear references to the ark of the covenant. In Psalm 78 the same expressions are used in relation to the ark on the occasion that it was taken by the Philistines: "(He) … delivered his strength into captivity, and his glory into the enemy's hand" (verse 61).

David had, only a short while before, sent the ark back to Jerusalem. It was not simply the ark itself, however, that caused David to express this yearning, but its association with the sanctuary and experiences that David had enjoyed in the past which he now longed to be renewed. There are several examples in the psalms that help us to understand David's fervent desires. For example:

"One thing have I desired of the LORD, that will I seek after; that I may dwell in the house of the LORD all the days of my life, to behold the beauty of the LORD, and to enquire in his temple." (Psalm 27:4)

So now David longed to behold God again as, in the past, he had seen (i.e., gazed upon) Him in the sanctuary. Note, in the passage quoted from Psalm 27, David did not simply wish to build a house for God. The thought that dominated his life was that he might actually dwell with God.

We have to ask ourselves just how we are to understand this language which David uses. Taking his description literally, and there seems to be no other way to regard it, he had on more than one occasion received visions of the glory of God. He had communed with God in the sanctuary – in fact in the Most Holy Place. Appreciating the ordinances of the law, that the high priest alone, and then only on the Day of Atonement, had access in this way, it is staggering to consider what manner of man this was who was granted such amazing and inestimable privileges. The expression a "man after God's own heart" must carry meaning beyond the simple, perhaps superficial, way in which we tend to regard it.

If some doubt that such were David's experiences, then the historical record adds weight to the psalm. After God had made His covenant with him it is recorded with stark simplicity:

"Then went king David in, and sat before the LORD."

(2 Samuel 7:18)

What follows is an outpouring of his heart before God for all He had done for him (verses 18-29).

With God's power and glory David links also His loving-kindness. This he had experienced in the depths of his despair after his sin in the matter of Bathsheba. To him it was better than life, for through it his hope of eternal life and everlasting fellowship with God was maintained. For this cause to know that loving-kindness was more precious than even this present mortal life as it is commonly enjoyed and which he would gladly have forfeited for it.

In all these things David found cause for praise. The joy of this praise is expressed in the words that follow:

"Thus will I bless thee while I live: I will lift up my hands in thy name. My soul shall be satisfied as with marrow and fatness; and my mouth shall praise thee with joyful lips: when I remember thee upon my bed, and meditate on thee in the night watches."

(Psalm 63:4-6)

So in a spirit of love and gratitude David would praise God throughout his life. In the traditional manner he would lift up his hands in prayer – an indication of the reality that he had in fact lifted up his soul to God (Psalm 25:1). His prayer would be in God's name and would be expressive of everything that David knew God to be, both from his knowledge of His word and from his experiences of God's care and revelation of Himself in deed. It was in the assurance that he was encompassed by God's loving protection that David's heart would be uplifted and his prayer offered.

The word rendered "marrow" is the usual word for "fat"as found in the offerings. It is specifically stated that "the fat is the LORD's" (Leviticus 3:16) and David is clearly not contemplating a literal meal. Nevertheless his soul is to be satisfied by what he perceives as a symbolic sacrificial meal. That which properly belongs to the Lord he will enjoy and be satisfied with. In other words, he would enter into the experiences of God; he would share the life of God. As he expressed it in another psalm:

> "As for me, I will behold thy face in righteousness: I shall be satisfied, when I awake, with thy likeness."
>
> (Psalm 17:15)

His joy would be full as he remembered and meditated upon his bed in the night watches. We have made the point before that it is in the night when we lie upon our beds that so often, as the body relaxes and the mind contemplates the experiences of life, the real man becomes apparent (see Psalm 36:4; Micah 2:1,2). What do we think about in the night watches? For David it was an opportunity to rejoice in his God and to cogitate upon the wonder of His character.

As a point of interest the Jews had three watches, whereas the Romans had four.

David completes his contemplation of God's loving care with a recollection of His continuing help:

> "Because thou hast been my help, therefore in the shadow of thy wings will I rejoice. My soul followeth hard after thee: thy right hand upholdeth me."
>
> (Psalm 63:7,8)

Because God had helped him hitherto and had brought him safely to this day he could rejoice in the knowledge that he was encompassed by God's loving care. The reference to the wings is, we believe, in keeping with the theme of the psalm, dwelling upon the overshadowing wings of the Cherubim. It spoke of the power and glory of God, of His presence that, in the trials and afflictions of life, had been with him and delivered him. He would follow God and cleave to Him (see Deuteronomy 10:20). The word rendered "hard" means literally 'to cleave'. Because of this he would be upheld by God's right hand – a mark of special privilege, an assurance of security; man was powerless to snatch him out of the grasp of his God.

Yet in all the wonder of his relationship with God, the knowledge of His continuing care, David was also aware that this did not mean that God would not allow his adversaries to afflict him, to triumph temporarily, to appear on occasions to gain the ascendancy. David's conviction, however, was that ultimately God would deliver him and that whatever hardship this life brought, his eternal future was assured. It was for this reason that he could say of his enemies:

"But those that seek my soul, to destroy it, shall go into the lower parts of the earth. They shall fall by the sword: they shall be a portion for foxes." (verses 9,10)

Because he was the Lord's anointed, David had a keen perception of the fact that his enemies were also God's enemies. For this cause, like Korah, Dathan and Abiram, they would be swallowed up in the pit. Their carcasses lying on the field of battle would become meat for the beasts of the field, for the foxes (lit. jackals) would feed upon them.

In contrast, David concludes his song:

"But the king shall rejoice in God; every one that sweareth by him shall glory: but the mouth of them that speak lies shall be stopped." (verse 11)

The king's enemies will be destroyed, therefore he rejoices in God as indeed do all those who are loyal to him. In this context, loyalty to the king, the Lord's anointed, is loyalty to God Himself who has chosen and honoured the king. It was an acknowledgement of the fact that His word was true. For this reason they that opposed the king had espoused lies. Their opposition to the king was an attempt to frustrate the purpose of God. There was only one possible outcome – their mouths would be stopped.

There is a final lesson to be learned. After the exalted theme of the earlier verses David turns to the plotting and hatred of his enemies. This was the background against which all his longings and desires had been expressed. These for David were the everyday experiences of life at that time.

So for us, if we would learn from David's spiritual life, we must appreciate that these longings and yearnings for God and the things that pertain to eternal life were not some mystical experience enjoyed by a recluse who had separated himself from the world. They were the outpourings of a man who loved God in the midst of all his wrestlings with very real problems, as his enemies sought his life. To understand this is to appreciate more fully what manner of man this was who was privileged to be described as "a man after God's own heart".

PSALM 64

AFTER careful reading and consideration of the contents of this psalm we were led to the conclusion that it would be very difficult for ordinary believers to relate the detail of the Song to their own personal experiences. For instance, a brief résumé of its contents presents us with the following picture.

The writer makes his prayer to God because of the way in which his enemies were plotting to harm him. They spoke against him secretly and devised their evil schemes, not just to discredit him, but that he might be utterly destroyed. Their words and thoughts are likened to arrows that they fired at him.

Suddenly, however, their slander and intrigue is turned back upon them, for God fires His arrows and through His providential hand they themselves are brought to confusion. In their destruction wise men, beholding the work of God, are instructed and learn to fear Him. For this cause, because God vindicates the righteous, all the upright in heart rejoice.

We do not say that there are not lessons to be learned from the detail of the psalm. The danger of the unbridled use of the tongue, the nurturing of evil thoughts and secretly plotting to bring about another's demise are characteristic of human nature. No doubt they can have their manifestations, although in an adapted form, in professing believers and then in ecclesial life. The real difficulty for us must arise from the response of God that was clearly perceived and understood by the Psalmist, for his enemies were publicly discredited and brought to confusion. Their fate was recognised by those who witnessed the hand of God at work and their destruction stood as a warning to all, like them, who were workers of evil.

How then are we to understand the psalm and what is its message for us today? We feel that reflection on the status of the author of the psalm, the circumstances that might have been the cause of him penning it and also its prophetic import in its relation to the Lord Jesus Christ, will help us to understand its meaning and also emphasise a wonderful truth that is conveyed by it for our comfort and consolation.

We believe unquestionably that the author was David, as we are advised at the head of the psalm. As to the time in his life when it was written, we cannot be absolutely sure, but there are only two periods to which it can refer. Other psalms we have considered have revealed the same attitudes of mind, the same intrigue, at the time that David was in the court of Saul and also in the events leading up to Absalom's rebellion. This view arises from a kind of intuition rather than any hard evidence, but the words of the psalm are appropriate to both periods in David's life.

The secret, of course, as with so many of the psalms, lies in the fact that David was the Lord's anointed. Consequently those who plotted and schemed to destroy him were in reality fighting against God – seeking, however clearly or not they might have perceived it, to frustrate the purpose of God. Thus, openly and manifestly, David was vindicated in the eyes of the people and his enemies brought to confusion – destroyed as they had sought to do him mischief.

Prophetically it can be clearly seen how those who "watched" the Lord Jesus Christ and secretly took counsel against him would fall into the same category. In his case he was vindicated by his resurrection from the dead and the assurance that was given to men thereby that one day he would rule the world (Acts 17:31).

The comfort and assurance that the psalm brings to us therefore, is the knowledge that nothing can frustrate the purpose of God. All men's machinations are utterly futile, for "I have set my king upon my holy hill of Zion" (Psalm 2:6). The truths we have espoused are beyond reproach and we can have the utmost confidence in them. Because the Lord has delivered His anointed we can be certain that the righteous will prevail, for the sinners shall be consumed out of the earth and the wicked shall be no more (see Psalm 104:35). For this cause "the righteous shall be glad in the Lord, and shall trust in him; and all the upright in heart shall glory" (Psalm 64:10).

For the purpose of exposition the psalm can be divided in the following way:

1. David's prayer to God (verses 1,2).
2. The plotting of his enemies (verses 3-6).
3. God's response to their intrigue (verses 7-9).
4. The joy of the righteous (verse 10).

David's Prayer to God

"Hear my voice, O God, in my prayer: preserve my life from fear of the enemy. Hide me from the secret counsel of the wicked; from the insurrection of the workers of iniquity." (verses 1,2)

In keeping with the conclusions reached above, there are undoubtedly echoes of Psalm 2 in these verses. The word rendered "insurrection" (RV, "tumult") is from the same root as the word used in that psalm, "Why to the heathen rage?" (verse 1). There, "the rulers take counsel together, against the LORD, and against his anointed" (verse 2) and although the Hebrew word is different, there is little doubt that it is a synonym of the word translated "counsel" in Psalm 64.

That David was experiencing great stress at this time is evident from the language he uses. The verbs are imperatives (i.e., "hear", "preserve", "hide") and convey a sense of urgency, the deep emotional need out of which his prayer sprang. This was "the fear of the enemy" – the alarm which they aroused in him because of their conspiracy against him.

The word rendered "prayer" is not the normal Hebrew word for such supplications. Indeed the RV renders it "complaint" which might give a totally wrong impression of David's attitude towards God. The word means literally, 'to meditate, to ponder, to converse with oneself'. In other words, out of the midst of his contemplation of the hatred of his enemies, his prayer emanates, 'Hear my voice, O

455

God and preserve me and hide me from their evil purposes'.

The plotting of his enemies (verses 3-6)

They whet their tongue like a sword, they had fired their arrows, even bitter words (verse 3). The language has already been observed in other psalms (57:4; 58:7; 59:7) and it is a vivid illustration of the mischief done by the tongue of the wicked as they sought to slander and discredit David. The word rendered "bitter" is interesting for it means literally 'venomous'. It is as if they had dipped their arrows in poison, so full of venom were the words they spoke, and so deadly were the schemes they hatched against him in secret.

What they did they practised secretly. The time was not right for them openly to show where their allegiance lay. The object of their hatred is described as "the perfect", that is 'the upright'. It is the same word that is used of Jacob (Genesis 25:27, and rendered 'plain') and Job (1:1 etc.). It recurs in the last verse of the psalm when "all the upright in heart shall glory". All they did was without fear either of God or man for they encouraged themselves (lit. 'made themselves strong'). That is, they hardened their hearts so that they were impervious to all divine influence. So determined were they to bring their schemes to a successful conclusion that they had said in their hearts, "Who shall see them?". This is an idiomatic way of saying "Who will see us?" – so sure were they that God did not care and would not reveal himself on behalf of David.

In effect they had whispered in their own ear, "there is no God" and their attitude is vividly reflected in another psalm:

"The wicked ... will not seek after God: God is not in all his thoughts ... He hath said in his heart, I shall not be moved: for I shall never be in adversity ... He hath said in his heart, God hath forgotten: he hideth his face; he will never see it ... Wherefore doth the wicked contemn God? he hath said in his heart, Thou wilt not require it." (10:4,6,11,13)

This is not the intellectual atheist. This the practical atheist – the man who does not wish there to be a God and who, in consequence, has convinced himself that if there is a God, He is not interested in how he behaves. God does not see or hear. Consequently there is no retribution, no judgement to fear. So he conceals his thoughts deep in his own heart where he imagines that none can search them out. Here indeed is a facet of human nature that can affect us all. The words of Jeremiah are particularly appropriate:

"The heart is deceitful above all things, and desperately wicked: who can know it? I the LORD search the heart, I try the reins, even to give every man according to his ways, and according to the fruit of his doings."   (17:9,10)

God's response to their intrigue

"But God shall shoot at them with an arrow; suddenly shall they be wounded. So they shall make their own tongue to fall upon themselves: all that see them shall flee away. And all men shall fear, and shall declare the work of God; for they shall wisely consider of his doing."   (Psalm 64:7-9)

There is a peculiarity about the Hebrew text that is not reflected in the AV. As God turns their evil designs back upon them, so His actions are spoken of as though they were immediate in their effect. Thus the verbs are not in the future but in the past tense (i.e., "God hath shot", "they have been wounded" etc.). It is as though the inevitability of God's judgement was emphasised in this way. It is as though He had already acted, so certain was His reaction to their secret counsels.

A play on words emphasises that they would become aware of God's actions "suddenly" (verse 7), just as they themselves "suddenly shot at (David)" (verse 4). The RV reads, "so they shall be made to stumble, their own tongue being against them" (verse 8). It is as though their own words, their own counsel was turned back against them to become the means of their destruction. An illustration of these words might be found in the actions and eventual fate of Ahithophel (2 Samuel 17:23).

Their fate is that of all those who seek to rebel against the will of God, imagining that they can frustrate His

457

purpose. Their end, like that of Korah, Dathan and Abiram (see Numbers 16:39,40) stands as a witness and a testimony to the faithfulness of God and the immutability of His purpose.

It is the message of the psalm for us. The judgement of God in David's experience is a matter of joy for the righteous because in it they find the proof that God is in control. Righteousness will prevail and in Him they have put their trust whom they have found a sure refuge. For this cause "the righteous shall be glad ... and all the upright in heart shall glory" (Psalm 64:10).

PSALM 65

THE psalm bears the inscription "A Psalm and Song of David". It is extremely difficult to discover a distinction between a 'psalm' and a 'song' for although they are different Hebrew words the lexicons indicate that they are synonyms. It is the first of four psalms described in this way and the only suggestion that we can make is that the term 'psalm' refers to the national worship of the people when the composition would have been sung in the sanctuary by the Levites. The term 'song' perhaps indicates that it was also customary for the words to be sung, initially by David and later by the people, in a less formal setting.

The majority of commentators dismiss the Davidic authorship on two counts: first the allusions to the temple (verse 4) and second a conviction that the psalm is connected with the reign of Hezekiah. We accept both the allusions to the temple and the association with events in Hezekiah's reign and yet remain convinced that it is a psalm of David.

Clearly, the reference to Zion (verse 1) would place it in the latter part of David's reign and we know that it was his consuming passion to build a house for God. It would be appropriate therefore for him to consider prospectively the time when that temple should be built. Indeed the references to "all flesh" (verse 2) would seem to indicate that the psalm is carrying us beyond the reign of David and Hezekiah to the consummation of the purpose of God in the kingdom of God. The psalm is in reality a prophecy and because of this, although springing out of circumstances in David's experience, it has a fulfilment in Hezekiah's day which itself was but a foreshadowing of its ultimate fulfilment in the work of the Lord Jesus Christ.

In this connection we think it appropriate to make some comments on the nature of prophecy. Sometimes, mistakenly, we believe, prophecies are spoken of as having 'double applications'. More correctly they have recurring fulfilments. That is, given a similar background and a like pattern of human behaviour, then God reacts in the same way. Thus when the heathen rage and the people imagine a vain thing, He who sits in the heavens always laughs and has them in derision (Psalm 2). We believe that we can identify five different occasions to which the words of Psalm 2 have an application and readers might like to consider what these might be.

The actual historic events in the life of David which occasioned the psalm are not identified positively in the text but we have a personal conviction the psalm was written in the year that Solomon was anointed king. The reasons for this suggestion will become apparent when we examine the text of the psalm. At this point we make the following observations about the background.

1. It was written concerning a momentous event in a specific year in David's reign, i.e., "Thou crownest the year of thy goodness" (RV & margin) – not a general statement but a reference to a particular year.

2. In that year God had subdued the tumult of the people (verse 7) and had filled the surrounding nations with fear at the manifest tokens of His power and might.

3. This year of blessing had been marked by the abundance of the harvest that had ensued – a token of God's loving-kindness that had produced joy and gladness in the hearts of His servants (verses 11-13).

The psalm appears to fall into three stanzas:

i. David's overwhelming desire for the people to praise God in His holy temple (verses 1-4).

ii. God's universal control over the natural world and all nations (verses 5-8).

iii. The rich blessings which flow, reflected in the abundance of the harvest, when the time to favour

Zion comes – the set time, the year that will be crowned by His goodness (verses 9-13).

Verses 1-4

"Praise waiteth for thee, O God, in Sion: and unto thee shall the vow be performed. O thou that hearest prayer, unto thee shall all flesh come. Iniquities prevail against me: as for our transgressions, thou shalt purge them away. Blessed is the man whom thou choosest, and causest to approach unto thee, that he may dwell in thy courts: we shall be satisfied with the goodness of thy house, even of thy holy temple."

It is these words primarily that convince us of the historical setting of the psalm. We note particularly there is reference to a specific vow (singular) that is to be paid. Almost without exception commentators, while acknowledging that 'vow' is singular, declare that it should be understood as plural because in other psalms it is plural. This we believe to be a major error.

We remember that almost throughout his life David's desire was to build a house for God. When he was told that he himself would not be allowed to undertake the work of construction, he was not deterred but gave himself wholeheartedly to the task of preparation to enable Solomon, his son, to perform the work of building at the earliest possible opportunity (1 Chronicles 29:2-5). We know that David was given the pattern of the temple by God and he delivered this to Solomon in writing (verses 11-19). Thus in the eventide of his life with Solomon anointed king, with the scene set and the preparations completed, David could say with confidence, "Unto thee shall the vow be performed".

That this was the scene is evident from the opening words of the psalm: "Praise waiteth for thee, O God, in Sion". The word rendered "waiteth" means literally 'is silent' and the idea conveyed is that of resting or the silence of waiting. There is a sense of intense expectation and excitement until the praise of God should burst forth in joyous acclaim when the temple was completed (2 Chronicles 5:11-14).

It is in the contemplation of this imminent event that David, through the Spirit, is carried forward to the kingdom age. God would hear the prayers of his servants who prayed "towards this place" (1 Kings 8:25-30 etc.) but eventually all flesh should come to Him. David appreciated that He was the "God of all the earth" and ultimately there would be a house of prayer for all nations (Isaiah 56:6,7; Psalm 86:9).

Thus David is able to say, "Blessed is the man whom thou choosest". Initially of course this was Solomon himself for God had said of him, "Solomon thy son, he shall build my house and my courts: for I have chosen him to be my son, and I will be his father" (1 Chronicles 28:6; see also 29:1). He would dwell in the courts of God's house. But although the immediate application of the words is to Solomon, running through David's words are undoubtedly references to the larger purpose of God. Ultimately God's chosen is the Lord Jesus Christ and it is in the day of his power that all faithful men will find their satisfaction and fulfilment in the appreciation of the goodness of God associated with His temple. There will, of course, be a literal building but we must not lose sight of the fact that there is also a spiritual house. Those who belong to the household of God belong also to the royal house of David and will find all that their hearts desire when that "habitation of God through the Spirit" is completed (Ephesians 2:22).

It remains but to consider the words about transgressors in this opening section. Iniquities had prevailed against him. Literally, the word rendered "prevail" means 'to be strong'. As he contemplated the house of God where He would dwell with man, David acknowledged that the great enemy that created a barrier between God and man was sin. Yet there was still joy and happiness in the knowledge that though sin was strong, God's grace abounded for He would purge away (lit. 'make atonement for') transgression that men might approach Him and walk in His courts.

Verses 5,6

A careful comparison of these verses with the language and thoughts of Psalm 46 shows obvious similarities. We have previously demonstrated the link historically between Psalm 46 and the events of Hezekiah's reign. In our considerations of Psalm 46 we demonstrated that it drew in its development from the theme and language of Psalm 2 (see also Isaiah 37:22,28,29). We believe that Psalm 2 was written to celebrate Solomon's coronation. The prophecy it contains had an incipient fulfilment in the reign of Hezekiah, hence the use of language in Psalm 46 that is reminiscent of that psalm. It should be apparent therefore that if our suggestion concerning the background of our present psalm is correct, it was written at approximately the same time as Psalm 2 and consequently has both verbal and thematic links with that song.

So in speaking of the supremacy of God both in nature and amongst the nations, David writes, "... which stilleth the noise of the seas, the noise of their waves, and the tumult of the people" (Psalm 65:7). The accession of Solomon to the throne was against a background of discord and rivalry within Israel. There were those who thought they had a better right to the throne than he. Outside of Israel also there would have been discord. Subject nations, with a new monarch ascending the throne would have flexed their muscle, been ready to probe for any sign of weakness in the young king. But God laughed, He had them in derision for "I have set my king upon my holy hill of Zion".

So David could say, "By terrible things (lit. 'great things', 'wonderful things') thou wilt answer us in righteousness (RV), O God of our salvation" (verse 5). All the rage of the nations, all the hope of the people, all their counsel against the declared will of God was futile. God heard and answered the prayers of His faithful servants. He acted in righteousness, for He was faithful, to effect their salvation. Such was His power, manifest in His control over natural phenomena that it struck terror into the hearts of all those that opposed His purpose. This power seen in the mountains, the raging seas, the tumult of the tempest were all tokens of His control over the nations.

463

Again, although having an immediate application, the words of the psalm are clearly projected to the kingdom age, for God is "the confidence of all the ends of the earth" (verse 5) and His fear is known amongst those "that dwell in the uttermost parts" (verse 8).

This section of the psalm has two interesting and enlightening links with the Gospel records. In each of the first three Gospel records (Matthew 8; Mark 4,5; Luke 8) the Lord Jesus stilling the storm is followed immediately by the miracle concerning Legion. In the first miracle the Lord stills the raging of the sea and calms the tempestuous winds. In the second he heals the madness, the tumult of the mind that Legion suffered for he was found "sitting … in his right mind" (Mark 5:15). Thus the Psalmist writes, "which stilleth the noise of the seas, the noise of their waves, and the tumult of the people" (verse 7).

Secondly, speaking of the universal recognition of the God of Israel David writes, "thou makest the outgoings of the morning and evening to rejoice" (verse 8). As one writer has said, "it describes the places where the morning and the evening have their birth". In other words, from the east and the west they come to sing. Fear at the signs of God's power turns to wonder and joy for "many shall come from the east and west, and shall sit down with Abraham, and Isaac, and Jacob, in the kingdom of heaven" (Matthew 8:11; see Malachi 1:11 for a more obvious reference to the Lord's words).

This section of the psalm can be summed up, appropriately by the words of David:

"Blessed be thou, LORD God of Israel our father, for ever and ever. Thine, O LORD, is the greatness, and the power, and the glory, and the victory, and the majesty: for all that is in the heaven and in the earth is thine; thine is the kingdom, O LORD, and thou art exalted as head above all. Both riches and honour come of thee, and thou reignest over all; and in thine hand is power and might." (1 Chronicless 29:10-12)

Verses 9-13

The psalm concludes with a vivid description of the bountifulness of the harvest in this most conspicuous of years in which God's blessing has abounded. First David describes the rains that have watered the ground and the manner in which God has prepared it for the corn to grow (verses 9,10). Truly He has crowned this marvellous year with His goodness (verse 11). The abundance of the crops was itself the crowning token of God's favour and so the final picture is of the "pastures of the wilderness", that is, the open uncultivated land used for pasturing, together with "the little hills, girded with joy" (verse 12, RV). The cultivated fields are clothed with sheep grazing and the valleys are covered with corn (verse 13).

In graphic language the wilderness, the little hills, the meadows and the valleys are presented as shouting one to the other. All nature is personified – filled with joy, singing God's praises. Words associated with the dedication of the temple provide a fitting conclusion to these thoughts:

"And they (the people) blessed the king, and went unto their tents joyful and glad of heart for all the goodness that the LORD had done for David his servant, and for Israel his people." (1 Kings 8:66)

Hezekiah

We have already indicated that we believe the prophecy contained in the psalm had an incipient fulfilment in the days of Hezekiah. When the host of Sennacherib besieged Jerusalem, the words which that tyrant's emissary used were described in terms recalling Psalm 2 (see passages in Isaiah 37 referred to above). But all their rage and tumult was utterly futile, for God had set His king upon His throne and He laughed them to scorn. The angel of the Lord went forth and destroyed the Assyrian host (2 Chronicles 32:21,22). This remarkable deliverance was linked with a wonderful promise regarding the harvest that was to be a sign to them of God's blessing (2 Kings 19:27-30). How remarkable the work of God was at this time is indicated by the blessings that were bestowed upon Hezekiah.

465

"And Hezekiah had exceeding much riches and honour: and he made himself treasuries for silver, and for gold, and for precious stones, and for spices, and for shields, and for all manner of pleasant jewels; storehouses also for the increase of corn, and wine, and oil; and stalls for all manner of beasts, and cotes for flocks. Moreover he provided him cities, and possessions of flocks and herds in abundance: for God had given him substance very much." (2 Chronicles 32:27-29)

Hezekiah could also say, "Thou crownest the year with thy goodness".

PSALM 66

THE psalm carries no indication of authorship, but the substance of the song gives clear indication as to the kind of circumstances in which it was written and, in our view, leads to the inevitable conclusion that it refers to the time of Hezekiah and was in fact penned by that righteous man.

The reasons for this conclusion will become more apparent as the contents of the psalm are examined, but at this juncture a brief analysis will indicate how appropriate the message is to the time of Hezekiah and his own life in particular.

In broad terms the psalm falls into two sections – the first (verses 1-12) characterised by the first person plural and the second (verses 13-20) changing to the first person singular. As far as structure is concerned the first section falls into three stanzas and the second into two, each indicated by the familiar "Selah" except at the conclusion of the sections.

The first section calls upon all nations to praise God and to acknowledge his sovereignty because of the marvellous way He had delivered His people, Israel, in the past. He had continued to watch over them even to that current time, when he had delivered them from an impending calamity in a most remarkable and effective way. Clearly this event to which the psalm refers could be the salvation from Assyrian tyranny and the wonderful manner in which God destroyed the host of Sennacherib.

The second section of the psalm is not national but personal. The author now speaks of his own experiences and it is evident that he too, like the nation as a whole, had cause to praise God and thank Him for a personal deliverance that he had known in his life. Again this would have an obvious fulfilment in Hezekiah's sickness and the extension of life that was granted to him.

These general observations may not be thought, of themselves, to be conclusive. The language, however, of the psalm contains so many allusions to other scripture which is associated with Hezekiah and his reign that we believe there can be no real doubt as to its historical background. These allusions will be noted when we deal with the text of the psalm.

Before coming to the psalm in detail, however, there is an important principle that we can learn from the two sections. The first is dealing with God's purpose with Israel, the second with Hezekiah's personal experiences. So it must always be in the lives of those who are called to the Truth. There is first the general understanding of the purpose of God – an intellectual assent to His work for the salvation of men, looking forward to the consummation of His purpose in the future. But that of itself is not enough. Out of that has to grow the conviction that we are part of the purpose, that we have a place in it. Because of that we shall come to appreciate more and more that not only is God working in the wider sense to fulfil that purpose, but also He is active in our lives. We can therefore be assured of His ability to save us. It was a lesson that Hezekiah had learned and the two sections of the psalm testify to this truth.

The five stanzas that comprise the psalm are as follows:

1. All nations are called to praise God (verses 1-4).
2. They are invited to behold God's work in the past (verses 5-7).
3. Also to recognise His recent deliverance of His people (verses 8-12).
4. The writer offers praise and thanks to God in the temple (verses 13-15).
5. He calls on all God-fearing men to witness the goodness of God in his life (verses 16-20).

Verses 1-4

"Make a joyful noise unto God, all ye lands: sing forth the honour of his name: make his praise glorious. Say unto God, How terrible art thou in thy works! Through the greatness of thy power shall thine enemies submit themselves unto thee. All the earth shall worship thee, and shall sing unto thee; they shall sing to thy name. Selah."

All the earth is summoned to praise God and acknowledge His power. The Hebrew word rendered "joyful noise" is rendered elsewhere as "shout" (e.g., Psalm 47:1; 1 Samuel 10:24) and is particularly associated with the recognition of a king (see Numbers 23:21 where the shout of a king is the recognition that God dwelt as a sovereign in the midst of His people).

Thus the first demand is that the nations recognise Israel's God as king. Three times the word "sing" is used. Some render the word "hymn" for it carries the idea not only of singing but also of playing music, literally 'to pluck the strings'. What they are urged to sing is "the honour of His name"; in other words to recognise in His acts, the characteristics of His holiness. This was to be the basis of their praise. They were to recognise "how terrible are thy works" (RV). Perhaps this is a reference to the destruction of Sennacherib's host, through the greatness of His power.

Because of this knowledge of His works, even His enemies will submit themselves to Him. This submission, however, is not a willing obedience. The word rendered "submit" means literally 'to lie (down)'. Hence it is a feigned allegiance, an unwilling homage such as might be given by a conquered people to their conqueror. The *Cambridge Bible* has "came cringing unto thee". The message is that those who will not willingly give Him the honour that is His due will be compelled by their own inability to stand before His power to recognise and acknowledge His sovereignty. Thus whether willingly or by compulsion, all the earth will worship and when the kingdom of men finally comes to an end then "every knee shall bow (and) every tongue shall swear" (Isaiah 45:23).

Before leaving this first stanza, note the similarity in the language of the psalm with the words of Hezekiah in Isaiah 37: "that all the kingdoms of the earth may know that thou art the LORD, even thou only" (verse 20).

Verses 5-7

Having expressed the inevitability of their ultimate submission to God, the Psalmist invites them to learn the lesson now. Those who would not respond must have their hearts stirred by a contemplation of God's works in the past, realising that their mighty acts are the token that He is still at work. "Come and see the works of God: he is terrible in his doing toward the children of men" (Psalm 66:5). Again there is a verbal link with another psalm which is undoubtedly connected with Hezekiah: "Come, behold the works of the LORD" (Psalm 46:8). The Hebrew word rendered "works" occurs only in these two psalms.

The preposition "towards" carries the idea of 'over', thus emphasising His supremacy "over the children of men", who can either recognise Him as their God or fear Him as their enemy. There is no escape for them – it is either the one or the other, and they are reminded of the wonderful and terrible works of the past, when God turned "the sea into dry land: (and) they went through the flood on foot" (verse 6). Note that the word "flood" is an archaic expression for a river (see Joshua 24:2,3,14,15); in this case obviously the Jordan.

The Psalmist says, "There did we rejoice in him". Notice that there is a continuity implied: "there ... we ..." There was an unbroken line from that time to the present. They had been and still were the people of God. It is an important lesson for us to learn also, for we belong to the family of God and as such are related in that same continuous unbroken line – to great men of faith like Noah, Abraham, Jacob, Moses, Joshua, David etc. If we can capture that sense of belonging, that consciousness of our heritage, then we shall appreciate more and more the privilege that is ours as the children of God.

The stanza closes with a reiteration of the message that by His power God rules forever and His eyes behold the nations (lit. 'keeps watch upon'). This is the assurance that Israel had received. He that kept them neither slumbered nor slept (Psalm 121:4) but was always alert to their need and to the intentions of the nations. Once again there is an allusion to Hezekiah's words in Isaiah 37: "Open thine eyes, O LORD, and see" (verse 17).

Therefore, "Let not the rebellious exalt themselves" (Psalm 66:7). It is a warning to men never to imagine that because God appears to be taking no positive action He is not concerned, for His eye is always upon His people. Once again there is a possible connection with Hezekiah, for God said to Sennacherib: "Against whom hast thou exalted thy voice, and lifted up thine eyes on high?" (Isaiah 37:23).

Verses 8-12
This particular stanza is remarkable in that in calling on the nations to recognise God's recent deliverance of His people it also emphasises two other aspects of His work. Firstly it draws attention to the way in which He had used their adversity to discipline and chasten them, but most remarkable of all God is telling the nations that He has done this because of Israel's responsibility to the world at large. His purpose with all the earth was to be carried forward and fulfilled through this people that He had created for himself. It is because of this great truth that the Psalmist cries: "O bless our God, ye people, and make the voice of his praise to be heard" (verse 8). Why must the peoples of the earth praise God in this way? Because He has preserved His people Israel, "which holdeth our soul in life, and suffereth not our feet to be moved" (verse 9).

When the Assyrian had swept into the land all nations had fallen before him, including the apostate northern kingdom of Israel. It had seemed inevitable that Judah would suffer the same fate. But as impending destruction loomed, God had intervened and not just delivered, but remembering His purpose with this people had preserved them. Note that the tenses of the verb in this verse are not general as the AV implies but specific in that they refer to the events described in the following verses. Literally, "who hath set our soul in life and not suffered our foot to be moved". To effect His purpose God had proved them as precious metals are tried to purge away the dross (verse 10). This of course is a common scriptural figure (see Proverbs 17:3; Jeremiah 9:7; Malachi 3:2,3), but significantly God had told them of His intention to use the Assyrian for this purpose through the prophet Isaiah:

471

"And I will turn my hand upon thee, and purely purge away thy dross, and take away all thy tin."

(Isaiah 1:25)

To appreciate the manner in which God tried them and purged them and the wonder of His deliverance it has to be remembered that the land of Judah, and all its cities, was ravaged by this savage aggressor. Only Jerusalem remained free for as Isaiah had prophesied, "he shall pass through Judah; he shall overflow and go over, he shall reach even to the neck" (8:8).

Thus it was that Judah could consider herself as delivered into the power of the enemy. "Thou broughtest us into the net; thou laidst affliction upon our loins. Thou hast caused men to ride over our heads" (Psalm 66:11,12). In a series of dramatic figures the calamities that had overtaken them are described. They had been caught in his net; like a great weight he had pressed down upon their land; in a figure his horses and chariots had ridden over their heads.

However, God's purpose with Israel remained inviolate. Their mission to the nations would still be fulfilled. Therefore God had delivered them from the furnace of affliction and from the flood that would have overwhelmed them (verse 12).

The language reiterates the assurance of the prophet and confirms to the nations who had been called upon to bless Israel's God that His purpose through this people would still bring blessing upon all peoples of the earth:

"But now thus saith the LORD that created thee, O Jacob, and he that formed thee, O Israel, Fear not: for I have redeemed thee, I have called thee by thy name; thou art mine. When thou passest through the waters, I will be with thee; and through the rivers, they shall not overflow thee: when thou walkest through the fire, thou shalt not be burned; neither shall the flame kindle upon thee." (Isaiah 43:1,2)

Verses 13-15

It is at this juncture that the second section of the psalm begins, marked as indicated, by the change from the first person plural to the first person singular. The first stanza (verses 13-15) of this section speaks exclusively of the manner in which the Psalmist comes into the house of God to offer sacrifice and to pay the vows he had made in the midst not just of Judah's distress but his own personal troubles:

"I will come (RV) into thy house with burnt offerings: I will pay thee my vows, which my lips have uttered, and my mouth hath spoken, when I was in trouble. I will offer unto thee burnt sacrifices of fatlings, with the incense of rams; I will offer bullocks with goats. Selah."

The passage might seem to be a straightforward statement of fact from which there is not a lot, beyond the obvious, that we can learn. However, there are several significant features that should not be missed.

First of all there does not appear to be any reference to sin offerings, but they are either burnt or peace offerings. Particularly interesting in this connection are the words translated "burnt" and "incense". In fact the word rendered "incense" is derived directly from that translated "burnt" and the literal meaning of the Hebrew word is 'to turn to incense or fragrance', and such offerings are always for "a sweet savour unto the LORD" (see Leviticus 1:9,13,17; 2:9). Of course, the fat of the sin offerings was also burnt for a similar purpose (Leviticus 4:31), but when the offering itself was burned a completely different word was used which signified 'to burn, or destroy utterly' (see Leviticus 4:12). The lessons that emerge are important. God requires sin to be utterly destroyed. But the burnt offering represented the complete devotion of a life to God and the peace offering the relationship with God that such an attitude produced. These were things in which God delights and, as such, rise as a sweet smelling savour. The Psalmist in his offerings was recognising that the deliverance that both the nation and he personally had experienced demanded that they give to God their wholehearted service. It is, of course, a lesson that we too need to learn in our lives. In delivering us from the tyranny of sin God expects no less than our wholehearted effort to spend our life in His service. It is this attitude towards life that rises to him as "a sweet smelling savour" in which He delights.

473

The particular offerings mentioned are significant in another way, for amongst them are sacrifices that could only be offered on behalf of the nation as a whole or by persons of distinction. Thus a ram could only be offered as a burnt or peace offering for the people, by their princes, by the high priest, an ordinary priest or a Nazarite (see Exodus 29:18; Numbers 6:15, for example). Again he-goats are only mentioned in connection with the burnt and peace offerings of the princes (see Numbers 7:17,23,35, etc.). Clearly offerings were made on behalf of the nation as a whole, but the emphasis upon his own personal trouble is an indication that the offerer was a person of distinction such as a priest or prince or, in the light of our considerations, Hezekiah himself.

Verses 16-20
Hezekiah had prayed for his life when the prophet had told him of his impending death (Isaiah 38:2,3). So now he calls upon all those who feared God to learn from his example:

"Come and hear, all ye that fear God, and I will declare what he hath done for my soul. I cried unto him with my mouth, and he was extolled with my tongue."
(Psalm 66:16,17)

When Hezekiah addressed his prayer to God he said:

"Remember now, O LORD, I beseech thee, how I have walked before thee in truth and with a perfect heart."
(Isaiah 38:3)

His prayer for God's mercy was based on the integrity of his life of service; the sincerity with which he could make his plea for deliverance. It is these thoughts that form the substance of the final words of the psalm:

"If I had regarded (RV margin) iniquity in my heart, the Lord would (RV) not hear me: but verily God hath heard me; he hath attended to the voice of my prayer."
(verses 18,19)

Here is a principle that is universal in its application. God only hears the prayers of those who approach Him in sincerity. If a man is a hypocrite, a play-actor who pretends to be righteous but in reality is not, then God will not hearken or answer his prayer. In our experience, words such as this cause many brethren and sisters very real distress and for this reason we feel it appropriate to give some consideration to the practical issue involved. We are, of course, all sinners and the conflict which we experience within because of our failure to overcome sin can be a most distressing emotion. There are habitual sins that can keep recurring, which however hard we try, somehow seem to be perpetual thorns in our flesh. It is these experiences that lead us to cry with the Apostle Paul, "O wretched man that I am! who shall deliver me from the body of this death?" (Romans 7:24).

Now we must never minimise sin; we must never take it for granted but must always strive, in the power of God's word to overcome it. Are, however, the experiences we have described what Hezekiah meant "by regarding iniquity in his heart?" We do not think so. The fact that we recognise our sins and the difficulties we experience in trying to overcome them is in itself an acknowledgement before God that we recognise our weakness. This is not, generally, the attitude of the hypocrite. The man who regards iniquity in his heart is, we suggest, he who delights in it; who, in effect, does not experience the conflict between right and wrong that distresses so many of us and, even if he does in a measure, feels no real concern when sin prevails. We must recognise that God alone is the judge but while never condoning sin, either in others or ourselves, if our desire is to please God and if we hate the sin that sometimes persists in our lives, then that is not regarding iniquity in our hearts and God will hear us in our prayers.

If we truly seek him with all our hearts then the day will come when we, like Hezekiah, will be able to say, because He has delivered us out of the hand of death:

"Blessed be God, which hath not turned away my prayer, nor his mercy from me." (verse 20)

PSALM 67

THIS short psalm is, we believe, directly related to the previous song, having the same historical background and, almost certainly, the same author. We suggested that Psalm 66 was written by Hezekiah against the background of God's deliverance of Judah out of the hand of Sennacherib and his own salvation from sickness and death. There was particular emphasis in the first part of the psalm upon the need for all nations to recognise the greatness of Israel's God and what He had done for them. Most significantly it was indicated that the reason why the nations should acknowledge God's power and sing His praise was because His deliverance of His people was not just for their own sake but for the benefit of all peoples of the earth. It was that Israel might fulfil their responsibility, in the purpose of God, to the world at large (verses 8-11). It is this priestly function of Israel to the nations of the earth that is the heart of the message of Psalm 67. To ensure that we appreciate this fully it seems appropriate that we should briefly outline precisely what this purpose is.

Israel in the Purpose of God

Many find it difficult to understand why God should have a special relationship with Israel. It is important to appreciate that this is not because Israel has some inherent worth or goodness that makes them superior to other nations, but they are "a chosen people" because God in His wisdom has used them to carry forward His purpose in the earth. This privilege carried commensurate responsibilities and their failure to fulfil these resulted in the overthrow of the nation, the scattering of the people and the suffering they have endured down through the centuries.

476

Israel were intended to be a witness for God in the earth. They were to be the custodians of divine truth for "unto them were committed the oracles of God" (Romans 3:2). They, amongst all the nations of the earth, were to have a unique relationship with the Creator that, through them, He might bring His purpose to fruition:

"... who are Israelites; to whom pertaineth the adoption, and the glory, and the covenants, and the giving of the law, and the service of God, and the promises; whose are the fathers, and of whom as concerning the flesh Christ came."   (Romans 9:4,5)

In determining to use a nation to witness for Him in this way God did not choose an existing people but He created a nation for Himself:

"But now thus saith the LORD that created thee, O Jacob, and he that formed thee, O Israel, Fear not: for I have redeemed thee, I have called thee by thy name; thou art mine."   (Isaiah 43:1)

In brief, we have only to think of the miraculous birth of Isaac and the early history of the family of Jacob, culminating in the deliverance from Egypt, to appreciate how true is this declaration of Isaiah.

When Israel came to Sinai God said:

"Now therefore, if ye will obey my voice indeed, and keep my covenant, then ye shall be a peculiar treasure unto me above all people: for all the earth is mine: and ye shall be unto me a kingdom of priests, and an holy nation."   (Exodus 19:5,6)

Israel's special status related to the fact that "all the earth" belonged to God. Their relationship to Him was directly connected to the fact that His purpose was concerned with the earth in its entirety. In relation to the nations of the earth Israel were a kingdom of priests. A priest has a dual function. He shows God to men and he brings men to God. In this sense, Israel, if they had realised their potential, would have fulfilled a missionary function in the earth. As God's witnesses (Isaiah 43:10-12) they would have shone as a light in the darkness of the world teaching and bringing the nations to recognise and acknowledge their God. This has a practical illustration

477

when the Queen of Sheba came to visit Solomon and is reiterated in the words of Deuteronomy:

> "Behold, I have taught you statutes and judgments, even as the LORD my God commanded me, that ye should do so in the land whither ye go to possess it. Keep therefore and do them; for this is your wisdom and your understanding in the sight of the nations, which shall hear all these statutes, and say, Surely this great nation is a wise and understanding people. For what nation is there so great, who hath God so nigh unto them, as the LORD our God is in all things that we call upon him for? And what nation is there so great, that hath statutes and judgments so righteous as all this law, which I set before you this day?" (4:5-8)

Israel failed to rise to their responsibilities and they have suffered the consequences. It is a paradox that what they failed to become willingly, they have become unwillingly through the events of their history. They have been and remain an abiding testimony to the reality and existence of God and to the truth of His word.

Amongst the nations they will yet fulfil their destiny in the kingdom age. We do not develop the theme but draw attention to the words of the prophet:

> "In those days it shall come to pass, that ten men shall take hold out of all languages of the nations, even shall take hold of the skirt of him that is a Jew, saying, We will go with you: for we have heard that God is with you." (Zechariah 8:23)

Against this background we return specifically to the words of the psalm which falls into three stanzas, the first and second ending with the familiar "Selah".

The Priestly Blessing

> "God be merciful unto us, and bless us; and cause his face to shine upon us." (verse 1)

These words are clearly taken from the priestly blessing in Numbers 6:

> "The LORD bless thee, and keep thee: the LORD make his face to shine upon thee, and be gracious unto thee: the LORD lift up his countenance upon thee, and give thee peace." (verses 24-26)

There is no indication as to when, specifically, Aaron and
his sons were to utter this blessing, although it seems
likely that one occasion when the words were used was
when Aaron and his sons began their priestly service. The
record in Leviticus 8 describes in detail the consecration of
the priests in the sight of all the people (verse 3). This was
clearly intended to impress upon them what the
responsibilities of priesthood really involved, for they were
a "kingdom of priests" and Aaron and his sons represented
them before the Lord. Aaron, in particular, was the
representative of the nation as a whole so that what was
true of him was true also of them. Chapter 9 describes how
Aaron, again before all the congregation (verse 5), offered
sacrifices both for himself and for the people, thus
indicating his association with them both in his need and
in the office held. Having thus entered into his priestly
service and discharged his responsibility he "lifted up his
hand toward the people, and blessed them" (verse 22),
surely in the words of Numbers 6.

Although thus reminded of the priestly responsibility,
both nationally and individually, the Israelite who wished
to please his God would know that only Aaron and his sons
could approach the altar and serve in the sanctuary
(Numbers 18:7). It was for this reason, that to encourage
those who took their priestly status seriously, God
provided the Nazarite vow. Space does not allow a detailed
consideration of this ordinance but just as Aaron was
given specific commandments with regard to strong drink
(Leviticus 10:8-11), bereavement (21:10-12), baldness
(verse 5), and was to wear the mitre, "the holy crown"
(8:9), so each of these elements was reflected in the
Nazarite vow of separation described in Numbers 6
(verses 1-8). It was a means whereby they could undertake
duties parallel to those of the high priest. As he was the
embodiment of the nation as a whole, so in this manner
they could assume priestly responsibilities in recognition
of their national and individual status.

It is surely not without significance that the priestly
blessing (Numbers 6:24-26) occurs immediately after the
description of the responsibilities undertaken by those
who took the Nazarite vow, for the blessing of God

479

pronounced by the priest had direct relevance to Israel's status as "a kingdom of priests and an holy nation".

It is thus particularly appropriate that this psalm which has as its theme Israel's responsibility towards the nations, should begin with this prayer drawn from the priestly blessing.

"Bless", writes the Psalmist, "that thy way may be known upon earth, thy saving health among all nations" (Psalm 67:1,2). That is, that Israel might be able to fulfil their national responsibility as outlined above. To express it in its simplest form, the effect of God's goodness shown to Israel is to be the conversion of the world.

Longing for the Fulfilment of God's Purpose

We have on several occasions drawn attention to the consequence of Judah's deliverance and Hezekiah's recovery of health:

"Many brought gifts unto the LORD to Jerusalem, and presents to Hezekiah king of Judah: so that he was magnified in the sight of all nations from thenceforth."
(2 Chronicles 32:23)

"And Hezekiah had exceeding much riches and honour: and he made himself treasuries for silver, and for gold, and for precious stones, and for spices, and for shields, and for all manner of pleasant jewels; storehouses also for the increase of corn, and wine, and oil; and stalls for all manner of beasts, and cotes for flocks."
(verses 27,28)

Two factors are emphasised. Firstly, the effect upon the nations who were drawn to Jerusalem and to Israel's God, and secondly, the abundance of the harvests reflected in the building of storehouses and housing for the herds and flocks. That these events were seen as a portent of the ultimate fulfilment of Israel's destiny seems clear and it is against this background that the Psalmist looks to the ultimate consummation of God's purpose in the earth.

"Let the peoples praise thee, O God; let all the peoples praise thee. O let the nations be glad and sing for joy: for thou shalt judge the peoples with equity, and govern the nations upon earth." (Psalm 67:3,4, RV)

The RV rendering correctly indicates that it is "peoples" not 'people'. That is, it is the nations of the earth rather than Israel that rejoice in the blessing of God. It is a desire for the kingdom age to be established for all nations to experience the righteous rule of God's king.

The longing for the nations to praise God in His kingdom is expressed again but this time linked, against the background of the bountiful harvests, with the abundance of the earth:

"Let the peoples praise thee, O God; let all the peoples praise thee. The earth hath yielded her increase: God, even our own God, shall bless us."

(verses 5,6, RV)

The closing verse of the psalm reiterates briefly the thoughts of the priestly blessing: "God shall bless us" and the outcome is that for which God created the nation of Israel, that they might be a kingdom of priests, "And all the ends of the earth shall fear him" (verse 7).

481

PSALM 68

AS we have done on previous occasions, we follow the suggestion of J. W. Thirtle in his book, *The Titles of the Psalms*, and relate the appropriate information at the head of the following psalm to that which precedes it. Psalm 68 is therefore one of two psalms (Psalm 44 being the other) which bears the inscription, "upon Shoshannim". There is little doubt as to the meaning of the Hebrew as almost all authorities are agreed that the word means 'lilies'.

This information, almost certainly, has some reference to its liturgical use and is an indication that it is a psalm that was associated with a particular time of the year in the temple worship. Speaking of flowers (i.e., lilies) would direct attention to Springtime, for:

"Lo, the winter is past, the rain is over and gone; the flowers appear on the earth; the time of the singing of birds is come, and the voice of the turtle is heard in our land." (Song 2:11,12)

It has been pointed out that the Hebrew preposition translated "upon" could also be rendered 'concerning or relating to' and given its relationship to the Springtime it does not seem inappropriate to relate the lily to the feasts of Passover and Weeks (Pentecost) (Leviticus 23:15-17; Exodus 23:14-17). Thus the association with these two feasts would speak of redemption (Passover) and ingathering (Pentecost).

The close connection between the two feasts in Jewish thought is indicated by Edersheim in *The Temple, Its Ministry and Services* – in a passage quoted previously:

"The 'Feast of Unleavened Bread' may be said not to have quite passed till fifty days after its commencement, when it merged in that of Pentecost, or 'of weeks'. According to unanimous Jewish tradition, which was universally received at the time of Christ, the day of Pentecost was the anniversary of the giving of the Law on Mount Sinai which the Feast of Weeks was intended to commemorate. Thus, as the dedication of the harvest, commencing with the presentation of the first omer on the Passover, was completed in the thank-offering of the two wave-loaves at Pentecost, so the memorial of Israel's deliverance appropriately terminated in that of the giving of the Law." (page 260)

These associations pointing to the significance of the title "concerning Shoshannim" indicate the theme and substance of the psalm for both Feasts could only be celebrated by a people settled in the land of promise, and Psalm 68 speaks graphically and dramatically of God's deliverance of His people from Egypt, of the giving of the law and of the establishment of Israel in the land.

It is, perhaps, appropriate to mention some of the contexts in which the lily is used as a symbol in scripture for it is part of the vivid imagery connected with the meaning of the feasts as outlined above.

It is linked with the pomegranate as an adornment of the two pillars of brass, Jachin and Boaz, that Solomon erected in the temple (1 Kings 7:16-22), and the brim of the sea (laver) of brass was also "wrought like the brim of a cup, with flowers of lilies" (verse 26). Similarly, the hem of the high priest's garment was to have pomegranates of blue and purple and scarlet and the pomegranate was to alternate with a golden bell: "a golden bell and a pomegranate, a golden bell and a pomegranate, upon the hem of the robe round about" (Exodus 28:31-35).

Clearly, the golden bells, like cups, represent flowers and it would be reasonable to suppose, given the connection with pomegranates elsewhere, that the flower thus indicated was a lily. The pomegranate would speak of a multitudinous seed whereas the lily stands as a symbol of God's people, redeemed through the forgiveness of their sins (see Hosea 14:4,5).

Historical Background

The circumstances which gave occasion to the writing of the psalm are, we believe, not as clear as many think. It has long been associated, together with Psalms 15, 24, 87, 96, 105 and 132, with David bringing the ark of God to its resting place in the tabernacle that he had prepared for it in Zion. This may well be so but the evidence that it was actually written at that time is inconclusive. That David had this event in his mind we do not doubt, but we think it possible that the joyous procession described in the psalm was recalled at a later date. It is indicated by the opening words of the psalm, "Let God arise, let his enemies be scattered", uttered by Moses when the ark set forward (Numbers 10:35) and reflected in the later parts of the psalm:

"They have seen thy goings, O God; even the goings of my God, my King, in the sanctuary. The singers went before, the players on instruments followed after; among them were the damsels playing with timbrels ... There is little Benjamin with their ruler, the princes of Judah and their council, the princes of Zebulun, and the princes of Naphtali." (verses 24-27)

The players of instruments went before, at the rear came the singers and between them the damsels playing their timbrels, while following all these came the representatives of the tribes (compare these verses with 1 Chronicles 15:14-22).

Clearly, David was recalling the bringing up of the ark to its resting place, but we suggest that it is possible he was moved to do this by a later event in his life, namely, the occasion when God made a covenant with him promising him the everlasting stability of his throne. Connected with the covenant was the promise of a seed who would build a house for God, thus David could anticipate the day when the temple would be erected. "Because of thy temple at Jerusalem shall kings bring presents unto thee" (Psalm 68:29). It is recognised that the word rendered "temple" is on some occasions used of the tabernacle, but we suggest that the tone and context of the psalm point to the more permanent structure built by Solomon which was but a portent of "the house of prayer for all people" yet to be erected in God's kingdom (Isaiah 56:7).

Bearing in mind the theme of the psalm, i.e., God establishing His people in their land, it should be noted also that when God made the promises to David He gave him this assurance:

"Also I will ordain a place for my people Israel, and will plant them, and they shall dwell in their place, and shall be moved no more; neither shall the children of wickedness waste them any more, as at the beginning."

(1 Chronicles 17:9)

This event seems to us to be more appropriate for the description of the grandeur of God manifest on behalf of His people which is the substance of this psalm, and it would be natural for David to think back to that joyous occasion in his own experience when the ark was brought from the house of Obed-edom to the tabernacle that he had prepared for it and God finally dwelt in Zion. But, wonderful though this event was, it remained a pale reflection of the manner in which God had led His people in times of old and the way in which He would yet lead them to their eternal rest in the triumphal procession of the Lord Jesus Christ and the saints at the time of the Lord's coming in glory.

A Man of the Word

We know that David was moved by the Holy Spirit to pen the words of the psalm. Yet one of the wonders of inspiration is that so often God allows the character and disposition of the writer to shine through the words he uses. The richness of scriptural allusion and quotation in Psalm 68 is truly amazing, and while acknowledging the power of inspiration it is also an indication of the manner in which David himself read and meditated upon the word of God.

"O how love I thy law! it is my meditation all the day."

(Psalm 119:97)

We cannot analyse all the references and allusions, but two passages of scripture and the events they commemorate clearly dominate the composition of the psalm. These are the blessing of Moses on the tribes of Israel (Deuteronomy 33) and the Song of Deborah and Barak (Judges 5).

We reproduce, for comparative purposes, some of the links between Psalm 68 and these scriptures. Other references and allusions to other scriptures will be noted as the study progresses.

Deuteronomy 33	Psalm 68
"The LORD came from Sinai, and rose up from Seir unto them ... he came with ten thousands of saints" (verse 2).	"The chariots of God are twenty thousand, even thousands of angels: the Lord is among them, as in Sinai, in the holy place" (verse 17).
"There is none like unto the God of Jeshurun, who rideth upon the heaven in thy help, and in his excellency on the sky. The eternal God is thy refuge, and underneath are the everlasting arms: and he shall thrust out the enemy from before thee; and shall say, Destroy them" (verses 26,27).	"Extol him that rideth upon the heavens" (verse 4) "To him that rideth upon the heavens of heavens, which were of old; lo, he doth send out his voice, and that a mighty voice. Ascribe ye strength unto God: his excellency is over Israel, and his strength is in the clouds" (verses 33,34).
"Israel then shall dwell in safety alone: the fountain of Jacob shall be upon a land of corn and wine" (verse 28).	"Bless ye God in the congregations, even the Lord, from the fountain of Israel" (verse 26).

Judges 5	Psalm 68
"LORD, when thou wentest out of Seir, when thou marchedst out of the field of Edom, the earth trembled, and the heavens dropped, the clouds also dropped water. The mountains melted from before the LORD, even that Sinai from before the LORD God of Israel" (verses 4,5).	"O God, when thou wentest forth before thy people, when thou didst march through the wilderness; the earth shook, the heavens also dropped at the presence of God: even Sinai itself was moved at the presence of God, the God of Israel" (verse 7,8).
"Awake, awake, Deborah: awake, awake, utter a song: arise, Barak, and lead thy captivity captive, thou son of Abinoam" (verse 12).	"Thou hast ascended on high, thou hast led captivity captive" (verse 18).
"Why abodest thou among the sheepfolds, to hear the bleatings of the flocks?" (verse 16)	"Will ye lie among the sheepfolds?" (verse 13, RV)

486

It is clear from a comparison of the passages that the verses from Judges 5 are themselves references to the Exodus when God marched at the head of His people, leading them from Egypt to Sinai and finally settling them in their place in the promised land. The language tells of God manifest in awful splendour and majesty. The presence of the God of Israel, accompanied by both natural and supernatural phenomena, was made known to Israel's enemies and to His people themselves as He revealed Himself to them.

The Theme of the Psalm

In short, it can be said that the psalm recalls God manifest in power on behalf of His people to deliver them and lead them to their promised rest. It anticipates further manifestations of God's power on their behalf and has rightly been regarded as one of the most grand and majestic of all psalms.

In summarising the theme of the psalm we believe that a key verse in unlocking its wonderful message of God-manifestation is verse 18: "Thou hast ascended on high, thou has led captivity captive".

Again we leave detailed consideration until later in the chapter, but we emphasise particularly the implications of the fact that God "hast ascended on high". It means, of course, in the language of scripture, that He has first come down and manifest Himself on behalf of His people. In the Old Testament the supreme example of this is the Exodus, which is at the heart of the message of this psalm. Thus we read:

"And the LORD said, I have surely seen the affliction of my people which are in Egypt, and have heard their cry by reason of their taskmasters; for I know their sorrows; and I am come down to deliver them out of the hand of the Egyptians, and to bring them up out of that land unto a good land and a large, unto a land flowing with milk and honey." (Exodus 3:7,8)

These words are quoted by Stephen in his defence of the Gospel (Acts 7:34).

Interestingly, the prophet Isaiah longing for God to manifest Himself as in times of old writes, "Oh that thou wouldest rend the heavens, that thou wouldest come down, that the mountains might flow down at thy presence" (64:1). His plea arises out of the fact "thou didst terrible things which we looked not for, thou camest down, the mountains flowed down at thy presence" (verse 3).

So the Psalmist describes God, having delivered His people from bondage and led them triumphantly to freedom, as "ascending on high" with the wonderful work of redemption accomplished.

It is this very figure that lies at the heart of John's Gospel record for it is coloured by the language of the Exodus. In the Lord Jesus, God wrought a greater deliverance than that from Egypt and, as on that occasion He came down. He was manifest now in the person of His only begotten Son. Thus the language, "he that came down from heaven" (John 3:13; 6:38,42, etc.), so often misunderstood, is in reality the language of God-manifestation. God, once again, had come down to redeem men from the power of sin through the work of the Lord Jesus Christ.

That our understanding is correct is corroborated by the testimony of scripture itself for verse 18 of Psalm 68 is, of course, quoted directly by the Apostle Paul and the same conclusions inferred that we have outlined above:

> "Wherefore he saith, When he ascended up on high, he led captivity captive, and gave gifts unto men. (Now that he ascended, what is it but that he also descended first into the lower parts of the earth?)"
>
> (Ephesians 4:8,9)

In the context of Ephesians the phrase in the psalm "thou hast received gifts for men" (to be considered later) is rendered "gave gifts unto men" and is clearly applied to the spirit gifts that were bestowed upon the first century believers, i.e., "And he gave some, apostles; and some, prophets; and some, evangelists; and some, pastors and teachers" (verse 11).

These gifts were also a form of God-manifestation, for it is recorded in Acts 2, "And suddenly there came a sound from heaven as of a rushing mighty wind" (verse 2), and Peter writes, "but unto us they (the prophets) did minister the things, which are now reported unto you by them that have preached the gospel unto you with the Holy Spirit sent down from heaven" (1 Peter 1:12).

Thus the wonderful theme of God-manifestation is described in the grandeur of the language as Israel's God came down to deliver them and His presence was known among men.

We now attempt the formidable task of expounding in more detail the substance of this magnificent psalm.

Structure

It is not an easy task to analyse the contents of Psalm 68 to determine its structure. A brief investigation of the attempts of various commentators will reveal how difficult they find it, for it is rare to find two who agree together. Our advice is to lay them all aside and read the psalm itself. Not once, but again and again and we believe that by this exercise the word of God will eventually enlighten the mind to the eternal truths contained in this wonderful song. Perhaps we can recommend this method of repeated reading for other parts of scripture that sometimes seem obscure and difficult to understand.

Since embarking on this study we have become increasingly aware that Psalm 68 is in fact a continuation of the theme developed in the preceding psalms.

It will be recalled that we emphasised that the purpose of Psalms 66 and 67, both written by Hezekiah, was to show how God had blessed Israel, not simply for their own sake, but that through them God's purpose with all the nations of the earth might be brought to its ultimate fulfilment. Psalm 68, although written by David, has been associated in the Psalter with these two psalms because in a most dramatic way it describes how God has been, and will be, active in the earth, in open manifestation of His power, to bring this purpose to fruition. Thus the psalm opens (verses 1-6) with a declaration of the Psalmist's desire that God would manifest Himself again as in days of old and continues (verses 7-18) with a contemplation of the manner by which God delivered His people and established them finally in Zion, His holy habitation. This is followed (verses 19-27) by a song of thanksgiving and a recollection of the triumphal procession when the ark was brought up to Zion. We are reinforced in our conviction that the psalm was actually written shortly after God made His covenant with David by the fact that it was in those promises that God confirmed the everlasting stability of David's throne and assured him that although he himself would not be permitted to build a house for God, a temple would be built by one in David's line of whom God said, "I will be his father, and he shall be my son". Thus the concluding part of the psalm (verses 28-35) expands into a consideration of Jerusalem with its temple, a house of prayer for all people (see Isaiah 56:6,7; Psalm 68:29,31), the centre of God's worldwide dominion when all the nations of the earth shall recognise Him and acknowledge His sovereignty.

David's longing (verses 1-6)

The opening words of the psalm, "Let God ('Elohim') arise, let his enemies be scattered: let them also that hate him flee before him" are an obvious reference to the words which Moses used (Numbers 10:35) when the ark of the covenant, the symbol of God's presence in the midst of His people, set forward on its journeys in the wilderness. Significantly, given the conclusions reached above concerning the manner in which God's purpose will eventually embrace all people, the covenant name "Yahweh" with its particular reference to Israel is replaced by the general title "Elohim". That the influence of the God of Israel who dwelt amongst them was not restricted to this nation and their borders, was indicated by the words of Joshua at their entry into the land when he referred to the ark as "the ark of the LORD, the Lord of all the earth" (Joshua 3:13). The record in Numbers 10 concerning the ark tells us that "the ark of the covenant of the LORD went before them" and the record in Judges tells how Deborah encouraged Barak with the words, "the LORD hath delivered Sisera into thine hand: is not the LORD gone out before thee?" (Judges 4:14). God has always gone forth before His people to ensure their victory. He prepares the way to ensure that in Him they will triumph. If we live in that confidence it remains true for us today.

This truth was reflected in the words of Psalm 68: "O God, when thou wentest forth before thy people ... the earth trembled" (verses 7,8, RV).

Returning to verse 1 of the psalm the phrase rendered "before him" is literally 'from his face' and it is the same word as that rendered "presence" in verses 2 and 8. The manifestation of God's presence brings terror to His enemies but joy and gladness to His people:

"As smoke is driven away, so drive them away: as wax melteth before the fire, so let the wicked perish at the presence of God. But let the righteous be glad; let them rejoice before God: yea let them exceedingly rejoice." (verses 2,3)

The wicked like smoke in the wind will be driven away. They will disappear before the fire of His wrath. But in an ever increasing crescendo of praise the righteous shall know joy and gladness. But if it is true that God goes before His people to ensure their victory, they must prepare the way for Him to act on their behalf for, as they sing praises to His name, they are exhorted also to "Cast up a high way for him that rideth through the deserts" (verse 4, RV).

There would appear to be no justification for the translation of the AV which reads, "Extol him that rideth upon the heavens". The Hebrew is almost exactly that of Isaiah's prophecy, "make straight in the desert a highway for our God" (Isaiah 40:3). The reference is to the practice whereby oriental kings sent messengers before them to prepare the way by clearing the path of all obstacles that might hinder or prevent the completion of the journey. No doubt this background can have more than one application, but in the context of our present thoughts, those who seek God to manifest Himself and go before them must themselves prepare the way by ensuring that lack of faith and faint-heartedness on their part do not impede the work of God.

The reference to the desert and the emphasis on His name of Yah (an abbreviated form of Yahweh) are clearly a recollection of the Exodus (see Exodus 15:2, RV margin). The exhortation is to "rejoice before him" for all that He has done which is, of course, comprehended in His name.

It is the contemplation of the character of Yahweh that causes the Psalmist to reflect:

"A father of the fatherless, and a judge of the widows, is God in his holy habitation. God setteth the solitary in families: he bringeth out those which are bound with chains: but the rebellious dwell in a dry land."

(verses 5,6)

Here is something truly remarkable. Earthly potentates, particularly in ancient times, were not renowned for their kindness to the poor and oppressed. They tended rather to be tyrants who surrounded themselves by the rich and the grand whom they imagined would add to the glory of their kingdom. In contrast, Israel's God is a defender and an avenger of the lonely and unprotected. The responsibility laid upon Israel in respect of the orphan and the widow was expressed in the most unequivocal terms (see Exodus 22:22-24). The contrast however, between earthly kings and the God of Heaven is so marked that it can be said truly that it turns human standards upside down. Deuteronomy 10 is particularly relevant for us:

"Behold, the heaven and the heaven of heavens is the LORD's thy God, the earth also, with all that therein is."

(verse 14)

"For the LORD your God is God of gods, and Lord of lords, a great God, a mighty, and a terrible, which regardeth not persons, nor taketh reward: he doth execute the judgment of the fatherless and widow, and loveth the stranger, in giving him food and raiment."

(verses 17,18)

No words of ours could possibly express adequately the greatness, the boundless might, the ineffable glory of Him to whom belong the heavens and the earth. All human dignity with its strutting arrogance fades into complete and utter insignificance before Him. Yet this is the God who has humbled Himself (Psalm 113:6) to execute the judgement of the fatherless and widow, from His holy habitation in heaven. These thoughts are particularly relevant to us for they are the words quoted by James in his Epistle:

"Pure religion and undefiled before God and the Father is this, To visit the fatherless and widows in

492

their affliction, and to keep himself unspotted from the world. My brethren, have not the faith of our Lord Jesus Christ, the Lord of glory, with respect of persons."

(1:27–2:1)

This loving care is extended also to the solitary (lit. 'lonely ones') whom God sets in families or literally 'a house or home'. Essentially this is God's family and it serves to emphasise the responsibility that we have towards one another in the house of God. There can surely be no greater indictment of our ecclesial life than to have amongst us, through no fault of their own, lonely brethren and sisters. The psalm nevertheless, is still dwelling upon the Exodus, for "He bringeth out those which are bound with chains" (i.e., "He leads captivity captive", verse 18). Thus he delivered Israel from the bondage of Egypt but the rebellious (the word used to describe the stubborn rebellious son – Deuteronomy 21:18,20) dwell in a parched and dry land for they perish in the wilderness (Psalm 107:4,40; Hebrews 3:7-11).

From Sinai To Zion (verses 7-18)

It was at Sinai that God first entered into covenant relationship with the people of Israel. It was on that mountain in awful splendour that He made Himself known to His people. Thus as verses 1 to 6 have introduced us to the thought of the Exodus, so verse 7, describing the beginning of the journey that should see the Lord enthroned in Zion, speaks of Him as if He were a military commander marching at the head of His people:

"O God, when thou wentest forth before thy people, when thou didst march through the wilderness. Selah."

The language of Exodus is immediately recalled:

"And the LORD went before them by day in a pillar of a cloud, to lead them the way; and by night in a pillar of fire, to give them light." (13:21)

The pillar of cloud and the pillar of fire were, of course, the visible tokens of God's presence in the midst of His people and the vivid and dramatic language of verse 8 describes the effects of His presence descending on the mountain of Sinai. Significantly there is a "Selah" indicating a pause for reflection and meditation at the end of verse 7 and

493

perhaps this can best be understood by the contrast presented by the warrior king who marches before his people and the shepherd who leads his people like a flock and provides for all their needs (see Psalm 77:16-20). This thought is reflected in the description of the continuing work of God presented in verse 9:

"The earth shook, the heavens also dropped at the presence of God: even Sinai itself was moved at the presence of God, the God of Israel. Thou, O God, didst send a plentiful rain, whereby thou didst confirm thine inheritance, when it was weary."   (verses 8,9)

As previously indicated, the language is drawn from Moses' blessings on the tribes (Deuteronomy 33) and the song of Deborah (Judges 5). We can readily appreciate the use of Moses' language but we might wonder why the Song of Deborah, which of course was itself drawing on the language of Moses, should play such a prominent part in the background of this psalm. There are two reasons that suggest themselves. Firstly the victory God wrought over Sisera and his host by the hand of Deborah and Barak was typical of the way God subdued all Israel's enemies that they might inherit the land. Secondly the emphasis upon women (Deborah and Jael) in this victory is a recurring theme in Psalm 68. It is surely an indication that there is no power in man to triumph over sin. It is of God and the seed of the woman is the means of God's triumph; just as ultimately it is the bride of Christ who will share the fruits of his victory.

The manifestation of God at Sinai struck terror into the hearts of the people. The earth trembled (RV) for there was an earthquake. The mountain itself "yon Sinai" (RV) shook at the presence of the God of Israel. There were thunderings and lightning, and the mountain top was covered in a cloud as the Lord descended in fire (Exodus 19:16-18). "But the heavens also dropped" and Judges 5 makes clear that the other phenomena were accompanied by a torrential rain (verse 4). But just as we have indicated above that God goes before His people to prepare the way before them, so also He prepared the land into which He would bring them. He sent upon the land a bounteous rain that it might be ready to be a home for

494

them when God established them there (see Exodus 15:17; Deuteronomy 11:9-12). This would not be a land like Egypt or the wilderness through which they passed, although that land also had known the weariness of drought in the past (Genesis 47).

So Israel came to dwell in the land. Again the fact that God had gone before and prepared the land for them is emphasised:

"Thy congregation dwelt therein: Thou, O God, didst prepare of thy goodness for the poor."   (verse 10, RV)

The Hebrew word translated "congregation" has been the cause of much discussion. The RV margin renders it "troop" and it is translated "company" in verse 30 of this same psalm. Together with the verb derived from it, it is used over 800 times in the text of the Old Testament and is most commonly translated 'life', 'live or living'. It is said that by derivation the word is used to describe a family, a class or group of people of one flesh and for our part we are happy to accept the translation "congregation" as describing the company of the people of Israel. We only mention this in detail because the word is also used in Ezekiel's prophecy where it is consistently translated "living creatures" (1:19,20,22; 3:13; 10:15,17,20) and this has led some to connect the verse in the psalm with the saints in glory.

This does not appear to us to be sound exegesis. It is not the way to compare the use of language in scripture and although the psalm is unquestionably Messianic and has a meaning for brethren and sisters in Christ the verse in question, in context, has clear reference to what God did for His people Israel in days of old. The word translated "poor" is directly related to that translated "affliction" in Exodus.

"I have surely seen the affliction of my people which are in Egypt."   (3:7)

"I will bring you up out of the affliction of Egypt … unto a land flowing with milk and honey."   (verse 17)

In a few graphic words, verses 11 to 14 describe the victories by which the land was won:

495

"The LORD giveth the word: the women that publish the tidings are a great host." (Psalm 68:11, RV) God has only to command and the victory is won. As in the beginning, God spoke and it was done. "And God said, Let there be light: and there was light" (Genesis 1:3; see also Psalm 33:6,9) The word translated "those" (AV) is in the feminine gender, hence the translation of the RV and it is in keeping with other scripture that the voices of the women should be heard celebrating the victory (see for example Exodus 15:20; 1 Samuel 18:6,7 and of course Judges 5). The result of the divine fiat was that "Kings of armies flee, they flee. And she that tarrieth at home divideth the spoil" (RV), "though ye may lie among the sheepfolds, the dove's wings are covered with silver, and her pinions with yellow gold" (*Cambridge Bible*) (verses 12,13).

The language draws heavily on the Song of Deborah and it has been suggested that they are the actual words that were sung by the women referred to in verse 11. Whether that conjecture be true or not we cannot say, but the plural "kings" recalls the words of Judges 5:19 and the vivid description of their panic stricken flight is illustrated by the double emphasis upon the word "flee". Again it reflects the language of Judges (4:15-17; 5:22). The title "King of armies" (lit. 'hosts') is unusual and would seem to be a direct allusion, by way of contrast, with Yahweh LORD of Hosts. Vast as their armies might be – all conquering perhaps, in human terms – they were impotent, powerless to resist Him who has at His command myriads of angels.

The return of the armies were looked for anxiously by those who waited at home. In anticipation they endeavoured to quell their fears by thinking of the spoil to be shared. So it had been with the mother of Sisera (Judges 5:29,30). As one writer has rendered part of her words "one coloured garment, two pieces of embroidery as spoil for my neck". With regard to verse 13 we have followed one of several suggestions to be found in the *Cambridge Bible* for it seems to us to capture the most reasonable sense of the words. Again there are clear references to the words of Deborah spoken concerning Reuben:

"By the watercourses of Reuben there were great resolves of heart. Why satest thou among the sheep-folds, to hear the pipings for the flocks? At the watercourses of Reuben there were great searchings of heart."   (Judges 5:15,16, RV)

Reuben was full of good resolutions. He searched his heart, he pondered over where his duty lay. But in the end it was the sound of the pipe and the bleating of the sheep that shut out the call to come and fight the Lord's battles. He stayed there at ease in his rustic life. It is a word of exhortation for all those who would engage themselves in the spiritual conflicts of life. So often we can be full of good intentions, having searched our hearts and yet still fail to answer the call because the everyday things of life are allowed to take precedence and shut out the call to fight the Lord's battles. We fall back into the same old rut. But though some like Reuben might show irresolution and cowardice, even these human failings had not prevented God from gaining victory. The evidence was to be seen in Israel, blessed by her God, established in the land He had promised. The dove is a symbol of the nation of Israel (see Isaiah 60:8; Hosea 7:11; 11:11; Song of Solomon 1:15; 2:14; 5:2). The quotations from the Song of Solomon were held dear particularly, for the book was esteemed because it was regarded by the Rabbis as demonstrating the intimacy of Israel's relationship with her God. So she was depicted in sweet repose, decked in silver and gold, reflecting the blessings God had bestowed upon her.

The imagery of verse 14 has perplexed most writers:

"When the Almighty scattered kings therein, it was as when it snoweth in Zalmon."   (RV)

The explanations offered are many but we suggest that perhaps one of the simplest is the most acceptable. The name Zalmon means 'dark or shady', almost certainly derived from its aspect. Thus the mountain clothed with snow would be transformed from its normal appearance by the glistering whiteness and would aptly serve as a figure of the manner by which God through the manifestation of His presence had lightened Israel's darkness by His victory over her enemies.

THE PRAISES OF ISRAEL (PSALMS 1–72)

So triumphantly the Lord comes to Zion. The surrounding hills and mountains which might have been thought by their eminence and grandeur to have prior claim to greatness are depicted as looking on in envy (verses 15,16). But, says David, "This is the hill which God desireth to dwell in; yea, the LORD will dwell in it for ever" (verse 16).

His entry into His rest is described in magnificent and dramatic terms. The march from Sinai (verse 7) is now completed.

"The chariots of God are twenty thousand, even thousands of angels" (verse 17). The Lord came from Sinai into the holy place (RV). So the great purpose for which God came down (Exodus 3:8) is now complete. He is enthroned in Zion and His people are settled in the land. This section of the psalm closes with the triumphant declaration:

"Thou hast ascended on high, thou hast led captivity captive: thou hast received gifts for men; yea, for the rebellious also, that the LORD God might dwell among them."   (verse 18)

We have already commented on the words, "He ascended up on high". The RV says "thou hast led *thy* captivity captive" indicating that it was the people of Israel delivered from their captivity in Egypt who became God's captive people, bondservants of the Most High. The deliverance was accompanied by other factors. He "received gifts for men". Paul writing in Ephesians says that He "gave gifts unto men" (4:8) and we have seen that this related to the gifts of the Spirit for "he gave some, apostles; and some, prophets; and some, evangelists; and some, pastors and teachers" (4:11). This apparent discrepancy has caused difficulty for many in understanding Paul's use of the psalm. However, closer examination of the psalm resolves the problem. The language has its origin in the provisions that God made for His people:

"Bring the tribe of Levi near, and present them before Aaron the priest, that they might minister unto him. And they shall keep his charge, and the charge of the whole congregation before the tabernacle of the

498

congregation, to do the service of the tabernacle ... And thou shalt give the Levites unto Aaron and to his sons: they are wholly given unto him out (on the behalf, RV margin) of the children of Israel." (Numbers 3:6-9)

"And I, behold, I have taken your brethren the Levites from among the children of Israel: to you they are a gift, given unto the LORD." (Numbers 18:6, RV)

At one and the same time the Levites were regarded as "a gift, given unto the LORD" and also as a gift given by Him to the people. So in the words of the psalm "thou hast received gifts for men". When the two aspects of the words are understood, the difficulty disappears. They are both present in the psalm but for his purposes Paul uses only the second sense that God gave gifts to men. All this was done "for the rebellious also". The goodness of God was manifest towards this people even though they were stubborn and rebellious (Numbers 20:24; Deuteronomy 1:26) and the reason for all this was, "that the LORD God might dwell among them". It was that there should be a dwelling place among the children of Israel – first in the tabernacle in the wilderness and finally in the temple that Solomon built at Jerusalem.

But these were but shadows of that spiritual house made up not of material things but of "living stones":

"built upon the foundation of the apostles and prophets, Jesus Christ himself being the chief corner stone; in whom all the building fitly framed together groweth unto an holy temple in the Lord: in whom ye also are builded together for an habitation of God through the Spirit." (Ephesians 2:20-22)

Verses 19-23

Although in our consideration of the structure of the psalm we connected verses 19 to 27 together, for convenience it seems appropriate to subdivide this section as the Psalmist turns from his review of God's triumphs on behalf of his people in the distant past, on the journey to His ultimate resting place in Zion, to more immediate events that culminated in the Covenant that God made with him concerning his house and his throne:

"Blessed be the Lord, who daily loadeth us with benefits, even the God of our salvation. Selah."

(verse 19)

The opening epithet, "Blessed be the Lord" recalls once more the language of Deborah's song for she rejoices in similar fashion as she contemplates the wonderful victory His hand wrought on behalf of His people (Judges 5:2,9).

The RV renders the latter part of the verse differently and it would appear, with more accuracy: "Who daily beareth our burden, even the God who is our salvation". The writer does not have a first hand knowledge of Hebrew but it does seem that on occasions some words are capable of two meanings and God, by His Spirit, uses them in certain contexts to convey a twofold meaning (see for example Psalm 32:6 with AV margin). Thus it is said of the word rendered "beareth our burden" in the RV, "This verb combines two meanings, (1) to put a burden upon another and (2) to bear a burden" (*The Psalms*, Vol. 1, Perowne, page 557). How true it is that God in the circumstances of life lays burdens upon His people to chasten and test them, but how true also that the God who is terrible in majesty is a God of tenderness and love for, in faith, he desires His servants to cast their burdens upon Him that He might bear them. Thus Psalm 37 reads literally "roll thy way upon the LORD" (verse 5, AV margin) and the Apostle Peter exhorts us, "casting all your care upon him; for he careth for you" (1 Peter 5:7). This is truly the God of our salvation and the "Selah" instructing us to pause and meditate before we continue, helps us to appreciate the wonder of all that God has done for those who put their trust in Him.

The theme is taken up again in the following verse:

"God is unto us a God of deliverances; and unto JEHOVAH (Yahweh) the Lord belong the issues from death." (verse 20, RV)

The passage is not specifically talking about the resurrection of the body. The God of deliverances (plural) is a God who can deliver out of all manner of circumstances. Even in the uttermost extremity when death threatens He has the power to save. Literally the Hebrew means "the ways from death" and it was not only

500

true of individuals such as David whom God delivered from Saul time and again but also of Israel nationally. Although Israel as a nation might be dead and her people scattered, God could breathe new life into them. There would be a national resurrection. (Hosea 6:1,2; Ezekiel 37).

For us, however, the hope of resurrection to eternal life, which is encompassed in the words, must be the primary significance. We look for the coming of the one who said:

"I am he that liveth, and was dead; and, behold I am alive for evermore, Amen; and have the keys of hell and of death." (Revelation 1:18)

In hope of life we heed the word of God:

"Keep thy heart with all diligence; for out of it are the issues of life." (Proverbs 4:23)

But if God is able to deliver, even from death, so also He is able to destroy those who oppose Him and show themselves to be the enemies of His people:

"But God shall wound the head of his enemies, and the hairy scalp of such an one as goeth on still in his trespasses." (Psalm 68:21)

It is possible that behind the words "God shall wound the head of his enemies" is the record of Judges 5 concerning the manner in which Jael killed Sisera (see verse 26).

Long hair is said to be representative of the strength and vigour of youth, as for instance, in the case of Absalom. Involved in this would also be the wilfulness and stubbornness of youth. A further suggestion is that in ancient times it was customary for warriors to consecrate themselves to the task before them by taking a vow which entailed leaving their hair to grow until victory was finally won. Thus "I will make mine arrows drunk with blood ... the blood of the slain and of the captives, from the hairy head of the enemy" (Deuteronomy 32:42, with RV margin). The scalp stands by metonymy for the man himself and the idea of going on still in trespasses conveys the idea of open defiance. The message is, however, that all man's persistence in opposing God and His people is futile for it is Israel's God who holds the issues of life and death and

He will destroy all those who seek to frustrate His purpose.

The next verse declares:

"The Lord said, I will bring again from Bashan, I will bring my people again from the depths of the sea."

(verse 22)

In the Hebrew, however, there is no object to the verb. Some supply, with the AV, "my people" and others with the RV "them". In the one instance the reference is to Israel, and in the other, given the context, to the enemies spoken of in verse 21.

The words "The Lord said" might imply that what follows is a quotation from earlier scripture, but there does not appear to be a passage that corresponds. It must therefore be regarded as a divine edict and following the RV we understand the words as a warning to those spoken of in the previous verse, that though they try to hide in the mountains of Bashan or in the very depths of the sea, they could not escape, for God would seek them out that His people may dip their foot in the blood of their enemies (verse 23). Before leaving this sub-section an interesting comparison can be found in Amos where similar language is used to describe how God will seek out sinful Israelites (9:2,3).

It is a sobering thought that in this context the judgement on the oppressor is the precursor of the deliverance of God's people and through this judgement and deliverance God's righteousness is vindicated. We know that in the day of the Lord's coming this will certainly be true for Israel after the flesh. They will be humbled by the oppressor before God judges these nations and delivers His people. Might it not be true also of the experience of Israel after the spirit that there must first be a period of trial and persecution before they too are delivered by the coming of the Lord Jesus?

Verses 24-27

The substance of verses 19 to 23 appears to establish principles whereby God reacts to the needs of His people and the cruelty of those who oppress them. In that sense it is descriptive of God's actions in the past, present and future. It had an immediate significance for David reflecting his own experiences prior to his establishment in Zion.

All this work of God in subduing his enemies culminated in the day when David finally brought the ark of God to the sanctuary he had prepared for it; when the journey Israel's God began at Sinai finally ended in His enthronement in Zion. Although this was a very real and substantial event it was nevertheless only a shadow of the glory to be revealed in the day when God consummates His purpose in the earth, and realising the incipient nature of the events the psalm records, we can appreciate more fully its prophetic import. It is this future aspect that becomes more apparent as the theme is developed and the psalm draws to its conclusion.

David recalls then that solemn yet joyful procession when the ark was carried from the house of Obed-edom to its resting-place in Zion:

'They have seen thy goings, O God; even the goings of my God, my King (into, RV) the sanctuary. The singers went before, the players on instruments followed after; among them (in the midst of, RV) were the damsels playing with timbrels. Bless ye God in the congregations, even the Lord from (ye that are of, RV) the fountain of Israel. There is little Benjamin with their ruler, the princes of Judah and their council (company, RV margin), the princes of Zebulun, and the princes of Naphtali." (verses 24-27)

As he had gone forth in triumph in days of old (see verses 7,8) so now, in the sight of men He comes into the sanctuary. David describes Him as "my God, my King" and the expression "my King" is emphatic, for He who is sovereign over His people leads the procession. First the singers then the minstrels, then on either side the damsels playing their tambourines and no doubt singing. Perhaps the words of verse 26 are part of the song that was sung. The word "congregations" is plural but it has been pointed out that this may be only to convey the idea of fulness (Gesenius). It was the full congregation, all the people of Israel, who gave their hearts to this project, for they were of the fountain of Israel. The patriarch Jacob

(Israel) was the source from which the whole nation had issued forth as a stream. It was a reminder to them of the privilege of their ancestry. The meaning, of course, looking forward from this time to the outworking of God's purpose was not confined to Israel after the flesh.

> "For they are not all Israel, which are of Israel: neither, because they are the seed of Abraham, are they all children: but, In Isaac shall thy seed be called. That is, They which are the children of the flesh, these are not the children of God: but the children of the promise are counted for the seed." (Romans 9:6-8)

Thus we are encompassed within the words of the psalm – numbered amongst those who shall accompany the King of Glory. "The LORD strong and mighty, the LORD mighty in battle ... the LORD of hosts (Psalm 24:8,10), when, manifest in the Lord Jesus Christ and a multitude of redeemed, He shall come to the place He has chosen to dwell, in Zion.

Following the singers and the minstrels come the tribes of Israel represented here by Benjamin and Judah from the southern kingdom and Zebulun and Naphtali from the northern kingdom. Clearly these are chosen to stand for all Israel for, united under David, the procession looks forward to the day when:

> "I will make them one nation in the land upon the mountains of Israel; and one king shall be king to them all." (Ezekiel 37:22)

Little Benjamin leads the way. So described because not only was he the youngest of Jacob's sons but he was also the smallest of the tribes (1 Samuel 9:21). It was to the inheritance of Benjamin that Jerusalem belonged (Deuteronomy 33:12; Joshua 18:6) and literally the text reads, 'There is little Benjamin their ruler, the princes of Judah, their company'. It hardly seems appropriate as some suggest that Benjamin is named as leader because Saul, Israel's first king, sprang out of him. More significant surely is the prophetic import of the events surrounding his birth, i.e., Benoni – the son of my sorrows and Benjamin – the son of my right hand (see Genesis 35:18 with Psalm 80:17). In this way it would point forward to the Lord Jesus Christ. Judah the largest and

504

strongest of the tribes follows. The word for company is associated with the word for stone, conveying the idea of compactness or strength. A bulwark amongst the tribes. Zebulun and Naphtali, the representatives of the northern kingdom are chosen perhaps because of their prominence in the defeat of Sisera's army and the place they occupy in the Song of Deborah (Judges 5:18).

Verses 28-35
The main theme of this final section is the subjugation of all nations and their recognition of the sovereignty of Israel's God over all the earth. In this respect Psalm 68, although written by David and not Hezekiah, is associated with the two previous psalms that have similar themes. The purpose of Yahweh's enthronement in Zion is that all the world might be converted to the hope of Israel and look to her God for deliverance.

Thus the Psalmist begins by calling upon Israel to recognise all that has been accomplished by the manifestation of His strength and power. "Thy God hath commanded thy strength" (verse 28). The supremacy which Israel now enjoys (i.e., her strength) has been ordained by God. Her exaltation among the nations has been accomplished by His power. This brief summary of the work of God is the basis of the prayer that follows, "Be strong, O God, thou that hast wrought for us" (verse 28, RV margin). In other words 'Complete the task already begun. Show thyself strong as in times past and bring all nations to yield to your authority'.

"Because of thy temple at Jerusalem shall kings bring presents unto thee." (verse 29)
As a consequence of God's word going forth from Jerusalem, nations shall willingly acknowledge Him and freely bring their gifts. There was an incipient fulfilment in the days of Hezekiah:

"And many brought gifts unto the LORD to Jerusalem, and presents to Hezekiah king of Judah: so that he was magnified in the sight of all nations thenceforth."
(2 Chronicles 32:23)

505

The words carry us forward, however, to the day when the Lord Jesus shall sit on David's throne (see Psalm 72:10,11; 76:11,12; Isaiah 18:7).

But not all kings will submit immediately so the prayer continues that God would compel those who oppose themselves to acknowledge His authority:

> "Rebuke the wild beast of the reeds, the multitude of the bulls, with the calves of the peoples (RV), till every one submit himself with pieces of silver: scatter thou the people that delight in war."   (verse 30)

It is natural to identify the wild beast of the reeds, thought by most to be either the crocodile or the hippopotamus, with Egypt. There does, however, appear to be something incongruous about symbolising Egypt by this beast and referring to Egypt directly as a representative of those nations that submit themselves to God in the very next verse (31).

Alternatives have been suggested and amongst them the idea that it is the lion which crouches amongst the reeds at river banks has a certain appeal, for it would then represent Babylon. This of course is not a matter of prime importance for the significance of the passage is not affected by the identity of the nation. The bulls and the calves probably stand for the leaders of the nations and those who follow them. Note that the word "people", a collective noun, is actually in the plural form, i.e., "calves of the peoples". Rebuked by God, their pride and arrogance abased they finally bring their gifts of silver and the nations which delight in war are compelled to submit. So the homage of all nations is expressed:

> "Princes shall come out of Egypt; Ethiopia shall soon stretch out her hands unto God."   (verse 31)

Egypt and Ethiopia are often linked together: Egypt, a neighbour of Israel, an ancient enemy; Ethiopia, a more remote nation of proud and formidable reputation. The use of these two nations in this context is to emphasise the fact that the most inveterate foes of Israel and the more remote nations, however noble their standing, will acknowledge the supremacy of Israel's God. That the nations mentioned are representative of all nations is evident for:

"Sing unto God, ye kingdoms of the earth; O sing praises unto the Lord; Selah."   (verse 32)

Once again the instruction to pause and reflect is most significant at this juncture for we have come to the conclusion of the whole matter. Israel's exaltation is intended that her God might be recognised and praised by all the earth. The God whom they are exhorted to unite in praising is then described in most graphic and awesome terms:

"To him that rideth upon the heavens of heavens, which were of old; lo, he doth send out his voice, and that a mighty voice. Ascribe ye strength unto God: his excellency is over Israel, and his strength is in the clouds. O God, thou art terrible out of thy holy places: the God of Israel is he that giveth strength and power unto his people."   (verses 33-35)

The heavens of heavens are the highest heavens and they are described as being "of old". The God who rode through the desert (verse 4) when He was manifest in the affairs of men, now exalted above all is depicted figuratively as riding in His chariot across the heavens. The heavens that were of old are those mentioned in Genesis 1:1, before the creation of the heavens that encompass the earth described in the remainder of the chapter. The RV translates, "he uttereth his voice and that a mighty voice".

The language is reminiscent of an earlier psalm: "The voice of the LORD is upon the waters: the God of glory thundereth" (29:3). He sends forth His voice and it is done, for with His word there is power to perform. It is for this reason that no man can frustrate His will or prevent His purpose from being carried out. Therefore says the song, "Ascribe ye strength unto God". Recognise His power and authority for because of it "his excellency is over Israel, and his strength is in the clouds". His power and majesty overshadow Israel to protect and bless them and His strength is not confined to the earth but extends throughout the universe, for He is everywhere present by His Spirit.

We have previously emphasised the allusions not only to Judges 5 but also to Deuteronomy 33 and the words of the two verses we have just considered are very clearly drawn from the words of Deuteronomy:

"There is none like unto God, O Jeshurun, who rideth upon the heaven for thy help, and in his excellency on the skies." (33:26, RV)

Truly all the nations of the earth could sing:

"O God, thou art terrible out of thy holy places: the God of Israel is he that giveth strength and power unto his people." (Psalm 68:35)

The fact that "holy places" (literally 'sanctuaries') is plural has been described as 'poetic licence'. Others speak of the plural as describing the various parts of the sanctuary, but surely the significance of the plural is obvious. The psalm has spoken of God manifest in the earth, finally coming to dwell in Zion His earthly sanctuary. But the psalm has also spoken in the grandest terms of the majesty and splendour of the God who, after delivering His people ascended on high (verse 18). He rideth upon the heavens of heavens. Not only did he have an earthly sanctuary from whence His authority and power was exercised, but He also had a heavenly sanctuary from whence His Spirit radiated throughout all space. Heaven was His dwelling place (see 1 Kings 8:30,34,36, etc.).

So the nations acknowledge the awful might of He who is the God of Israel, the source of their strength; by whose power they will be exalted amongst the nations that through them all the earth might turn to their God.

In this grand consummation of God's purpose in the earth, both Israel and all nations can only respond in humble acknowledgement of all that He has done.

"Blessed be God." (verse 35)

PSALM 69

THE psalm bears the inscription "of David", and that the "Sweet psalmist of Israel" was indeed the author is confirmed by the Apostle Paul when citing verses 22 and 23:

"And David saith, Let their table be made a snare, and a trap, and a stumbling block, and a recompence unto them: let their eyes be darkened, that they may not see, and bow down their back alway."

(Romans 11:9,10)

The attitude of most commentators and their approach to scripture generally can be summed up in the words of one: "When this psalm was written we have no certain clue to guide us" (Perowne – *The Psalms,* Vol. 1, page 560). Generally they seek to ascribe a late date to the psalm, possibly after the captivity, although there is a strong body of opinion that believes that Jeremiah was the author.

If there were no inscription or word of scripture in support of the Davidic authorship one could understand the support for Jeremiah. We know of at least one Christadelphian writer who offered an ingenious but unconvincing argument in an attempt to circumvent the references to David and maintain the connection with Jeremiah. The appropriateness of the psalm to Jeremiah's life and experience will be discussed briefly later.

The fact remains, however, that although we cannot be completely certain that the ascriptions of authorship were part of the original compositions of the psalms they are beyond doubt of very ancient authority and personally we do not know of a single instance where there are grounds for calling their credibility into question. The Apostle Paul's quotation should remove any lingering doubts that any have. It is hardly sound exposition to claim that in ascribing the words to David, Paul meant to say no more than 'The Book of Psalms saith' as though he believed that all the psalms were written by David. It appears to the writer that the main problem that the psalm presents to many who have attempted to expound it, is that in their view it does not readily lend itself to the circumstances and events of David's life – a view that we hope to show conclusively is totally without foundation.

Structure

The psalm consists in the AV of 36 verses. In endeavouring to discover the structure of a psalm we usually read it several times and look for natural breaks or changes in theme or emphasis. However, remembering we are reading a translation it is wise to check reliable commentators to ensure that the original text does not indicate natural divisions that are not apparent in the English translation. Our experience is that usually commentators have followed the same method as we have adopted, often agreeing in general terms but sometimes offering alternatives that are worthy of consideration.

We mention this because perusing *The Speakers Commentary* a little while ago we read the introduction to Psalm 69. This work is one of the few which, accepting the inspiration of scripture, dismisses all other suggestions and affirms steadfastly the Davidic authorship. In this connection, however, the authors made the following comment:

> "The metrical system is highly artistic, a fact nearly conclusive against the supposition of a late date; it consists of strophes responding to each other in reverse order, with 4,8,9,8,4 verses severally; with a liturgical close, verses 34 to 36." (Volume 4, page 325)

We are not qualified to offer an opinion on the Hebrew text but, following the English translation, we found that the psalm could certainly be divided in the way indicated and, giving our own headings, we have decided to follow this structure.

The psalm is clearly Messianic with more passages quoted or alluded to in relation to the Lord Jesus than any other. Much of its relevance to the Lord Jesus, even when it is not directly quoted, arises out of the psalm's appropriateness to events in the life of David. For this reason we propose to examine the psalm first in an analytical fashion without reference to the life of David or the Lord Jesus Christ. We shall endeavour to relate the psalm to both David and his greater Son after we have completed this task.

A Flood of Adversity (verses 1-4)
It is important to appreciate that the language of verses 1 and 2 is metaphorical in its use and not as some maintain a direct reference to the experiences of Jeremiah (Jeremiah 38:6).
"Save me, O God; for the waters are come in unto my soul. I sink in deep mire, where there is no standing: I am come into deep waters, where the floods overflow me." (verses 1,2)
The language, of course, is a common Biblical metaphor for tribulation and adversity, particularly in the psalms. (see Psalms 18:16; 32:6; 124:4; see also Lamentations 3:54). In the opening words the Psalmist likens himself to a drowning man. The language of Jonah (2:1-5) should be compared where the words have both a literal and symbolic meaning in the experience of that prophet.

In the words that follow, the Psalmist uses graphically two similar but diverse figures. The first refers to what we might describe as 'quick-sands'. In illustration some have quoted the words of Thomson in the *Land and the Book* (page 360) when he speaks of quagmires being common in Palestine and treacherous in the way the unwary could sink in them. The second figure, while maintaining the idea of being swallowed up by the waters, conveys the idea of a man being swept away by the current into deep waters which threaten to engulf him. Just a point of interest: the Hebrew word rendered "flood" in this passage is the "Shibboleth" (Judges 12:6) which the men of Ephraim found so difficult to pronounce.

The picture presented by these two verses is clear. It is of a man who finds himself in circumstances that threaten his life which appears to hang in the very balance. The floods of trouble and adversity had well nigh swept him away and in the midst of the roaring of the waters against which all human effort seemed utterly futile he cries unto his God to save him. His plight was desperate:

"I am weary of my crying: my throat is dried: mine eyes fail while I wait for my God. They that hate me without a cause are more than the hairs of my head: they that would destroy me, being mine enemies wrongfully, are mighty: then I had to restore (RV margin) that which I took not away." (verses 3,4)

The cause of the Psalmist's troubles is made clear. He is surrounded by implacable enemies who desire only his destruction. Their hatred is unjustified, there is no cause for it. They are powerful men who wrongfully (lit. falsely) accuse him. Their hostility was based upon misrepresentation and slander. They had accused him of extortion, of seizing that which was not rightfully his and were demanding restitution. So numerous were they that the Psalmist describes them as "more than the hairs of my head". Perhaps if we ever feel like the Psalmist we can find comfort in the words of the Lord Jesus that "even the very hairs of your head are all numbered" (Luke 12:7) and again "But there shall not an hair of your head perish" (Luke 21:18. Compare also verses 16,17 with Psalm 69 verses 8,9). God is in complete control. He has counted the very hairs of our head and those who might hate us without a cause are also numbered in more senses than one.

In his dilemma the Psalmist had cried to God and there had been no apparent response. He still waited upon God and felt a sense of bodily and spiritual exhaustion. Weak from long hours of crying, his throat was dry and burning from the wrestlings in prayer that maintained him during this crisis in his life.

The Cause of His Persecution (verses 5-12)

This section takes us to the very heart of the psalm's message, for it makes clear the reasons for the hatred that his enemies bear towards him.

First, however, he acknowledges that in all his troubles he has no cause for bitterness towards God, for he confesses that he has behaved foolishly and sinned. God has searched him and known him (verse 5). His primary

concern nevertheless is that God will show mercy and
deliver him, that faithful men who seek God might not be
ashamed and confounded through his demise (verse 6).
Perhaps this was because they had been associated with
him in his endeavour to maintain his fidelity to God and
in his zeal and enthusiasm for the things in which Israel's
God delighted. His appeal, in the titles and Name that he
uses is an acknowledgement of the sovereignty of God and
of His faithfulness to the covenant that He had made with
His people.

"Lord (*Adonai*) Yahweh of hosts (*Tzvaoth*) ... God
(*Elohim*) of Israel." (verse 6)

He feels that dishonour must fall upon those that wait
upon God if he is abandoned to his enemies, for it is for
God's sake that he suffers in this way and if it appeared
that God had deserted him their hope would also appear
to be vain.

"Because for thy sake I have borne reproach; shame
hath covered my face." (verse 7)

They were his enemies because in fact they were God's
enemies. They hated him, whatever the pretext might
have been, because of his faithfulness to Israel's God.
Even his close family relations had separated themselves
from him:

"I am become a stranger unto my brethren, and an
alien unto my mother's children." (verse 8)

And the reason for all this antipathy? Perhaps the
answer is given in a key verse of the psalm:

"For the zeal of thine house hath eaten me up; and
the reproaches of them that reproach (RV) thee are
fallen upon me." (verse 9)

His love for God's house like a consuming fire had eaten
him up. Like the burnt offering, his devotion ascended like
a sweet-smelling savour before God, but his jealousy for
the dwelling place of God had brought only reproach.
Family and friends reproached him because of his love for
God's house; in effect they were reproaching God. It was
because of his zeal for God that they reviled him; it was
their antagonism towards the things in which he
delighted that was the cause of their hatred. The

513

Psalmist's reaction to their bitter words was to mourn that men who belonged to God's covenant people could so lightly regard their heritage:

"When I wept, and chastened my soul with fasting, that was to my reproach. I made sackcloth also my garment; and I became a proverb to them."

(verses 10,11)

He fasted and wore sackcloth in his distress. Their response was to make pithy (Strong's) comments about him. The word carries the idea of jesting. He had become a joke, an object of derision. Even the judges and rulers, those that sat in the gate, spoke about him and against him. It was the main topic of gossip. At the other end of the spectrum he had become the target of the comic songs of the drunken revellers (verse 12). Uppermost in the Psalmist's consciousness was his realisation that he was hated above all things because of his devotion to Israel's God.

He Lays His Cause Before God (verses 13-21)

"But as for me, my prayer is unto thee, O LORD, in an acceptable time: O God, in the multitude of thy mercy hear me, in the truth of thy salvation."   (verse 13)

In the face of all his trouble the Psalmist has only one recourse, to turn to his God. So his desire is that his prayer might ascend before the Lord in an acceptable time, that is that God would accept his pleading. He could not be sure that the time was right for God to deliver him. Literally the phrase means 'a time of good pleasure' and the words of Isaiah are particularly enlightening. "In an acceptable time have I heard thee" (Isaiah 49:8).

He depends totally on the faithfulness of the God who had shown Himself gracious in his past experience, and recalls the qualities that were characteristic of Him when He declared His Name to Moses "abundant in goodness (lovingkindness) and truth" (Exodus 34:6, compare also with Psalm 69:16). The intervening verses (14,15) repeat the vivid imagery of the psalm's opening verses as he pleads that the deep might not swallow him up. His plea is "Turn unto me (verse 16) ... And hide not thy face" (verse 17).

514

Turning carries the idea of 'looking unto' and contrasts naturally with the hiding of the face, which he fears. Surely God must hear him for he is totally committed to His cause.

"Hear me speedily. Draw nigh unto my soul, and redeem it: deliver me because of mine enemies."
(verses 17,18)

Again the emphasis is upon the fact that if his enemies triumphed then they would regard his trust in God as unfounded and His Name would be dishonoured.

Once more the Psalmist reiterates his plight recalling the words he has used earlier "Thou knowest (RV) my reproach and my shame, and my dishonour" (verse 19). Apparently there is tremendous emphasis upon the word "know" for the Psalmist realises that God is in control. All his enemies are in His sight (verse 19) for they are all known of Him.

His sufferings have brought him to the depths of despair resulting not just in mental anguish but also in physical suffering.

"Reproach hath broken my heart; and I am full of heaviness." (verse 20, RV margin, "sore sick")

His enemies were implacable, there was no pity. They were determined to isolate him and discredit him.

"And I looked for some to take pity, but there was none; and for comforters, but I found none." (verse 20)

But not content with merely refusing him sympathy, they sought to aggravate his sufferings,

"They gave me also gall for my meat; and in my thirst they gave me vinegar to drink." (verse 21)

In their original setting the words are not to be taken literally. They describe in a metaphorical way the manner in which his enemies sought to add to his sufferings. It was as though they put bitter gall in his food and gave him vinegar to intensify his thirst.

Reward them according to their works (verses 22-29)

This section, no doubt, causes difficulty for many because of what they perceive to be the vengeful tone of the sentiments expressed. It comes into the same category as the imprecatory psalms and they feel it to be contrary to the spirit and tone of the New Testament.

This, of course, is to misunderstand the intentions of the Psalmist who, directly because of his love for God, has been subjected to the most intense hatred. Once we appreciate that the writer was David we must acknowledge also that he was the Lord's anointed and that as such he was God's representative upon the throne of Israel. It was the reproaches of those who had reproached God which had fallen upon him. Thus he cries:

> "Let their table become a snare before them: and that which should have been for their welfare, let it become a trap." (verse 22)

The language, of course, is contrasted with the previous verse. As they had sought to aggravate the sufferings of God's servant so now his plea is that that which should have been for their pleasure should become the means of their ruin. The table was a symbol of fellowship and prosperity and it was to become a snare to them. What they thought was for their benefit was to become a trap in the midst of their security ("welfare", Hebrew, *shalom,* peace). The picture is of men who have done their worst and rest at ease without care or thought for the wickedness they have wrought, only to be overcome by sudden destruction (see 1 Thessalonians 5:3). As they have loved darkness so let darkness overtake them, let them be confirmed in the choice they have made. Let their strength, in which they delighted, depart from them (verse 23).

> "Pour out thine indignation upon them, and let thy wrathful anger take hold of them. Let their habitation be desolate; and let none dwell in their tents."
> (verses 24,25)

The figure is taken from the nomadic life with which men of Israel would be well acquainted. What we have to understand is that there was no greater disaster than the blotting out of the family name and that is the picture presented of a desolate habitation and empty tents. It is the reward of the wicked, for sinners shall be consumed out of the earth and the wicked shall be no more (Psalm

104:35). This was to be their reward for persecuting him whom God had smitten, foretelling of the grief of those whom God had wounded (verse 26). Therefore he cries:

"Add iniquity unto their iniquity: and let them not come into thy righteousness. Let them be blotted out of the book of the living, and not be written with the righteous." (verses 27,28)

Let their iniquities accumulate and let not forgiveness (thy righteousness) be extended to them. They have no place in "the book of life" (RV). Their names will not be enrolled amongst the righteous.

If these sentiments were provoked by personal animosity it would be difficult to understand them, but these are the words of the Lord's anointed, spoken through the influence of the spirit, describing the fate, not only of those immediately involved, but of all those like them in every generation who reproach God and those who seek to serve Him.

In contrast the prayer of the Psalmist is:

"But I am poor and sorrowful: let thy salvation, O God, set me up on high." (verse 29)

Though now oppressed, his faith would be vindicated and he would be exalted when his enemies were laid low.

The Offerings of the Righteous (verses 30-33)

The Psalmist turns now in his concluding thoughts to his worship of the God for whom he had suffered reproach.

"I will praise the name of God with a song, and will magnify him with thanksgiving." (verse 30)

He will lift his voice in a hymn of joy in which he would recognise the greatness of God (i.e., magnify him) in his outpouring of thanksgiving. This would be more acceptable than any animal sacrifice, better than an ox or bullock that had horns and hoofs. The horns indicate that the animal was full grown, i.e., more than three years old, and the hoofs indicate that the animal was clean and suitable for sacrifice (see Leviticus 11:3). But spiritual sacrifices were far more acceptable than even the most perfect of beasts (Psalm 50:9-15).

When the humble see this they will rejoice and their hearts will be revived (made alive) because they seek God (verse 32).

> "For the LORD heareth the poor, and despiseth not his prisoners." (verse 33)

The references to God's prisoners does not mean that they have literally been cast into the prison house. It is almost certainly an allusion to the Hebrew idiom whereby suffering and affliction is referred to as captivity (see Job 42:10). God had loosed the bands of their sufferings and delivered them out of all their tribulations.

A Final Paean of Praise (verses 34-36)

The Psalmist calls all creation to praise the Lord (verse 34) for He will save Zion and build the cities of Judah, so that the righteous may possess them and dwell in them for ever. It is those who are Israelites indeed that will enjoy this blessing, the true seed who love the Name of the Lord their God (verses 35,36).

The Life of David

We believe that a careful reading of the historical background and appropriate psalms will show that David was a man with an overwhelming desire to build a house for God. He had talked about it with those of like mind when he had kept the sheep at Bethlehem (Psalm 132:3-6). This zeal was initially fulfilled when he built his tabernacle and brought the ark home to Zion. But this was not sufficient for David and his thoughts were soon dwelling on the erection of a more permanent structure (2 Samuel 7). Although David was not to be the one who should build the house, his enthusiasm was unabated and he spent the remainder of his life preparing and gathering the necessary materials and treasures for his son to build that house (see 1 Chronicles 22).

It may not be readily apparent but we believe that David's zeal for God's house was not shared by the majority in Israel. In fact there was active opposition to the proposal, particularly by many who were powerful and influential. It is interesting to note that Joab who stood with David through all his trials did not support Solomon. Ever the opportunist he had his finger on the pulse. He knew that the people were not of a mind to make the necessary sacrifices to build a house for God. Foolishly, forgetting that it was impossible to frustrate the word of God, he gave his support to Adonijah.

David's desire to number Israel was also, we suggest, motivated by his zeal for God's house. The revenue raised from the census was to be devoted to that cause. It is significant that it was this event that led to the selection of the threshing-floor of Ornan the Jebusite as the site of the future temple. Note that throughout this event the anger of the Lord was kindled against Israel, not David (2 Samuel 24:1; 1 Chronicles 21:7), although David's concern, as a good shepherd, was for his sheep (2 Samuel 24:17). In this event also, Joab, knowing the hearts of the people and their unwillingness to pay the half-shekel of the sanctuary, sought first to persuade David not to undertake the numbering (24:2-4), and then to frustrate the king's purpose by not numbering the people in the appointed manner (1 Chronicles 27:24). Indeed at this very time it would appear that Joab was plotting with Adonijah (1 Kings 1:5-7). The people and those who were powerful in the land were disillusioned with the ageing king. They had no enthusiasm for what they saw as an old man's foolishness. Against this background it has to be remembered that David, following his sin in the matter of Bathsheba and Uriah the Hittite, suffered both physical illness and mental stress. He lost his former decisiveness and his enemies, who were many, waited hopefully for him to die (see Psalms 38,39,41, etc.).

Knowing of his sin it is not hard to imagine how they would regard these things that befell him as a punishment, a curse from God. When he sought to encourage the people to share his zeal for God's house they would use them to discredit him, to reproach him; to contend that God was not with him, thus indicating, not His approval, but His displeasure that David should treasure these ambitions in his heart. Their real motive was that they did not share David's love for God, and self-interest drove them to seek to frustrate God's purpose by either deposing David or preventing Solomon from ascending the throne.

THE PRAISES OF ISRAEL (PSALMS 1–72)

So it was eminently true of David, "the zeal of thine house hath eaten me up; and the reproaches of them that reproached thee are fallen upon me". A brief reference in 1 Chronicles 22 sums up the background to the psalm:

"Now, behold, in my trouble I have prepared for the house of the LORD ..."   (1 Chronicles 22:14)

The Lord Jesus Christ

The Messianic nature of the psalm is plain. So many of David's experiences were replicated in the life of the Lord Jesus and as stated the psalm has more passages than any other either quoted or alluded to in the New Testament. We list below some of those we have identified.

"I am become a stranger unto my brethren, and an alien unto my mother's children" (N.B. implicit reference to virgin birth) (verse 8).	Mark 3:21,31-35
"The zeal of thine house hath eaten me up" (verse 9).	John 2:17; 7:3-5
"The reproaches of them that reproached thee are fallen upon me" (verse 9).	Romans 15:3
"They that sit in the gate speak against me; and I was the song of the drunkards" (verse 12).	Mark 15:29-32
"Thou hast known my reproach, and my shame, and my dishonour" (verse 19).	Matthew 27:29,30
"Reproach hath broken my heart; and I am full of heaviness: and I looked for some to take pity, but there was none" (verse 20).	Matthew 26:36-40
They gave me also gall for my meat; and in my thirst they gave me vinegar to drink" (verse 21).	Matthew 27:34,48; John 19:28-30
"Let their table become a snare before them" (verses 22,23).	Romans 11:9,10
"Let their habitation be desolate; and let none dwell in their tents" (verse 25).	Acts 1:20
"Let them be blotted out of the book of the living, and not be written with the righteous" (verse 28).	Compare Luke 10:20

520

Apart from the passages listed, the psalm in its entirety uses language that is particularly appropriate to the Lord Jesus Christ, and his perfect life was foreshadowed in the words and experiences of the man after God's own heart.

Jeremiah

In conclusion we briefly draw attention to the connection between Jeremiah and this psalm. A careful use of a concordance will establish the affinity that Jeremiah had with this psalm. He did not write it, but he quoted it and saw in it a reflection of his own experiences, for he too had the spirit of David (see Jeremiah 15:15-18; 20:9,10).

Reproach is the inevitable experience, at some time in their life, of all who are truly zealous for God's house. When we are reproached we too can take comfort in the knowledge that our God will vindicate us; exalt us when those who hate God are brought low.

PSALM 70

THIS short psalm repeats with some variations the last five verses of Psalm 40. For reasons that will become apparent we are confident that Psalm 40 was the first to be composed although both psalms relate to the latter part of David's life. Writers on the psalms give little, if any, space to this short song usually pointing out its connection with Psalm 40 and suggesting that it has been plucked out of that psalm and amended slightly for liturgical use at a later date. As to its liturgical significance we cannot comment as we have no evidence, but this ready explanation for the inclusion of this short song in the Psalter is typical of the paucity of thinking that many manifest when dealing with apparent problems. We cannot claim to know all the answers but we are confident that there is far more to the inspired word of God, preserved for all subsequent generations, than this.

Psalm 40

We feel it appropriate to recall, briefly, what we wrote about the background to Psalm 40. We endeavoured then to demonstrate that the song was composed some little time after David's sin in the matter of Bathsheba and Uriah the Hittite, when the king was experiencing some of the consequences of his sin in the reaction of the people, and particularly his enemies, towards him. In that study we discussed the reasons why men hated David so much and presented arguments that were replicated, although from a different standpoint, in our consideration of Psalm 69 in the previous chapter. Their hatred was rooted in their antagonism to the kind of life that David lived. They did not share his love for God nor the manner in which he pursued spiritual aims in his rulership over the kingdom. These things were not just irksome to them but they saw them as a positive hindrance to the fulfilment of their own

522

fleshly ambitions. They saw their opportunities in David's sin and eventually Absalom's rebellion, to seek to depose him from the throne and, as we saw in Psalm 69, this same spirit manifested itself not just towards David, but also towards his chosen heir Solomon over the question of building a house for God's dwelling place.

Without elaborating in detail, we drew attention in Psalm 40 to the striking verbal links between these last five verses and Psalm 35 which was written much earlier when David was fleeing from the hand of Saul. We indicated then how it was self-interest, their desire to ingratiate themselves with Saul, the king, that motivated those who hated David. We reproduce now some of these verbal links with Psalm 35 as an aid to our understanding of the relevance of Psalm 70.

Psalms 70 & 40	Psalm 35
"Let them be ashamed and confounded that seek after my soul: let them be turned backward, and put to confusion, that desire my hurt" (verse 2; Psalm 40:14).	"Let them be confounded and put to shame that seek after my soul: let them be turned back and brought to confusion that devise my hurt" (verse 4; see also verse 26).
"That say, Aha, aha" (verse 3; Psalm 40:15).	"Aha, aha, our eye hath seen it" (verse 21).
"Let all those that seek thee rejoice and be glad in thee: and let such as love thy salvation say continually, Let God be magnified" (verse 4; Psalm 40:16).	"Let them shout for joy, and be glad, that favour my righteous cause: yea, let them say continually, Let the LORD be magnified" (verse 27).
"I am poor and needy" (verse 5; Psalm 40:17).	"The poor and the needy" (verse 10).

There are other points of contact between Psalms 35 and 40 which we have not developed (see for instance Psalms 35:18 and 40:9). It is evident then that the language of Psalm 35 forms the basis of the structure of both Psalm 70 and the relevant section of Psalm 40. There is nothing strange about this. Indeed it is appropriate that when men hated the Psalmist and sought his hurt as they did in the period leading up to Absalom's rebellion, his thoughts should have gone back to that time when men hated him wrongfully because of their self-motivated allegiance to Saul, and to be led by his recollections to reproduce in Psalm 40 the language of Psalm 35.

Why then reproduce the language of Psalm 40 in Psalm 70? Further comparisons between the language of Psalm 69 and 70; Psalms 40 and 69; and Psalms 35 and 40 with Psalm 71 demonstrate clearly we believe, that Psalm 70 is drawn out of Psalm 69 and is the bridge between that psalm and Psalm 71.

Indeed these somewhat complex comparisons reveal, we suggest, a thread of thought, a common theme which runs not just from Psalm 69 but, beginning in Psalm 68 continues to Psalm 72 which brings what is generally regarded as the second book of the Psalms to a conclusion. Firstly we set out some of the points of contact between the various psalms mentioned above.

Comparisons

First Psalms 69 and 70

Psalm 69	**Psalm 70**
"Make haste to hear me" (verse 17, AV margin).	"Make haste to help me, O LORD" (verse 1). "Make haste unto me … O LORD, make no tarrying (verse 5).
"But I am poor and sorrowful: let thy salvation, O God, set me on high. I will praise the name of God with a song, and will magnify him with thanksgiving" (verses 29,30).	"Let all those that seek thee rejoice and be glad in thee: and let such as love thy salvation say continually, Let God be magnified. But I am poor and needy" (verses 4,5).

524

Secondly Psalms 40 and 69.

Psalm 40	**Psalm 69**
"I waited patiently for the LORD" (verse 1).	"While I wait for my God" (verse 3). "Let not them that wait on thee ... be ashamed" (verse 6).
"He brought me ... out of the miry clay" (verse 2).	"I sink in deep mire" (verse 2). "Deliver me out of the mire" (verse 14).
"Many, O LORD my God, are thy wonderful works which thou hast done, and thy thoughts which are to us-ward: they cannot be reckoned up ... they are more than can be numbered" (verse 5).	"O God, in the multitude of thy mercy hear me" (verse 13; see also verse 16).
"He hath put a new song in my mouth, even praise unto our God" (verse 3). "Sacrifice and offering thou didst not desire" (verse 6).	"I will praise the name of God with a song, and will magnify him with thanksgiving. This also shall please the LORD better than an ox or bullock that hath horns and hoofs" (verses 30,31).
"Withhold not thy tender mercies from me, O LORD: let thy lovingkindness and thy truth continually preserve me" (verse 11).	"Hear me, O LORD; for thy lovingkindness is good: turn unto me according to the multitude of thy tender mercies" (verse 16).
"Innumerable evils have compassed me about ... they are more than the hairs of mine head" (verse 12).	"They that hate me without a cause are more than the hairs of mine head" (verse 4).
"Let them be ashamed and confounded that seek after my soul to destroy it" (verse 14).	"Let not them that wait upon thee, O Lord GOD of hosts, be ashamed for my sake: let not those that seek thee be confounded for my sake, O God of Israel" (verse 6).
"Let them be desolate for a reward" (verse 15).	"Let their habitation be desolate" (verse 25).

525

The connections between Psalm 70 and Psalm 69 would of course also be appropriate to the last five verses of Psalm 40.

Finally connections between Psalms 35 and 40 and Psalm 71. We hope to show that the substance of the song is very relevant indeed to the theme running through these five Psalms (68 to 72).

Psalms 35 and 40	Psalm 71
"Let them be confounded and put to shame that seek after my soul" (35:4,26; 40:14).	"Let them be confounded and consumed that are adversaries to my soul; let them be covered with reproach and dishonour that seek my hurt" (verses 13,24).
"O LORD, make haste to help me" (40:13).	"O my God, make haste for my help" (verse 12).
"O LORD be not far from me" (35:22).	"O God, be not far from me" (verse 12).
"And my tongue shall speak of thy righteousnes" (35:28).	"My mouth shall show forth thy righteousness" (verse 15).
"I have preached righteousness in the great congregation" (40:9).	"My tongue also shall talk of thy righteousness all the day long" (verse 24).
"Many, O LORD my God, are thy wonderful works … thy thoughts which are to us-ward: they cannot be reckoned up in order unto thee … they are more than can be numbered" (40:5).	"My mouth shall show forth thy righteousness and thy salvation all the day; for I know not the numbers thereof" (verse 15).

The Message of the Comparisons

In some senses comparisons of this kind can be tedious and perhaps some points of contact may strike some as a little tenuous. If, however, the psalms concerned are read carefully then the repetition of similar language and thought patterns establishes a conclusive link in the mind. As already stated Psalm 35 was written when David fled from Saul. Psalm 40 was composed in the period between David's great sin and Absalom's rebellion. Psalm 69 was written in the last years of David's life.

They have one thing in common – the hatred that influential men bare towards David, motivated primarily by their own self-interest and their antagonism towards his way of life and spiritual values. It was natural that in writing Psalm 40 David should recall the words of Psalm 35 written during a similar crisis in his life. Psalm 40 is different from Psalm 69 although the language connects the two. In Psalm 40 David is able to speak of God's deliverance from his enemies. "I waited patiently for the LORD; and he inclined unto me, and heard my cry" (verse 1). In Psalm 69 David still waits for the acceptable time when God would hear his cry (verse 13). It is perfectly reasonable therefore that David should recall this similar experience and find comfort in the deliverance obtained on that occasion. Psalm 70 is a prayer taken from Psalm 40, that God would show himself active on his behalf as he had done then. Psalm 71 will be seen now as an enlargement of the short prayer of Psalm 70, beseeching God that as he had cared for him in his youth and indeed throughout his life, He would not cast him off in old age, in the time of grey hairs (see verses 5,6,9,17,18).

The Theme of the Songs.

We are now able to set out below the thread that runs through the last five songs of this second book of Psalms.

Psalm 68: A song that celebrated the covenant God made with David with its emphasis upon a son who would build a house for God's name.

Psalm 69: David's overwhelming desire to prepare for the building of that house and the hatred engendered amongst those who did not share his spiritual ambitions.

Psalm 70: A prayer arising from this situation for God to make haste to deliver him.

Psalm 71: An enlargement of the prayer of Psalm 70 recalling the blessings of earlier life and asking God to respond now as in the past.

Psalm 72: A prayer for the fulfilment of God's purpose written on the accession of Solomon to the throne. Although written in the language of prayer it is nevertheless a prophecy describing the ultimate fulfilment of the covenant that God made with him, in the person of his greater son, the Lord Jesus Christ.

We finally turn our attention to the substance of the five verses of this short psalm.

To Bring to Remembrance.

This prefix is used at the head of just one other psalm (38) and is undoubtedly intended as a plea to God to remember David in his distress and deliver him. The RV margin, correctly we believe, renders the words "to make memorial" and the allusion is almost certainly to the meal offering (Leviticus 2); to that portion of it that was mixed with oil and frankincense and burnt upon the altar (verse 2). It was described as "the memorial" and it was to be "of a sweet savour unto the LORD". The connection between prayer and incense is well established (see Luke 1:9-11; Revelation 8:3,4) and the lesson is that when in trouble one shows faith and trust in God by crying to Him for deliverance. That prayer, as a sweet savour, rises as a memorial before God and God remembers the plight of His servant. In scriptural language when God remembers, then He acts (see Genesis 8:1: Exodus 2:24; 1 Samuel 1:19 etc.). Thus David's prayer was a cry to God to remember him and deliver him.

"Make Haste, O LORD"

The idea behind the word "haste" is that of hurrying (Strong's) and whenever God's servants find themselves in distress and God does not appear to answer their cry then their prayers take on an urgency and immediacy that looks to God with an intensity of emotion that He would manifest Himself to deliver and help (verse 1). It was David's desire that those who falsely accused him and derided him should be shown for what they really were, men who opposed not just the king but the purpose of God in him. Let them be ashamed, their slanderous accusations shown to be without excuse. Let them be confounded, all their arguments and malicious intentions shown to be without foundation, so that they blush (this is the root meaning of Hebrew word – Strong's) in the confusion of being shown in their true colours (verse 2).

"Let them be turned back" or literally 'let them turn back'. Let them retreat in ignominious dishonour "by reason of their shame" (verse 3, RV).

They had said "Aha, aha" – an exclamation of malignant delight in anticipation of the king's downfall. But his prayer was that all those who seek God might be vindicated and rejoice and be glad in Him for; "let such as love thy salvation say continually, Let God be magnified" (verse 4).

We magnify God in our lives when we make Him great, give Him the reverence and place in our lives that He deserves. If we are numbered amongst those who love His salvation we will also look beyond this present day to the time when He will be magnified in all the earth.

In his distress David could hardly bring himself to think that he was numbered amongst such for, he cries "I am poor and needy". Therefore make haste to deliver. "O LORD, make no tarrying" (verse 5).

Such must be the spirit of all those who look for God's deliverance both for themselves and for the earth at large in the fulfilment of His purpose. Herein must lie our deepest longing and desires as we in our day and age take to our hearts the words of the Lord Jesus, "Surely I come quickly" and respond in the spirit of David, "Even so, come, Lord Jesus" (Revelation 22:20).

PSALM 71

THERE is no title of authorship at the head of Psalm 71 but there can be no doubt given the connections established with the preceding psalms in the last chapter, that it was written by David.

As indicated, it is an enlargement of the prayer of Psalm 70 as David looks back over his past experiences in life and beseeches God that, as He had proved Himself faithful in previous crises, so now He will, once again, deliver him from those who seek his hurt. Beyond doubt David penned this psalm in the latter part of his life as old age and grey hairs loomed ominously near. His words nevertheless encompass each stage of his life.

"Thou art my trust from my youth. By thee have I been holden up from the womb: thou art he that took me out of my mother's bowels."   (verses 5,6)

"Cast me not off in the time of old age; forsake me not when my strength faileth."   (verse 9)

"O God, thou hast taught me from my youth."
          (verse 17)

"Now also when I am old and grayheaded, O God, forsake me not."   (verse 18)

As David thus reflects on his experiences it is natural that the language he uses should recall that of earlier psalms written at different periods of his life. We compared the psalms that had a direct connection to Psalm 71 in the last chapter but there are other psalms alluded to; particularly the first three verses seem to be a repetition of the opening words of Psalm 31. We shall comment on the link between these verses when we come to consider the content of the psalm in detail.

As far as structure is concerned it is difficult to divide the psalm into recognisable sections. We have, however, endeavoured to trace certain themes that we believe help to establish patterns of thought that can be discerned in the psalm.

Analysis of themes

1. Prayer for God to Deliver
    a. "Deliver me ... and cause me to escape" (verse 2)
    b. "Save me" (verse 2)
    c. "Given commandment to save me" (verse 3)
    d. "O God, be not far from me" (verse 12)
    e. "Make haste for my help" (verse 12)
    f. "O God, forsake me not" (verse 18)

2(a). David's Trust in God
    a. "In thee ... do I put my trust (verse 1)
    b. "For thou art my hope" (verse 5)
    c. "Thou art my trust" (verse 5)
    d. "I will hope continually" (verse 14)

2(b). David's Faith in God for Protection
    a. "Be thou my strong habitation" (verse 3)
    b. "For thou art my rock" (verse 3)
    c. "And my fortress" (verse 3)
    d. "Thou art my strong refuge" (verse 7)
    e. "I will go in the strength of the Lord GOD" (verse 16)

3. God's Righteousness
    a. "Deliver me in thy righteousness" (verse 2)
    b. "My mouth shall show forth thy righteousness" (verse 15)
    c. "I will make mention of thy righteousness" (verse 16)
    d. "Thy righteousness also, O God, is very high" (verse 19)
    e. "My tongue also shall talk of thy righteousness" (verse 24)

These themes provide a framework in which to study the message of the psalm. His prayer for God to deliver him from his enemies gives us an insight into the extremity of his plight, and the urgency with which he pleads for God to act to save him. As David saw things there was a need for swift and immediate action if he were not to be overcome by his enemies.

The basis of David's prayer was his faith. He had an implicit trust in God and his hope in Him never waned. Whilst this was expressed in simple straightforward terms – see 2(a), there was also a recollection of past blessings. He remembered his flight from Saul and so interspersed in the declarations of trust there is the imagery of those earlier days. God was still, he assured himself, his rock, his cliff, his fortress, his stronghold – see 2(b), and consequently those that hated him would not prevail.

It will be observed that these first three themes are primarily to be found in the first half of the psalm, whereas the emphasis on God's righteousness is to be found predominantly in the latter half. Here perhaps, is an indication that the first half of the psalm, say verses 1 to 12, has a different emphasis from the second half, verses 13 to 24, and we can perhaps, for convenience, divide it in this way as an aid to our understanding.

The Grounds of Faith (verses 1-3)

As indicated above the first three verses of the psalm are a repetition, with some variations, of the opening verses of Psalm 31. That psalm was concerned with the dangers that David encountered from Saul and the use of the words here is an indication of how David's faith was sustained by this recollection of past trials and the manner in which God had delivered him from them.

He had put his trust in God; alternatively the Hebrew is rendered, "I have taken refuge in thee". Consequently he pleads, "let me never be put to confusion". More accurately the word rendered "confusion" means 'ashamed'. In effect he says, Let me never know the shame that would come if it were to appear in the sight of men that my trust had been misplaced and my faith without foundation (verse 1). So he continues, "Deliver me in thy righteousness, and cause me to escape: incline thine ear unto me, and save me" (verse 2).

The construction of the Hebrew text is interesting. *Young's Literal Translation* renders the words "In Thy righteousness Thou dost deliver me, and dost cause me to escape". The emphasis is upon the word "righteousness", a thought which, as we have seen, is developed later in the psalm. Because God is righteous He will not abandon His servant. He will be true to the promises that He has made.

"Incline thine ear" cries David or "bow down" as Psalm 31 (verse 2) and the RV render it. That is "bend a listening ear" and deliver me. "Be thou to me a rock of habitation, whereunto I may continually resort" (verse 3, RV).

Psalm 31 reads "strong rock" and there is some manuscript evidence for translating "stronghold of habitation" in Psalm 71. But there is no confusion in the meaning and nothing substantial is lost from the prayer of David, however the words might be translated. God was his rock, a place of safety; a place to give shadow from the heat of the day. This is a fitting symbol for those enduring qualities that belonged to the Eternal God with whom David had made his home. This thought of making one's dwelling (i.e., habitation) with God is a most intimate figure to describe the relationship we can have with the Almighty. Our fellowship with Him is likened to our home. That is we feel comfortable, secure, at ease with Him. The figure is of course found elsewhere in the psalms (90:1; 91:1) and is carried over into the New Testament also:

"If a man love me, he will keep my words: and my Father will love him, and we will come unto him, and make our abode (i.e., our home) with him."

(John 14:23)

The use of such imagery to illustrate the closeness of our fellowship and association with God should cause us all to search our hearts to discover if indeed we have developed such a relationship with our Father in heaven.

David continues,

"Thou hast given commandment to save me; for thou art my rock and my fortress." (verse 3)

With all the means at His disposal the commandment given by God could be open to any number of explanations but given the assurances of scripture that "the angel of the

533

LORD encampeth round about them that fear him" (Psalm 34:7) and "for he shall give his angels charge over thee, to keep thee in all thy ways" (Psalm 91:11), it does not seem inappropriate to consider the commandment as given to the angels who had responsibility to care for and protect David in his life. Once again, David's language recalls his earlier perils when he fled from Saul, "For thou art my rock and my fortress" (verse 3). The Hebrew word translated "rock" is different from that used in the first line of this verse. Literally 'my cliff' (Hebrew, *sela*) perhaps recalling particularly the events of 1 Samuel 23 when David in extreme peril was surrounded by Saul and his men in the wilderness of Maon (verses 25,26) and escaped by the providential hand of God. For the Philistines invaded the land and Saul was compelled to turn away to confront this new danger (verse 27). Because of these events they called the name of the place Sela-hammahlekoth (i.e., "the cliff of escape") (verse 28).

Prayer for Deliverance (verses 4-12)

"Deliver me, O my God, out of the hand of the wicked, out of the hand of the unrighteous and cruel man."

(verse 4)

We know that David was a man beloved of God. We know also that he inspired great love and loyalty among men who were of a kindred spirit. Yet throughout his life there were men who hated him for reasons we have discussed at some length in previous chapters.

These men were always there looking for opportunity to discredit him, to turn the hearts of the people against him. We might wonder sometimes why David, the king, did not take decisive action against them for they were seeking to subvert the kingdom. It has to be remembered, however, that they were powerful and influential men in Israel, princes of their tribes, and much of their treachery was conducted not in an open manner but in a clandestine way. To have taken action against them would have aroused the anger of their families and could have destroyed the unity of the kingdom. David, ever the shepherd of his people, sought to avert such an outcome whatever the cost might be to him personally. So his prayer was that God would rescue (RV) him from these implacable foes, "the unrighteous and cruel man", almost certainly meant to be understood in a collective sense.

"For thou art my hope, O Lord GOD: thou art my trust from my youth". God was his hope and his trust. His deepest longings, the things he yearned for, were all of them connected with his God and the purpose He would bring to pass in the earth. It was David's confidence in these things that made the God of Israel both his hope and his trust. As we read the psalms such sentiments must cause us to search our hearts and examine what motivates us in life. Certainly popularity, for its own sake, was never something that David courted; and the record of his life, and indeed that of almost every man of God of whom we have detailed information, the Lord Jesus Christ in particular, indicates that it was not something that they enjoyed in their pilgrimage.

David recognised the goodness of God in all his past experiences:

> "By thee have I been holden up from the womb: thou art he that took me out of my mother's bowels: my praise shall be continually of thee."　　　　　(verse 6)

He had stayed himself from birth on God (*Cambridge Bible*) and God had been his benefactor from his mother's womb (see RV margin). For these reasons his praise of God never ceased. So he declares:

> "I am as a wonder unto many; but thou art my strong refuge. Let my mouth be filled with thy praise and with thy honour all the day."　　　　　(verses 7,8)

There have been a number of explanations offered for the sense in which David had become "a wonder unto many". However, the following phrase, "But thou art my strong refuge" must surely direct our thoughts. Many had looked upon the troubles that had overtaken him and concluded that they were a token of God's displeasure, a sign that the wrath of God was upon him. In this sense we understand the word "wonder" in the same way that it is used in Deuteronomy 28 regarding the curses that would be brought upon Israel: "And they shall be upon thee for a sign and for a wonder" (verse 46).

Nevertheless, through all these things that he had suffered, David's faith had remained unshaken and his mouth would be full of God's praise and honour all the day (RV). Having contemplated the goodness of God in his earlier years, David now looks forward to the eventide of his life and prays for God to maintain His loving kindness towards him.

"Cast me not off in the time of old age; forsake me not when my strength faileth. For mine enemies speak against me; and they that lay wait for my soul take counsel together, saying, God hath forsaken him: persecute and take him; for there is none to deliver him." (verses 9-11)

We often think of great men of God as individuals who somehow never experienced the doubts and anxieties so characteristic of our lives. We have used words in this study in which we have described David's "unshaken faith". Truly we consider in the pages of scripture, spiritual giants, with whom we rightly compare ourselves as pygmies. But we make a mistake if we think that men like David knew no doubt or weakness. The words of his prayer mirror our own uncertainties. "Cast me not off", he cries, "Forsake me not when my strength faileth". David knew the weakness of his nature; how constant was his need of God's help if he were to prevail. But he knew also that he could not presume on God's goodness. He had no right to divine protection for it was of God's grace that he was not consumed. Thus although his life to that point in time gave him an abundant assurance of God's goodness and fidelity, he still felt the need to plead his cause before God, and his "unshaken faith" is seen in the way in which he constantly overcame all his doubts and uncertainties and lived in the confidence of God's love towards him.

So it was that his enemies, typifying the attitude of the Pharisees and Herodians towards the Lord Jesus (Mark 3:2-6) spoke against him, and they that watched (RV) for his life took counsel together. Why they said, "God hath forsaken him". It seems that they had deluded themselves. They were convinced that right was on their side therefore let us "pursue and take him for there is none to deliver"

(RV). To the attitude of his enemies David had only one response:

"O God be not far from me: O my God, make haste for my help." (verse 12)

The Enemies of David and the Righteousness of God (verses 13-24)

As David began the psalm praying that God would not let him be ashamed before his enemies so now he contrasts his own expectations, based on the righteousness of God, with theirs.

"Let them be confounded and consumed that are adversaries to my soul; let them be covered with reproach and dishonour that seek my hurt." (verse 13)

It must be appreciated that there is no vindictiveness in the expression of these sentiments. It is not a desire for personal revenge that motivates David. Either they were right in their assessment of him, in which case he had been forsaken by God and was doomed, or the truth of God as he had perceived and embraced it would be seen to prevail. Fundamentally it came down to the question; Who was really on the Lord's side, and who ultimately would be ashamed because of the attitude they had adopted? David's plea that they should be confounded (ashamed, RV) and consumed – covered with reproach and dishonour – was based upon his experience of God's goodness throughout his life. If they were right his whole life would have been a sham and his conception of the righteousness of God would be shown to be false. But David had no doubts in this matter:

"But I will hope continually, and will yet praise thee more and more. My mouth shall shew forth thy righteousness and thy salvation all the day; for I know not the numbers thereof." (verses 14,15)

Righteousness and salvation are linked together for the one is the outcome of the other. The man who is worthy to ascend into the hill of the Lord is the one who shall receive the blessing, even righteousness from the God of his salvation (Psalm 24:3-5). The outcome of God's work of salvation is righteousness, for we shall be like Him, having entered into the very life of God itself. Not only in

THE PRAISES OF ISRAEL (PSALMS 1–72)

the physical sense of being immortal and incorruptible but also in the moral sense having assumed all the ethical qualities of the Divine nature.

There is in verse 15 a play in the Hebrew upon the words rendered "shew" (RV, tell) and "numbers". The *Cambridge Bible* renders it as follows (meanings of words confirmed in Strong's); "My mouth shall tell of thy righteousness, and of thy salvation all the day; for I know not the tale thereof".

The words "tell" and "tale" are derived from the same root. And as 'tell' in old English means both to count and to recount, so it is with the Hebrew word. Not only is it impossible to count God's mercies but also it is impossible adequately to tell of them in words; "God's mercies are an inexhaustible theme" (*Cambridge Bible*).

As a consequence, says David, "I will come in the strength of the Lord GOD. I will make mention of thy righteousness, even of thine only" (verse 16, RV with margin). The picture is of David coming into the tabernacle having derived strength from the knowledge of God's righteousness before the people. That past mercies are the grounds of David's hope is evident for he continues:

"O God, thou hast taught me from my youth: and hitherto have I declared thy wondrous works. Now also when I am old and grayheaded, O God, forsake me not; until I have shewed thy strength unto this (RV, the next) generation, and thy power to everyone that is to come." (verses 17,18)

From his youth he had been taught in the school of God, learning daily from the interaction of his experiences with the word of God. Hitherto he had been declaring the wondrous works of God and the tense of the verb indicates that this had been his habitual and constant preoccupation. So now in old age he pleads that these experiences might continue – not just for his own sake but also that he might be able both by example and precept to instruct the next generation.

This is a responsibility laid upon us as brethren and sisters in the Lord Jesus Christ. It is one of the dominant themes of scripture – the need to teach the young that the chain of truth might be maintained in the earth. The point is illustrated by examples from both Old and New Testaments. See for example Psalm 78 (verses 1-7) noting particularly the words,

"That they should make them (God's testimony and God's law) known to their children: that the generation to come might know them, even the children which should be born; who should arise and declare them to their children." (Psalm 78:5,6)

Similarly Paul reminded Timothy of his responsibility to "Hold fast the form of sound words, which thou hast heard of me" (2 Timothy 1:13) and those things which he had heard among many witnesses the same he was to commit to faithful men who shall be able to teach others also (2:2).

Returning to David's words, his desire was to show God's *strength*. Strong's indicates that the original word means "arm" in the sense of being outstretched to act. Kay (*Psalms with Notes*) observes that the word's associations indicate the thoughts of guidance, support, protection, government, chastisement and victory. All these things would be evident from the Word of God in the revelation of God's acts in previous generations, but evident also in the life of David himself which, for those with spiritual discernment, would be like a book where men could read in terms of human experience all the wonderful things which God's arm had wrought. So David could sum up the work of God in his life.

"Thy righteousness also, O God, is very high. Thou who hast done great things. O God, who is like unto thee?" (verse 19, RV)

God is incomparable in His power and goodness and David's desire was that He would continue His work in his life.

"Thou, which hast shewed me great and sore troubles, shalt quicken me again, and shalt bring me up again from the depths of the earth. Thou shalt increase my greatness, and comfort me on every side." (verses 20,21)

It might appear that David was at the very point of death. It was as if the "gates of Hell" were opened to receive him.

But he was confident that God would quicken him and bring him up from the depths of the earth. He had experienced great troubles but was certain that eventually God would exalt him again so that men would acknowledge his greatness and in this he would find comfort and consolation.

Apart from one instance in the Book of Esther the word rendered "greatness" is used only of God himself. This has led some to doubt the text. This however is typical of so many orthodox commentators. Our understanding of the man David points unquestionably to the conclusion that it was not his own personal dignity that concerned him, but the fact that as the Lord's anointed, he was God's representative on the throne of Israel. Any greatness ascribed to David was but a reflection of the glory that belonged to the King Eternal on whose behalf he reigned.

Having made his prayer unto God, having expressed his trust that in His righteousness God would deliver him out of the hand of his enemies, David closes the psalm with a declaration of his intended response to all that God had done for him.

"I will also praise thee with the psaltery, even thy truth, O my God: unto thee will I sing with the harp, O thou Holy One of Israel. My lips shall greatly rejoice when I sing unto thee; and my soul, which thou hast redeemed. My tongue also shall talk of thy righteousness all the day long." (verses 22-24)

Praise is perhaps, one of the aspects of our worship that deserves more thought and consideration. We praise God in our hymn singing but it is more than that. So often a good tune, a rousing chorus can move us and uplift us and yet fall short of real praise. For it is primarily not about our emotional response, although of course we cannot separate that from our praise for it springs out of our joy, our thankfulness to God for what He is and for what He has done. But essentially praise is directed towards the One who is worthy to receive it whether in word or song.

Consequently the words of our praise must be words of Truth, words soundly based on the impregnable rock of holy scripture. David said "my tongue also shall talk of thy righteousness". The word "talk" means literally 'to ponder, to converse with oneself' (Strong's), that is, to meditate. Here is an insight into praise that does not necessarily have anything to do with the words being uttered. Rather our meditations upon the righteousness of God, our contemplation of the wonder of His character and of all that He has done for us, if it fills our hearts with joy and wonder then it is a form of praise that is acknowledged and recognised by God. How often is it that such meditations cause us to break forth spontaneously into spoken words or songs of praise? Surely the truest and purest form of praise arises from such contemplative experiences as this.

The final sentence of the psalm is once more an expression of David's faith. The fate of his enemies was so certain that he could speak of it as though it were already accomplished.

"For they are confounded, for they are brought unto shame, that seek my hurt."   (verse 24)

PSALM 72

THERE could be no grander finale to the Second Book of Psalms, or to the sequence of thought that we have pursued through the last five psalms it contains, than this prayer of David for the purpose of God to be consummated in the reign of his son. It is surely one of the most well known of psalms amongst us and is probably read more than any other portion of scripture at our meetings to proclaim the good news of the kingdom of God.

It bears the title "A Psalm for Solomon" and it is our conviction that it was written when Solomon was anointed king. In that event David saw an incipient fulfilment of the promises that God had made to him, but as the language of the psalm makes clear David saw those events as but a shadow of the glorious reign that should ensue when his greater Son should sit upon his throne for ever. While the psalm begins as a petition for God to grant the gifts necessary for the king to reign in justice and righteousness, almost immediately it becomes prophetic as David describes the blessings that will accrue as a consequence of God establishing the throne of his son. That the psalm is looking beyond Solomon to the reign of the Lord Jesus Christ is evident, not only from the description of the reign which far surpasses Solomon's kingdom in all its particulars, but also from the indications within the psalm itself that this king is going to reign for ever (see verses 5,15,17,19).

Structure.

It might appear at first sight that part of the second half of the song (verses 12-14) is a repetition of the thoughts expressed at the beginning of the psalm (verses 3,4), but a careful reading makes clear that although the deliverance promised to the poor and needy is the same, the individuals referred to are different. In verses 2-4 the poor

542

and needy are described as "thy people" and "thy poor" – in other words, the people of Israel. However, verses 12-14 describe in similar language benefits bestowed on the poor and needy following a section that deals with the worldwide dominion of the king (verses 8-11), and are thus a description of blessings enjoyed by the Gentiles – by all peoples of the earth. The construction of the psalm is not difficult to discern.

verse 1	David's Prayer
verses 2-7	The beneficent consequences of the king's reign for Israel
verses 8-14	His worldwide dominion
verse 15	The people's response
verse 16	The earth blessed
verse 17	His everlasting name
verses 18-20	Doxology

David's Prayer

This first verse of the psalm is clearly a petition. It is a request that God would bless the king with His righteousness that he might rule and judge with equity. It should be noted that many writers maintain that the psalm in its entirety is a prayer, arguing that the verbs throughout are what are known as 'optatives', e.g., "*May* he judge thy people with righteousness" (verse 2); "*Let* the mountains bring peace to the people" (verse 3) etc. Others, however, maintain that the verbs are simple futures. We have noted that those who wish to make the whole psalm a prayer are mainly of a critical disposition and one cannot escape the conclusion that some of them at least are seeking to remove the predictive element from the psalm. Not, of course, that this is a correct assumption even if their interpretation of the Hebrew text is correct. Through inspiration David would then be expressing his desire for the fulfilment of all that God had promised concerning his son and the prayer would naturally become a prophecy of all that God would do in faithfulness.

It is so easy to think of the poetic element of the psalm and to imagine that "thy judgments" and "thy righteousness" are but different expressions of the same thing, parallel descriptions of the same truth. One writer

543

has observed that whereas "judgments" refers to the decisions that the king will be called upon to make which, when uttered, David prays may be in accordance with the will of God, "righteousness" refers to the mind and spirit, the wisdom that resides within.

David's longing for his son(s) was fulfilled first in Solomon of whom it is recorded:

"And all Israel heard of the judgment which the king had judged; and they feared the king: for they saw that the wisdom of God was in him, to do judgment."

(1 Kings 3:28)

Again the Queen of Sheba exclaimed:

"Blessed be the LORD thy God, which delighted in thee, to set thee on the throne of Israel: because the LORD loved Israel for ever, therefore made he thee king, to do judgment and justice." (10:9)

It was only completely true, however, of one Son:

"There shall come forth a rod out of the stem of Jesse, and a Branch shall grow out of his roots: and the spirit of the LORD shall rest upon him, the spirit of wisdom and understanding, the spirit of counsel and might, the spirit of knowledge and of the fear of the LORD; and shall make him of quick understanding in the fear of the LORD: and he shall not judge after the sight of his eyes, neither reprove after the hearing of his ears: but with righteousness shall he judge the poor, and reprove with equity for the meek of the earth."

(Isaiah 11:1-4)

His Reign Over Israel (verses 2-7)

Endowed with divine authority the king now reigns as the Lord's representative upon the throne of David. The word rendered "judge" in verse 2 is different in the Hebrew from that similarly translated in verse 4. The first (*din*) means 'to rule, to umpire (i.e., decide the cause)'. The second (*shaphat*) means 'to dispense justice, to pronounce sentence, to punish the wrongdoer'. Hence the *Cambridge Bible* renders the phrase in verse 2: "He shall give sentence to thy people with righteousness" and the NKJV renders verse 4, "He will bring justice to the poor of the people".

The word rendered "poor" is the same Hebrew word on each occasion it occurs in the AV of Psalm 72. While carrying the idea of those of a humble disposition (i.e., the poor in spirit), it is these who would most naturally be oppressed by the rich and powerful and therefore the word carries also the idea of the afflicted. It is this latter meaning that seems to be pre-eminent in the context of this psalm.

The divine rule, exercised through the power of His Son will bring justice to the afflicted and protection to the needy (verse 4). The whole land, represented by its characteristic features, the mountains and the little hills, will enjoy peace and all Israel benefit from the righteousness of his rule.

When Isaiah speaks of a king "reigning in righteousness", he proclaims:

"Then judgment shall dwell in the wilderness, and righteousness remain in the fruitful field. And the work of righteousness shall be peace; and the effect of righteousness quietness and assurance for ever."

(Isaiah 32:1,16,17)

The result of Messiah's just reign is this: "they shall fear thee as long as the sun and moon endure, throughout all generations" (Psalm 72:5). Note the change in pronoun from "he" to "thee". It is not the king who is addressed but God his Father. As a consequence of the king's righteous reign, men come to fear God and reverence Him. The reference to the sun and moon should be noted, for this is repeated on another two occasions in this psalm:

"In his days shall the righteous flourish; and abundance of peace so long as the moon endureth."

(verse 7; see also verse 17)

The reference to the heavenly bodies as a figure of God's fidelity to the things He has promised in His covenant is most appropriate, for in another psalm (89), rejoicing in the faithfulness of God (see verses 1,2,5,8,24) the writer says:

"My covenant will I not break, nor alter the thing that is gone out of my lips. Once have I sworn by my holiness that I will not lie unto David. His seed shall endure for ever, and his throne as the sun before me. It shall be established for ever as the moon, and as a faithful witness in heaven." (verses 34-37)

Thus God was to declare at a later date, when the overthrow of the kingdom was imminent:

"Thus saith the LORD; If ye can break my covenant of the day (i.e., the sun), and my covenant of the night (i.e., the moon), and that there should not be day and night in their season; then may also my covenant be broken with David my servant, that he should not have a son to reign upon his throne." (Jeremiah 33:20,21)

Sun and moon are constant reminders to us of the authority of God's word, of the everlasting stability of the throne and kingdom of David.

The righteous flourish and enjoy abundance of peace because He comes down like rain upon the mown grass and as showers that water the earth (Psalm 72:6). The rain and the dew are, of course, figures of sound teaching (see Deuteronomy 32:1,2; 2 Samuel 23:3,4). Because truth prevails the righteous are blessed and the earth is filled with peace.

The King's Worldwide Dominion (verses 8-14)

It might be thought that this particular section of the psalm can have little significance as far as Solomon is concerned, but in fact the reign of Solomon provides a wonderful background for the description of the worldwide dominion of David's greater Son and the homage paid to him by all nations of the earth. The reign of the Lord Jesus Christ was marvellously foreshadowed by the splendour of Solomon's reign and the honour bestowed upon him by the kings of the earth. We recommend that 2 Chronicles 9 be read concerning the visit of the Queen of Sheba and in particular note the following verses:

"And all the kings of the earth sought the presence of Solomon, to hear his wisdom, that God had put in his heart. And they brought every man his present ..."
(2 Chronicles 9:23,24; see also 1 Kings 4:20-25)

However, the language of Psalm 72:8 goes far beyond the dominion of Solomon and recalls the language of other scripture (Psalm 2:7,8 which we believe was written shortly before Psalm 72 and Zechariah 9:10, for instance).

"He shall have dominion ... from the river unto the ends of the earth."

The expansion of the promise made to David, who ruled over the house of Israel, to encompass the whole earth may seem strange at first but it actually follows logically from that promise. He was not only to be David's Son but God's Son. As the only begotten Son of the great Un-Create, the Most High, "possessor of heaven and earth" (Genesis 14:19,22) he was the heir. If the earth belongs to God why should He not give it to His Son for an inheritance?

The language that follows describes the subservience of the mighty and the deliverance of the poor (on which we have already commented).

"They that dwell in the wilderness shall bow before him; and his enemies shall lick the dust." (Psalm 72:9)

It is strange that the people of the wilderness should be particularly identified as they might be regarded as the most insignificant amongst the nations. Yet perhaps there is a great truth underlying the words, for such as lived in this way were those who would separate and free themselves from the authority and power of those who lived a more social and organised life. These were "the free" who recognised no king or human authority but lived as they pleased in the wilderness places. But even such as these who sought freedom to indulge their own desires in any way they pleased would bow in homage before him, and those who would not, from wheresoever, should "lick the dust". "Dust shalt thou eat" (Genesis 3:14) was God's curse on the serpent. Similarly the prophets declare, "Dust shall be the serpent's meat" (Isaiah 65:25) and "The nations ... shall lick the dust like a serpent" (Micah 7:16,17).

In other words, sin in all its organised forms is to be humbled; it shall not stand before him:

"The kings of Tarshish and of the isles shall bring presents: the kings of Sheba and Seba shall offer gifts."
(Psalm 72:10)

Tarshish and the isles represent the great maritime and merchant nations of both the west and the east. Sheba, of course, represents Arabia and those nations in closer proximity, while Seba has been identified with Africa. It is worth noting, however, that after the Flood it is recorded of Shem, Ham and Japheth, the sons of Noah, that "by these were the nations divided in the earth after the flood" (Genesis 10:32). If we look more closely in Genesis 10 we shall discover that Tarshish was of the sons of Japheth (verses 2,4); Sheba was of the sons of Shem (verses 21,28) and Seba was of the sons of Ham (verses 6,7). In other words they were representative of all the nations of the earth and in case any reader should have missed the point, verse 11 reinforces it: "Yea, *all* kings shall fall down before him: all nations shall serve him."

The reason for this obeisance is that as He blessed the poor of Israel, now His mercy has been extended to the oppressed of all nations. No more shall the cruelty and tyranny of man bring misery and despair to his fellows, but right, not might, will prevail (verses 12,13). The hallmarks of human dominion, deceit (RV margin, fraud) and violence shall be eradicated from the earth. Men will be redeemed from these evils and although the words apply to the mortal population of the earth the idea of redemption is appropriate, for all these blessings spring out of the perfect sacrifice of the Lord Jesus Christ. It is because he was obedient even to the death of the cross that all the promises of God are yea and amen in him. Perhaps also it is because these things were accomplished by the shedding of his "precious blood" that the psalm emphasises "that precious shall *their* blood be in his sight" (verse 14).

The People's Response (verse 15)

The *Cambridge Bible* renders the opening words of this verse, "so may he live". It was no doubt a prayer that found an echo in the hearts of all those who benefited from the beneficence of Solomon's reign. How much more shall those who enjoy the blessings accruing from the reign of David's greater Son express their longing that his reign might never end. Their gratitude shall overflow from willing hearts and they shall bring their gifts, i.e., "the gold of Sheba". Not only so but, "Prayer also shall be made for him continually; and daily shall he be praised".

Recognising his greatness, rejoicing in the blessings that flow from his hand, he is praised continually. There is nothing inappropriate in this outpouring of praise to the Lord Jesus Christ for the song of the redeemed (Revelation 5) is also sung in recognition of his victory.

"Worthy is the Lamb that was slain to receive power, and riches, and wisdom, and strength, and honour, and glory, and blessing." (verse 12)

The Earth Blessed

"There shall be an handful of corn in the earth upon the top of the mountains; the fruit thereof shall shake like Lebanon: and they of the city shall flourish like grass of the earth." (Psalm 72:16)

The word rendered "handful" is translated "abundance" in most other versions and commentators generally follow this meaning. However, Gesenius (*Hebrew-Chaldee Lexicon*) points out that the literal meaning of the word is 'diffusion' and lends support to the translation of the AV in the sense of an handful, i.e., as much as the hand can hold, hence an abundance for scattering and diffusion over the earth. We feel that the context requires this translation and the significance of the words is enhanced by it. A handful of corn on the top of a mountain, the most barren and inhospitable of places where no man would normally scatter his seed, is going to produce a wonderful harvest. The fruit is going to shake like Lebanon, like the most fertile and productive of wheatfields. No more shall men suffer famine for even the barren places shall bring forth abundantly.

The blessings are not confined to the countryside but those who live in the city will also have their lives enhanced for they shall flourish like grass of the earth. Here grass, often used for the brevity of human life, is used for its freshness and abundance of growth, for in every respect the quality of human life will be improved, whether it be in the fertility of the land or the prosperity of those who dwell in the city.

549

His Everlasting Name

"His name shall endure forever: his name shall be continued as long as the sun: and men shall be blessed in him: all nations shall call him blessed."   (verse 17)

Within His name, Yahweh, was enshrined the whole purpose of God. "He who will be" was manifest in His Son. In him, in the life he lived and in all that he accomplished the name of the Father was revealed. It is a name of salvation.

For there is none other name under heaven given among men, whereby we must be saved."   (Acts 4:12)

By his victory over sin and death he has proved himself worthy to bear that name forever:

"And being found in fashion as a man, he humbled himself, and became obedient unto death, even the death of the cross. Wherefore God also hath highly exalted him, and given him a (the, RV) name which is above every name: that at the name of Jesus every knee should bow, of things in heaven, and things in earth, and things under the earth; and that every tongue should confess that Jesus Christ is Lord, to the glory of God the Father."   (Philippians 2:8-11)

To these great truths the opening words of verse 17 of the psalm testify.

The second phrase, "His name shall be continued as long as the sun" might appear to be a repetition of the first but the word rendered "continued", occurring only this once, carries the significance of 'issue or propagation'. Pusey wrote: "His name shall propagate, gaining, generation after generation, a fresh accession of offspring" (Quoted by J. Perowne – *The Book of Psalms*, Vol. 1, page 592). We are reminded of the words of Exodus, "This is my name forever, and this is my memorial unto all generations" (3:15). We quote these words of Pusey, however, not because we believe that he explains the verse, but for the way in which he enlarges our understanding of the meaning of the word. A footnote in the *Speaker's Bible* renders the word "to regenerate" and referring to the writings of the Rabbis comments, "They rightly apprehended the meaning of regeneration involved in the word, applying it, however, not to the creation of a

550

new people, but to the resurrection which our Lord calls the regeneration" (see Matthew 19:28).

God's name is perpetuated from generation to generation by the manner in which faithful men take that name upon themselves and experience the salvation it embodies. It is perpetuated throughout the kingdom age by the resurrection to life of those, out of all generations, who have espoused the name. Yet even in the kingdom amongst the mortal population men will still call His name upon them. The purpose enshrined in the name will still be perpetuated, producing offspring from generation to generation until the second resurrection leads to the consummation of the purpose of God.

Thus "men shall be blessed in him, all nations shall call him blessed" (Psalm 72:17). Here is a clear allusion to the covenant that God made with Abraham: "In thy seed shall all the nations of the earth be blessed" (Genesis 22:18; see also 12:3; 18:18). The Apostle Peter quoted these words in Acts 3 and his exposition of them helps us to appreciate how they grow so naturally in the psalm out of the expressions used regarding the name of God:

"Ye are the children of the prophets, and of the covenant which God made with our fathers, saying unto Abraham, And in thy seed shall all the kindreds of the earth be blessed. Unto you first God, having raised up his Son Jesus, sent him to bless you, in turning away every one of you from his iniquities."   (verses 25,26)

The words of the psalm, however, are not precisely the same as those of Genesis; literally the words are "men shall bless themselves in him" (RV margin). It implies that they live in the consciousness and awareness of the blessing they enjoy (Kay – *Psalms with Notes*).

The Doxology (verses 18-20)

Each of the five books of the Psalms concludes with a doxology and it is almost universally assumed that these words are the work of an editor who added the paean of praise to indicate the division between the conclusion of one book and the beginning of another. In this instance, however, the doxology is followed by another sentence: "The prayers (lit. 'hymns or songs') of David the son of Jesse are ended" (verse 20).

Again writers presume that these are the words of an editor who because most of the psalms in Books One and Two were written by David, added the words. This conjecture, of course, does not take account of the fact that there are many psalms written by David in the remaining three books of the Psalms. It is our conviction that in this instance the doxology and the final words were written by David himself.

The doxology needs little comment.

"Blessed be the LORD God, the God of Israel, who only doeth wondrous things. And blessed be his glorious name for ever: and let the whole earth be filled with his glory; Amen, and Amen." (verses 18,19)

Could we imagine a more appropriate ascription of praise to conclude this wonderful psalm? It sums up everything that the psalm contains. It was the hope that David treasured in his heart and the joy he felt overflowed in this song of praise. The words will find an echo in every faithful heart and with David they will exclaim in their confidence that God will fulfil His word, "Amen and Amen".

What then of the final words? We go back to our introduction where we suggested that David wrote this psalm on the accession of Solomon to the throne of Israel. It was very shortly before David's death, and the words are his own for this is the very last psalm that David wrote. They have no relevance to the place where the psalm occurs in the Psalter but it is David's recognition that, after this song he laid down his pen and the "Sweet Psalmist of Israel" wrote no more.

How fitting that his final song should speak so wonderfully of the covenant that God had made with him.

"He shall build me an house, and I will stablish his throne for ever. I will be his father, and he shall be my son: and I will not take my mercy away from him, as I took it from him that was before thee: but I will settle him in mine house and in my kingdom for ever: and his throne shall be established for evermore."

(1 Chronicles 17:12-14)